9/97

The essays in this volume explore the ways in which traditional philosophical problems about self-knowledge, self-identity, and value have migrated into literature since the Romantic and Idealist periods. How do so-called literary works take up these problems in a new way? What conception of the subject is involved in this literary practice? How are the lines of demarcation between philosophy and literature problematized? The contributors examine these issues with reference both to Romantic and Idealist writers and to some of their subsequent literary and philosophical inheritors and revisers. Their essays offer a philosophical understanding of the roots and nature of contemporary literary and philosophical practice, and elaborate powerful and influential, but rarely decisively articulated, conceptions of the human subject and of value.

CAMBRIDGE STUDIES IN PHILOSOPHY AND THE ARTS

Series editors

SALIM KEMAL *and* IVAN GASKELL

Beyond representation

CAMBRIDGE STUDIES IN PHILOSOPHY AND THE ARTS

Series editors

SALIM KEMAL *and* IVAN GASKELL

Advisory board

Stanley Cavell, R. K. Elliott, Stanley E. Fish, David Freedberg, Hans-Georg Gadamer, John Gage, Carl Hausman, Ronald Hepburn, Mary Hesse, Hans-Robert Jauss, Martin Kemp, Jean Michel Massing, Michael Podro, Edward S. Said, Michael Tanner.

Cambridge Studies in Philosophy and the Arts is a forum for examining issues common to philosophy and critical disciplines that deal with the history of art, literature, film, music and drama. In order to inform and advance both critical practice and philosophical approaches, the series analyses the aims, procedures, language and results of inquiry in the critical fields, and examines philosophical theories by reference to the needs of arts disciplines. This interaction of ideas and findings, and the ensuing discussion, brings into focus new perspectives and expands the terms in which the debate is conducted.

Beyond representation

Philosophy and poetic imagination

Edited by
RICHARD ELDRIDGE
Swarthmore College

CAMBRIDGE
UNIVERSITY PRESS

Published by the Press Syndicate of the University of Cambridge
The Pitt Building, Trumpington Street, Cambridge CB2 1RP
40 West 20th Street, New York, NY 10011–4211, USA
10 Stamford Road, Oakleigh, Melbourne 3166, Australia

© Cambridge University Press 1996

First published 1996

Printed in Great Britain at the University Press, Cambridge

A catalogue record for this book is available from the British Library

Library of Congress cataloguing in publication data

Beyond representation: philosophy and poetic imagination / edited by Richard
Eldridge.
p.   cm. – (Cambridge studies in philosophy and the arts)
Includes index.
ISBN 0 521 48079 5 (hardback)
1. Philosophy in literature. I. Eldridge, Richard Thomas, 1953–   . II. Series
PN49.B49   1996
809′.93384–dc20   95–18227
CIP

ISBN 0 521 48079 5 hardback

Contents

List of contributors   *page* ix
Editor's acknowledgments   xi

1 Introduction: from representation to *poiesis*   1
   RICHARD ELDRIDGE

2 Confession and forgiveness: Hegel's poetics of action   34
   J. M. BERNSTEIN

3 The values of articulation: aesthetics after the aesthetic
   ideology   CHARLES ALTIERI   66

4 In their own voice: philosophical writing and actual
   experience   ARTHUR C. DANTO   90

5 Poetry and truth-conditions   SAMUEL FLEISCHACKER   107

6 Fractal contours: chaos and system in the Romantic
   fragment   AZADE SEYHAN   133

7 The mind's horizon   STANLEY BATES   151

8 Kant, Hölderlin, and the experience of longing   175
   RICHARD ELDRIDGE

9 Wordsworth and the reception of poetry   197
   MICHAEL FISCHER

10 Self-consciousness, social guilt, and Romantic poetry:
   Coleridge's Ancient Mariner and Wordsworth's Old
   Pedlar   KENNETH R. JOHNSTON   216

11 Her blood and his mirror: Mary Coleridge, Luce Irigaray,
   and the female self   CHRISTINE BATTERSBY   249

Contents

12   Scene: an exchange of letters   273
     PHILIPPE LACOUE-LABARTHE AND JEAN-LUC NANCY

     Index   303

Contributors

CHARLES ALTIERI
University of California, Berkeley

STANLEY BATES
Middlebury College

CHRISTINE BATTERSBY
University of Warwick

J. M. BERNSTEIN
University of Essex

ARTHUR C. DANTO
Columbia University

RICHARD ELDRIDGE
Swarthmore College

MICHAEL FISCHER
University of New Mexico

SAMUEL FLEISCHACKER
Williams College

KENNETH R. JOHNSTON
Indiana University

PHILIPPE LACOUE-LABARTHE
University of Strasbourg

JEAN-LUC NANCY
University of Strasbourg

AZADE SEYHAN
Bryn Mawr College

Editor's acknowledgments

Salim Kemal has provided a great deal of timely advice and help in preparing this volume, at several stages. Several readers for the Press made numerous specific, timely, and apt suggestions for improvements to the individual essays, at various stages of their compositions. I am grateful to these readers for their advice, and I especially thank the volume's contributors for being continuously willing and prompt in responding to editorial suggestions, both from myself and from others.

Some of the editorial work was done during a sabbatical year at the Stanford Humanities Center. I thank the Center and Swarthmore College for sabbatical support, and I am grateful to Wanda Corn, the Center's director, Charles Junkerman, its associate director, and its staff for providing such pleasant and fruitful conditions of work and daily life.

Samuel Fleischacker's essay is a somewhat revised version of an essay entitled "Frustrated Contracts, Poetry, and Truth" that appeared in *Raritan* 13: 4 (Spring 1994), and it appears here in its present form with the author's and the journal editor's permission. The essay by Philippe Lacoue-Labarthe and Jean-Luc Nancy first appeared in French as "Scène: un échange de lettres" in *Nouvelle revue de psychanalyse* 46 (Autumn 1992). Its translation for its first appearance in English in this volume was very ably done by Maiko Behr. The essay appears here with the permission of the authors. Christine Battersby's essay forms part of a projected larger work, and she retains its copyright.

At Cambridge University Press, Joanna West and then Judith Ayling, Hilary Gaskin, and Ann Martin efficiently helped to move the volume from a proposal to an accomplished fact. At Swarthmore College, Jackie Robinson produced disk versions of some of the essays in a standard format for typesetting very quickly and ably.

I am grateful to Joan Vandegrift for her editorial advice, particularly concerning the introduction and my own essay, as well as for accommodating cheerfully the demands on my time and attention that regularly arose in the course of preparing this volume and distracted me from family life.

Introduction: from representation to *poiesis*

RICHARD ELDRIDGE

I

Twice upon a time, in both the seventeenth to eighteenth centuries and again in the twentieth-century heydays of logical atomism and logical positivism, the task of philosophy – so Richard Rorty[1] and Ian Hacking[2] have reminded us – was to provide a critical theory of representations of the world. By sorting representations – mental or linguistic, as may be – into the accurate and well-founded vs. the inaccurate and ill-founded, different cultural practices might be submitted to critical judgment. This is possible insofar as "culture *is*," in Rorty's words, "the assemblage of claims to knowledge,"[3] or perhaps, more weakly, in so far as cultural practices as various as preparing food, making paintings, building houses, and telling stories about ancestors all presuppose claims to knowledge. If the representations or knowledge-claims that a given bit of culture either is or presupposes are themselves in good order, then that bit of culture is itself well-founded; if not, then not. If *that* – foxglove – is *in fact* a poisonous plant, then (given a desire to avoid the poisonous) one ought not to eat it; if *mass* is in fact an essential property of physical objects, then one will do best to understand how physical bodies will move under certain conditions by, among other things, weighing them. Out of a critical theory of representations, philosophy, it was hoped, would derive a critical theory of culture.

As Rorty, Hacking, and numerous other writers on the death of epistemology have suggested, however, this project has also twice foundered on a dilemma. What is the status of the intended theory of representations itself? Either it is simply taken for granted that this theory of representations itself represents representations correctly and that the privileged set of first-order representations of the world that it favors is likewise accurate, in which case it is dogmatic and uncritical; or this theory of representations is itself taken to be in need of some guarantor of its accuracy and of the accuracy of the first-order representations that it favors, in which case an infinite regress ensues and the theory fails to provide a basis for assessing culture and cultural practices. In Hegel's trenchant image, if reality "is supposed to be brought nearer to us through this instrument [a theory of representations together with a set of favored, first-order representations], without anything in it being altered, like a bird caught by a lime-twig, it [reality] would surely laugh our little ruse to scorn, if it were not with us, in and for itself, all along, and of its own volition."[4]

Not only does the effort to construct a critical theory of representations founder between dogmatism and skepticism, it also arguably both reposes on inconsistent assumptions and misrepresents human interests. Developing a line of argument that he sees as realized in various ways in the writings of Kant, Hegel, Heidegger, Wittgenstein, and Merleau-Ponty, Charles Taylor has claimed that the epistemological project of constructing a critical theory of representations rests on an incoherent picture of the single human knower as primitively and self-sufficiently a subject or bearer of representational states. Within the epistemological project, Taylor writes, the state of having a representation in mind (whether mental or linguistic) is conceived of as "an ultimately incoherent amalgam of two features: (a) these states (the ideas) are self-enclosed, in the sense that they can be accurately identified and described in abstraction from the 'outside' world ... and (b) they nevertheless point toward and represent things in that world."[5] Only if both (a) and (b) are true does the project of stepping back from all presuppositions and commitments, and thence reflectively *testing* representations for their accuracy, make any sense. Yet the amalgam is incoherent. To the extent that representations do present or point to things in the world, they are – arguably – shapes or sound patterns or images that are themselves in use in the world. Moreover, the interests that human beings have in using representations to form judgments may well be much wider than cognitive interests alone, and may be interests the pursuit of which is effectively undermined by taking cognitive interests to be of paramount importance. By attempting to stand back from all presuppositions and commitments, in the cognitive interest of identifying unprejudiced and well-founded representations, we may not only get nowhere: we may also distort and repress genuine but less obviously cognitive interests that we do have – interests in justice or freedom, say. In this way, as Hegel observes, "fear of error [within the epistemological project] reveals itself rather as fear of the truth [as truthful living and the satisfaction of genuine interests]."[6]

One way out of this impasse faced by representationalist epistemologies is to consider representations *not* as self-standing, reality-related packets in either mind or language, but instead as markers or signifiers in use in a population. In this way it becomes possible to connect the uses of representations or signifiers with other actions in practice that are carried out in the pursuit of other interests. Thinking, or entertaining representations in mind, and using linguistic representations in speaking and writing then become subsets of the many things that human beings do in pursuing many and various interests. Thought and language-use are reset within wider frameworks of human practical life.

Depending, however, on what wider interests human beings are taken to have and on how these wider frameworks of practical life are taken to be set, this way of thinking about representations can yield wildly different stances on human life and thought. Are there any interests that are simply given, and, if so, how? Or are all interests predominantly set by local and personal facticity, without deeper constraints? Are human subjects capable of an adequate and clear consciousness of their interests, however they are set? Or do these interests, bound up with the possibilities of life that culture affords, remain always in part opaque to reflective intelligence? Different answers to these questions will yield radically different ways of moving beyond Cartesian representationalism. Three broad kinds of anti-Cartesian stances have been especially prominent of late.

(1) *Naturalism*: It might be held that certain human interests – pre-eminently those in food, clothing, shelter, freedom from pain and misery, and so on – are simply given biologically. Human action is dominated by these interests that are given naturally, and by other, later interests (for example, in nurturing pride, in decoration) that grow out of these earlier ones according to natural patterns of growth and development. Theorists of thought, language, and action as different from one another as Noam Chomsky, W. V. O. Quine, Bernard Williams, J. L. Mackie, and E. O. Wilson all hold views of this kind, differing only about which specific interests are first given naturally and about the mental or neural mechanisms through which those interests are implemented and developed. Behind our lives

with representations, it is suggested, lie our lives as evolved, biological systems within a larger system of physical nature.

(2) *Linguistic idealism*: It might be held that nothing governs our actions, thoughts, and uses of language beside our own creations. Concepts such as *rightness, piety, goodness, honor, efficiency,* and *duty*, that human agents have typically, but variously, used to describe and assess courses of action, are not built into the order of nature, either in our brains or as part of reality. The fact that these concepts vary widely in how they sort actions, without having a common core, suggests that nothing but our own creativity as it plays itself out in linguistic-social life lies behind them. As Rorty observes, defending this view, "the notions of criteria and choice (including that of 'arbitrary choice') are no longer in point when it comes to changes from one language game to another. Europe did not *decide* to accept the idiom of Romantic poetry, or of socialist politics, or of Galilean mechanics. That sort of shift was no more an act of will than it was a result of argument. Rather, Europe gradually lost the habit of using certain words and gradually acquired the habit of using others."[7] It may not be that our words causally create electrons or geological formations. But our words may be responsible for dividing things up into the categories under which we take them to fall in the course of pursuing our interests (themselves thus created). Behind this life of language lies no punctual, individual, cognizing subject, no given order of nature, and no God. Our complex, conflicting, and always evolving habits of usage themselves determine how we classify and identify things – how we represent them to ourselves – in ways that are then not under the control of either reality or individual knowledge and will. Views of this kind have been prominent in strains of recent literary theory that have been influenced by Saussure's claims (themselves detached from Saussure's program of generating a semantic science of how conventional connections between signifiers and signfieds are laid down) about the arbitrariness of the signifier. As Catherine Belsey puts it, the thought is that "the world, which otherwise without signification would be experienced as a continuum, is divided up by language into entities which readily come to be experienced as essentially different."[8]

(3) *Cultural materialism*: Partly making use of post-Saussurean hostility to kinds written into the order of nature, but partly in disappointment with idealism and in pursuit of the thought that *something*, but not nature, must constrain human actions and the

4

development of systems of representations (what would it be to "experience the world as a continuum" anyway? – the thought makes little sense), the thought arises that human acting, thinking, and language-using are constrained or determined by sociological configurations of power. Moving from Saussure to Marx, Foucault, and Althusser (often by way of Freud and Lacan), the thought is that human beings live out their lives, and take up courses of thought and action, within social frameworks. These social frameworks are above all frameworks of opposition and domination. In any known or imaginable form of social life, certain rights and privileges are somehow allotted differentially to members of opposed groups. Women may not inherit property, while men can. Owners of the instruments of production may "steal" embodied labor through the mechanisms of capitalist production, while wage-workers cannot. Gays may be diagnosed as mentally ill and subjected to courses of medical treatment, while heterosexuals are regarded as normal and healthy. These kinds of divisions – determined socially and histori- cally, not by physical or biological nature alone – affect how people think about themselves and their courses of action. The systems of representations that people use to think about themselves and their lives thus reflect their positions within one or another framework of social antagonisms. No one thing – not nature, not consciousness and will, not a history of technological development, not God – stands behind the development of social frameworks that embody domination. Rather, power is fluidly manifested in all social struc- tures, without source and without a possibility of cure. As Foucault puts it,

Power's condition of possibility, or in any case the viewpoint which permits one to understand its exercise, and which also makes it possible to use its mechanisms as a grid of intelligibility of the social order, must not be set in the primary existence of a central point, in a unique source of sovereignty from which secondary and descendent forms would emanate; it is the moving substrate of force relations which, by virtue of their inequality, constantly engender states of power, but the latter are always local and unstable. The omnipresence of power: not because it has the privilege of consolidating everything under its invincible unity, but because it is produced from one moment to the next, at every point, or rather in every relation from one point to another. Power is everywhere; not because it embraces everything, but because it comes from everywhere. And "Power," insofar as it is permanent, repetitious, inert, and self- reproducing, is simply the over-all effect that emerges from all these mobilities, the concatenation that rests on each of them and seeks in turn to arrest their movement.[9]

Against Cartesian conceptions of a punctual subject, self-sufficiently sorting through its representations for reliability one by one,
each of these stances has considerable charm and power. Surely it is
right to see human action, thought, and language-use arising within
a natural framework; surely language evolves, often in ways that are
unpredictable by appeal to either natural processes or individual
will; surely the presence of changing varieties of domination in
social life is an historical fact that is of significance for how we act,
think, and use language. But each position also suffers from two
limitations. Within each stance a metaphysical scheme is dogmatically assumed. Either the ultimate authority of nature over the
formation of thoughts and desires and social life is taken for granted,
or idealism is embraced, or power is cast as an ineliminable, but in
principle uncentered, unintelligible, and unassessable metaphysical
fact. Moreover, against the force of these metaphysical assumptions,
no morality of aspiration is articulable. In each case, the governing
way of thinking about action, thought, and language forces us toward
explaining how in fact human beings act, think, and use language,
without articulating how they might do these things better than they
do now. No routes toward partial, further rational independence and
social freedom are either discerned or discernible. The very ideas of
rational independence under norms and of social freedom become
nearly unintelligible. Thinking of our systems of representations,
and of our lives with them, as somehow *determined* – by nature, by
nothing, or by power, as may be – we then alternate between
(inconsistent) reversions to Cartesian voluntarism and clarity in
choice, ecstatic embraces of a post-modern sublime, of what Lyotard
calls "the unpresentable in presentation itself, that which denies
itself the solace of good forms,"[10] and submission to natural or
cultural fate.

And this, we may think, cannot be right. Perhaps our lives and
thoughts and expressions are not our own as punctual, clairvoyant,
Cartesian, originative subjects, either actually or potentially. But can
it be that behind our lives and thoughts and expressions there is only
either physical-biological nature, or nothing, or power? Can we
simply know one of these metaphysical stances to be true? Or is it
rather that all at once, as beings who possess cognitive interests,
moral interests, and natural endowments, and who are set within
cultural matrices of both interest and domination, we nonetheless
dimly but actively refigure our representations and rearticulate our
interests?

To think about the human subject in this way, as departing from multiple natural and cultural interests and endowments, thence actively to refigure representations and effectively to rearticulate interests, is to conceive of the human subject as a subject of and within *poiesis*.[11] As Plato and Aristotle use the term, *poiesis* is the name for any activity of making, as opposed to *theoria* (observing, theorizing) or *praxis* (acting, doing). More narrowly, it specifically means the making of any *imitative representation* (*mimesis*), no matter whether in prose or verse or painting or music (as a *mimesis* of emotions).[12] So used, *poiesis* is not solely the making of something that is merely fictional or unreal, since a *mimesis* or imitative representation presents aspects of things that are. As Paul Shorey usefully remarks, "Imitation means for [Plato and Aristotle] not only the portrayal or description of visible and tangible things, but more especially the communication of a mood or feeling, hence the (to a modern) paradox that music is the most imitative of the arts."[13]

Poetic imitation is distinguished from the construction of a *logos* (definition or account) through *theoria* in the interests of knowledge or science (*episteme*). Thus the metaphysical-biological account of man as a rational animal will be a part of *episteme* and a product of *theoria*, not a poetic imitation. But poetic imitation is the means of representing appearances, moods, characters, human moral and political interests, and actions and their meanings, among many other things. These are, we might say, things that are *portrayed* by us in our speech – figurations of how things appear to us, of what our interests are, of what our actions mean – not things that are captured by us in the course of our scientific theorizing about nature. They are representations of subjects, their characters, their interests, and their possible stances in culture that are made by subjects and that in turn help to make them, insofar as they make available certain routes of self-construal and of action and identity in culture. Such figurations will be, in Plato's and Aristotle's terminology, *poetic representations*, *mimemata* that are products of *poiesis*, and they are far from insignificant for human life, far from idle objects of aesthetic delectation.

The forming of poetic imitations, hence engaging in the activity of *poiesis*, is arguably central to the life of any human subject. We articulate and evince our characters in our actions, and we respond continuously to our senses of the characters of others. We articulate our interests – things that are not simply given in the order of physical nature, in material culture, or by personal situation and individual will – as we envision courses of action and character formation that are fulfilling for us. These articulations of interests and of possibilities of action and identity are the vehicles of our cultures' various lives in us and of our lives in cultures, in such a way that it is a mistake to think of these articulations as either simply given, simply discovered, simply invented, or simply willed. As products of *poiesis*, these articulations both *represent* subjects and their interests, and yet also fail to do so: as products of imaginative power calling to ways of cultural life not yet in being, they allude to an ongoing and unmasterable historicity of human life. We appear to ourselves and to one another under certain roles, within plots of character development and of the pursuit of interest that we inhabit. We appear to ourselves and to one another, multiply and variously, as sons or daughters, as members of certain political parties, as bearers of certain tastes or interests in the arts, as lovers and co-workers, consumers and laborers, bosses and correspondents.

These roles are in conflict with one another in the culture, and so also in us, we who multiply inhabit them. Being a daughter, a painter, a boss, and a politically engaged citizen calls for casts of mind and ways of thinking about actions and their meanings that are not easily reconciled with one another. The tensions or oppositions here are so great that many recent writers – aware of the proliferation of cultural roles and of the antagonisms that lie between such roles – have begun to doubt whether there is any unity to the subject at all, to doubt whether there is any locus of rational freedom within the subject that embraces and organizes how one participates in the multiple roles one occupies. Perhaps the subject is a nothing, particularly if there is no self-present punctual subject, able effectively on its own to pursue cognitive interests that are central to any other interests it also has.

And yet we seem to wish effectively to integrate our various roles with one another as coherent and complementary expressions of our humanity and free personality. *We appear to ourselves* as having various interests and desires and characters, as caring about various things and occupying various social roles, and we wish to achieve coherence and integrity in freely and reasonably bearing these multiple cares and concerns, whose coherence and integrity are readily, and painfully, felt to be lacking. Or, as Hegel remarks in characterizing the sort of self-consciousness that comes with having a propositional, judgmental consciousness, wherein *one takes oneself* to be following rules in judging the contents of experience:

The antithesis of [consciousness'] appearance and its truth has, however, for its essence only the truth, viz. the unity of self-consciousness with itself; this unity must become essential to self-consciousness, i.e. self-consciousness is *Desire* in general. In this sphere [of self-consciousness as involving an effort to achieve its coherence, integrity, and unity] self-consciousness exhibits itself as the movement in which this antithesis is removed, and the identity of itself with itself becomes explicit for it [German: *wird*: becomes or comes about].[14]

For Hegel, the overcoming of the antithesis between self-consciousness' housing in multiple roles, on the one hand, and its unity to be achieved, on the other hand, involves at least the development of a fully coherent culture, within which subjects will *recognize* or *acknowledge* one another's rational humanity and free personality as they are expressed in roles that are no longer brutely at odds with one another. It is in and through these recognitions or acknowledgments that are won from those with whom one shares a coherent culture of rational freedom that one's own unity of self-consciousness is achieved. "Self-consciousness exists in and for itself when, and by the fact that, it so exists for another; that is, it exists only in being acknowledged [*es ist nur als ein Anerkenntnes*: it *is* only as an object of recognition] ...The detailed exposition of the Notion of this spiritual unity in its duplication will present us with the process of Recognition [*Anerkennung*]."[15]

Even for Hegel, however, no substance or agency that is external to human subjectivity guarantees that the achievement of a unified self-consciousness in and through a coherent culture of rational freedom will come off. To suppose there is some such substance or agency would be dogmatically to assume a cosmological-metaphysical stance, in advance of a critical examination of human subjectivity and its always emerging possibilities of development. Though Hegel himself looked forward to the imminent inauguration of a coherent culture of freedom, whose structural institutions and predominant modes of activity he undertook to describe, there is nonetheless, in his thinking, nothing external to our own collective, divided subjectivities and their efforts that is to bring such a culture about. *Geist* or Spirit is, for Hegel, fully immanent within human subjectivities in their natural and cultural situations, somewhat in the way in which a personality is immanent in the ways in which one takes an interest in, and responds to, things. A personality just *is* certain patterns of shifting interest and responsiveness, partly latent and partly actual in consciousness, not a separate something that is behind them. Just so, for Hegel, with *Geist* or Spirit and human subjectivities, together with their possibilities of development, in their cultural and natural situations. The extent to which the lack of any substance external to human subjectivities might, contrary to Hegel's optimism, leave these subjectivities ever at odds with one another and internally divided, without fully unified self-consciousness, is perhaps a topic that is best left to us to dwell on, as we consider our own possibilities of development, just as various of Hegel's precursors and contemporaries did.

Strikingly, in rejecting the existence of any substance or agency external to our collective, partially unified, partially divided subjectivities – in rejecting dogmatic reliance on a metaphysical cosmology – Hegel is in fact taking up a line of thought that is already powerfully developed by Kant. Kant tells us that the law of duty – the law which commands the formation of a rational-moral culture of freedom as an earthly kingdom of ends, within which reciprocal respect and recognition, and with them lived rational self-consciousness, are achieved in daily routines – has no basis other than free human personality itself, in its present, and persisting, partial unity and partial self-dividedness.

Duty! Thou sublime and mighty name that dost embrace nothing charming or insinuating but requirest submission and yet seekest not to move the will by threatening aught that would arouse natural aversion or terror, but only holdest forth a law which of itself finds entrance into the mind and yet gains reluctant reverence (though not always obedience) – a law before which all inclinations are dumb even though they secretly work against it: what origin is there worthy of thee, and where is to be found the root of thy noble descent which proudly rejects all kinship with the inclinations and from which to be descended is the indispensable condition of the only worth which men can give themselves?

It cannot be less than something which elevates man above himself as a part of the world of sense, something which connects him with an order of things which only the understanding can think and which has under it the entire world of sense, including the empirically determinable existence of man in time, and the whole system of all ends which is alone suitable to such unconditional practical laws as the moral. It is nothing else than personality, i.e., the freedom and independence from the mechanism of nature regarded as a capacity of a being which is subject to special laws (pure practical laws given by its own reason), so that the person as belonging to the world of sense is subject to his own personality so far as he belongs to the intelligible world.[16]

One way to sum up the thought that we are thus elevated by our free personalities – in their partial unities and in their struggles to submit inclinations to the law of freedom – above the world of sense, the thought that we are able to articulate and envision, albeit in specific ways, impersonal ideals of free activity and ways of pursuing of them, is to say that human subjects are subjects in and through *poiesis*.

It is just this sense of the human subject as a subject in and through *poiesis* that has been decisive for literary and poetic practice, now regarded *not* as the production of idle amusements, *not* as controlled by the movements of material nature, *not* as arbitrarily conventional, and *not* as reflecting only brute external realities of power, but instead as a practice in and through which possibilities of free human cultural activity are recalled, envisioned, and criticized. In their groundbreaking *The Literary Absolute: The Theory of Literature in German Romanticism*, Philippe Lacoue-Labarthe and Jean-Luc Nancy sum up the Kantian sense of the human subject as a subject in and through *poiesis* that has been decisive for serious literary practice, now regarded as that into which philosophical thinking about our possibilities of development necessarily migrates. Kant rejects the existence of intellectual intuition, but retains a sense of the human subject as dimly capable of rational self-consciousness and self-legislated free action, out of its own resources. What results is a sense of the human subject as bearing, intensely, the problem of forming its own rational unity in and through the forming of a rational culture. As Lacoue-Labarthe and Nancy put it,

The first and foremost result [of Kant's transcendental Aesthetic or theory of sensibility in the *Critique of Pure Reason*] is that there is no *intuitus originarius*. Whether it was situated as *arche* or as *telos*, within the divine or within the human (as either pure intellectual self-consciousness in Descartes or pure empirical sensibility in Hume), what had heretofore ensured the philosophical itself disappears. As a result, all that remains of the subject is the "I" as an "empty form" (a pure logical necessity, said Kant; a grammatical exigency, Nietzsche will say) that "accompanies my representations." This is so because the form of time, which is the "form of the internal sense," permits no *substantial* presentation. As is well known, the Kantian "cogito" is empty.

... This weakening of the subject is accompanied by an apparently compensatory "promotion" of the *moral subject* which, as we know, launches a variety of philosophical "careers." ... As a moral subject, in sum, the subject recovers none of its substance. Quite to the contrary, the question of its unity, and thus of its very "being-subject," is brought to a pitch of high tension.

... [One result of this conception of the subject is] the infinite character of the process of human *Bildung* (with which Kant, in the eighteenth century, departing radically from the *Aufklärung*, represents the first view of history that refers its *telos* to infinity).[17]

11

The subject is caught up in this movement of infinite *Bildung*, in continually seeking to become unified and free, in and for itself and in and for others. So conceived, the subject is both more than an interference point set up by intersecting waves of cultural discourse and less than free and transparent to itself, in bearing the problem of achieving a not yet existent situated freedom.

Our subjectivity, as the locus of a project of freedom and a power of poetically forming and critically assessing new visions of new cultural routines, of itself commits us to this movement of *Bildung*. Human subjectivity *is* free activity partially coming to be, in forming a partially unified self-consciousness, its connected representations, and the cultural routines in which it is to find itself. The movement of poetic *Bildung* here is deeper than, or logically prior to, any epistemological testing of already formed representations for corre-spondence to reality or for coherence. It is a movement that is, for us, not optional, but rather one we are always already caught within. As Robert Pippin cogently remarks,

Kant attempts to show that in all empirical experience, or representation of objects, and in all intentional activity, there simply are, necessarily, sponta-neously self-legislated rules or conditions, that human awareness and action is spontaneously self-determining, whether recognized as such or not. On this reading, the Kantian "revolution" is not, at least not originally or primarily, something we reject or join as a practical matter and so ... does not involve (again, at least not originally) getting the unenlightened to start doing something or acting differently. The first step is to realize what has been involved all along in thinking, judging, and acting.[18]

The problem that human subjectivity bears, and is, is, one might say, a problem simultaneously of the remembrance (overcoming repres-sion and oppression), release, and perfection of its latent rational spontaneity or freedom, in and along with others.

The products of such poetic, self-forming, self-shaping, efforts in *Bildung* will naturally display a certain performativism, a certain literariness or writerliness, freed from dogmatic or uncriticized constraints of correspondence and coherence. Instead of testing self-standing representations for their reliability, subjects here imagina-tively remake their representations and themselves. The theoretical, spectatorial standpoint is supplanted by engaged, conditioned activ-ities of poetic making and remaking, in which subject and object are inextricably caught in play. Inherited languages are infused with exoticisms so as to introduce new powers of cultural formation. The textual forms of the ongoing, poetico-critical refiguration of the

12

subject and culture shift away from the closed treatise and toward more occasional, improvisatory, open, and uncontrolled forms – the fragment, the poem under continual revision, the polyphonic novel, and critical readings of other texts. Sometimes there will be what Kant called a "prevailing mood ... of weariness and complete *indifferentism*,"[19] or alternatively a certain lingering in the agonies of not yet unified subjectivity, a lingering that will sometimes appear politically quietistic and excessively self-absorbed. Sometimes there will be the ecstasies of responsiveness to the not yet presentable becoming present in culture and in oneself. *Indifferentism*, subjective *agonism*, and openness to sublimities here present themselves as alternating moods and modalities of attention. Acts of *poiesis*, carried out under these alternations, here aim at being what Kant called "the origin, or at least the foreplay, of an approaching Recreation-Rebirth and Enlightenment of themselves [der Ursprung, wenigstens das Vorspiel einer nahen Umschaffung und Aufklärung derselben[20]]" – where the foreplay (das Vorspiel) of this Recreation of the subject and culture lasts a long time.

In and through this performative movement of *poiesis* aiming at the *Bildung* simultaneously of human subjectivity and culture, there will be also always a movement of remembrance or recollection (*anamnesis*, *Erinnerung*; not *mneme*, *Gedächtnis*, not the personal recall of events one has experienced), a kind of recollection of the powers and possibilities of a unified self-consciousness that has already been partly achieved, and of a culture that is already partly expressive of freedom. Backward-looking moments of meditative recollection will sit alongside, chasten, and contest forward-looking moments of the unleashing of spontaneity in new directions. The subject will try to recall or recapture a partial *Bildung* and self-integration and also to unbind itself, to overcome dogmatic captivity by anything that is given.

Poiesis so conceived is obviously an incoherent, unstable, self-cancelling, and inconclusive form of subject activity. It will present resistances to any immediately moralizing form of interpretation or appropriation, and in doing so it will frustrate formulized receptions. But, despite its frustrating and inconclusive character, it is a kind of thinking – a scrutiny of our dim possibilities of freedom in culture and of self-unity – that we may do ill to do without. As Adorno says about what he calls *open thinking*:

The uncompromisingly critical thinker, who neither subordinates his conscience nor permits himself to be terrorized into action, is in truth the one who does not give up ... Open thinking points beyond itself. For its part, such thinking takes a position as a figuration of praxis which is more closely related to a praxis truly involved in change than is a position of mere obedience for the sake of praxis.[21]

Not only, moreover, might we do ill to do without *poiesis* or open thinking so conceived, it is also the case – if the Kantian–Hegelian conception of the human subject as inherently a subject of and in *poiesis* is right: and how are we to tell, except by entering into its projects? – that *poiesis* is something we can do without only at the price of the self-stultification and self-repression of our inherent powers, of our very nature as subjects.

II

Each of the essays that are collected here moves broadly in the orbit of the Kantian–Hegelian conception of the human subject as a subject of and in *poiesis*. They track various modes – often themselves involving gender, class position, and national tradition – of the uncovering and exercise of human poetic powers creatively to envision a just and free culture, drawing on, but also against the grain of, forms of cultural life that are already in place. At the same time, these essays follow out moments of self-interrogation and self-criticism in the uncovering and exercise of poetic powers, moments in which the very sense that one possesses these powers is blocked by an awareness of the force of antagonisms in culture, present and foreseeable. In each essay there is a pronounced emphasis on the priority of the process of the continual refiguration (blending discovery or acknowledgment with construction, in ways that are not readily parted) of subjects and their cultures over the completed and substantial nature of the subjects and the cultures that are thus refigured. A sense of independence and nascent autonomy continuously competes with a sense of incompleteness, fragility, and self-dividedness. This is true both of the protagonists that are presented or implied in the writings that these essays take up and, curiously, of these essays themselves, so the writers of these essays participate in just the agonistic logic of always refigurative self-consciousness that they are undertaking to describe.

In chapter 2 "Confession and forgiveness: Hegel's poetics of action," J. M. Bernstein elaborates Hegel's view of the self's ongoing refiguration of itself, blending acknowledgment and projection. It is in and through action, where action essentially involves the taking up and (at least sometimes) the conscientious recasting of norms, that we are what we are. "It is," Hegel tells us, "the linguistically actualized expressive dimension of action which is the means whereby the self comes both to reveal and to take a stand upon itself as a conscientious agent." Since there is in human action an essential moment or dimension of taking a stand upon oneself and against existing norms, it follows that human action as such is inherently evil. Hence it inherently defeats the subject's efforts to secure full, stable, and universal recognition of its expressive power and full, self-recollective, self-identity. It always partly unmakes what it would otherwise make. "Each act through which we would affirm ourselves dispossesses us of the self we are and want to be."

As a result, for Hegel, transgression and the failures both of full self-closure in self-recollection and of the perfection of human community are neither accidental nor surpassable, but rather part of the structure of human life. "Transgression is not the denial of a positive norm but the creation of a breach, rent, tear or wound in the body of united life (that, of course, exists in part through the continual activities of rending and tearing) – which is what positive norms are and represent if they but knew themselves aright." Existing as human subjects only within this thus always torn, always reforming body of united life, the only modalities of action through which we might achieve such moments of recognition, self-recollection, and community with others as we are capable of are the modalities of confession and forgiveness. Confession "is attempting to establish the common" by allowing it to declare itself in oneself; forgiveness lifts action out of the cycle of particular self-assertion and revenge in which otherwise it would remain caught. But because forgiveness, too, "is a performative act of recognition," it too bears the stain of transgressive self-assertiveness that marks all human action. "Forgiveness must express my particularity as well as renouncing it." Together, then, confession and forgiveness are "categorial modalities of all actions that provide them with their spiritual shape." One result of this shape of all human action is that we must be open to the work of mourning, as opposed to the vengeful denials and resentments of melancholia, as we are aware of those, both living and dead, with whom we have achieved partial (albeit only partial: there is no "uncontaminated universality") reciprocal recognition. Within "contaminated universality" there will be, for us, only vengefulness and violence, internal and external, in the absence of confession and forgiveness – the modalities of action under which alone "united life" is possible.

Charles Altieri takes up the Hegelian thematics of action as inherently involving *poiesis*, confession, and forgiveness in chapter 3, "The values of articulation: aesthetics after the aesthetic ideology." Altieri begins from a certain dissatisfaction both with what he calls "the aesthetic ideology" – the view that art is a phenomenon essentially of aesthetic pleasure – and with recent efforts to overturn that aesthetic ideology in favor of a conception of the work of art as primarily a political instrument. Without denying either the pleasures or the political instrumentality of art, Altieri nonetheless finds both these stances to be rooted in modernity's rejection of the abilities of art and poetry to serve as vehicles of truth. As Adorno and Horkheimer notoriously observe in their *Dialectic of Enlightenment*, "To the Enlightenment, that which does not reduce to numbers, and ultimately to the one, becomes illusion; modern positivism writes it off as literature."[22] Once legitimate truth-seeking is seen as the preserve solely of the sciences, art and poetry are immediately reduced either to the status of providers of gratuitous, *belle-lettristic* pleasures or to instrumentalities of power. (Bernstein powerfully characterizes and criticizes modernity's reductions of art's significances in his *The Fate of Art*, and he points to Kant, together with Heidegger, Adorno, and Derrida, as gesturing towards ways of reconceiving and recovering those significances.[23])

Instead of accepting these reductions, which now present themselves as mirror-images of one another, of art to either the aesthetic or the political, Altieri suggests that we might better revert to a premodern conception of the powers of art – the view of Longinus that sees the work of art as carrying out a "work of articulation" that makes routes of expressive power available to us. (In developing this suggestion, Altieri is powerfully extending the lines of thinking of his collection of essays *Canons and Consequences: Reflections on the Ethical Force of Imaginative Ideals*.[24]) Unlike a *measurement* or *reproduction* of something that is already in existence, an *articulation*, as Altieri develops the term to describe the work and product of *poiesis*, involves a movement from potentiality to actuality, a work of forming and testing the subject and its commitments. Articulation partially, but only partially, resolves the "inchoate pressures" of multiple desires within specific settings by affording them modes of release, expression, and development. When the work of poetic articulation is carried out well, as Altieri suggests it is in Yeats'

"Leda and the Swan" and in Shakespeare's *Othello*, then the poet may be seen to be arriving at witness to our cultural failures, to historical traumas, and to the brutalities of power, but in arriving at this witness also to be bearing an affirmative power of judgment and of the vision of something different. Altieri acknowledges that there is a certain danger that thus thinking of poets as exemplary strong articulators of judgment, vision, and routes of expression and desire will itself be received as a "reactionary fantasy" that worships art while leaving regnant political powers in place. In embracing this danger, however, Altieri intimates that it is only by accepting certain models of strong articulation, witness, and poetic vision – models that might provoke us to our own originalities – that we might hope to lead our lives as fallen subjects in culture and in political life affirmatively. "Participation in how another mind makes use of language ... carries a significant model of our own freedom" to be achieved in our own expressive acts.

Arthur C. Danto has been a powerful and prominent critic of the Cartesian conception of the human subject as a punctual processor of representations, themselves taken to stand in a problematic relation to some external thing that causes them in us. Urging a variant of the argument that Charles Taylor has elicited out of Hegel, Heidegger, Wittgenstein, and Merleau-Ponty, Danto has argued that just to the extent that we can identify anything as a representation at all, we are thereby committed to accepting the thought that there is a real world apart from our representations, perhaps even a world of which we are a part.[25] In place of the Cartesian conception of the human subject and of the primacy of cognitive interests in the life of the subject, Danto has elaborated, in both his philosophical and his critical writings on art, a conception of the human subject as coming to its distinctively representational consciousness and self-consciousness only in and through its formed social world, to which it then reacts.[26] The work of the artist, Danto writes, is that of "inventing modes of embodying meanings she or he may share with communities of very large circumference ... [M]eanings more or less come from the world in which the artist lives."[27]

In chapter 4, "In their own voice: philosophical writing and actual experience," Danto takes up philosophically the ontology and the practical ethics of the production of philosophy itself. Most "star-philosophers," Danto notes (and surely this category includes pre-eminently himself, who possesses an extraordinarily distinctive, lapidary style), "have pretty distinct voices." Does it follow from this

17

fact that their writings are products of merely personal, or perhaps situated historical-personal, voice or style and vision? Embracing this thought, Danto suggests, "vaporizes philosophical writing into poetry" – an unhappy result – in so far as a concern for standing truth, truth that survives changes in fashion, is lost.

That the traditional philosophical pursuit of standing truth can be sustained is evident, Danto argues, in the writings of Wittgenstein and Cavell. While these are two of the most writerly, most idiosyncratic, philosophical intelligences who have ever lived, and while much of the substance of their thinking is pre-eminently conveyed in their respective styles, there are nonetheless some theses that can be abstracted from their writings. Whether accepting limits is a good thing, as Wittgenstein urges, or whether as Cavell claims "all selves are sided," are matters that can be argued about. A concern for truth, not just for voice, informs their quite stylized writings, and as readers we must bring our own concern for truth to bear on the claims that they urge on us.

But, while this is true, it is also true that not any thought can be expressed in any voice. Certain voices and styles, themselves partly personal and partly historically situated and generated, make certain regions or aspects of truth available to us. In pursuing a neutral, impersonal style for the formulation of theses, what Danto calls "bottom line philosophy" – surely thinking of the routinized academic performances that compose much so-called professional philosophy, analytic and Continental alike – is "abstract and distorted and surrealistic." "We really do experience the world and life as gendered beings" and as otherwise specifically historically situated beings, "which means that the suppression of our facticities means a distorted representation of the world, the world according to Nobody." Instead of being anonymously professional and neutral, or written by Nobody, the work of "creative philosophers ... carries what they have written and what they hope to write as the aura of a total vision." It is impossible here not to think of the aura of the total vision of Danto's writing as itself providing us a certain persuasive articulation (in Altieri's terms) or poetic representation of how we might bring our personal-historical styles and experiences into fruitful engagement with our concern for truth. As simultaneously a writer and a philosopher, Danto hopes, it seems, both to engage us with his own writerly voice and also to say something true, in a standing way, about the importance and possibility of blending voice with truth-telling.

Chapters 5 and 6 as it were split this suggestion, taking up respectively the sides of the object of our characterizations and the subject who does the characterizing. In chapter 5, "Poetry and truth-conditions," Samuel Fleischacker takes up the topic of how things are present to us at all. In trying to make sense of our world, we are, he notes, caught within "the general human situation of being limited creatures who must always live beyond their limitations." Surprising things can happen, in the arts, in the sciences, in politics, and in daily life. Jackson Pollock produces a drip painting, or the position and velocity of an electron turn out to be unmeasurable simultaneously, and we do not know what to say. Nor are we at ease with this. When some bit of experience thus challenges our concepts and our capacities to make sense, then we construe that experience as presenting a problem for us. Fleischacker persuasively analogizes our need to make new sense of surprising experiences to our need to arrive at a judgment about whether a contract may be enforced in various kinds of unforeseen and largely unforeseeable circumstances. Something must be said, a verdict must be reached, but what, and how?

Here, Fleischacker suggests, is where poetry comes in, and is hence part of our normal equipment in responding to our worlds. In such unforeseen and unforeseeable circumstances, what is needed are creative judgments, employing indeterminate, not yet fully worked out, concepts with indeterminate truth-conditions – the kind of indeterminate concept that Kant says "beauty" is. Poetry helps to provide us with such concepts, with new, indeterminate ways of looking at new things that can help to support creative, reflective judgments of our experiences and lead us toward new ways of making sense. (In chapter 8, I similarly elaborate how art, in Kant's terms, "bodies forth to sense" certain indeterminate ideals.) "Poetry," Fleischacker claims, "thrives ... at these margins ... concentrates on, and derives its power from ... the fact that we must always project our commitments beyond what, strictly, we know." Crucially, however, and in acceptance of something like Danto's thoughts about the possibility of philosophical truth, this is not quite the simpler Rortyan thought that, in Shelley's terms, "poets are the unacknowledged legislators of the world,"[28] for the work of poetry is not prior to and independent of, but rather in its turn also presupposes, the works of science and of ordinary, "literal" assertion. "Poetry and science make each other possible"; we must embrace "both the determinacy of concepts of truth and their vulnerability to revision." In their dialectical interaction, poetry and science jointly serve as open, self-correcting vehicles of the continual represencing to us of the world.

Azade Seyhan takes up this theme of the continual, open-ended, self-correcting represencing to us of the world under certain forms of attention to it in chapter 6, "Fractal contours: chaos and system in the Romantic fragment." Suppose, in the wake of Kant, we reject dogmatism and strong forms of metaphysical and epistemological realism, so that there is no certain method for limning the ultimate structures of reality and for defending one's characterizations of what is ultimate. But suppose also that we retain a sense of our critical powers and possibilities, rather than accepting the Humean views that nature, of which we are a part, is too strong for principle and that our condition is whimsical. What forms of attention and expression, Seyhan asks, will then be appropriate for subjects thus situated, who retain powerful expressive aspirations but yet cannot stably and securely grasp the ultimate under a method? How can standing openness and a self-correcting character come to inhabit our forms of attention and expression themselves?

Seyhan suggests that the Romantic fragment, particularly as it was theorized and developed by Friedrich Schlegel, presents a persuasive answer to these questions. "The fractured reality of the world" – at the very least a world resistant to ultimate metaphysical characterization – "found its coincidental form of expression in the fragment." Its value as a form lies in its disseminating power, its provocativeness, its presentation of continuing energies of transformation in both the subject and the world that do not arrive at *stasis*. "Fragments are symbolic markers of a 'chaotic' progression that strives toward the cognition of an 'infinite reality.' Their open resistances to redemptive attempts at final restorations of unity and harmony embody an impetus for self-transformation." The Romantic fragment manifests a tendency toward irony, incomprehensibility, and the enactment of a sense of sublime powers never able to be housed. Yet it functions less as a simple embrace of disorder and chaos than as vehicle for coming to terms with always changing new orders of possibility in our cultural lives. "The fragment, then, mediates between system and systemlessness, attempts to function as a critical instrument for the review of apperceptual regimes, and renegotiates the status of the poetic in the anatomy of philosophical discourse." It presents its author, and implicitly presents human subjects in general, as always cast on routes of self-revision, partly of their own making, and always containing unanticipatable turnings.

In chapter 7, "The mind's horizon," Stanley Bates likewise takes up the theme of the continuously self-revising character of the human subject, likewise beginning from the Kantian "problematic of the subject unpresentable to itself" enunciated by Lacoue-Labarthe and Nancy. When one reviews Kant's sometime attempts to gesture toward an ultimate, noumenal reality that is never present to us in distinct existents or in our representations of them – the only objective representations we are able to form – then one discovers that there are "internal strains" that trouble this attempt. "From what perspective could one be in a position to say what Kant says in these passages ... We seem to be both within and beyond our own experience, simultaneously." A similar internal strain, Bates argues, also troubles Hegel's efforts to combine a conception of human subjects as always acculturated, acculturating self-revising subjects with the claim that we have arrived as human subjects at Absolute Knowledge that includes our full and final knowledge of ourselves.

Once we trace out the internal strains that trouble these Kantian and Hegelian efforts to characterize our position once and for all, while yet acknowledging our lack of direct and unmediated contact with anything ultimate, then we can see, Bates suggests, that our position as subjects in nature and culture, as well as how to enact that position, is always a problem for us. Awareness of this forces certain themes on us:

(1) the idea that reason is not the most fundamental mode of human being in the world but that something else, variously characterized as practice, doing, passion, feeling, etc., is, (2) the idea that there is a kind of division in the self, so that one may not know oneself fully (an idea something like that of the unconscious), (3) the idea that the individual self is not a given entity, but a goal to be sought in a process, potentially progressive, in which the self constitutes itself ... (4) the idea that certain experiences, which might be described as moments when the self-as-it-would-be transcends the self-as-it-is, provide intimations of the directionality of this process – and that these experiences fit comfortably under the rubric of the sublime, (5) the fact that many of the subsequent authors who express these themes do so, not in traditional (Descartes to Hegel) philosophical forms, but in other literary genres – essays, fictions, parables, polemics, pseudo-scriptures, etc.

Bates then concludes by tracing "the dialectic of exaltation and ordinariness, and the possibility of finding exaltation in ordinariness" that is played out in Emerson's essays. What emerges there is that "the moments of exalted awareness" that are achievable "cannot be sustained." Hence we bear a kind of "double conscious-ness" of ourselves and our possibilities, as we are caught, in "relations of self-succession" between moments of exaltation, self-collection, integrity, and at-homeness, on the one hand, and moments of doubt, despair, self-dispersion, and alienation, on the other.

Following Lacoue-Labarthe and Nancy, both Bates and Seyhan suggest that this kind of double consciousness, emerging out of the reception of Kant, has massively informed much of the most com-manding literary and philosophical work of the last two centuries, including at least the English and American Romantics, Kierkegaard, Marx, Nietzsche, Heidegger, Derrida, and poets of the American sublime such as Wallace Stevens and William Carlos Williams, among many others. In "Kant, Hölderlin, and the Experience of Longing," I undertake to track this sort of double consciousness as it manifests itself in the texts of both Kant and Hölderlin. Each of them enacts, I claim, "a sense of the human person as caught between an aspiration toward the ideal and the standing defeat of that aspira-tion." Focusing in particular on Kant's historical essays, where his conception of the perfection of the subject toward the always deferred full articulation and release of its rational capacities in lived, historical time is worked out, and on Hölderlin's "Dichter-beruf," "The Poet's Vocation," I argue in chapter 8, "Kant, Hölderlin, and the experience of longing," that a sense of one's own identity and power is internally related to one's sense of the possibilities of a culture of affirmative moral freedom. Hence the standing deferral of the achievement of such a culture, while its call for us remains present, throws one's own identity and integrity, perhaps one's very sanity, into question. Whether elegiac consciousness of moral freedom never quite coming to realization can itself sustain a kind of measured, always shifting, self-integrity and sense of cultural possi-bilities (rather than madness), therein motivating confession and a sense of shared identity (as Bernstein describes them) and gratitude (rather than revenge), presents itself here as an always open, and perhaps unavoidable, question.

Michael Fischer hopes for a culture that, while imperfect and suffused with antagonisms, is also informed by gratitude and a sense of shared, affirmative possibilities. In chapter 9, "Wordsworth and the reception of poetry," he suggests that Wordsworth's conception of his poetry and his own poetic practice can help to nurture this hope. In a pluralist age of multiple cultures, and of antagonisms within all cultures, it is rightly easy to distrust ethico-political universals and claims to culture-transcendent rationality. But it is equally hard to see how to inherit, revise, and share a culture affirmatively in the absence of a common articulate conception of what is worthwhile.

Here, Fischer, suggests, is where Wordsworth can help us. He is a universalist – he seeks guiding ethico-politico-religious conceptions for himself and for others – but he is not a transcendent or dogmatic universalist. He seeks not to impose his judgments on others, but instead to lead readers to decide for themselves, along his tracks, what is worthwhile. He seeks "to affect readers without coercing them." This leads Wordsworth, in his poetic practice, to solicit others to sing with him, as he seeks to articulate "conditional or provisional universals." "He wants readers to tap in themselves the imaginative energy that he himself has employed in writing the poem."

Because, however, Wordsworth has no independent metaphysical conception of the nature and proper objects of imaginative energy, hence no rationally demonstrable standards for its appropriate exercise (apart from whatever fitfully shows itself in that exercise itself), an enormous anxiety about the inheritability of his work, and beyond that about "the transmissibility of culture itself" results. "Will readers – many of whom will be quite different from me – exercise their imaginative energies along my routes, with anything like my provisional results?" Wordsworth wonders, agonizes. Two ways of responding to that anxious, self-interrogative wonder then present themselves. One might foreclose it through violence, seeking to force the agreement of others with one's valuations, as Robespierre did, or as Wordsworth is tempted to do in fantasizing that he might himself murder Robespierre. Or instead one might write, continuing therein to articulate conditional universals and to acknowledge the doubts that inevitably attach to doing so (thus bearing the kind of double consciousness that Bates describes and that I see in Kant and Hölderlin). "Though Wordsworth feels the allure of the violence he is contemplating, he rejects this option, turning instead to writing." The provisional articulations of values (in Altieri's sense) that then result from his writing are a way of continuing the traditional philosophical dream of substituting reason for violence in human relations, but now a poetic, nondogmatic reason – the very sort of reasoned but poetic pursuit of valuations, Fischer suggests, that also informs the best present feminist criticism, theory, and pedagogic practice.

In chapter 10, "Self-consciousness, social guilt, and Romantic poetry: Coleridge's Ancient Mariner and Wordsworth's Old Pedlar," Kenneth Johnston likewise scrutinizes how Wordsworth and Coleridge bear a double consciousness both of their identities as subjects and of cultural possibilities. By the end of 1797, both Wordsworth and Coleridge bear a "profoundly troubled commitment to the cause of human possibility, democratically defined." Each of them had for a time identified himself as a subject with the advancement of the democratic promise of the French Revolution. Here Johnston reminds us how powerful the association is between democratic ideals and Enlightenment conceptions of human subjects as individual bearers of representations. As the promise of the French revolution collapses into terror, however, Coleridge and Wordsworth find themselves forced to reconsider both their conceptions of themselves and their senses of the nature of the human subject generally. Direct political action by individuals, alone or massed, based on their representations of the world no longer seems a promising route toward freedom. But withdrawal from all action seems to acquiesce in the rule of the powers that be and to forego any sense of oneself as a self-forming subject, potentially effective in historical time.

Johnston characterizes the strategy at which Coleridge and Wordsworth then arrive – that of becoming a poet "radically": that is, with a new sense of oneself, one's commitments, complicities, and interests – as involving first bearing a sense of guilt and second trying to define oneself as one who goes on nonetheless in bearing that sense, principally by writing it out so that others may find themselves in it. (Here Johnston echoes Bernstein on the logic of confession and forgiveness as a vehicle for finding and forming a shared identity.) Their writing involves not the purveying of a doctrine, but rather "efforts at self-definition" of how one can be both guilty (for one's impotences) and yet an affirmative human subject.

These efforts are evident first of all in the story-tellings on the parts of the Ancient Mariner and the Old Pedlar. But the guilts that they bear (the Mariner for killing the albatross; the Old Pedlar for doing nothing in the face of Margaret's decline) and seek to acknowledge are in turn both figurations, and provocations, of guilt in their auditors (the Wedding Guest and the young Poet – for being themselves transfixed by stories and caught within their own stories, rather than attentive to material suffering). The guilt that all these figures thus share in turn figures the guilts that Coleridge and Wordsworth themselves bear for the failures of their own political involvements, aspirations, and commitments. In acknowledging these guilts through their story-tellers, who then provoke a like sense of guilt in their auditors, Coleridge and Wordsworth provoke a similar acknowledgment of guilt in us, *their* readers. Such ackowledgments (confessions in Bernstein's sense) of failures and guilts are a central modality of such self-understanding and expiation as there can be. "Each [Coleridge and Wordsworth] thus presents not a metaphysical explanation for human suffering, but a metapoetical situation that literally *articulates* the need for constant telling (including revising) of tales of human suffering." In this telling and revising, one, along with others, as an active human subject who bears responsibilities and guilts (rather than being in possession of political self-sufficiencies) – persists, Johnston suggests, as a bearer of a quasi-secularized version of original sin. Recognizing that one is a subject of this kind – as these poems prompt us to do – is, Johnston argues, less the path of political quietism than it is the way to any sense of human life, political or otherwise, that is worthy of the name.

Each of the contributions so far has dwelt on a conception of the human subject as divided within itself. Human subjects have been cast as bearing a double consciousness of aspirations and their defeat. They are seen as possessing a partly accomplished power to transform culture, but also as suffering guilt over failures of attention and responsiveness. Is this sort of sense of the human subject simply parcelled out among all of us, so that any poet, possessed of and enacting enough self-consciousness, might speak for us, might express a shared sense of subjectivity? Or does it make a difference to the sense one has of oneself as a subject that one is a woman? "What is it," Christine Battersby asks, in chapter 11, "Her blood and his mirror: Mary Coleridge, Luce Irigaray, and the female self," "to write as a woman?"

Here Battersby finds that there are indeed some important specificities to the female subject position. It is not that there is an ahistorical feminine style – involving, say, gentleness and emotional attunement – into which woman writers naturally fall. To think this, Battersby argues, is to essentialize away history and its possibilities of alternative subject positions. But there is nonetheless a specifically female, not feminine, subject position that is evident in the poetry of Mary Elizabeth Coleridge and the theoretical writings of Luce Irigaray. This female subject position is specifically historically allotted to members of the female sex, who are forced by their sex (itself partly a constructed, partly a given category, involving – Battersby suggests – an interfusion of metaphysics and history) to react against a specific literary and philosophical tradition.

Traditionally, Battersby argues, in male-dominated philosophy and letters, one became an accomplished, exemplary, fully self-conscious human subjectivity – a genius – by becoming an androgynous or feminized male. (Here Battersby draws on her powerful analysis of gendered Romantic genius in her *Gender and Genius: Towards a Feminist Aesthetics.*[29]) Occupying this position is evidently impossible for women. Both Mary Elizabeth Coleridge and Luce Irigaray note "their own incapacity as female to occupy that subject position," and they seek therefore to "reconstruct a female subject position." While they cannot take up the modes of the bearing of affirmative, expressive power that have been typical in our culture, they nonetheless refuse to abandon the pursuit of expressiveness and a sense of oneself as a subject who bears power in and through culture.

Caught between the appeal of their literary-philosophical tradition in offering models of cultural power, on the one hand, and that tradition's specific rejection of them as female subjects, on the other, Coleridge and Irigaray enact a specific awareness of their "indeterminate desire" and of their "incompleteness" and "woundedness," as they find themselves unable to enter into the routes of transcendence of the given that our culture has traditionally held open for some. "The female poet," Battersby writes, "retains the horror of the flesh whilst simultaneously blocking traditional models of transcendence." Coleridge "seems entirely caught up with the paradoxes and the contraries of the other within," in possession of indeterminate desire and a distress that is "unsanctified" by any vehicle for its working through and overcoming.

Yet what Coleridge experiences as the woundedness, indeterminate desire, and unsanctified distress of the female subject position may also, Battersby argues, itself be productive and affirming. Elaborating Irigaray's work on the Thesmophoria festivities, Battersby suggests that "what was celebrated in these all-female spaces was a form of identity in which the self was relational, and in which otherness extruded out of (and was then reincorporated within) the female self via relationships of gift, birth, ripening and (productive) decay." Perhaps, Battersby intimates, female subject-position writing that is continuous with such ritual celebrations can provide a more persuasive model of the sustenance of human identity generally than the post-Platonic male models of transcendence of the given that we have mostly inherited from our traditions.

Whether, how – under what modalities of practice –, and to what extent self-integrity is possible for us, through coming to achieve reciprocal recognition in a perfected culture, where both self-integrity and the perfection of culture are envisioned through *poiesis*, is the issue around which all the contributions to this volume center. How, if at all, might we come to be affirmatively free human subjects in culture? Is this either possible or desirable? These questions are the focus of attention in chapter 12, "Scene: an exchange of letters," the contribution of Philippe Lacoue-Labarthe and Jean-Luc Nancy. In moving through this field of concerns, Lacoue-Labarthe and Nancy are meditating, roughly fifteen years later, on the fundamental issues raised by their epochal 1978 book *L'absolu littéraire* – the book from which Seyhan and Bates explicitly, and several other contributors implicitly, take their points of departure.

That book – we may now recall from these other contributions – enunciates the Kantian and post-Kantian problematic of the subject not present to itself. That is, in *The Literary Absolute* Lacoue-Labarthe and Nancy describe the post-Kantian sense of the human subject as always in process, bearing a kind of decentered subjectivity always in reformation, in and through its poetic and critical envisionings of itself and its situation. Those who bear this sense of themselves as subjects – pre-eminently Friedrich Schlegel – hence find their philosophical concerns for self-integrity, freedom, and the perfection of culture migrating into poetry, or better yet into a kind of philosophico-poetico-criticism, wherein disciplinary distinctions break down. In this way, these figures continue the concerns of philosophy by another means. For the modern, Romantic subjects who bear this sense of themselves – for those who have become poets radically, Johnston would say –

programmatically, the philosophical *organon* is thought as the product or *effect* of a *poiesis*, as work (*Werk*) or as poetical *opus* ... Philosophy must effectuate itself – complete, fulfill, and realize itself – as poetry ... [L]itera-ture, as its own infinite questioning and as the perpetual positing of its own question, dates from romanticism and as romanticism. [This means that] the romantic question, the question of romanticism, does not and cannot have an answer. Or, at least that its answer can only be interminably deferred, continually deceiving, endlessly recalling the question ... This is why romanticism, which is actually a moment (the moment of its question) will always have been more than a mere "epoch," or else it will never cease, right up to the present, to incomplete the epoch it inaugurated ... Romantic criticism – and indeed criticism and poetics since romanticism – conceives of itself as the construction of the classical work to come. This is also why, with regard to romantic poetry "itself," criticism in turn possesses its own superior and as yet unactualized status: that of this "divinatory criticism," which alone (again in *Athenaeum* fragment 116) "would dare to characterize" the ideal of such a "poetry."[30]

In their present meditation on what it is like to bear this sort of subjectivity, scrutinizing itself and its possibilities through this form of philosophico-poetico-critical thinking, Lacoue-Labarthe and Nancy begin from a question about the meaning and importance of *opsis* – staging or spectacle (it makes a difference which term we choose) – in Aristotle's *Poetics*. Tragic drama, Aristotle claims, essentially takes place through staging, yet staging as spectacle is nonetheless secondary and inessential to tragedy and its proper effects.

For Lacoue-Labarthe and Nancy, this issue in the *Poetics* about the nature and importance of staging is but one side of a much larger issue: what is the nature and function of performance in the construction of a human subjectivity and its life? Their turn to this larger issue is motivated by the fact that the French word "scène," which translates one sense of Aristotle's *opsis* (stage or staging, not performance or spectacle) is also the word in psychoanalytic theory in French that describes the place of the formation of subject identity: *la scène originaire*, the primal, Oedipal scene. (Their essay was first published in French in a 1992 issue of *Nouvelle revue de psychanalyse* devoted to "The Primal Scene and Some Others.")

Against the background of their post-Kantian concerns, Lacoue-Labarthe and Nancy then see the scene (primal and otherwise) as the place of the continual coming-to-be of the subject. The work done in this scene is characterized by a dialectic of order and disorder (Seyhan), by a mixture of coercion and free consent (Fischer), by productive imagination acting under constraints set by materiality and tradition (Danto, Fleischacker). It is a place of the performance (Altieri) of identity, including gender identity (Battersby) and voice (Danto), wherein subjects bear both a double consciousness of their possibilities (Bates, Eldridge) and guilt (Johnston), wherein they are locked in relations of confession and forgiveness, sustained or refused (Bernstein).

Given all this, how is the work of subject formation best to be done? Here Lacoue-Labarthe and Nancy divide themselves in their exchange of letters. ("A dialogue is a chain or garland of fragments. An exchange of letters is a dialogue on a larger scale," as Lacoue-Labarthe and Nancy cite Schlegel's *Athenaeum* fragment 77 in *The Literary Absolute.*[31]) "I always," Nancy writes, "take the side of the *opsis* and you the side of the 'solitary reading.'" As Nancy develops this stance, it emerges that this side, the side of *opsis*, involves a commitment to the values of spectacle, free performativism, and the enunciatory gesture (wherein meaning is not readily parted from effect or from touch) in the enactment of subjectivity. Occupying this stance means conceiving the subject as itself not a fixed point of origin of performances, but instead as something wholly caught up and constituted "in a game, in an exchange, in a circulation, and in a community which depends on an economy completely different from that of subjective representation [i.e. from a unified, punctual subject's having of ideas]." Here we may think naturally of Nietzsche in *The Birth of Tragedy* on the Dionysian and its form of fragmented, collective subjectivity.

Against this stance, Lacoue-Labarthe urges "a principle of restraint in art." Lacoue-Labarthe does not deny that we are always becoming what we are in and through scenes of performance. There is no reversion to a Cartesian conception of subjectivity. "I am ... fully convinced that we are at the end of a subjectivity understood as a self-presence which supports presentations and brings them back as one's own – this subjectivity being, precisely, unpresentable," Nancy writes, enunciating the Kantian and post-Kantian conception of the subject described in *The Literary Absolute*, and Lacoue-Labarthe apparently accepts this. But, while accepting subjectivity as always coming to be in and through a scene of its staging, Lacoue-Labarthe nonetheless resists the values of performativism and open, unleashed figurality. Such unleashed figurality, an attempt to think and embrace the figurality of figure, involves, according to Lacoue-Labarthe, a potentially dangerous, Heideggerian "sacralization or mythologization" of figural breaks from the tradition and the ordinary – figural breaks that threaten to undo everything that is, all partial identity and all partially free culture, far too apocalyptically. Unleashed figurality as a positive value threatens to make "a religion of the unpresentable," threatens to enact an empty and dangerous sublime. At the very least, too much figurality and openness in performance, and too little concern for tradition, for the ordinary, and for the real as it has so far presented itself in and through culture, supports, Lacoue-Labarthe suggests, a certain "sentimentality" and "an expressionistic weakness" in thinking about our possibilities of character and culture. We would be better off, Lacoue-Labarthe asserts, to keep to a certain normative principle of sobriety and restraint in our performances of ourselves and our culture – a stance that we can recognize as urging the values of the Apollonian sensibility as Nietzsche describes it in *The Birth of Tragedy*.

Is there, then, any way to reconcile these stances on the performances of subjectivity and of culture, any way to resolve the question about how being-in-common (*être-en-commun*), both within oneself and with others, might best, even if fitfully, be achieved? Near the end of their exchange, Nancy writes that "an antinomy, if you will, of perceptions and affections" inhabits their exchange and makes there to be this scene – this staging of oneself for and to and with another – between them. This seems right, as their exchange enacts the sense that questions about how best to go on reforming our partially integrated, partially free, but also partially self-opposed, partially unfree, subjectivities and cultures as they stand must always remain open for us.

III

Many of these essays – and most especially the exchange between Lacoue-Labarthe and Nancy – display a critical and philosophical performativism, particularly when contrasted with more routinized forms of professional philosophical thinking and expression. Truth is here pursued through criticism, and articulation, and envisioning, not through any attempt neutrally to measure and trace what is independently materially real. In these pursuits, varieties of voice and sensibility become strongly evident, as the writers of these essays enact – stage, Lacoue-Labarthe and Nancy might say – their respective subjectivities.

A certain careful, materialist cast of mind will find these pursuits suspicious, and it will seek, perhaps, to reduce these enactments of sensibility to the expressions of mere preferences (it will say) somehow formed elsewhere – in either material nature or material social life. One ambition of this collection is to make that reduction harder to sustain, by presenting essays – enactments or stagings or envisionings – of such depth and richness that it is hard to reduce them away and to deny the reality of always enacted-enacting subjectivity. On their showings, we are human subjects in and

through the tangled, self-opposed, work of *poiesis*, aimed at ourselves in our culture and our culture in ourselves, and the work of
poiesis lasts a long time.

Notes

1 Richard Rorty, *Philosophy and the Mirror of Nature* (Princeton University
   Press, 1979). See especially Rorty's characterization of the role of philosophy as it was conceived of by Descartes, Locke, Russell, and Husserl,
   among others: "Philosophy can be foundational in respect to the rest of
   culture because culture is the assemblage of claims to knowledge, and
   philosophy adjudicates such claims. It can do so because it understands
   the foundations of knowledge, and it finds these foundations in a study of
   man-as-knower, of the 'mental processes' or the 'activity of representation'
   which make knowledge possible. To know is to represent accurately what
   is outside the mind; so to understand the possibility and nature of knowledge is to understand the way in which the mind is able to construct such
   representations. Philosophy's central concern is to be a general theory of
   representation, a theory which will divide culture up into the areas which
   represent reality well, those which represent it less well, and those which
   do not represent it at all (despite their pretense of doing so)" (p. 3).
2 Ian Hacking, *Why Does Language Matter to Philosophy* (Cambridge
   University Press, 1975), p. 187: "At any rate, I have one answer to the
   question of why language matters to philosophy now. *It matters for the
   reason that ideas mattered in seventeenth-century philosophy*, because
   ideas then, and sentences now, serve as the interface between the
   knowing subject and what is known." Hacking then goes on to look
   forward to a situation in which discourse is "that which constitutes
   human knowledge" (p. 187), without dependence on either a knowing
   subject or a given external reality. Here he anticipates the subsequent
   work not only of Rorty, but of such post-structuralist literary theorists as
   Catherine Belsey.
3 Rorty, *Philosophy*, p. 3.
4 G. W. F. Hegel, *Phenomenology of Spirit*, trans. A. V. Miller (Oxford:
   Clarendon Press, 1977), para. 73, p. 47.
5 Charles Taylor, "Overcoming Epistemology," in *After Philosophy: End or
   Transformation?*, eds. Kenneth Baynes, James Bohman, and Thomas
   McCarthy (Cambridge, MA: The MIT Press, 1987), p. 474.
6 Hegel, *Phenomenology*, para. 74, p. 47.
7 Rorty, *Contingency, Irony, and Solidarity* (Cambridge University Press,
   1989), p. 6.
8 Catherine Belsey, *Critical Practice* (London: Methuen & Co., Ltd., 1980), p.
   40.

9 Michel Foucault, *The History of Sexuality, Vol. 1: An Introduction*, trans. Robert Hurley (New York: Random House, 1978), p. 93.

10 Jean-François Lyotard, *The Postmodern Condition: A Report on Knowledge*, trans. Geoff Bennington and Brian Massumi (Minneapolis: University of Minnesota Press, 1984), p. 81.

11 There is controversy about how this word ought to be spelled. The Greek word is ποιησει, later transliterated into Latin as *poesis*, as in Horace's *Ars poetica*, and it is this latter, Latin spelling that has been familiar from schoolboy classical educations for several hundred years. There is also controversy about whether the e in poiesis (however spelled) should carry a macron, no accent, or even a circumflex. Insofar as the philosophers, poets, and critics who will be under consideration are themselves trying to recover and refigure certain wide-ranging senses of the nature of poetic activity and its value in the life of a subject that are principally evident in the Platonic and Aristotelian texts, it seems apt to prefer a direct and simple transliteration of the Greek. I owe the information about the history of the spellings of *poiesis* to my colleagues in Greek and Latin Studies, Gilbert Rose and William Turpin.

12 See the discussions of *poiesis*, *theoria*, *praxis*, and *mimesis* in the Glossary to Aristotle, *Poetics*, trans. Richard Janko (Indianopolis: Hackett Publishing Company, 1987), as well as Janko's helpful section of his Introduction on "Aristotle's Concept of Representation" (pp. xiv–xv).

13 Paul Shorey, notes to Plato, *Republic I*, trans. Paul Shorey (London: William Heinemann Ltd. [Loeb Classical Library], 1930), p. 224, note c.

14 Hegel, *Phenomenology*, para. 167, p. 105.

15 *Ibid.*, para. 178, p. 111.

16 Immanuel Kant, *Critique of Practical Reason*, trans. Lewis White Beck (Indianapolis: The Bobbs-Merrill Company, Inc., 1956), p. 89.

17 Philippe Lacoue-Labarthe and Jean-Luc Nancy, *The Literary Absolute: The Theory of Literature in German Romanticism*, trans. Philip Barnard and Cheryl Lester (Albany: State University of New York Press, 1988), pp. 30, 31, 32.

18 Robert B. Pippin, *Modernism as a Philosophical Problem* (Oxford: Basil Blackwell, 1991), p. 50.

19 Kant, *Critique of Pure Reason*, trans. Norman Kemp Smith, 2nd edn. (London: The Macmillan Press, Ltd., 1933), Ax, p. 8.

20 Kant, *Kritik der reinen Vernunft*, ed. Raymund Schmidt (Hamburg: Felix Meiner, 1956), Ax, p. 6. My translation.

21 Theodor Adorno, "Resignation," *Telos* 35 (Spring 1978), 168.

22 Max Horkheimer and Theodor W. Adorno, *Dialectic of Enlightenment*, trans. John Cumming (New York: Continuum, 1972), p. 7.

23 J. M. Bernstein, *The Fate of Art: Aesthetic Alienation from Kant to Derrida to Adorno* (University Park, PA: The Pennsylvania State University Press, 1992).

24 Charles Altieri, *Canons and Consequences: Reflections on the Ethical*

Force of Imaginative Ideals (Evanston, IL: Northwestern University Press, 1990).

25 Arthur Danto, "The Representational Character of Ideas and the Problem of the External World," in *Descartes: Critical and Interpretive Essays*, ed. Michael Hooker (Baltimore: The Johns Hopkins University Press, 1978), p. 295.

26 See especially Danto, *The Transfiguration of the Commonplace* (Cambridge, MA: Harvard University Press, 1981), especially chapter 7, "Metaphor, Expression, and Style," pp. 165-208; and "Narrative and Style," *The Journal of Aesthetics and Art Criticism* 49: 3 (Summer 1991), 201-209.

27 Danto, *Embodied Meanings: Critical Essays and Aesthetic Meditations* (New York: Farrar Straus Giroux, 1994), p. xii.

28 Percy Bysshe Shelley, "A Defence of Poetry," in *The Norton Anthology of English Literature*, Vol. 2, 3rd. edn., ed. Abrams *et al.* (New York: W. W. Norton & Company, Inc., 1974), p. 632.

29 Christine Battersby, *Gender and Genius: Towards a Feminist Aesthetics* (London: The Women's Press Limited, 1989).

30 Lacoue-Labarthe and Nancy, *The Literary Absolute*, pp. 36, 83, 112.

31 *Ibid.*, p. 84.

2

Confession and forgiveness: Hegel's poetics of action

J. M. BERNSTEIN

CONSCIENCE: BETWEEN IRONY AND LIBERAL COMMUNITY

In writing a "phenomenology" portraying the fundamental forms or shapes of human consciousness, tracing them through their internal struggles and eventual self-generated dissolutions, Hegel must be construed as intending his philosophy to depart from the foundational, deductive, and naturalistic ambitions that constitute modern philosophy. Only through "experience" (*Erfahrung*) (86)[1] that is, through the self-induced transformations of historically and socially mediated forms of consciousness, is philosophical insight possible. Yet, because he calls the knowing that results from this history of consciousness "Absolute," and because he goes on to provide us with a "logic," it has been almost universally supposed that his poetics of spirit (*Geist*), his account of the creative self-overcomings of consciousness, its "way of despair" (77), is only a "ladder" (26) to the standpoint of the Absolute which is to be cast away once it has been achieved; and with that achievement Hegel's philosophy, however circuitously, however deferred in approach, rejoins the tradition of subsumptive rationalism his phenomenological practice had bracketed. The phenomenological analysis of the modern conscientious self decisively challenges the thesis that with Spirit's coming to be acknowledged as Absolute we could cease having experiences and our exposure to despair be overcome.

Conscience is the third and final self in the history of Spirit through which it comes to awareness of itself as the ground and condition of human experience.[2] Whatever Hegel means by his notions of Spirit and Absolute is hence to be revealed by how the self of conscience comes to understand itself. As it first emerges, the conscientious self claims direct awareness of itself as Absolute truth

34

and being. In the apperceptive "takings" of its all-too-human will (*Willkür*) the individual conscience claims immediate awareness and certainty of its action as what it is universally and objectively obligated to do; subjective conviction and objective duty coinciding (633). In opposition to this original claim, the actual experience of conscience (*das Gewissen*) is of its continual loss of certainty (*Gewissheit*). Conscience could only be certain that what it claims as its duty is what is objectively required if it had complete knowledge of the circumstances and consequences of action, and if the meaning of its action were uniquely determined by its apperceptive relation to it; neither condition is satisfiable. Our knowledge of the conditions and consequences of our actions is always parochial and limited (642), and we cannot be privileged determiners of the meaning of our actions without discounting the experience of other conscientious selves in determining what for them those actions might mean (647–649). Yet, despite the fallibilism of all moral knowledge and ineliminable interpretive pluralism with respect to the meaning of all moral actions, we cannot as modern selves give up the claim of conscience without surrendering our conception of ourselves as subjects who freely and self-consciously give shape to our lives and the world we inhabit. If we are in any sense self-determining, then we must be conscientious selves, selves who determine for ourselves, on the basis of judgment, reflection, and deliberation, what is morally (universally and objectively) required.[3]

Where conscience initially goes wrong is in regarding its conscientious belief that X is its duty as a constitutive criterion which would immediately make X what is objectively required. Construing the deliverances of conscience as criterial in this way makes each individual conscience into an a priori and thus empty form, structurally homologous with the formalism of Kantian universality that conscience meant to overcome. This is Hegel's point in using the same terms of criticism against conscience ("displacing" and "dissembling") he had previously deployed against Kantian moralism (648 and 616–631). Salvaging the claims of conscience while acknowledging fallibilism and interpretive pluralism requires discriminating the truth of an action from its intended meaning. Conscience properly belongs to the doing of an action and hence to the agent's determination of itself through that doing. Conscientious action thus comes to involve both a content, what is done, and a reflexive form of performance, the doing, with the latter being equivalent to "the self-expression of an individuality" (650). Only in being recognized as a conscientious *self* by others, affording action a distinct expressive dimension apart from its actual content, does it become possible for an action to be recognized as both conscientious and wrong. And it is only through language, through the performative declaration of conviction, that the expressive dimension of action achieves actuality, and so a being there for others. Equally, however, it is the linguistically actualized expressive dimension of action which is the means whereby the self comes both to reveal and to take a stand upon itself as a conscientious agent (652–653). Hence, only in a community of conscientious agents, who recognize one another as conscientious selves, are acts of conscience, which here must be taken as equivalent to any non-routine, significant human action, possible.

Although this provides the rough contours that Hegel's resolution of the problem of conscience will take, it oversimplifies the aporia of conscience in two respects. First, while mutual recognition of one another as conscientious selves may afford release from the burden of existential solitude implied by the demand of conscience (656), the idea of an immediate (romantic) community of conscientious selves simply eludes or suppresses the question of conscientious action: the universality of the mutual recognitions forming the community of conscience leaves blank the question of determining the objectivity of the actions of those agents. How could mutual recognitions remove the negativity in virtue of which an action is a "this one" and "mine"? Secondly, if significant action is expressive, and that expressive dimension reflexively determines the character of the self performing the action, then the moral worth of the self, its standing for itself and for others, cannot be recognized independently of its actions, actions which reveal and determine the self in opposition to the community. These considerations threaten the certainty of the (Romantic) consensus.

In response to these difficulties, two strategies emerge. On the one hand, the moment of community itself may be embraced by means of the collective and conscientious adoption of rules and principles for the co-ordination of action. Mutual recognition of one another as conscientious selves is actively and reflectively affirmed and structured through the construction of rules and principles that are themselves expressive of this mutual recognition. We may conceive of this constructivist programme as involving the employment of, say, the Rawlsian veil of ignorance or the adoption and employment of Habermas' principle D.[4] Hegel denominates the self who adopts this strategy first "universal consciousness" (663), and then "judging consciousness" (665) since it displaces the burden of significant action into the procedures employed for generating universal principles of action, and hence into the principles themselves; all that is then left for it to do is judge the correspondence between particular actions and collective principles. In this way judging consciousness preserves its moral purity by not having to act, in any weighty sense, at all. In making this charge, Hegel will not mean to deny the ideals of modern liberalism (freedom, equality, mutual respect, etc.) that are presupposed throughout by the standpoint of conscience, albeit unreflectively. What he will contest is liberalism's self-understanding, its mode of justification, its claim to self-sufficiency, and hence its philosophical ultimacy. The ideal of a deliberative community does not exhaust the claims of conscience.

On the other hand, conscience may despair of the possibility of providing a final and stable set of norms and principles, since any such set, given the real social and historical complexity of the moral universe, would necessarily repress the individual conscientious self's right to judge and legislate for itself what is morally required. But, if no communal principles for action can capture or coincide with self-determining and self-legislating activity, then it follows that no individual set of rules and principles can either; what makes communal norms inadequate for the articulation and expression of self-determining individuality equally ruins any settled configuration of principles for action. Hence, only the reiterated activity of judging and acting conscientiously in relation to all events and circumstances, and never identifying oneself with either the community as a whole or the principle revealed through any particular action, is compatible with the claims of conscience. It is through the moment of non-identification of itself both with others and with what is realized through its own actions, and thus through the maintenance of the separation of its apperceptive self-relation from the actualized putative universality of its actions, that this form of conscience sustains its moral purity, and hence the certainty of its conscience. This is the position of "acting consciousness" (659).

If the stance of judging consciousness can be identified with contemporary liberal communitarians like Rawls and Habermas, the position of acting consciousness finds expression in modern projects for autonomy and authenticity which depend upon the self realizing itself in opposition to achieved communal consensuses and any

achieved self-identity. Acting conscience's insistence on its apperceptively conceived individuality thus anticipates Mill's defence of
eccentricity versus what is customary, Heidegger's defence of
authenticity against the "chatter" of *das Man*, and even Nietzsche's
Zarathustra's defence of the project of self-overcoming: "Whatever I
create and however much I love it – soon I have to oppose it and my
love: thus will my will have it."[5] Hegel would identify each of these
as forms of romantic irony in which the negativity of apperceptive
self-awareness, the self-positing of the Fichtean ego, is taken as
essential in relation to any content created by it: "But in that case the
ego can remain lord and master of everything, and in no sphere of
morals, law, things human and divine, profane and sacred, is there
anything that would not first have to be laid down by ego, and that
therefore could not equally well be destroyed by it."[6] The quint-
essence of this project, Hegel avers, is "living as an artist and
forming one's life *artistically*."[7] Such artistically formed living, in
comparison to the case of the "simply deceived, poor limited
creatures," those who live the customary life of *das Man* or who are
embroiled in the fate of passive nihilism, the "herd" of mass society,
achieves its infinite worth from the *process* of creation and formation
with respect to which everything else is only an "unsubstantial
creature, to which the creator, knowing himself to be disengaged and
free from everything, is not bound, because he is just as able to
destroy it as to create it,"[8] "to bind and to loose" (646). Acting
consciousness is thus an active nihilism, an identification of the self
with its negating/creating capacity.

Romantic irony for Hegel is just principled disengagement from
content. From this angle, his critique of the ironist is unsurprising.

I live as an artist when all my action and my expression in general, in
connection with any content whatever, remains for me a mere show and
assumes a shape which is wholly in my power. In that case I am not really in
earnest either with this content, or generally, with its expression and
actualization. For genuine earnestness enters only by means of a substantial
interest, something of intrinsic worth like truth, ethical life, etc., – by means
of a content which counts for me as essential, so that I only become essential
myself in my own eyes in so far as I have immersed myself into conformity
with it in all my knowing and acting.[9]

The practice of creation constituting the life of the ironist both
reiterates and provides the fullest articulation of the categorical
separation of negating activity (transcendental consciousness) and
passivity (empirical consciousness) that results from the sceptic's

attempt to secure the independence and essentiality of himself as a self-consciousness (204–205). Thus, etched into the project of the ironist is that form of sceptical self-consciousness which attempts to secure itself as free and self-determining by disavowing its dependence on the deliverances of its senses which afford it the opportunity of exercising its capacity for negation. In both forms of consciousness all contents are conceived of as being logically incommensurable with the essential autonomy of the self: to be self-determining is to be in perpetual and necessary excess to any content. If only the determining activity of self-consciousness is essential, then contents are mere vehicles for self-expression. But if the contents are only vehicles, worthless in themselves, then the activity of creating them becomes equally worthless. Contents cannot be mere vehicles, mere instruments, without their emptiness reverberating back on the processes generating them – which is what logically presses Nietzsche toward some form of vitalism, the achievement of "more life," as the indirect content of the process of creation itself. But even this solution must fail since there is no logical difference between "more life" and "more freedom"; if contents are only ever means and instruments, if all the worth of a creation lies in its expressive features, its being created, and none in its content, then the process of creation becomes an instrumentalizing of the self. Nonetheless, even if we concede that the autarky of the ironist can only be overcome through a commitment to a content, we may still wonder about Hegel's contention that such a content must possess "intrinsic worth." How does "intrinsic worth" relate to the negative powers of the self? How can it come to "count" for me as "essential"? Why is not the affirmation of such a content an act of bad faith through which I surrender my right of self-determination to others? Why is not the immersion of oneself in, say, the content of ethical life reducible to judging consciousness' avoidance of action? If the position of judging consciousness does involve a suppression of action, then must not the act of immersion in a content *include* the negativity of "forming one's life artistically" in order to be valid?

In the *Phenomenology* Hegel broaches these issues indirectly. Both judging and acting forms of conscience are "beautiful souls," souls whose beauty is co-extensive with their (desire for) certainty, a certainty that for them is a condition of their moral purity. Placing judging and acting consciousness in this frame reveals that neither has truly accepted the analysis of moral action leading to their formation: if the contents of action may always be falsified later and by others, then no action can be free of the possibility of deliberative reproach. But if the moral worth of actions is always subject to censure, then the dual strategies of shifting the locus of purity from action to self must involve a disavowal of the expressive dimension of action, of our taking a stand upon ourselves through the actions we perform. No formation of self or community can underwrite or secure their authenticity and universality a priori. The moment of creative negativity will become contentless, mere capricious self-affirmation, the hollow and anxious singing and dancing of a deluded Zarathustra, and the community a structure of universality indifferent to the claims of individuality, if either is reified and made independent of the other. The "beauty" of the "beautiful souls" of acting and judging consciousness thus echoes the illusory "beauty" of the "stable equilibrium" (462) of Greek ethical life that was shattered by Antigone's deed. So the figure of acting consciousness is a modern Antigone, still holding out the claims of individuality and its "unwritten law"[10] against the claims of the publically recognized, universalistic laws of community; and the figure of judging consciousness a modern Creon, still placing the universality of the community before the claims of individuality. Thus the *agon* between acting and judging consciousness means to resolve the matter between Antigone and Creon, between individuality and universality, unwritten and written law, where this resolution must turn on pressing the issue of the negativity of human action, the loss of certainty, in relation to the claim for purity made by modern beautiful souls, their beauty the sign of what they affirm uncondi-tionally or refuse: "the tremendous power of the negative ... the energy of thought, of the pure 'I' " (32).

Death, if that is what we want to call this non-actuality, is of all things the most dreadful, and to hold fast what is dead requires the greatest strength. Lacking strength, beauty hates the understanding for asking of her what it cannot do. But the life of spirit is not the life that shrinks from death and keeps itself untouched by devastation, but rather the life that endures it and maintains itself in it. It wins its truth only when, in utter dismemberment, it finds itself ... Spirit is this power only by looking the negative in the face, and tarrying with it.   (32)

These evocative phrases from the "Preface" of the *Phenomenology of Spirit* are shown in the experience of the conscientious self to refer to the negativity of self-consciousness in relation to all contents that is revealed through the discovery that conscientious action cannot have its objective worth prospectively secured. The dilemmas represented by moral fallibilism and interpretive pluralism are components of an analysis of human action generally that demonstrate it as always a re-creation, a reconfiguration of existing norms and practices, and hence as always negating those contents, and thus the community that is bound and constituted by them, in the very acts that are meant to be their realization and concretion. This unsurpassable "moment" of negativity is reified in the artistic life of the ironic self. Because that moment is consubstantial with our embodied individuality, because it realizes itself always against given truth and given norms, because in transgressing against given norms we are transgressing against the achieved universalities through which those around us gather their worth and dignity as individuals, judging consciousness denominates the moment "evil."

CONFESSING EVIL, BREAKING THE HARD HEART

The conflict of duties between the judging consciousness and the ironic self is not only a clash of ideas, but a clash of wills in which the modern, conscientious Antigone can only, but equally must, stake herself in pressing her claim. Conscience begins with this: it does not act for the sake of the law, but in its individual response to wrong, which here is just the community's disavowal and non-recognition of passionate negativity and thus individuality. It must place itself, its ends, and the ends of others, against an inert universality that claims to be devoid of all individuality (because a perfected expression of it). In so placing and taking a stand upon itself, acting consciousness appears to judging consciousness as only a self, an individual posing its individual claims in opposition to those of the community at large. Do we know if Antigone is acting out of love for her brother or from religious duty? Is the passion of her act suppressed erotic fascination or a passionate claim on behalf of the rights of the individual? Is she not, in her passion and conviction, putting herself, her desires, needs, inclinations, and interests in the place of the universal laws of the state? These admittedly anachronistic questions are the ones asked by the liberal, modern Creon who seeks evidence for the impersonal point of view as criterial when considering the validity of the ironist's deeds (665). Finding none, he condemns her: she is evil because she rejects the universalist standards of the community; because these standards are constitutive of what is universal "in us," she is evil because she

41

denies what makes her a conscientious self. Further, she is a hypocrite because she self-servingly paints her individualist claims in the colors of conscience (660).

The condemned ironist does not see herself as she is seen. For her the questions of the impartial moralist are moot. Her passion and her duties are intertwined: if duties do not issue from any source beyond the self, and the self can only be through its claiming, each claim being an expression of the self as conscientious and hence a self-affirmation, then every claim is interested, a claim of the self through which it can hope to find itself confirmed (665).[11] It is he who judges who is the hypocrite, who denies that he is in his judgment, who falsely believes that in judging he is doing nothing, that judging is not acting, but merely surveying from an indeterminate place the correspondence between universal and particular. But, given her self-understanding, the ironist cannot condemn her judge as evil, only as base and hypocritical since the judge conceived as acting and interested is formally equal with her (666).

Although we may not feel pity and fear in anticipation of this moment, it nonetheless involves a reversal and recognition, however partial. In being judged and being condemned, we might imagine that what the ironist comes to see is that what is called universal or right or justice is not an independent truth, but an expression of her, a figure of what will count as her self-realization and her relations to others. Hence, we might imagine that the ironist perceives the good as her good as it is made possible through her interaction with others, including the judge; and hence, that the idea of *the* good is a fiction, there can only be *our* good, the one that first emerges through creative activity and is realized by being recognized and tokened by others. But how might she say this? How might she convince the judge that this is how things are? What form of insight would be involved in pressing this claim?

In fact, Hegel does not take the ironist, the modern Antigone, down this logical road; and he does not because an insight of this kind would be abstract, theoretical, an insight about the nature of the good rather than, say, a concrete moral insight, a judgment and an act of conscience. Rather, what the ironist sees, and sees in virtue of what is done to her, is that the judge is no better than herself in his judging. She sees only this equality (*Gleichheit*) between herself and her judge: they both must realize their conscientious ends through themselves, acting passionately and interestedly (666). Being cast out and condemned, she comes to see through the judge's eyes her non-identity with her proclaimed universal; because she nonetheless does not doubt her moral claim, she simultaneously sees in her judge's condemnatory judgment his non-identity with his moral claim. The moment of apperception in each, each being bound to enter ethical life through their individuality, itself becomes the source of what is shared or common or universal between them. The ironist thus gives utterance to this, confesses this commonality "and equally expects that the other, having put himself on the same level, will also respond in words in which he will give utterance to this equality with [her], and expects this mutual recognition will now exist in fact" (666). What is significant here, is the replacement of the theoretical insight that might have been with a confession: she not only perceives her equality with her accuser, but enacts it. Her judgment of equality and her consequent confession of evil are exemplary of a re-formed conscience: only as an act of conscience there for everyone, hence ethical in itself, does the creative act realize its legislative intention; only by living artistically, by being opposed to others and the other in ourselves, the moment of dead universality, can the universal proclamations of conscience matter.

In confessing her evil, her particularity, and yet meaning that confession itself to be a claim of conscience, she departs from the ironic perspective: no longer disengaged, she enters ethical life, the matter of ethical life, her confession to and for the judge the performative identification of herself with her act, an act of self-expression through which who she is comes to be lodged in the act she performs (662). In confessing the evil she perceives as adhering to all conscientious action she radically fuses, or aims to fuse, universality and particularity, realizing thereby the claim of con-science itself. With the charge of hypocrisy thus cancelled, but evil in the form of the ineliminable negativity of action avowed, the ironist becomes a self-perfecting conscience, a conscientious self who must form her life artistically, as it were.

In order to gauge what this identification amounts to, we must first examine the confession through which it first emerges. This is a wholly secular confession; it is not a confession of a sin that requires God's forgiveness if the self is going to be redeemed, saved, realized. The perfectionist challenges that notion of confession because she perceives the utter entwinement of her passions and her moral beliefs in herself and in the other; thereby, she perceives that there is no radical evil in us. We are not divided creatures, half angel (reason) and half beast (inclinations), torn between selfishness and altruism (although we can find ourselves so torn), individuality and universality. Her judge's attempt at universality or impartiality is as active and interested as her disobedient deed; and such acts of judgment can themselves be as transgressive and divisive as any act she might do (Creon's was). There is then at this level no evil to confess. What she confesses to is only her finitude, that her life, its meaning or failing to mean, come from her, what she does and says as expressions of what she knows and wants. There can be no abstract, infinite arbiter or judge of her since there exists no independent universal to which her deeds might correspond or fail to correspond.

Secondly, through her judge she sees herself, and hence her equality with and her difference from him. In confessing this, she is attempting to establish the common; which is to agree that what is common or shared between them is not some fact upon which she can rely, as if the fact of their finitude, their inescapable common individuality were itself sufficient to establish a world between them. There is no ultimate fact of the matter, even this fact of their common predicament. Confessing is letting the common bind and matter by making it common – something actually shared and agreed. Hegel has this in mind when he gives to the perfectionist the insight that her language of confession "is the *existence* of Spirit as an immediate self." Confessing reveals, or means to reveal, what is shared *as* shared. The language of confession hence replaces the language of conviction; and it replaces it because the language of conviction disowns its expressive dimension by wanting what is expressed to play a formal role, validating the goodness of the self in acting in a certain manner. In opposition, the language of confession aims simply at solidarity, commonality. And this solidarity itself is meant to replace the errant abstract and formal universal. Ethical universals are not independent existences, but forms of mutual recognition, hence solidaristic in themselves. Confession is the mode through which the entanglement of universality, recognition, and solidarity is made actual; confessing, as an exposure before the other and invitation to respond in kind, intends the binding of us one to another through the acknowledgement of our shared condition.

The act of secular confession has an exemplary status since it is both cognitive, by virtue of what is expressed, and affective, itself an expressive performance soliciting a response. What conscience has discovered is that it does not necessarily speak with a universal voice, that nothing guarantees or underwrites its claims to generality, and that its sayings and doings are necessarily and only potential candidates for being claims that speak for the community and her. To confess this is equally to admit that the negativity of my deeds reveals that I am unsure to what extent I am in agreement with myself (because I never am fully); hence in confessing I am testing myself, seeking to find myself in my words and deeds by testing whether you can find yourself in them. If I can speak for you, confess what I take as our shared condition, and you can recognize yourself in my words and deeds, and so recognize me, then we will have found (both discovered and established) the common: Spirit.[12]

By this juncture we should be unsurprised by Hegel's claim that we cannot be morally self-identical or morally self-certain. The impossibility of my being immediately at one with myself, immediately certain of my possession of universality, has been what the entire discussion of conscience has been about, its point. Hence, my being dependent on others in coming to know what is truly mine and what is not mine is the non-skeptical way of reading the significance of the account of conscientious action as incapable of maintaining its certainty, the immediate identity of particularity and universality. If there exists an irrevocable prospective opacity in my knowledge of the circumstances of action; and if the entwinement of self-realization and moral pursuit, the entanglement of individuality and universality in moral action, entails the prospective reproachability of deliberation, as does the fact that the meaning of moral principles is dependent upon their application; if there is the possibility of different interpretations of the same act; and yet, if my acts are nonetheless expressive of me, then all these qualities that give to my acts a quality of testing, asserting and interrogating ethical space, reverberate back on me as an ethical subject. What becomes of my acts and my standing, even in my own eyes, as an ethical subject must wait upon an answering voice: Antigone cannot be without Creon and the community he represents and misrepresents.[13]

This is what the act of confession means here, but only *retrospectively*; it is not what the perfectionist means to say in her confession or what she actually says. To the accusation that she has acted from passion and interest, and that she has transgressed upon the shared norms of the community, she, for the reasons given, simply confesses that all this is indeed the case, for herself *and* the other (667). Her implicit invitation to the judge to confess in return, to make the confession mutual, is rebuffed: "This was not what the judging consciousness meant: quite the contrary. It repels this community, and is the hard heart that is for itself, and which rejects any continuity with the other." Even if this rebuff is, at the end of the day, wrong, it is motivated. And some of that motivation needs to be seen in the act of confession itself.

The perfectionist in confessing did not intend her act as an "abasement, a humiliation, a throwing-away" of herself, but as an expression of mutuality and equality between her and her judge. But if this is so, then the confession is "the renunciation of particularity, rather than its expression."[14] There is, then, a Rousseauian conceit here, as if in confessing all, in revealing her humanity as she sees it, there should be mutuality because her judge is no better than she. To put the point another way, she does not ask for forgiveness because her humanity is not evil; hence, there is no difference between her and her judge, just a shared humanity. So Rousseau on the opening page of *The Confessions*: "Let them groan at my depravities, and blush for my misdeed. But let each one of them reveal his heart at the foot of Thy throne with equal sincerity, and may any man who dares, say 'I was a better man than he.'"[15] If one holds to the principle "To confess all is to be forgiven all," then one does not really confess to anything, transgression is levelled to acts of human nature; and actual forgiveness, forgiveness as something spontaneously given to substantive trespass, is suppressed, as if forgiveness followed confession as B follows A if A entails B. The ineliminability of passion, interest, and desire does not entail, a priori as it were, their moral innocence; and hence does not entail that confessing to a shared humanity itself deserves recognition, deserves an answering confession. Finally, the content of the confession, shared non-identity with one another, itself covers over rather than reveals mutual dependency, attempting to institute equality or similarity in the place of dependency. *Pace* Rousseau, confession and forgiveness belong to different "logics," different modalities of action, independent spontaneities whose inner articulation can never be written without displacing the ethical force of the acts involved. The silence of the hard heart is the caesura with confession which reveals its moments of particularity and universality as non-identical with one another.

Although the rebuff of the confession is "hard," it is not untoward: to accept and return the confession would be to avow "community," like-mindedness, as if the confessor had not transgressed, as if her individuality (inclinations and desires, again) could be discounted by being shared. Perhaps we can say: enjoining community in this way disavows autonomy, its difficulty, the fact that in acting I individuate myself, act against the community (and so myself as constituted through it) in my desire to realize myself and it. If the judge becomes the "hard heart" in refusing to return the confession, he has moral reasons for so doing. Indeed, one final reason we might offer in support of the hard heart is that in her expectation that her judge will return her confession with his own and will thus "contribute his part to this existence" (666), the perfectionist treats her confession as a form of moral payment or investment through which she should receive payment in kind. Her expectation of payment in kind takes away from the confession its moral attributes and gives to it a prudential character. And perhaps it is because she has this expectation that she does not consider her confession "an abasement, a humiliation, a throwing-away." The perfectionist wants a moral *logic* to support her actions: to confess all should automatically entail being forgiven all; to confess should entail a confession in return. And this hope for a logical resolution to ethical life underlies central moral concepts like "desert" and "merit"; confession merits forgiveness, a confession deserves to be returned. With these terms we are back to the language of "ought" as existing above and independently of our activities: a sincere confession ought to be forgiven, a sincere confession ought to be responded to in kind. Our realist intuitions and desires run deep. If recognition, mutuality and reciprocity are morally important as Hegel clearly believes they are, then our presumption is that there is a logic of recognition that exists independently of its actuality, its performance. But to believe that would be to detach ethical insight, moral knowing, from ethical activity, substance from subject.

The hard heart rejects the confession. As a consequence, the confessing perfectionist, seeing herself repulsed, comes to see the hard heart as being in the wrong, as wicked or evil. He, after all, gives her no place to stand, no way of measuring her words and deeds, but simply judges in silence. With no answering words from him, her dependence on him becomes frozen, their relation incapable of being moved, shifted, straightened or bent. He is "beyond" her absolutely. But this dependence is no longer the dependence of an individual on a universal (the moral law) before which it is always in the wrong (radically evil), but a relation of selves, one of whom, the hard heart, pretends to the empty space of universality, wishing to install himself in it. It is just this, moral transcendence reinscribed as mute silence, like the silence of a transcendent God, that the perfectionist perceives. When seen finally in the human dress it always was, this uncommunicative universality cannot be regarded as anything but self-asserting particularity and hence wicked. He makes of her an unhappy consciousness.

The theological and anti-theological contours of Hegel's text here are overt. The hard heart "contrasts the beauty of his own soul with the penitent's wickedness, yet confronts the confession of the penitent with his own stiff-necked unrepentant character, mutely keeping himself to himself and refusing to throw himself away for an other" (667). Above we criticized the perfectionist for taking her confession as a moral investment, and thus not an act of throwing herself away. It is through the hard heart's silent refusal that what was, perhaps, a prudential calculation is revealed as or *becomes* a "throwing away," an act of freedom for which no logical or empirical grounds provide sufficient reason. The hard heart's non-response is thus central to unlocking the meaning of confession: she can only come to herself, gain self-possession, through throwing herself away on the other. Confession is this throwing-away, a risk of abasement and humiliation. And the abasement and humiliation she feels in response to the hard heart's silence reveals both her absolute dependence upon him and the depths of his separateness. It is that separateness that destroys both moral (universalistic) and prudential reasons for ethical action. She cannot have good moral or prudential reasons for confessing to him, because it is only in virtue of recognizing and being recognized, relations of mutual recognition, that the conditions under which there can be moral or prudential reasons arise. Recognition is not an isolable act, the "perceiving" of similarity which *then* is expressed, avowed or admitted – the conceit of the contemplative/theoreticist paradigm; hence confession is not a mere avowal or admission (*Geständniss*), but the ethical renunciation of particularity through an act, confession (*Bekenntniss*) as a "throwing away" of the self in relation to the other, that presages universality through dissimilarity.[16]

Always presupposing our likeness as moral or happiness maximizing agents, traditional moral or prudential good reasons for action necessarily come too late because my having reasons comes through others whose separateness from me is as radical as our mutual dependence. This is why acts of conscience obey always only the "unwritten law," and hence why confession in its retrospective understanding becomes exemplary of conscientious action. Perceiving the likeness or equality of our individuality (our unlikeness with one another) suppresses the fact that difference is independence and negativity. Difference is misrecognized if universalized as shared by all. Hence, there cannot be a logical transformation of particularity into universality through an act of perception. The ethical meaning of individuality is not universality but ungraspable dependence: each act through which we would affirm ourselves dispossesses us of the self we are and want to be. The silence of the hard heart is *the* non-recognition of this; his silence makes the perfectionist, her life, unhappy.

These thoughts explicate the status of Hegel's treatment of the hard heart and what might have been anticipated as the disappointment of that treatment. One might have hoped that Hegel's account of conscience would terminate by providing us with good reasons for recognizing others, for example, because only through such recognition and participating in certain collective projects (like the state) can we attain the very freedom and happiness we most desire. Prudential accounts of this all fall afoul of some version of the free-rider problem, while the internal difficulties with the Kantian account reflect its detachment of reason from motivation (as the metonymy of our embodiment). Hegel is not attempting to provide a better version of prudential or moral "good reasons for action" accounts. No such account is possible; the marker of that impossibility, which is equally the last throw of the dice of a philosophy which would insure us of the world's reasonableness a priori, is acting consciousness' (prospectively understood) confession. We acquire good reasons through participation in certain types of recognitionally structured practices, hence too late to lead us on the basis of them to recognize ourselves in others. The "law" obligating us to the other must remain "unwritten." Hence, Hegel can only show that each such proffered good reason, each written law, each moral logic involves a turning of one's back upon those others to whom one is already bound. As he exhausts all the possible varieties of good reasons, then the refusal to recognize others as providing the grounds for one's activity becomes more and more radical. The appearance of the hard heart will not, finally, give us the good reason we have been missing; rather, he exemplifies *all* our refusals, rejections and blindness. In him is expressed in its "extreme form the rebellion (*Empörung*) of the spirit that is certain of itself" (667). The hard heart, who now stands in the space of intransigent particularity through clinging to his idea of universal truth, mimetically enacts the angelic/satanic rebellion against God. Hegel thus reverses the tradition: the most extreme rebellion against Spirit is revealed to be what personifies the pure universal, the beautiful soul of modernity.

The most extreme form of the rebellion of Spirit, because most immediate and direct, is the simple refusal to recognize another who has exposed herself, risked herself in confession and thus acknowledged her dependence. Without the conceptual mediations simultaneously encoding and disavowing our recognitional dependencies, for example, the moral law, the language of rights, and religious doctrines, all of which have been dissolved in the apperceptive cauldron of conscience, the perfectionist's dependence on her judge becomes immediate and personal, as the slave was dependent upon the master, and as each of us is before those we most love. It is the coldness of the "beautiful soul" of the hard heart which echoes in Hegel's repeated mention of its "uncommunicative" character. The hard heart remains for-itself, locked in its pure, because uncommunicated, moral knowing. The secret rage of the omnipotence of thought – the belief in omnipotence a correct evaluation of the fact that nothing can resist the understanding's reflective and analytic reach; the rage a premonition of the impotence of that same power – that attempts to compensate inability to act in the world is the violence which the beautiful soul enacts upon itself and its other; in denying her he denies himself.

Because the hard heart's refusal is immediate and personal, because his stand on himself as an individual and as a moral self have become identified, because his moral stand towards the perfectionist encapsulates his standing toward her as a figure of all others, then the reversal of fortune he undergoes is itself immediate and literal in Hegel's treatment: "lacking an actual existence, entangled in the contradiction between its pure self and the necessity of that self to externalize itself and change itself into an actual existence, and dwelling in the immediacy of this firmly held antithesis ... this 'beautiful soul' ... is disordered to the point of madness" (668). What the beautiful soul loses through his refusal to recognize acting consciousness by confessing to her, his remaining locked up within himself, is his self. The suppressed rage and silence of the hard heart's silence, silence being the only possible form of refusal to the naked and abased figure of the confessing self, turns upon him. The suffering of the tragic hero has become the madness of the modern subject. Still, for Hegel, the thesis remains: because we suffer, through our madness, we acknowledge we have erred. Madness, in modernity, is perhaps the only adequate metaphor we have for the self-destruction that is consequent upon the refusal of the other, if equally a not implausible empirical consequence. To concede this is to acknowledge that the ethical arena of modern self-consciousness includes an all but unpresentable interiority and subjectivity whose connectedness with others as a condition for its selfhood is sustained through nothing but words and deeds – hence the ethical depth of silence; and that nothing quite like the causal sequences of Greek tragedies is available to us to image the tragic contours of experience that potentiate our losses of self (although as *images* they remain potent). The languages we do possess, psychoanalytic or ethical discourses construed descriptively (as novelists do), lack the compelling empirical qualities that the causal sequences of tragic narratives possess – thus the continuing appeal of the novel of plot. The interiority and reflective expressivity of the modern self entails that its reversal of fortune involves not a loss of happiness (*eudaimonia*) but, figuratively, a loss of self in madness, with King Lear as the transitional figure enacting both forms of loss.[17]

The madness of the hard heart is both symptom and symbol of his withdrawal from actuality. It is equally the "breaking of the hard heart" (669); this "breaking," which will raise him from individuality to the universality of recognition is, Hegel informs us, "the same movement which was expressed in the consciousness that made confession of itself," that is, the movement from opposition to a perception of "continuity with the other as a universal" (667). Now in both these cases we find not a heretofore hidden reality becoming apparent (as in the Greek *hamartia* model), but a turning around of the self, the shift to a different standpoint, from unconditioned subjectivity to intersubjectivity, from ontological atomism *and* moral individualism to ontological holism *and* (some form of) ethical collectivism. This is Hegel's version of tragic recognition. My reason for calling this recognition tragic will emerge shortly.

In signalling earlier how Hegel's language here is more and more bound to religious language (confession, penitent, stiff-necked, hard heart), I was anticipating the "breaking" of the hard heart. The breaking of the hard heart permits a change of heart, a conversion. And it is because it is a conversion of one standpoint (atomism, individualism) to another that Hegel must himself turn away from Greek vocabulary. The breaking of the hard heart which leads to his turning around, his change of heart, is not an arbitrary structure, but one necessitated by the conception of subjectivity Hegel is inscribing. We do not suffer (only) from the kind of recurrent ignorance implied by the idea of *hamartia*;[18] and this because there is no information we are lacking or paths of reasoning we might adopt that would take us from our entrapment within our beautiful souls into the world. Both sides of our modern selves – both our apperceptive particularity and our habitation in a feasible, unrestricted universality – are structurally subject to a denial of dependence on their opposite. Hence, if any significant action we perform either potentially or actually transgresses the possibilities of prospective justification, and hence transgresses what can, at that very moment, be recognized as of worth, thus transgressing what till that moment others conceive of as providing their worth and dignity, therein transgressing against *them*, then we are as conscientious subjects always evil, always false, always lost (47). For Hegel "the status of the subject as such is evil."[19] We need to be turned around. But this is simply the darker side of the fact that since every significant action transfigures the meaning of given principles and norms, then coming to recognize these *new* claims and ideas involves undergoing a conversion to the outlook they alone make possible. But if this requirement for conversion is consequent on the significance of negativity for all action, then all contentful claiming is bound to the spiritual logic of negativity and conversion, which, of course, is just what Hegel methodologically identifies as "experience" in the "Introduction" to the *Phenomenology*. Whether it is a truth claim or a moral claim, claiming occurs through transgressive action. In order to claim I must turn around, as acting consciousness did in confessing; and in order to recognize a novel claim I must be converted, as the hard heart was in his breaking. All this, Hegel believes, follows from a consistent denial of realism. The logic of conversion, the movement of "spiritual" life itself, is coextensive with Hegelian objective idealism. Hence, the central claim of that idealism, the recognition of self in absolute otherness, occurs through the conversions undergone by acting and judging consciousness.

Despite his deployment of religious language and logic, Hegel's thought is radically secular. Even in the final turning of the hard heart, we are not ultimately restored to united life, for that life exists only in virtue of the apperceptive negations that move us and it forward. There is no moral purity or unconditionality here, no safety, no resting place. Justice (as an image of united life), we might say, exists *only* through the injustice, the evil, of the perfectionist and her like. Each of us is Antigone and Creon, and each of us continually rehearses and inhabits the moments of individuality and universality they represent. To imagine otherwise would be to imagine that there was something other THAT IS ABSOLUTE than united life and the freedom of negating/creative action that is its medium.

The conversion of the hard heart then is not final or ultimate, except symbolically and for the epistemic purposes of revealing just what is "absolute." Because I must turn away from united life in order to confirm for myself what in it confirms me and through me us, and because this turning away is driven by the desire to underwrite, to make alive, the life given to me, then both my turning away and my turning back are *equally* conversions, movements from darkness into light which is the harbinger of a future darkness. This, we might say, is the shape of a conscientious life lived artistically. What Hegel identifies as the "specific quality of the ethical life" (468), the self-certainty and harmony presumed by a set of collective practices, is just that moment in which every community takes its practices as natural and immediate. Without the presumption of naturalness and hence immediacy, no socialization would be possible. But to remain mired in such naturalness would be to fail even to ask the question as to whether the life it offers is one I can affirm and be affirmed by. Modern self-consciousness, with its accomplished sense of individual autonomy, makes Ismene's option of non-action impossible; or rather, to be an Ismene would be a refusal of a kind, an effort to remain within practices whose claim to be worthy have not been questioned or tested. Conversely, because our social world permits and encourages extremes of individuation as matters of style, proof that what we have attained is really our own, that it is me who is apperceptively tokening its worth, becomes ever harder to achieve. It is by this means that proof of autonomy comes to lie in idiosyncrasy: "The problem completes itself when we no longer know whether we are idiosyncratic or not, which differences between us count, whether we have others."[20] By this route, perfectionism would collapse back into the romantic irony it meant to have left behind.

FORGIVING EVIL

We make concrete confessions, as opposed to making excuses for ourselves or explaining or justifying ourselves, when it feels important both that we stand in or by what we have done, that burying or denying what has occurred would be burying and denying ourselves and our relations with the person to whom we are confessing, and that our action has produced a breach in our relationship with respect to which any attempt at justification is either unavailable or inappropriate: "I had my reasons for doing why I did, I did what I had to do, my duty, but that cannot now matter or register for you, count, given what has occurred." Confessions occur, then, when there has been a breach in the continuity between us, and no silence or dissimulation will revoke that fact. Even more, these are cases when reparative activities are insufficient or dissimulating: "I have broken what you held most dear, what you took as absolute; nothing can change that, neither apology or glue will hide the tear. I say I did it and do not deny it." There is something desperate and distressed in our confessions, wanting our continuity to be re-established, yet possessing only our nakedness (we must confess all) and impotence (we can do nothing to repair the breach) with which to accomplish this end.

Hegel captures all this when the confessing conscience is forced to acknowledge that her confession was a throwing herself away for someone else. I take this throwing away, with its attendant dangers of abasement and humiliation, to reveal that in confession we stake ourselves through nakedness and impotence. Confession then is an activity through which we reveal and acknowledge our utter passivity and dependence. When we confess, we are not positively asking for (requesting, supplicating) forgiveness, for to ask for forgiveness is too active, too demanding, too much like claiming that one deserves forgiveness because one is human. And were the other to refuse here, then *a fortiori* they would be denying that your humanity does provide a good reason for forgiving you. And this belief, we have seen, is both true and false: it is true because not reciprocating is a denial of you and the humanity in you; it is false because forgiveness is not anything anyone deserves, has a right to, or is entitled to expect in the deontological sense of those moral terms. Confession perfectly realized the limits of reason, demand, desert, and entitlement in finally and powerfully imaging the *aporetic* character of recognition: because it is the ground of our freedom and selfhood, then we can never give the other adequate reasons to recognize us because those reasons will only count as reasons for them to the degree to which they have already recognized us as continuous with or part of them. Therefore, we have nothing else we can offer them except our nakedness and impotence, no further bargaining chip. We throw ourselves away.

Everywhere in his writings, Hegel images the relation of will against will, the situation in which there is misrecognition, the continuity between us broken, as transgression eliciting transgression, as trespass meeting with revenge. And we should now be able to understand why the vicious cycle of revenge remains a potent image. If human action is transgressive in character, and there is no binding union between persons, then all we have in order to respond to what has infringed upon us and our beliefs and world is the capacity to respond in kind. The cycle of revenge images this process of transgression as infinite: "Thus revenge, as the positive action of a particular will, becomes a new infringement; because of this contradiction, it becomes part of an infinite progression and is inherited indefinitely from generation to generation."[21] For Hegel, any conception of punishment that conceives of it as grounded in a universal law or norm independent of the wills of the agents involved equally must be construed as an act of revenge. The reason for this apparently perverse view is simply that whenever and wherever universality is conceived of as independent of the activities of the agents involved, then the will of every agent is only particular, a brute *Willkür*, and hence, keeping in mind the skeptical worry about whether any agent has ever acted on the moral law, each individual is entitled to perceive in the will of the other only its subjective interest, only its self-assertion, and, in punishment, only a secret will for revenge. The ontological indifference of moral norms to concrete experience, their logical separation from it, yields a space where only particular wills reign; if all action is negating, then under these conditions it will be negating only other particular selves. Creon in holding to his law can only be seen as avenging himself against Antigone; and because only revenge is possible when the law is separate then only tragedy can result. The remorseless structure of Greek tragic action as epitomized by *Antigone* (and perhaps available only in it), its fateful and natural unfolding, is the logic of revenge which cannot end. Revenge thus becomes the type of all action within a realist metaphysics. For Hegel, on the contrary, transgression is not the denial of a positive norm but the creation of a breach, rent, tear or wound in the body of united life (that, of course, exists in part through continual activities of rending and tearing) – which is what positive norms are and represent if they but knew themselves aright. This is how criminal activity is *felt when* one is

55

its direct or immediate victim. The criminal attacks us, the fabric of our lives, tearing it, violating its integrity, leaving behind the gaping wound (158–160).

Whatever the pros and cons of Hegel's retributional conception of punishment, at the intimate level we are examining here, we are hence faced with the question of what, if anything can be done to heal the breach having learned that there is now nothing the transgressor can do. Once again, in calling upon the power of forgiveness, Hegel draws upon the Christian tradition in order to make his secular point. The peculiarity of forgiveness is that it treats what appears as irreversible, and is indeed irreversible from the perspective of the transgressing agent, as capable of being reversed. No one has seen better into this than Hannah Arendt.

In this respect forgiveness is the exact opposite of revenge, which acts in the form of re-acting against an original trespassing, whereby far from putting an end to the consequences of the first misdeed, everybody remains bound to the process, permitting the chain of reaction contained in every action to take its unhindered course. In contrast to revenge, which is the natural, automatic reaction to transgression and which because of the irreversibility of the action process can be expected and even calculated, the act of forgiving can never be predicted; it is the only reaction that acts in an unexpected way and thus retains, though being a reaction, something of the original character of action. Forgiving, in other words, is the only reaction which does not merely re-act but acts anew and unexpectedly, uncondi-tioned by the act which provoked it and therefore freeing from its conse-quences both the one who forgives and the one who is forgiven.[22]

Hegel conceives of forgiveness in precisely these terms, namely, as reversing the apparently irreversible, as lifting action out of its causal nexus (the process of action and re-action) and realizing it as part or moment of united life. So, what the hard heart does not know is that "The wounds of Spirit heal, and leave no scars behind. The deed is not imperishable; it is taken back by Spirit into itself, and the aspect of individuality present in it, whether as intention or as an existent negativity and limitation, straightaway vanishes" (668). Or: "Spirit, in the absolute certainty of itself, is lord and master over every deed and actuality, and can cast them off, and make them as if they had never happened [*ungeschehen machen kann*; make them undone]" (667). These words describing the work of spirit almost exactly parallel those quoted earlier that Hegel uses to criticize the ironist (the ego that "can remain lord and master of everything"). Spirit's power of forgiveness must thus be seen as inhabiting the same conceptual space of negativity as that which dissolved the worth and actuality of all meaning structures.

In urging the significance of the act of forgiveness, the stakes are very high for Hegel both ethically and metaphysically. The metaphysical issue is there in the distinction between the "bad infinity" of revenge and the "good infinity" of the act of forgiveness that undoes the natural conditions of action, annulling thereby the passing time which is the medium of vengeful action, and making actions moments in a self-determining "spiritual" (which is just another way of saying "self-determining") totality. What is equally clear is that the way in which the act of forgiveness raises metaphysical questions is intended to demonstrate that our metaphysical insights are to be bound by an ultimately ethical set of categories. If revenge is the type of all action within a naturalist and realist metaphysics, forgiveness is the type of all action within Hegel's idealist metaphysics since in it the "natural" order of events is "reversed," "sublated," provided with an accent necessarily unavailable from a realist perspective. What is "absolute" in Hegel is ethical life itself with its capacity to tarry with the negative, hold on to negation and death as the condition of its universality in which no wounds or scars, the things in themselves of realist metaphysics, are left behind. The act of forgiveness explicitly raises this claim.

Do we have the power of forgiveness: What are we claiming for ourselves in self-ascribing this capacity? Can we forgive anything? everything? Might not the claim for this power be an act of self-mystification, a merely psychological strategy for averting our eyes from the irreversibility of human action? Could there be evidence for this power other than its exercise? If not, then what would count as a vindication of our possession of it?

Both Hegel and Arendt conceive of punishment retributionally as accomplishing the same end as forgiveness, namely, a putting an end to a course of action and thereby mending the fabric of society by immediately (through punishment) reintegrating the criminal into it. Yet if the end of punishment is (ideally) reintegration, then the criminal who returns is no longer a criminal, therefore no longer an individual outside society, therefore the punishment has been the process of undoing the original criminal deed. We have forgiven him. So, as Arendt claims, "men are unable to forgive what they cannot punish and ... are unable to punish what has turned out to be unforgivable."[23] We cannot truly punish anyone for acts that cannot be forgiven. Perceiving the ultimate coincidence between punishment and forgiveness is important for the under-standing of each. Punishment cannot but appear vengeful, a secret desire to harm the criminal, if it is detached from the effort of repairing the rent in society and returning the criminal to it. Without these ends, punishment collapses into revenge. But equally, to return the criminal to society with the stigma of his crime remaining would push punishment back into revenge. If the criminal was not participating in the mending of his deed, what were we doing to him when punishing? Hence, it must be part of the intent of having an institution of punishment that we intend to "undo" the criminal's action. The completion of that undoing would be forgiving, where forgiving involves our no longer identi-fying the doer with that past deed. The doer is here with us, one of us, while the deed is left behind.

Having admitted that we cannot actually reverse the deed (literally turning the clock back), the naturalist may well object at this juncture that the language of forgiving amounts to no more than our selfish interest in forgetting the deed in order that we can get on with things as normal. The naturalist is right in linking forgiving with active forgetfulness, which, I wish to suggest, is coextensive with the "power" to mourn, to lose and grieve and continue acting. Revenge is to melancholia as forgiveness is to mourning. Melancholia holds on to the dead past, the dead, not letting them pass, hence endlessly bound to revenging itself for a loss that can never be compensated or overcome simply in so far as it is a loss and something past. Conversely, forgiveness completes mourning by acknowledging the particular as something that must pass away, be lost, is always already lost in its particularity, as a condition of it having presence or meaning at all. Antigone must be able to mourn Polyneices, make his death a "work" (452), something done, and so sublate his crime and death. Creon, in melancholia and rage, anticipates metaphysics in wanting to keep separate transgression and death on the one hand, and united life on the other: "Never the enemy, even in death, a friend." Metaphysics, the revenge against time, is melancholia.[24]

Thus where the naturalist must be wrong is in thinking that we can or do actually forget the transgressive deed. If there is a forgetting here, it is an ethical forgetting: the broken bowl with its glue slightly showing remains, but it is no longer part of my meaning, my presence for you. You release me from my deed by letting me, naked and impotent, into your presence and thus giving me back mine. The recognition which forgiveness is has its force in giving the one forgiven back their self from out of the deeds they have done. What is forgiven is not the actual deed, the loss, but its expressive relation to the subject; but then, nothing else could be either forgiven *or* unforgiven since the actual deed almost instantly recedes into the temporal and causal past. That actions should be accorded an expressive dimension, reverting back into the doer, already includes this fact. Revenge, which trades deed for deed, misrecognizes the recognition it already accords the doer of the first deed by holding him responsible. The vengeful person passionately and unknowingly must indeed love his enemy.

The temporal and causal specificity of actions ill consorts with our regard for their enduring meaning in relation to the individuals doing them unless we regard united life as an on-going product of activity whose fundamental end is free human activity itself. Arendt, again, shares this vision with Hegel. Individuality and apperception enter her lexicon as "beginning something new," and recognitional universality she calls the "web" of human affairs or relations:

> But trespassing is an everyday occurrence which is in the very nature of action's consistent establishment of new relationships within a web of relations, and it needs forgiving, dismissing, in order to make it possible for life to go on by constantly releasing men from what they have done unknowingly. Only through this constant mutual release from what they do can men remain free agents, only by constant willingness to change their minds and start again can they be trusted with so great a power as that to begin something new.[25]

Because they take trespass and transgression as routine occurrences in cultures in which some version of the apperceptive principle has made its appearance, Hegel and Arendt come to regard innocent trespass, individuation through transgressive appropriation, creative transgression, and criminal transgression as points along a continuum bound on one end by routine or habitual actions, actions without negativity, and on the other by absolute transgressions which negate the "whole." This is the conception of action implied by conscience's loss of certainty and purity since it is only through the strategies of conscience to maintain certainty and purity that any significant action can be salvaged from the taint of negativity. It is only when the claim of conscience can be raised, the claim that the apperception of each immediately delivers them into universality, that the connectedness and separation between negativity and universality, the emergence of universality out of an original negativity, can be revealed. Conscience's loss of certainty is the revelation of the negativity, the transgressivity, which adheres to all human actions.

Central then to Hegel's entire argument, ethical and metaphysical, is the continuity hypothesis concerning the multiplicity of forms of human transgression, and hence the fact that the acts of punishment and forgiveness come explicitly to occupy the same conceptual space: forgiveness completes punishment, making the punishable a species of forgivable transgressions. Hegel adopts this focus to indicate both that there is a certain type of space – united life – and what the texture of that space is: complex recognitional structures. Forgiveness for Hegel is not a special or rare ethical gesture, but exemplary of our constant negotiation of the fact that those whose recognitions compose our world, give us a world by giving us ourselves as agents in it, can only be themselves, as we can only be ourselves, by departing from existing forms of mutual interaction, by putting themselves, the acts through which they claim universality for themselves, in the place of the whole of which they are part, and thus by not giving or offering a place or space to us. Transgressions, small or large, are always the removal of the self from shared space and hence always a displacement of us, their recipients, since that space has no substantive existence independently of the persons and acts composing it. Forgiveness is the genus or type of all routes of re-entry and re-integration.

Forgiveness is a performative act of recognition. In forgiving you I call you back to my presence and so return yours to you. Figuratively, forgiveness reverses the vengeful, metonymic shift of taking your action for you: I turn away from the act toward you, as you in confessing had turned away from your act and exposed your (whole) self to me. The "throwing away" that confession is, and the release and recognition that forgiveness is, makes of these not only types of human action, not only paradigms of spiritual action, enactments of the entwinement of dependence and independence of subjectivity, but categorical modalities of all actions which provide them with their spiritual shape. To act is to "throw away," to risk abasement and humiliation, to expose oneself, naked and impotent, before the other; *all acting is confessing.* But if all acting negates the other and the other in the self, then in judging all action we are already releasing the agent from the trespass that makes their doing an action; *all judging is forgiving.*

In stressing the role of forgiveness and the type of recognitional act it performs, we have been tacitly examining it from the perspective

of the person forgiven: the transgressing perfectionist as the realization of individuality, the moment of slavery and Antigone. Yet it was
to be the hard heart, as realizing the moment of universality first
embodied in mastery and Creon, that does this forgiving. It is central
to Hegel's argument that the belief by the hard heart that it occupies
the place of universality is illusory. Once existing generality has
been transgressed, then because that generality was nothing but
mutual recognitions, universality disappears. The hard heart is
revealed as a particular will with its claim to universality opposing
the equally particular claim of the perfectionist. There is hence a
symmetry between the two; they are two wills standing opposed to
one another, their backs at first turned away from one another. The
perfectionist turns toward the hard heart and confesses.

Can we make sense of this scenario? Is not the hard heart he who
was transgressed against? Why place him in the same space of
individuality as the transgressor? What are we doing, with respect to
ourselves, when we forgive another? What prompts our act? What
makes the hard heart hard? Hegel says its hardness involves not
perceiving the individual act, the self-assertion against the other, in
its judgment of condemnation. That does not help much since, I
think, it misidentifies the origin of that self-assertion. Our hardness
is internally well motivated. You have transgressed upon me and I
have been injured. My injury, my hurt and pain and anger, are what
turn me away from you, lock me within myself – as we collectively
turn our back on the criminal in hurt and anger. Whether it is myself or our-self here matters little. What matters is the hurt suffered,
and in my suffering I become lost within it, which is to say, within
myself. Hurt, injury, pain, and their corollaries – anger, hatred, rage,
resentment and the like – are the forces that turn selves inwards. We
nurse our grievances.

The injured self is hence as captured by its injury as the confessing
self was trapped by her deed. This capture is also a loss of self, a
petrification of the self in what it has passively suffered; it is the
pining away till death of the beautiful soul and the rage unto death of
Creon. Above all, we must understand that there is nothing we can
do with our injury, any more than the transgressor could herself
repair what she had broken. And yet, remaining within our injured
sense of self disables us from going on, from acting again; either we
are broken or die. Our need is great, but nothing will answer this
need, perhaps because the need itself is constitutive, not a particular
need that another action or object might answer, but the need for my

61

humanity and autonomy to be returned to me. What is wanted, as Arendt states, is a new beginning. Only I can give myself that new beginning. It may be said that what allows me to forgive the other is seeing their confinement in their misdeed as equivalent to my confinement in my hurt. But to see this identity of myself with the one who has injured me is already implicitly to have forgiven them. Until, "in my heart" as they say, I have forgiven her I can not perceive the continuity between us. The act of forgiveness must then, like confession, have a cognitive component *in* it. The act of forgiveness is an act of recognition through which, by releasing the transgressor from her deed I release myself from my hurt. Forgiveness must express my particularity as well as renouncing it. Forgiving obeys the "unwritten law" which inscribes my originary debt to the other, my having my meaning and being through her. This originary debt to the other, this side of melancholia, call it philosophy, and death, is always both to be redeemed and always already acknowledged as the continuous exchange of misrecognition and recognition. The claim of particularity, of negativity and death, that Antigone acknowledges through transgressing against the *polis* and burying Polyneices, is not complete until Creon too learns to "love the dead,"[26] to make death and negativity – "the enemy" – a friend, mourning and forgiving Antigone. Creon's lesson is the avenging history of spirit, its tragic unfolding, that can terminate only in and with the hard heart's final release. In that release, universality, and judgment, call it philosophy once more, come to have a history and a world that is their own, a history and world that is Spirit's work of mourning.

In order to forgive I must throw myself away, that is, give up the hurt and anger that confine me in melancholic rage. Forgiving is the act of throwing myself away, of overcoming my particularity and (re-)instituting a commonality by recognizing the one there: "The forgiveness which it [the hard heart] extends to the other is the renunciation of itself"(670). In releasing the conscientious Antigone from her deed, the hard hearted Creon – who is also, as judge, the philosophical, transcendental "I" – releases himself from his absorption in pain and anger. Mourning the loss of purity as uncontaminated universality, as in mourning the death of that other without whom in the bliss of love I did not believe I could be without and survive, I complete my mourning by forgiving the other (for their transgression, for dying and leaving me behind, for the world being infinitely separate from me), and so forgive myself (for living and surviving and having a world); hence, the sense in which forgiving is a self-overcoming. I regain myself by allowing the other (the world) back as a presence to me in order that I may be a presence for her (and so again for myself). Thus, as we saw that each confession invoked a confession of a common humanity, so "each instance of forgiveness constitutes in small a forgiveness of being human, a forgiveness of the human race."[27] With each such act of forgiveness we record, as we live and breathe and act anew, an infinite mourning, our measureless love of the dead.

Notes

1 All references in the text are to the paragraph number of A. V. Miller's translation of the *Phenomenology of Spirit* (Oxford: Clarendon Press, 1977).

2 The first self is the Roman legal person, the second the self of absolute freedom that appears as the principle and goal of the French Revolution. Legal persons are wholly constituted by the powers they are given, and hence in the way in which they are acknowledged by others; while the self of absolute freedom abrogates all meaning to itself and denies the possibility of significant otherness. Legal persons may hence be construed as selves without individuality, and free selves as wordless individuals. Only with the moral self of Kantian thought do the moments of individuality and universality begin to mesh and syncopate.

3 In "Conscience and Transgression: the Persistence of Misrecognition," *Bulletin of the Hegel Society of Great Britain* 29 (Spring/Summer 1994), 55–70, I argue in more detail than is possible here that the analysis of conscience is, in fact, an account of Hegel's conception of the negativity of action, which needs to be seen in relation to the fleeting and unstable emergence of individuality entailed by Antigone's deed of opposing the "universal," written laws of the *polis* with the "unwritten laws" of religion. I was anticipated in this take on the meaning of conscience by Benjamin C. Sax, "Active Individuality and the Language of Confession: The Figure of the Beautiful Soul in *Lehrjahre* and the *Phenomenologie*," *Journal of the History of Philosophy* 21: 4 (1983), 437–466.

4 *A Theory of Justice* (Cambridge, MA: Harvard University Press, 1971), chapter 3; *Moral Consciousness and Communicative Action*, trans C. Lenhardt and S. W. Nicholsen (Cambridge, MA: MIT Press, 1990), pp. 76–109.

5 *On Liberty* (Harmondsworth, Middlesex: Penguin Books, 1985), chapter 3, "Of Individuality," pp. 125–132; *Being and Time*, trans. John Macquarrie and Edward Robinson (New York: Harper & Row, 1962), sections 27 and 53; *Thus Spoke Zarathustra*, trans. R. J. Hollingdale (Harmondsworth, Middlesex: Penguin Classics 1961) , "Of Self-Overcoming," p. 138.

6 *Aesthetics: Lectures on Fine Art*, vol. 1, trans. T. M. Knox, (Oxford: Clarendon Press, 1975), pp. 64–65. For pointing out this connection between conscience and romantic irony I am indebted to Terry Pinkard's *Hegel's Phenomenology: The Sociality of Reason* (Cambridge University Press, 1994), p. 215.

7 *Ibid.*, p. 65.

8 *Ibid.*, pp. 65, 66.

9 *Ibid.*, p. 65.

10 *Antigone*, trans. Elizabeth Wyckoff, in *Greek Tragedies*, vol. 1, edited by David Grene and Richmond Lattimore (University of Chicago Press, 1960), p. 196, line 455.

11 *Lectures on the Philosophy of World History: Introduction*, trans. H. B. Nisbet (Cambridge University Press, 1975), pp. 68–71.

12 See also: Stanley Cavell, *The Claim of Reason* (Oxford: Clarendon Press, 1979), p. 28.

13 The question of the "answering voice," the question of when I speak only for myself and when I speak "for us," can be tracked in *Antigone* through the shifting allegiances of the chorus and Haemon. Arguably, the modern Antigone's confessional voice is at one with the confessional voice of the modern poet. Consider John Berryman's "anxious Henry" (hoping against hope to find love or community in order to end the cycle of the revenge against life exemplified by his father's suicide) and his chorus, Mr Bones.

14 Robert Bernasconi, "Hegel and Levinas: The Possibility of Forgiveness and Reconciliation," *Archive di Filosofia* 54 (1986), 338. I am indebted to Robert Bernasconi for first drawing my attention to the potential significance of the "deferment" of mutual reconciliation in the refusal of the hard heart.

15 *The Confessions*, trans. J. M. Cohen (Harmondsworth, Middlesex: Penguin Classics, 1954), p. 17.

16 I want to thank Liz Goodstein for suggesting to me that the shift from *Geständniss* to *Bekenntniss* might be interpreted in order to support my reading of conscience. Implicitly in what follows I am suggesting that, in part, the history of Spirit can be construed as precisely the transformation of *Geständniss*, which is equivalent to Antigone's defiant "confession" of guilt (lines 441ff., ending with "I say I did it and I don't deny it") into the (Christian) "throwing away" of *Bekenntniss*. That is the core of her "spiritual" transfiguration.

17 For a "light" fleshing out of this shift from Greek tragedy to modernity, see my "Conscience and Transgression," pp. 65–67. Richard Eldridge suggests an analogous account in his "How Can Tragedy Matter for Us?" *The Journal of Aesthetics and Art Criticism* 52: 3 (Summer 1994), 291–292. For the "modern" aspect of Lear see Stanley Cavell, "The Avoidance of Love: A Reading of *King Lear*," in his *Must We Mean What We Say?* (Cambridge University Press, 1969), pp. 267–353.

18 For a helpful interpretation of *harmartia* see Nancy Sherman,

"*Harmartia* and Virtue," in *Essays on Aristotle's Poetics*, ed. Amelie Oksenberg Rorty (Oxford: Princeton University Press, 1992), pp. 177–196.

19 Slavoj Zizek, *Tarrying with the Negative*, Durham: Duke University Press, 1993, p. 98. Of course, Hegel cannot stop with this; so at 780 he states: "If Evil is the same as Goodness, then Evil is not just Evil, nor Goodness Good: on the contrary, both are suspended moments – Evil in general is self-centered being-for-self, and Goodness is what is simple and without a self. When thus expressed in terms of their concept, their unity is at once evident."

20 Stanley Cavell, *The Claim of Reason*, p. 464.

21 *Elements of the Philosophy of Right*, trans. H. B. Nisbet (Cambridge University Press, 1991), 102, p. 130. For the most recent reflections on Hegel's conception of punishment see Allen W. Wood, *Hegel's Ethical Thought* (Cambridge University Press, 1990), chapter 6, and, especially, Stephen Houlgate's review of Wood in the *Bulletin of the Hegel Society of Great Britain*.

22 *The Human Condition* (Garden City, New York: Doubleday Anchor Books, 1959), p. 216. For an analogous use of Arendt with respect to Hegel see Robert R. Williams, *Recognition: Fichte and Hegel on the Other* (State University of New York Press, 1992), p. 209.

23 *Ibid.*, p. 209. Reasons of space have forced me to cut a discussion of the unforgiveable in Hegel and Arendt. In broad terms, for both, "absolute transgressions," those that can be neither punished nor forgiven, are ones attacking the conditions of ethical life as such rather than a part. For Hegel the line is drawn at murder; for Arendt it is drawn at genocide.

24 *Antigone*, line 522, p. 198. I am here lightly brushing against Heidegger's reading of Nietzsche's account of time and metaphysics in *What is Called Thinking?*, trans. J. Glenn Gray (London: Harper and Row, 1968). My implicit critique of Heidegger here depends upon holding fast to the phenomenology of ethical revenge as a more than metaphorical substratum for the comprehension of the "will's revulsion against time and its 'It Was'" (p. 93), and hence insisting that phenomenological categories – revenge and forgiveness, misrecognition and recognition, melancholia and mourning – must carry "metaphysical" weight that cannot be "logically" cancelled.

25 *The Human Condition*, p. 216.

26 *Antigone*, p. 198, line 523.

27 Stanley Cavell, *Conditions Handsome and Unhandsome* (London: The University of Chicago Press, 1990), p. 120; see also his *This New Yet Unapproachable America*, Alburquerque, New Mexico: Living Batch Press, 1989, pp. 106–107. My treatment of melancholia and mourning dovetails with Gillian Rose's critique of Walter Benjamin's "aberrated mourning" (my melancholia) and construal of "inaugurated mourning" in "Walter Benjamin – Out of the Sources of Modern Judaism," in her *Judaism and Modernity: Philosophical Essays* (Oxford: Blackwell, 1993).

3

The values of articulation: aesthetics after the aesthetic ideology

CHARLES ALTIERI

All our current instruments agree that we are working in the wake of an "aesthetic ideology" that is less a fixed set of beliefs than a set of malleable assumptions deriving from Kant and then from Romanticism about what works of art make available for society. But that very malleability makes it very difficult to get the kind of handle on the past which will allow us to test the degree to which we can escape the hold of this ideology without losing an entire cultural heritage. In fact this malleability creates a condition in which that ideology continues to haunt those who would reject it, especially those who seek to build a new politics on notions of person, text, value, and community, since such notions tend to be covertly shaped either by that ideology directly or by problematic oppositions it generates. Therefore trying to work somewhat free of this ideology requires arguing on two fronts – against an oversimplified political dismissal of some fixed version of this aesthetic ideology and also against those theorists like Eagleton and Derrida who hope to correlate versions of post-modern politics with ideals recuperated directly from that ideology. My ultimate ambition is to elaborate alternative ways of providing a language of value for the arts, and hence for the ways that the arts contribute to social life. But before I take on that conceptual task I want to set the contemporary scene by rehearsing a narrative that I hope clarifies some of the basic underlying factors affecting our conceptual commitments.

I

On the most general level, we need to understand the aesthetic ideology as part of an overall cultural struggle to provide vital alternatives to the perspectives on value established by empiricist and utilitarian conceptual frameworks:[1] emphases on particularity, intuition, and interpretation were seen as countering scientific method; idealization would at least complement analysis; and efforts to construct community would struggle against the levelling abstract individualism basic to society in large democracies. Since the problems remain, twentieth-century theory has continued the struggle, often with less direct borrowing. So rather than review a series of thinkers, I hope to isolate the four basic conceptual topoi that still give resonance and respectability to most philosophical efforts to locate value within aesthetic experience. I must admit that few artists and even fewer in their audiences would put the case quite the way that the philosophers did, and do, but by concentrating on philosophical discourse we can quickly locate the logic underlying the full range of investments elaborated within the various art worlds, especially the domain of literary criticism. And we can then begin the slow work of developing workable alternatives.

For the first topos I want to look at the rhetorics used to account for those pleasures that might be distinctive to aesthetic experience. Theorizing about pleasure proved crucial to isolating aesthetic experience as a subject about which one could philosophize – in part because the theme of pleasure helped secure the psychologizing of aesthetic discourse that took place during the eighteenth century, and in part because that theme leads into the more important domain of how attention to the arts might allow a culture to develop versions of subjective agency not bound to empiricist and utilitarian models of human needs, interests, and desires. Within the aesthetic ideology, the pleasure provided by the arts is not simply a passive reaction to stimuli, nor is it merely an immediate subjective excitement. Rather this aesthetic pleasure pushes against the limits of empirical subjectivity. Pleasure located in the object follows the model of the sublime, a domain where some version of excess challenges the understanding and opens the agent to imaginative speculation on what lies beyond the boundaries of common sense. Such pleasure elicits an intensity and a mobility of self at odds with the versions of duty and decorum imposed on us as part of the socializing process. And aesthetic pleasure located in the responder becomes the basis for claiming that there are interests within the act of judgment that are not content with merely subjective reactions. In aesthetic experience we let our pleasure depend on our efforts to cast our judgments so that they elicit agreement from other agents, and hence become exercises in our capacity to identify freely and fully with what we take to be communal attitudes. Pleasure then is not merely a reaction, but a projection of what is possible for a self that submits itself to the discipline of tracking forms and exploring how it might be bound to other agents. This pleasure becomes a symbolic display of what is possible for me as a moral agent capable of identifying with rationality.

The more stress that is put on principles of pleasure, the greater the imperative to elaborate features of the art object that can be sufficient causes of those distinctive qualities (or sufficient vehicles for the sociality that these theories weave into their accounts). Therefore claims for art as cognitive work provide a second, complementary topos. Not only do art works appeal to special psychological traits, they also offer unique ways of linking those traits to the world, because they allow us cognitive relations to objects that are not subordinated to the epistemic criteria imposed by the demands of discursive practices. The arts offer intuitions that stay intuitions, and hence connect us to determinate singularities not cognizable by any established empirical method. Where scientific practical knowledge must deal with types, not with individuals, and where such knowledge must be tested by repeated experiment, the arts are claimed to offer knowledge in the form of concrete universals: the more richly one grasps the particular contours of a work, the more fully one comes to appreciate how the details might serve as general exemplars. In other variants of this topos, the arts are claimed to provide actual knowledge of particulars (as in a photograph) or to define what is involved in particular emotional states (as in what Cézanne teaches us about the life of the eye).

The third topos tries to explain how the arts might have such distinctive cognitive status. It represents the art as produced by "genius," that is by certain powers that can be seen as achieving a deeper, more intense hold on the actual world than anything science or virtue could offer. Concepts of genius then proliferate, given how much might be claimed for it. Some theorists stress the power of genius to create dense internal formal relations and organic structures that in some way transcend the empirico-practical; others trade on connections to older notions of the wisdom of the artist and hence use the notion of genius to explain how art may carry the kind of insight requiring distinctive cognitive claims. This logic produces the almost magical effect of combining that traditional wisdom role with idealizations of madness and alienation – all now perhaps synthesized once more in terms of a rhetoric of resistance.

All three topoi prepare the ground for a fourth, most problematic set of claims: conceptions of genius as working to enhance cognition and to afford a distinctive mode of pleasure also invite arguments that the arts carry a unique moral force. Because art involves a range of specific visions, that moral role could not be defined in terms of any single set of moral beliefs. But if art could not dictate moral principles, it could nonetheless shape how its audience engaged in the processes of forming moral responsibility. Works of art do not argue for moral values; rather they embody modes of attention that help shape our relation to whatever moral system governs our social reality. Therefore the aesthetic ideology linked the fostering of responsibility to the shaping of how we directed our responsiveness. That idealized responsiveness could then be put to work in a variety of philosophical contexts ranging from Schiller's concern for an active moral attention to complex particulars to Kant's interest in how agents bind themselves to thinking in terms of universal judgments.[2]

In order to bring this story forward to the contemporary scene we have to understand how the dominant theoretical positions managed to make adjustments enabling them to pursue the pedagogical and critical ideals fostered by the aesthetic ideology while finessing the conceptual problems that plagued the underlying philosophical program. As Romanticism illustrates, the aesthetic ideology first took hold because it promised to continue Christian humanism by other, less overtly metaphysical means. This ideology's concern for distinctive modes of cognition maintained faith in powers to form judgments and make interpretive discriminations that could not be generated by any "method," and the link of the arts to moral education and moral perfectionism made them crucial to the cultivation of those best selves that might survive the effects of democratic levelling everywhere evident in the fabric of social life. However this humanism was haunted from the start by a manifest social impotence: whatever knowledge art did produce failed to have visible social consequences, and whatever moral cultivation it produced seemed indistinguishable from the imposition of class values.

So there soon emerged as alternatives two extreme attitudes (each breeding several particular theoretical positions). At one pole, theory could retain its ambitious claims about the powers that art conferred so long as it could redirect its idealizations: the arts matter not because they enhance social life, but because they provide powerful alternatives to the social marketplace. This logic leads directly to nineteenth-century aestheticism, but it also provides the basic impetus for positions like Schopenhauer's and Adorno's – the one positing the domain of art as an escape from the ravages of will, the other casting beauty as a power of negation making visible the limitations of what truth had become under capitalism.[3] At the other pole, those eager for direct social application of the arts – either for Marxist programs or for some general ideal of moral edification – proved impatient with the focus on specificity and analogical powers emphasized by Kant and Schiller and the Romantic poets. Educators and critics had, and have, good reasons for translating the singularity of art works into some kind of allegorical framework that makes that singularity carry a more determinate universal import – both as representing social traits to be cultivated and as suggesting or earning some moral ideal.

My story follows the course of these pedagogical appropriations of the aesthetic ideology, since there we find most clearly the source of contradictions that continue to plague us, largely because the only means of preserving a sense of the vital singularity of art works seemed to be submitting that singularity to practices of thematic reading that inevitably impose allegories as their means of showing how the particular work deserves to be taught. Therefore it should not be surprising that within the academy pleasure claims got ignored, knowledge claims subsumed particularity under a more generalized exemplarity, and genius claims were folded into efforts to show how artists were in fact moral agents whom society could honor (and employ). In the classroom, and in writing shaped by classroom ideals, singular purposiveness becomes thematized as concrete universality and the cultivation of moral sensibility becomes an allegorical moralizing sustained by these thematic readings. Only interpretation can save us from the excesses of interpretation, and only views of agency that privelege interpretation over pleasure can have give art the clout necessary to win resources in a university environment.

Now the plot thickens. These efforts at academic appropriation simultaneously weaken the aesthetic ideology and make it more desperately necessary as the only way to mask that weakness, the only way not to have to subject one's weaknesses to the criticisms that other discursive practices based in the social sciences might bring to bear on it. One source of the weakness is a wandering from the original idealizations; an even more disturbing source is the effect of the academy's turning what was suggestively vague into demands for rigor specific enough to make visible the limitations of the entire project. The effort to find usable, generalizable meanings puts at risk whatever is truly distinctive or uniquely powerful in works of art. And, more important, attributing concrete moral content to works of art simultaneously exposes the interests beneath the purported universalizing and reveals how ineffectual art is in making good on the ideology's claims for it.[4]

So we come to the present, at least in American literary criticism. We cannot escape the failure of the moral claims basic to our educational ambitions. But we are also the heirs of traditions insisting on the social importance of aesthetic education, so we (at least those of us who make a living on it) cannot dismiss the art in the same way that we dismiss the moral claims. Instead, where abstract universalizing fails, concrete politicizing rushes in, promising that it can both explain and direct the powers that art works possess. If we cannot make clear claims about how art offers a distinctive kind of knowledge, we can try to show that we can treat the works as part of the knowledge system sustained by various kinds of socio-historical inquiries. Or we could fuse the knowledge claim with the genius claim to insist on art as a source of resistance. Then even the pleasure claims can be co-opted as a version of utopian vision. Finally, once moralizing allegories seem little more than idealist evasions of specific historical struggles, it is hard not to turn to stances that promise direct political relevance for the art. These promises then take two forms: historically, individual works can be treated as actual participants in producing ideologies and fostering group identities, and practically these works afford materials that can be used by critics to organize shared interests and foster political agendas. The failures of the moral define what become the possibilities of the political.

II

Let me be as specific as I can about how I am using the notion of "the political." I mean by political that criticism which prefers contexts to texts, then insists on either of two ways of using those contexts.[5] Criticism can concentrate on the historical analysis of how the art serves particular embedded interests that continue to exert repressive forces on democratic social life, or it can use literary readings to take on the roles of advocate or adversary in trying to shape an audience's orientation towards specific institutional commitments in the present.

I need this specificity because I now must add a further claim. The more we perform these historico-political analyses, the more we seem haunted by their failure to grant art most of the power, or authority, that the aesthetic ideology claimed for it. Having exposed the limitations of that ideology, we have little warrant for the critical attention we continue to give to particular works of art or for the pleasure we have in reading and teaching that concentrates on the particular situations unfolded within an artist's work.[6] That, I submit, is why we now witness so many of the theorists once influential in dismantling aesthetic ideology now returning to that ideology in the hope of salvaging something that may sustain a plausible contemporary discourse for valuing the arts. At one pole we find Terence Eagleton's Marxist efforts to recuperate a politicized version of the moral idealizations Kant and Schiller attributed to the aesthetic, and at another there are efforts by Jacques Derrida and Jean-Luc Nancy to adapt the aesthetic ideology's claims about cognition into a thematics that provides a post-structural version of Heideggerean ontology. (One could also note the interest literary critics now place in Martha Nussbaum's and Stanley Cavell's versions of art's moral claims, as well as in Richard Rorty's celebrations of art as the domain of the private ironist.)

But I do not think we can establish substantial values for the arts along any of these lines. Efforts to recuperate parts of the aesthetic ideology are likely to take place in an impoverished conceptual universe, since contemporary theory can no longer rely on the psychology or models of value or even the sharp opposition to empiricism that originally sanctioned the aesthetic ideology's claims about pleasure, cognition, genius, and moral sensibility.[7] Eagleton, for example, cannot connect what he claims about the version of freedom sustained by ideas of aesthetic agency to any specific properties of aesthetic experience, so he subordinates that version of agency to purely political value models. And Derrida turns from specific cognitive claims about art as distinctive knowledge to ontological versions of that claim celebrating art's disrupting all conceptual categories. But then his victory is pyrrhic because such singularity will not lead back to much of a psychology or morality. Moreover, as I try to show in another essay, each of these four topoi is riven with conceptual fault lines, so any effort to base value claims for art upon them is likely to end up in serious trouble.[8]

For now I hope the following formula can suffice to summarize this critique: any effort to recuperate the aesthetic ideology's versions of pleasure and of genius must be so severely underdetermined as to collapse all the corollary distinctions needed for making cogent claims about values, while, as Derrida shows, ambitious versions of that ideology's claims about cognition and morality in the arts are inescapably overdetermined by the philosophical or social scheme we use to specify what counts as knowledge and as an adequate moral vision. Pleasure and genius are vague abstract notions that have very little concrete force, unless one builds meaning for them within the very notion of art that they are then invoked to clarify. Pleasure, for example, is too general a notion to provide any specific guidance in our view of art, while "aesthetic pleasure" only makes sense as a distinctive mode because of the definition we give to the aesthetic. Similarly genius is a very general term that in itself offers no distinctive notions of form-giving etc. that the aesthetic ideology imposes upon it.

Claims about cognition and morality, on the other hand, are always laden with cultural meanings, since they depend on assumptions shaped by cogent practices. So, when applied to art, these notions impose on the art the force of the frameworks specifying how particulars count as epistemic or carry moral value. And such impositions in turn influence how we postulate significant internal relations within the art work, even if these have little to do with what artists intend or even with what the manifest surfaces offer. Suppose, for example, I want to talk about the kind of knowledge *Othello* provides, or I want to say that it somehow serves ethical functions. Then my model of knowledge shapes how I read (usually tempting me to impose some kind of allegory that can have the generality necessary for speaking about knowledge – even if the allegory is about the value of specificity). And the desire for moral meaning requires my bringing to bear both models and ancillary discourses warranting different kinds of allegories. Under this pressure, contemporary theory tends to posit a morality that resists allegory, but that imposition has the same dependencies on general moral models (like Lacan or Levinas or Rorty) which pull against a more particularized engagement in the play's deployment of moral feelings. Such allegories against allegory in fact ironically lead us back to ideals shaped by doctrines about pleasure and genius, as we see in Derrida's developing a morality of art based on idealizing the very difficulty of developing any adequate categories of judgment.

III

In criticizing the ideals shaped by the aesthetic ideology I am not denying that they call our attention to aspects of art that many of us care about. Nor do I deny that one can claim significant values distinctive to the experience of works of art. I deny only that we can use these four topoi as the basis for a coherent philosophical account of those cares and values. That, of course, is not a small denial, in part because it also entails suspending, if not rejecting, any effort to make the concept of "the aesthetic" or of aesthetic properties do significant work in these domains. But such a denial may also make it possible to recast the languages we use to attribute values to the arts, so that we can more directly resist those models of value that insist on equating art's social force with the roles it may play in overtly political practices.

I suggest that we suspend discourse about "the aesthetic" because that concept simply carries too much baggage (and in literary studies contains too little substance). Relying on the concept of the aesthetic forces us to concentrate on properties like unity (or even like institutional sanction) so abstract as to apply to the full range of art works, whether or not they are actually central to the various modes. And, more important, for the universalizing discipline of aesthetics to have much practical force, it must rely on systematic equivocation between what we predicate of art objects and what we attribute to the modes of response the objects can be said to elicit from us.[9]

Developing an alternative need not entail a nominalism devoted only to particular cases. We may be able to concentrate on constructing models for values that can be attributed to wide ranges of experiences made available by the arts and by the social practices they foster, without our having to argue for their universal validity. To accomplish that we have to shift our focus from describing those properties to accounting for the functions that we see served by various sets of such properties. For then we can derive values in relation to those functions, and we can speculate on how similar functions might be afforded by quite different particular structures. Dance, painting, and poetry may give similar delights or even similarly affect dispositions by affording very different concrete experiences, and very different long-term patterns of engagement.

What do we put in the place of "aesthetics"? I suggest we take our cue from the line of thinking that Bernard Williams worked out for moral analysis in his *Shame and Necessity*.[10] For Williams the basic problem facing contemporary moral philosophy is the pervasive influence of Kant's stance on moral obligation. Even Kant's opponents seem to have accepted his reliance on a notion of rationality as at once the means of discovering obligations and the internal principle that binds us to them. So to develop an alternative stance not contaminated by that notion of rationality Williams has to go all the way back to a pre-Socratic ethics in which many of our basic moral concepts played central roles, but without that problematic obsession with impersonal and transpersonal obligation. In this effort at imaginative recuperation Williams is clear that we cannot simply return to pre-Socratic thinking, but we can learn from it how to shape concepts that may fit our needs without trapping us in the structure of oppositions inescapable within post-Kantian theorizing.

Williams cannot be applied directly to the philosophy of art. In that field we cannot settle on any one cultural formation, nor can we find any one source of confusion with the power and scope that Williams shows is the case with the ideal of rational obligation. But we can use his example to strengthen the possibility that we can learn a good deal by trying to recover in contemporary terms those lines of attributing value to the arts which got supplanted by the idealist orientations shaping the aesthetic ideology (and perhaps reshaping much of Kant's specific case in the process). I hope ultimately to make the case for three of these pre-Kantian orientations, which we then have to find ways of putting into conjunction with each other – the Longinian position on the sublime (which connects the work of articulation to a language of ethos), the Plotinian position on what exceeds representation (which calls attention to two modes of excess often central to our interests in the arts – immediate fascination and a concern for something transcendental or mysterious), and the neoclassical discourses on the passions (which enable us to speak about pleasure and about emotional impact without our having to rely on discourses of knowledge and of morality, and without the contemporary emphasis on interpretation as something close to the final goal of engaging works of art). Aristotelian theory provides an obvious fourth candidate, but I have nothing interesting to say about it. For, while it can readily be allied with Kendall Walton's efforts to treat representation as an intellectual, reflective task that need not buy into any empiricist concerns about truth and displacement,[11] most theory in this vein also adapts Aristotle's biologically rooted organicist metaphors to idealist concerns about unity and coherence, so that it is difficult to separate it from the aesthetic ideology.

Here I have time only to develop the first of these possibilities, the ways in which the Longinian sublime helps us develop a language of values stressing the powers of articulation pursued by most works of art (albeit in different registers).[12] However this one possibility proves so incompatible with much of contemporary theory that it provides a good starting-point for exploring the range of possibilities that emerge if we can break with what the aesthetic ideology has now become. For example, stressing articulation enables us to honor the worldly effects of the labor that goes into art without our having to invoke any special cognitive claims: all we need is reminders like Paula Modersöhn-Becker's "the strength with which a subject is grasped, that's the beauty of art."[13] Articulations matter not for their truth, but for the senses of power they make available, both in our appreciation for how the artist works and in our senses of who we can become by virtue of our provisionally taking on the stances toward the world that the artist makes articulate. We can appreciate such power without claiming that it is in some sense an adequate picture of facts, so that articulation offers a way of connecting art to the world that does not invite deconstruction (in fact deconstruction is itself a process of making articulate the slippages in our languages claiming truth values). All we have to say is that much of the work artists do involves making clear through particular images and events what is involved in how modes of desire emerge in our experience and orient us towards certain ways of engaging the world.

The simplest formulation of this mode of value consists in treating our art practices as encouraging attention to how particulars achieve a vivid "thisness" relative to some set of needs or drives foregrounded in the art work or by the context that the art work is placed in. And the measure of the adequacy of the "thisness" is not a referential standard but one that involves ethos. "Thisness" satisfies to the degree that a person takes responsibility in and through it – either by identifying with a given formulation or by trying to make it do certain kinds of work. Articulation is the mark of power in relation to a medium, and it is the precondition for those modes of responsibility that the medium makes possible.

By stressing thisness we have a means of recognizing what has been at stake in a variety of realisms – from Tintoretto's pride in painting backs to Balzac's pride in skewering French social life. In various ways this art sees itself as providing a means of clarifying both how art can engage the world and how those engagements become means of testing and acknowledging authorial investments. Those same principles then help us see what is also at stake in struggles like Cézanne's against such realism in order to shift the focus from getting the world right and to getting right how we engage the world with an intensity that makes us care about rightness. In fact we can use the same ideal of articulation to describe the use to which we can put pure constructivist features of art – ranging from the thematic brilliance of Shakespeare having the true Richard II visible only in a broken mirror, to Gertrude's Stein's amazingly precise self-proclaimed realism with respect to the event-quality of language engaging a topic, to the expressivist thisness of Pollock's wandering line. Even deconstruction or deliberate indeterminacy matter to the degree that they clarify the lines of force (or over-determination) making any more positive thematizing of sense impossible.[14]

It will take considerable work if this principle is to become itself fully articulate as something other than a reactionary fantasy. But I think I have said enough to establish a context for showing how this effort to recuperate Longinus may afford us a conceptual instrument capable of dislodging one of the pillars of contemporary faith that I think is as problematic as it is fundamental. I refer to a range of ways that articulation now is seen as necessarily displacement and disfig-uration of some unrepresentable but nonetheless easily alienated primary reality. From anti-Hegelian work like Blanchot's that treats dialectics as death work to Lacan's treatment of representation as castration, ideals of articulation become highly suspect because articulation necessarily objectifies. And whatever is objective cannot be subjective. Therefore it seems reasonable to argue that whatever purports to make anything about a subject articulate in fact deprives that person of subjective agency. What might live as a first-person process is displaced by any set of signs that can be handled in the third-person categories of the understanding that we adapt in treating language as determinate. The subject of the enunciation is different from the subject that is announced in the message, so that the public sign is irreducibly both a mask and a castrating force denying the subject the very difference its speaking tries to make.

In my view this framework denies without fully taking on what I call an expressivist model of articulation. In that model articulation is not primarily a means of representation, although signs can always be used pragmatically (not pictorially) to stand for certain phenomena. Rather articulation is a making visible what it is that one wants to be represented by – whether that be an effort to evoke one's own emotions or an effort to fix some phenomenon so that others can see why one cares about it or can do some kind of work because of how the particular gets encoded in a sign system. This model allows for the work of science, but it does not make scientific realism its basic ontological ground, and hence it is simply not open to standard post-structural critiques engaging that ontological model. Within expressivist thinking the primary concern is for how certain ways of rendering the world help realize certain needs and desires that inform the signs or that are made compelling within them, as is often the case in art. Such concerns cannot be handled adequately by relying on a simple binary between objective and subjective. References to the world are inseparable from activities within and upon it, so we try to give articulate existence not to objects or to subjects but to the efforts of subjects to specify their interests in particular ways of negotiating aspects of experience. Even efforts at pictorial representation must be seen simply as tools subjects use to define aspects of their own purposive relations to time and to change.

From this angle it seems that the Lacanian view is far too narrowly spatial. Lacanian theory makes it appear that at each moment we cut into the stream of experience we find a dynamic structure of desire threatened by efforts to stabilize it within an image. And because there are only these two terms – the fixed and the dynamic, or dead positivity and vital negativity – we are forced into having to deny objects in order to save subjects, even if the cost is to deny subjects any world worth being subjects for. However, once we treat subjective agency as always working within time, its struggles are not definable simply as negativity versus objectivity. Considered as a function within temporal sequences, negativity is always positioned: it is not some purely indefinable force. As positioned, it is always in the process of rejecting or changing some position for another one. Subjective agency has orientations, and it has a stake in being able to locate itself in relation to the unfolding of investments that begin as simply inchoate in those orientations. Agency can become self-reflexive to the degree that it identifies with what it can make articulate about its own investments, which range from the work to realize long-term commitments to the pleasure one can take in simply feeling itself focused by and within certain recognitions.

And, because it operates within time, this subjective agency need not stake everything on single images that then displace it. Rather it tries to be as clear as possible about what in its own activity it can identify with as it works through various challenges to its desire to give meaning to its own activities.

IV

I will prepare for specifying the most important traits of this emphasis on articulation by turning to the somewhat melodramatic yet brilliantly intricate lyrical rendering of this entire expressivist project that we find in Yeats' "Leda and the Swan":

> A sudden blow: the great wings beating still
> Above the staggering girl, her thighs caressed
> By the dark webs, her nape caught in his bill,
> He holds her helpless breast upon his breast.
>
> How can those terrified vague fingers push
> The feathered glory from her loosening thighs?
> And how can body, laid in that white rush,
> But feel the strange heart beating where it lies?
>
> A shudder in the loins engenders there
> The broken wall, the burning roof and tower
> And Agamemnon dead.
>   Being so caught up,
> So mastered by the brute blood of the air,
> Did she put on his knowledge with his power
> Before the indifferent beak could let her drop?[15]

This poem is probably offensive to many contemporaries, and not without good reason, since any metaphorizing of rape seems insensitive to the enormous concrete suffering of those who experience it literally. And Yeats not only metaphorizes rape, he makes the woman's position his vehicle for a highly generalized effort to understand how consciousness can dispose itself towards those forces of events, of history, that shatter its dominant frameworks. But, having said this, I also have to insist that rape by a god introduces a scenario somewhat more difficult to politicize. The poet is forced to take up the woman's position, at least provisionally, in order to make articulate a possible response to the sense of powerlessness that consciousness experiences before absolute forces.

For Yeats not even the god can understand what drives and

contains him. So this struggle for articulation cannot be equated with any epistemic means of making distinctions between true and false statements. But the complex relation between response and responsibility need not rely on such crutches. Instead Yeats turns to the strange dynamics of empathy that are set in motion by his realization that the very conditions of his own poem mime the relation to history that Leda embodies. The pressure of historicity here requires his transforming the sonnet form into a structure marked by emphatic breaks in syntax and lineation. We can no longer hope that an argument will be performed, as in Shakespeare and Milton, that accounts for the pressure and dialectically restores at least the appearance of discursive coherence. Instead the poem must explore positions from which the actual replaying of the trauma becomes a means of adjusting to it.

In "Leda and the Swan" these positions are shaped largely by the foregrounding of two repeated syntactic structures. The first consists simply in the similar participial constructions that dominate the poem's opening and closing stanzas. The opening confronts us with a participial nominative absolute followed by gerundive present participles that cannot be placed in direct syntactic relation with any of the main grammatical units of the sentence registering the rape. It seems then as if the emergence of this god requires our working through several kinds of contingency, only to be forced to recognize that this mode of power need not depend on any of our qualifiers for its existence. Instead divinity may simply be the power to generate such syntactic diffusiveness.

Yeats needs to return to this syntactic key in order to suggest that the responding mind need not be helpless before such power, at least when it occupies the poet's retrospective position. By the end of the poem another string of past participles emerges, this time capable of serving as modifiers of the subject, and hence suggesting that this way of working through Leda's trauma can establish a mode of reflective agency capable of at least some significant response to history's violence. Even if one cannot answer the poem's daunting question about knowledge and power, one can come more fully to appreciate what conjunction of forces, sympathies, and fears makes the asking of that question an important act in its own right. One can realize one's own deep contingency before history, while also deepening one's grasp of the modes of sympathy, and even of self-definition, called forth by such recognitions.

A second syntactic parallel considerably deepens our understanding of what is involved in so modifying the role played by subjective agency. Notice that the concluding question echoes a set of interrogatives in the second stanza. In that stanza questions are necessary in order to open some space for the powers of consciousness within an event dominated by the god's refusal to be bound by any human standards or rationales. Unable to make sense of the god, the poem tries questions as its mode of at least reaching out to what torments Leda in her confrontation with the divine presence. The speaker's questions become vehicles for exploring the possibility of making identifications – initially with Leda's efforts to resist, then, more intensely, with her visceral response to the beating of his heart, that is with the most intimate site where she was actually connected to that divine strangeness.

The metonymic reference to his heart soon gives way to a more general string of metonymies tracing the consequences of this rape. Then, to get beyond a world reduced to such metonymies, the poem turns once more to the interrogative. But now the trauma is so expansive that consciousness cannot simply be an engaged witness; it must find some stance that enables it to respond, to adapt its sense of will and responsibility to what overwhelms it. If the questioning itself can carry the participial modifications, then it becomes possible for the poem to treat its own response to powerlessness as its vehicle for appreciating the complex interrelations among Leda's victimage, the god's power, and whatever dictates the "could" to that power. The interrogative preserves the absolute strangeness of this incarnation, but it also provides a means of identifying with those who must encounter that strangeness – both as Leda does and as Zeus eventually does. So the questioning itself may constitute the version of knowledge required to engage fully what living in history entails: to register the full plight of those Leda comes to represent requires this constant effort to identify with suffering that cannot be described by any positive knowledge without being displaced into something it is not.

And yet such questioning need not reduce us to Leda's victimage. Questioning also becomes a means of rivalling the god because the syntax of questioning can be transformed simply by intensity into the syntax of exclamation – at once intensely itself and in strange contact with a "could" whose power extends beyond its ken. The intense identification which questioning can establish becomes in its own gathering and self-grounding power the only mode of knowledge that history's victims *could* achieve.

V

There could be simpler examples (pre-eminently Stevens' marvelous "Adult Epigram"). But I do not think these would prove as helpful in spelling out the four features basic to the complex of values we can attribute to the work of articulation accomplished in the arts. The first feature consists of the ways in which articulation binds what we say about objects to some set language of motives necessary for contextualizing and characterizing the performative activity. Articulations matter because they satisfy certain desires by providing those desires a means of expression placing them in some ongoing practices. This means that defining articulation involves speculating on what had been the inchoate pressures that get at least partially resolved in those expressions. These pressures can be located in several dimensions, each with a somewhat different mode of inquiry: Yeats' poem can be seen as working out an idea, as a desperate encounter with his own powerlessness in the Irish political theater, or as a symptomatic reflection of social forces and interests within which he is fundamentally a medium.

There are obvious temptations to rest with this one stance towards articulation, since then we could argue that some one critical language like psychoanalysis or cultural criticism best specifies the relation between inchoate need and artistic product. But in order to have at least a principled way of distinguishing among relevant contexts we need to see how the ideal of articulation also involves specific semantic conditions that must be addressed in our attribution of motives. Articulations that matter for the arts offer singular configurations which I think are best treated as performative acts concretely foregrounding specific qualities and interpreting their relevance for the action. Let us call this second feature the rhetorical aspect of articulation, because it consists in the ways that artistic production manipulates a set of historical possibilities and hence turns what was merely potential into an actuality that then opens onto a range of future uses.

As "Leda and the Swan" shows, this correlation is not a simple matter, since the question of "couldness" complexly positions intentional actions against a background where claims about individual wills come to seem somewhat silly. And we see that our most passionate actions tend to reveal far more than the performing consciousness takes account of. But at the same time, we only arrive at a point where clear knowledge of what has power over us becomes thinkable when we let ourselves dwell provisionally on what the agent might have been intending in the expressive actions. Art becomes a witness to history by defining moments where the intensity of individual will modulates into a submission to what goes beyond that will – as necessity in history and as necessity within what the medium can be stretched to allow.

But how can art be witness to anything if our prevailing critical languages insist that the only domain of readerly freedom consists either in reading against a text or in finding texts that defer their own purposiveness in order to elicit the reader's making sense of what otherwise is only indeterminate potential? In other words, we encounter another serious limitation within contemporary criticism: its distrust of articulation seems inseparable from its insistence that the reader's participation is only intense when it is understood as a capacity to refigure or constitute meanings. In contrast, a third feature of articulation in the arts (as well as in practical life) invites a very different model of audience participation. Works of art make demands on audiences that they come to appreciate how the specific movements within the art flesh out what becomes their own passionate concerns. Surely coming to understand how Yeats' language functions requires far more intense participation than simply refiguring the poem or working out our own emotional responses to its overt features. And one might say that such participation in how another mind makes use of language even carries a significant model of our own freedom – not to make meanings but to submit ourselves to other intelligences and to identify with, even celebrate, the community that becomes available among those who can specify what they admire or find useful in that complex authorial labor. The very process of engaging another's articulation of emotions allows us to see how deeply our own structures for intense, passionate life are woven into those figures.[16]

My fourth and final feature consists in a perlocutionary component that makes it possible to flesh out the values involved in this witnessing of authorial witnessing. Articulation need not be an end in itself. It is also a means by which authors and audiences spell out what might be involved in taking new imaginative stances or pursuing new imaginative directions. We might even consider the articulation itself as producing an inchoate pressure for us to explore what it opens. Understanding Leda's plight required that Yeats' speaker come to terms with the relation of his own will to the tragic conditions she epitomizes, and understanding Yeats' stakes in that process involves also reflecting on the values we then place on what he defines for us. Therefore we have to develop two quite different dimensions of this perlocutionary process. The most general one is historical: in what ways does an expression open a range of corresponding acts which can take it as a message to be responded to, as a challenge to be faced, or as some kind of exemplar that then creates possible interpretive and practical uses. (Such uses need not be adulatory; Yeats' poem also enters history as a provocation, leading poets like June Jordan to sharp criticisms of what the poem reveals about male attitudes towards rape.) Then each historical possibility requires fixing personal responsibilities to and for what gets articulated. For ultimately articulation is not simply a modification in language, it involves a modification in selves who have to interpret why they find satisfaction in it and who have to indicate what consequences might follow from that act of identification. Articulation raises the possibility that every interrogative might become an exclamation without passing through truth functional analysis. Therefore concerns for articulation are inseparable from matters of ethos. In an anti-foundational age, this process becomes the basis for a full range of ethical judgments, since it specifies how first-persons offer themselves to second- and third-person assessments of how their actions conform to their self-projections.

VI

In my view we must preserve Kant's sense that the richest accounts of art manifest powers that carry over into the moral realm. This is quite different from saying that works of art ought as individual pieces carry some specific moral burden. The Kantian position can be understood as asking simply that our characteristic engagements with art sustain or even generate certain senses of ourselves which carry over into our practical actions. Therefore I will close by using a literary example to articulate the ethical dimension of the values articulation can be said to foster. Consider the ending of *Othello* (and by implication the way Shakespeare concludes all his tragedies). The hero's final confrontation is with himself: he must face the fact of what he has made of his life. Can self-consciousness generate a mode of willing adequate to the emerging knowledge of what the person has become? And, more generally, can acknowledging the ways in which all self-knowledge tends towards having to come to terms with tragic limitations help us appreciate more richly the values involved in taking responsibility for those limitations?

Othello wooed Desdemona by his narratives, with their exuberant sense of his living up to various challenges and loving it. But once he has killed Desdemona, he enters a world entirely dominated by one narrative, by the one set of facts he cannot any longer not know about himself. The freedom to tell stories gives way to an inescapable self-image all too articulate in its power to generate a self-disgust so deep that any other torture would be a relief:

> Here is my journey's end, here is my butt
> And very sea-mark of my utmost sail.
> Do you go back dismay'd? 'Tis a lost fear
> Man but a rush against Othello's breast
> And he retires. Where should Othello go?
> Now – how dost thou look now? O ill-starr'd wench,
> Pale as thy smock. When we shall meet at compt,
> This look of thine will hurl my soul from heaven ...
> Whip me, ye devils
> From the possession of this heavenly sight!
> Blow me about in winds! Roast me in sulphur!
> Wash me in steep-down gulfs of liquid fire! (5.2.267–280)

The tragic event has produced absolutely no general wisdom, in contrast to much of Greek tragedy. Tragedy here consists in the increasing loss of all options – both for action and for locating ways of regarding oneself. What had been a divided mind is now all too unified by the ways Othello must see himself being seen – first by Desdemona, then by his own ineradicable self-consciousness. Any pain would be easier than this clear vision of himself. And any sound, even the pure moan at the very end of the speech, would be preferable to these repeated "me"'s that no vision of punishment can quite alleviate. Finally any vision would be a relief from the contrast between "this heavenly sight" that was Desdemona and this raging bull "that was Othello," but now is nothing more than a function condemned to endlessly repeating "Here I am" (5.2.284).

Othello's challenge is to transform the pure shifter function of that "Here I am" into a means of actively taking responsibility for what he has irreducibly become. What he has made articulate about himself entails damnation, but there remain several possible attitudes towards that damnation. Othello dwells on its particularity, refusing any consoling abstractions. So he must die, but not as passive object of the state's justice. Instead he makes his dying an absolutely concrete singular judgment, taking action in response to his lucid sense of what he has come to deserve. As he is to be led off to his fate as a condemned prisoner, Othello tries first to make a public appeal that they "speak of me as I am ... who loved not wisely but too well." Then others might know him as he would like to know himself. But his pain cannot be reconciled to such idealization, or to such theatrics. Othello is no Hamlet, and no story could bring out what is unknown in order to heal his wounded name. For Othello, story must give way to action. His very telling of his story, of the story that now is his life, requires his literally dividing himself in two so that he can take responsibility for the "me" that the "I" everywhere confronts. So divided, however, he can find an action which seems to restore a sense of identity, even as it fully interpellates himself into the Venetian society that never could quite accept him. Othello the murderer is nothing better than a Turk, a "circumcised dog" who "beat a Venetian and traduced the state." But Othello can still assume the role of soldier – now no longer as adventurer or captain, but as pure revenger, capable at least of sacrificing himself to purify the state of its ugliest canker.

In this case becoming fully articulate as a subject makes Othello an object with which he cannot bear to identify. But, through the imaginative world that the play makes visible, we also come to understand the painful joy involved in achieving precisely that moment of responsibility, before the indifferent beak could let this too drop.

Notes

1 As will be evident, my discussions of aesthetic ideology will ignore both analytic and pragmatist perspectives, on two grounds – that most of the positive claims they make derive from Kantian concerns, and that as locales of aesthetic theory they have not had much influence on the practices of literary and art criticism. And my discussions will ignore Paul de Man's writing on aesthetic ideology on the grounds that he has had too much influence. I joke, but there is a sense in which de Man's linking of the aesthetic ideology to fascism mirrors standard easy moves within the academy and does not give the aesthetic ideology a fair hearing. For a good critical analysis of de Man's case, see Ian MacKenzie, "Terrible Beauty: Paul de Man's Retreat from the Aesthetic," *Journal of Aesthetics and Art Criticism* 51: 4 (1993), 551–560. I should also note that Richard Wollheim's work proves an important exception to my claims about the

influence of Kant, and hence is very helpful in thinking about alternatives to the aesthetic ideology because it is so completely focused on style as agency and so free of moralizing impulses.

2 Stanley Cavell, *Conditions Handsome and Unhandsome* (University of Chicago Press, 1990), has recently argued that we can directly adapt Kant's aesthetics as a means of deepening our ethical thinking, and I have just completed *Subjective Agency* (Oxford: Basil Blackwell, 1994), a book largely based on the premise that Kant's aesthetics provides concepts fundamental to a workable expressivist ethics. But the fact that the concepts he developed for aesthetics help construct an ethics is not a good reason to rely on his aesthetics as an aesthetics. For a contrary view attempting to reconstruct Kant's aesthetics as the basis for a critical, politically responsive view of the arts see Paul Crowther, *Critical Aesthetics and Postmodernism* (Oxford: Clarendon Press, 1993).

3 Anthony Savile's essay on Adorno, "Beauty and Truth: The Apotheosis of an Idea," in *Analytic Aesthetics* ed. Richard Shusterman, (Oxford: Basil Blackwell, 1989), pp. 123–146, provides a powerful and subtle account of how Adorno's thinking was mobilized by, and ultimately trapped within, traditional or "archaeological" notions of truth and beauty that have been characteristic of aesthetic theory.

4 John Guillory's *Cultural Capital* (University of Chicago Press, 1993) tells another version of this story which is far more willing than I am to treat the weaknesses as sufficient evidence for reading other interests concealed by the ideology as actual driving forces. I think this becomes another untestable allegory, so we have no choice but to stay on the level where we take reasons seriously and argue in terms of overt claims rather than hypotheses about covert interests.

5 I am aware that critics often use "political" more loosely, as a term simply for the side that one is on by virtue of one's actions, even if they are not intended politically and do not have any more direct concrete social consequences than serving as instances of one's general commitments. Thus one is being political by what one does not do as well as by what one does. But this way of imposing identities holds for any practice: one is making a religious statement in not going to church, and one is making an economic statement by what one does not buy. When value claims get this general, one is making a theoretical statement by demonstrating what has very little theoretical force.

6 At best these situations become instances of more general socio-psychological traits, and that means we are always faced with the challenge that the very details we isolate require some ancillary analytic discipline which we only gesture towards. (There is a further irony that we become the repository of analytic disciplines like psychoanalysis which seem anachronistic to academic specialists, and yet which keep alive precisely the kind of hermeneutic values that we once could use the arts to defend and to exemplify.)

7 I work out these claims, as well as the critiques of Eagleton and of Derrida

on which I rely here in my still unpublished "Antiaesthetics." One might note as a contrast to this entire discussion the powerful argument in Tony Bennet's *Outside Literature* (London: Routledge, 1990) that for his political purposes the most honest and most productive move is simply to give up the category of the aesthetic because otherwise politics always functions as a set of default values. Eagleton's case, on the other hand, will always surrender the aesthetic to those default values. Derrida manages to escape such surrender, but only by making default itself his model for the basic values that art might represent or produce: both desire and responsibility can only live as fault lines not assimilable to any general expectations.

8 Perhaps the single most useful reminder of the limits of such work is David Summers, *The Judgment of Sense: Renaissance Naturalism and the Rise of Aesthetics* (Cambridge University Press, 1987). This book offers a powerful and remarkably precise account of how post-Romantic concepts of the aesthetic go back to classical and Renaissance ideals, so we must see these aspects as not dependent on the emergence of bourgeois capitalism. My *Subjective Agency: A Theory of First-Person Expressivity and its Social Implications* (Oxford: Blackwell, 1994) also makes a case for those limits by dealing at length with problems in Eagleton's efforts to treat Kant's aesthetics as congruent with bourgeois social interests, so, while we can speak of an aesthetic ideology in an Althusserian sense, we cannot cogently link that ideology to the work that Marx's own theory attributes to ideology.

9 The controversies generated by Frank Sibley's arguments about the relation between aesthetic and non-aesthetic properties seem to me a clear example of the dangers I refer to. The very form of the debate depends on problematic ontological assumptions. Similarly the form of current debates about art-world definitions of art seems shaped by inescapable difficulties in moving from what we can say about particulars to what we must locate as conditions of our training and long-terms effects of our habits.

10 Bernard Williams, *Shame and Necessity* (Berkeley: University of California Press, 1993).

11 Kendall Walton, *Mimesis and Make-believe: On the Foundations of the Representational Arts* (Cambridge, MA: Harvard University Press, 1990). Ironically, when Aristotelian theory resists being aestheticized in this manner, the aesthetic ideology tends to respond by treating this mode of theorizing as if concerns for issues like unity condemned it to being a bad version of empiricist ideals of representation. What the aesthetic ideology cannot make its own, it consigns to the only locus of opposition that it takes seriously.

12 On the value of the Longinian sublime as opposed to Romantic and contemporary versions of the topic (but without reference to articulation) see my "Plato's Performative Sublime and the Ends of Reading," in *Canons and Consequences* (Evanston: Northwestern University Press,

1990), pp. 163–187.

I should also note that I concentrate here on articulation because I find it the easiest of the three domains to discuss. It is the closest of the three to the values of Kantian aesthetics, although I think I can show how it also proves compatible with quite different perspectives. Historically one might say that classical mimetic theory tried to subordinate a rhetorical model of articulation to one that did invite an epistemic framework, if only an Aristotelian contemplative one. That theory managed to show how this desire for articulation has real effects on how people think about the world. But the theory could not survive empiricist renderings of the powers and obligations involved in making representations of the world. Those accounts replaced the ideal of knowing by questions about who knows for what interests, and, in relation to the arts, they stressed ways that articulation masks interests rather than allowing agents to accept the stakes involved in wanting a particular realization. Idealism did have an account of such desires, since articulation becomes the work of Spirit (whether the Spirit be Kantian or Hegelian). And now our task is to redefine that work so that Spirit itself enters a pragmatic domain for linking questions to exclamations.

13 Alicia Ostriker quotes this statement in her "Surviving" from *The Imaginary Lover* (University of Pittsburgh Press, 1986), p. 49.

14 I cannot deny that there remain problematic cases, like that of John Ashbery's poetry, where the emphasis is on making vividness itself a fluid state emerging only at moments within an otherwise indeterminate flow of associations. Yet even here Ashbery's power lies largely in how he produces those moments of sudden insight or fresh conjunctions of language. And one could argue that the play with indistinctness is part of his articulating an overall attitude which the poems interpret so as to take overt responsibility for the stance they define.

15 W. B. Yeats, *The Poems of W. B. Yeats*, ed. Richard Finneran, (New York: Macmillan, 1983), pp. 214–215.

16 These specifyings of possible shared emotions play a crucial role in contemporary culture because we have to come to understand how naturalist accounts of the relation between brain and consciousness can balance a sense of individual *qualia* with an awareness of the ways that other aspects of these *qualia* are fundamentally shareable. I am moved to this formulation by the argument of Owen Flanagan, *Consciousness Reconsidered* (Cambridge, MA: MIT Press, 1992).

4

In their own voice: philosophical writing and actual experience[1]

ARTHUR C. DANTO

In contemplating the prospect of having to undergo Congressional scrutiny in connection with her confirmation as director of the National Endowment for the Arts, the esteemed actress, Jane Alexander, said – half in jest and half as boast – "It's the first time I've had to audition for an awfully long time." She had attained that level of professional acclaim where those with parts to give out came to *her*, hoping she would consider accepting them, knowing her participation in a play would enhance its success, as art and as enterprise. There are those in philosophy of whom something like this is true as well, who do little or nothing by way of writing "on spec," but nearly always in response to requests to give keynote addresses, symposium papers, named lectures, invited papers, contributed essays – and whose books themselves are often simply gatherings of these. Donald Davidson once told me that of the then close to forty papers he had published, none had been refereed – none had been *submitted* for publication and subjected to the processes of editorial or peer review, and exposed to requests for revision. Instead, those parts of his papers which an editor might peremptorily have written "Clarify!!!" next to in the margin have given rise to mighty rivers of commentary and analysis, and doubtless have seen more than one critic through to tenure as a specialist in the philosophy of Donald Davidson. There are exceptions, some surprising, but what is true for Davidson is in large measure true for philosophers of any reputation to speak of. It is difficult to imagine most of them submitting to the indignities of audition, exposing themselves to the humiliation of having their work turned down, or, if accepted, then on terms set by unnamed referees. They are *stars*.

Most of these star-philosophers have pretty distinct voices, possibly in consequence of the fact that so much of what they have written has been composed to be read before audiences, and hence is filled with devices of a kind calculated to hold an audience: turns of phrase, ingenuity of examples, sparks of wit, and an aura of presumed intimacy between speaker and hearer. In general, I should think, most who are literate in contemporary philosophy would be able to identify the authors of sample anonymous texts, as much by voice as by the positions they advance – would be able to say that this passage must be by Jerry Fodor or that by Richard Rorty or Hilary Putnam or Daniel Dennett or Saul Kripke or John Searle, let alone Quine, Goodman, Davidson, or Chisholm. The jokes, the asides, the syntax, the punctuation (like parentheses), the vocabulary, the imagined cases, the authorities appealed to, the *tone*, give the author away. This familiarity of voice perhaps comes from having heard these philosophers speak, so that one can virtually hear them as one reads, whatever may be the problems with logocentrism and its relationship to *l'écriture*. The presence of these philosophers gives one a reason to attend the lecture, the panel, the disputation, the meeting – and this is no less true of the apostle of *l'écriture*, M. Derrida, who is as much a philosophical presence as the individuals cited. We may not always admire these personal styles; we may in fact wince at the jocularity, the confessional disclosure, the flaky examples, the feigned simplicity, the flaunted technicalities, the contrived analogy, the fruity metaphor – or the aggressiveness, the mock humility, the pedagogic sneer. But it seems to me incontestable that to have evolved a philosophy sufficiently marked that the author is exempt from audition is also to have evolved a philosophical style and personality which is readily marked and easily imitated. It is even possible to suppose that the strongest philosophers of our era possess the strongest styles, to the point where no one would think of writing in their voice, let alone the voices of the towering masters of writing like Heidegger, or Wittgenstein, or Dewey. To do so would straightaway be reckoned imposture. Does that mean that philosophy and philosopher are inseparable? Or that there is a deep connection between philosophy and voice?

It is reported that, as early as 1920, Hans-Georg Gadamer heard that Heidegger, in a lecture of extraordinary originality, used the phrase "it's worlding."[2] And it became a matter of international scandal, at least among the Positivists, that Heidegger used what they regarded as the paradigm of nonsense in connection with the word *das Nichts*, namely that *es nichtet*.[3] To transform nouns into the verbs one needs is certainly more than a style – it is the very substance of a metaphysics, and one is very grateful – one is in any case if one admires Heidegger at all – that he was not obliged to submit the manuscripts of his lectures to some arbiter of editorial correctness. But is style always and invariably internally related to substance in this way? Admittedly, it would at the very least be difficult to imagine Heidegger – or Wittgenstein for that matter – using the literary style, hence speaking in the voice of, another philosopher, like John Dewey or A. J. Ayer, hence as exploratory, the way an animal explores a field, leaving an involuted trail, or as supercilious. But are these thinkers' thoughts so involved with their voice that we cannot state a Heideggerian or Wittgensteinian "truth" without using the Heideggerian or Wittgensteinian style to do it with? Thus Wittgensteinian "truths" – I am employing quotation marks because I want to leave the reader a bit edgy with the idea that there are such things as Heideggerian or Wittgesteinian truths rather than truths which happen to have been uttered by Heidegger or Wittgenstein – often appear by way of responses to vivid questions in little scenarios. Does this circumstance in any way penetrate the "truth" that comes as a response? And we report "it" by saying, perhaps, "Were someone to ask – or think ... then one might say ... " So that Wittgensteinian "truths" are things one might say in certain choreographed circumstances, in case a worry arose which it then helps mute. It is almost medicinal, bearing a tacit label "To be taken in the case of mental cramp." As if only to someone genuinely provoked to make the query does the "truth" come as an answer. I am not comfortable with this idea, but it strikes me that something like it has been advanced by Stanley Cavell, who is one of the few to have made philosophical voice a central concern of his philosophy.[4]

Here, a propos a well-known argument of Kripke's based on a no less well-known thought (or "thought") of Wittgenstein, Cavell

[s]uggests a piece of advice [he has] for one who (for a moment, or from now on) has freed himself or herself from Wittgenstein's spell, and would like to believe that the writing, while no doubt distinguished, is not really essential to the teaching; not just that it fails sometimes, which is inevitable, but simply that it cannot matter *that* much, as much, say, as its fervor continually seems to declare. My advice is to take the writing of the *Investigations* as perfectly straightforward – or as straightforward (say undigressive) as any can be with spade turned, empty of theses, no agenda to complete. It is Wittgenstein's posture of philosophy, always arriving at a standstill ("peace"), as if there were no (other) goal. That there is limitation in this

manner I would not deny, but the unstraightforward is as much part of its power as of its impotence. Images associated with the turned spade, the unassertive pen, will continue to return[5]

That is to say, the unstraightforward in Wittgenstein's writing is *in its own way* straightforward, once we grasp what the posture is. Kripke, on the other hand, had supposed that all the backing and forthing was a kind of ornamentation, and that it could be erased in favor of asserting a straightforwardly straightforward proposition which can be discerned behind or beneath the style. "So Wittgenstein perhaps cagily might very well disapprove of the straightforward formulation given here. Nevertheless, I choose to be so bold as to say: Wittgenstein holds, with the skeptic, that there is no fact as to whether I mean plus or quus."[6] And Cavell is disapproving on Wittgenstein's behalf. Getting rid of the "unstraightforward," saying flat out in robust Anglo-Saxon terms what one is getting at, is a project as misguided as that of the Walrus and the Carpenter, who see the sand as a form of dirt, making the beach disagreeable, when in fact the sand *is* the beach. "Holding" is not something Wittgenstein does ("empty of theses"). He is not seaching for a thesis but for peace. There are sentences in Wittgenstein which look like theses (which in the *Investigations* look like the propositions in the *Tractatus*): extractable, detachable, capable of being set down in a kind of breviary and bound in red and titled in gold lettering: *Wittgenstein's Philosophical Thoughts.* So one might even imagine Wittgenstein using the very words Kripke uses: "There is no fact as to whether I mean plus or quus." But that would not be a thesis of Wittgenstein's as it is *the* thesis of Kripke in his text on rules. Rather, there is something in Wittgenstein as a writer, in his mode of presentation, which could ("I fancy," Cavell writes, leaving it open as to whether or not he "holds") "have given the words a voice that prompts a countervoice." And so Kripke's view "cannot just be right."[7]

The thought, if I follow Cavell, is that it is inconsistent – it is an inconsistency of philosophical practice – to believe that as a philosopher Wittgenstein held or could have held anything, writing the way he did. And this in effect means: you cannot free yourself from the spell of his writing, and bear away a nugget of philosophy. That would be like rationally expecting to find in your hand the coin you dreamt you found. No: to read Wittgenstein, on Cavell's view, is to enter into a peace-bringing discourse as one of the voices sooner or later expresses a worry and the counter-voice administers relief. It is like entering a poem. You cannot flatly say "Frost said 'And miles to go before I sleep.' " Of course the words were his. But he said them in a poem, and that line has to be reached by reading through the poem which it closes, resolving the tensions of the poem by its repetition. It is not separately assertable, not something Frost *held*. This is to treat philosophy as if oblique. It is indeed to treat it as *literature*! Is this just true of Wittgenstein or is it generally true of philosophy? Is it true of Cavell, for example? Few writers are less straightforward than he, but in the end he is making a claim about how Wittgenstein is to be read which is true or false. Cavell reads Wittgenstein the way a gifted literary critic would read him. Consider the passage in Wittgenstein to which the phrase "As straightforward ... as any can be with spade turned" refers:

"How am I able to obey a rule?" – if this is not a question about causes, then it is about the justification for my following the rule in the way I do.

If I have exhausted the justifications, I have reached bedrock, and my spade is turned. Then I am inclined to say: "This is simply what I do."[8]

The word "justification(s)" occurs twice in this passage, Cavell notes, but a different German word is translated each time. In the first paragraph the German is *Rechtfertigung.* In the second the German word is *Begründungen.* By translating the two terms the same way, the English version "misses the chance to register that the metaphorical strain in *Begründung*, that is, grounding, or following, is followed out as this sentence in which the image of ground occurs continues the image by invoking hard rock and the spade it turns back."[9] One might even go further: the sound of *Grund* could have awakened the thought of *Grund*, and hence the powerful metaphor of the turned spade. This is a wonderful way of having one's text read, but not, I think, if it vaporizes philosophical writing into poetry. That is not the way I want to think about philosophical writing or voice, nor is it the way with the prominent philosophers I began by citing, who are beyond audition, but have burning truths to transmit whatever the poetics or rhetoric of their discourse – about reasons being a class of causes, about consciousness being the essence of mind, about the existence of a language of thought which it makes sense for scientists to look for. Having listened to Cavell's advice, does Kripke not in the end have to make his mind up whether or not he was right, hence whether or not Wittgenstein holds that there is no fact by which I can tell which of two things I mean? He may be wrong, but not for the Cavellian reason that there is no holding in the *Investigations*, but for the reason that Wittgenstein does not hold *this*.

Wittgenstein's *Philosophical Investigations* has, rather rare among philosophical works, a claim as a work of literary art, not so much because of its vivid and compelling imagery – its "fervor," to use Cavell's expression – but because it somehow embodies what it is about. Digging is not deflected by bedrock, it is a search for bedrock; and bedrock itself is defined by the kinds of tools one has for digging of this sort and for this purpose. It is bedrock only for the spade it turns, and there is no value in the suggestion that one can easily go deeper with a pneumatic drill or a back-hoe, or, as Nietzsche liked to say about his own writings, with dynamite. If I were an engineer, charged with digging a tunnel, bedrock would be an obstacle to get round: saying my spade had been turned would be a call for heavier equipment. The point is not to make a hole of a certain depth, come what may, but to find where bedrock is, using a spade. For Wittgenstein, the plain and simple tools of manual labor are metaphors for the plain and simple tools of philosophical investigation, the ordinary methods of inquiry where probes are made in the search for limits, where digging has to stop. In its own way, the *Investigations* is composed in the Kantian spirit of finding the boundaries, beyond which we are unable to pass, however great our appetite for doing so, and where our spades are turned. And when he says "This is what I do" he refers to the common practices for which the simple tools are metaphors. He means: This is where I am, this is how it is, this is what my house – my life, *my being* – rests on and is confined to: This is *what I do*. A counter-voice – Don't you need a better shovel? Are you sure this is what you were looking for? Do you not want to try digging a foot or so to the left? – would come only from a philosophical kibitzer whose ambition is to deprecate our powers. But the kibitzer is the nemesis of peace, and the *Investigations* demonstrates how to shut him up, not how to allow him to flourish. Peace comes with the finding of limits we then learn to live within, which is a kind of stoicism. And this fits in with so much of what Wittgenstein wrote, in *On Certainty* and elsewhere, that one feels it has to have been the project of his life. The writing *shows* what can also be *said* (even if Wittgenstein, famously but to another purpose, said: "What *can* be shown *cannot* be said"[10]). And what can be said can be detached and asserted. As Doctor Johnson said, "The mind can only repose on the stability of truth."[11] It could not be more reassuring to learn that there is bedrock, a point beyond which digging cannot go. There is also a certain comfort in seeing the digging done, embodied in the way the text is written. But the spirit of the *Investigations* in seeking the foundations of the world is finally not that different from that of the *Tractatus*, which also seeks bedrock. Finally, let's face it, we know enough of Wittgenstein's life and personality to appreciate that it would be as a man with a spade that he would want to be perceived. Not with a shovel – he was not moving dirt or manure. He was a digger.

One cannot imagine Cavell with spade in hand, and this is reflected, or inflected, in his chosen voice, which is easy to recognize – he perhaps holds the record for the largest number of parentheses to appear in a single paragraph – but difficult to condense into an image other than the image, perhaps, of a conversation in which different voices occur and concur and diverge. "Becoming intelligible to oneself," he writes, "may accordingly present itself as discovering which among the voices contending to express your nature are ones for you to own here, now. (The contention among voices may shift without settling once and for all.)"[12] Regarding his own "sound" he writes "It may help to say that while I may leave ideas in what may seem a more literary state, sometimes in a more psychoanalytical state, than a philosopher might wish ... I mean to leave everything I will say, or have, I guess, ever said, as in a sense provisional, the sense that it is to be gone on from." But he adds "philosophy should sometimes distrust its defenses of philosophical form." But this mistrust of form together with what one must call an advertisement for his own form, acts to soften up the anticipated opposition to his urging us to take Emerson, a favorite philosopher of his, as philosophically seriously as he does. But (of course in a parenthesis) "Emerson's prose exists as a kind of conversation with itself." Given his voice, it is natural, or at least understandable, that the texts he admires are conversational, and that in consequence he shall listen for the essential counter-voice between the lines in the *Investigations*, and that it be essential there that the conversation go on – and hence that nothing be held, that everything be provisional, so that if conversation stops it does not end. He invents a conversational theory of justice in order to accommodate Rawls, and he all but apotheosizes J. L. Austin for having licensed recognition of voice, without which conversation is impossible. Curiously, one sees – or, not having read every word, I have seen – very little celebration of Paul Grice, who after all devoted his major effort to what one might call the ethics of conversation: Cavell is interested in conversing, not in the theory of conversation. I can see him, eccentrically so far as the philosophical canon is concerned, extravagantly admiring Emerson, who has opposed views on certain matters, so that his writing is by way of transcript of the internal conversation, of one side of him trying to get the other side to see things in a certain way, it not greatly mattering which side comes out on top – it almost being a shame if one side in fact comes out on top if that means conversation ending.

Cavell has a certain investment in that conception of the self as something with different sides, between which the life of the self is conversational (it is not a split self where the sides are incommunicado). He, for example, cites Thoreau with approval for having written "With thinking we may be beside ourselves in a sane sense."[13] Cavell indeed rather pounces on "beside ourselves," which he paraphrases as "ecstasy," which really is not so much being beside as outside ourselves. Generally, a person is said to be "beside himself" when the pressures are of a degree that he is unable to cope – who is "beside himself with worry." But I in any case do not know what ecstasy "in the sane sense" would amount to, just because one is really outside oneself in the ecstatic moment, which is a little bit of controlled madness. But I concede that philosophers have used "ecstasy" in a non-ecstatic sense – Heidegger, for example, in his discussion of the temporal dimensions of Dasein.[14]

I surmise that what Thoreau meant, sticking his tongue out at the reader or at least sticking it in his cheek, was that thinking involves putting my thoughts at a certain distance – it means in effect reflection. Not just having thoughts, which everyone does, but directing my thoughts, which is a form of regimentation into syllogisms of theory and practice, and the very opposite of ecstasy. Cavell has a somewhat different and perhaps deeper view, which he throws out as an aside by locking it into a parenthesis: "(Thinking does not start from scratch: it as it were sides against and with the self there is and so constitutes it. The question is what must that be in order to be sided, to be capable of asides, to require parentheses.)"[15] This in effect is a comment on Descartes' thesis of the thinking nature of the self, with the emendation that if the self is essentially thought, it is essentially sided, for thinking is conversational. But does that mean that one has to write that way, with all those parentheses and asides? It could be that the style expresses the writer's self, but, if the theory is any good, all selves are sided, however they write. And on this perhaps a few words of commentary will not be amiss.

An aside is a speech outside the action of the play and unheard by the characters in the play, the action of which in no way turns on what the aside says or on the fact that it is said. It is addressed to the audience, who are not part of the action at all. The aside-deliverer has to be part of the action, except when in the posture of aside-delivering. Through delivering it he underscores his complex status as within and without the action of the play. He mediates between audience and the action of the play exactly by putting the play at a certain distance, and by settling the audience in a different relationship to that action than when it is in the action's grip. Usually, asides are scripted, but I suppose I can imagine the possibility of a conversation between aside-deliverer and audience about the meaning of the action: but it would require the other actors to freeze until the conversation stopped. It in any case is not a conversation between the aside-deliverer and the other characters. It can happen only when the action stops. So it is a bad model for conversation. If I were at this point to deliver an aside to the reader, it would be at right angles to the text. Cavell's asides, his paren-theses, are delivered not to the reader but to himself, or to one side of his self from another: the reader, in fact, is ignored. That is why, because internal to the prose, they are so annoying and distracting, keeping the reader's mind off the flow, unable to follow what is action and what is not. Or they are a bit like the patter of the magician, distracting us from seeing how the rabbits are pulled from the hats, with the difference that no one can tell hat from rabbit, action from aside, except that they do not fall into the linearity of good expository prose. It divides the self of the reader into sides, perhaps, as if the style were a kind of ontological proof of what the author says the self is, since reading itself becomes as fissured as the self described and exhibited by the prose. And that is the point: described and exhibited. But philosophical descrip-tions of the self do not have to be mirrors of the self described, they do not have to show what the text also says. But in any case even if they do show that, this contributes not a shred of evidentiary support for what the text says. So, in even the extreme case of Cavell, I am uncertain there is an internal connection between style and philosophical substance, even if the style exemplifies the substance in a literary way. Of course there may be this connection: the style is the man and the theory was evolved in order to justify what Cavell is as a person, a thinker, a talker. But then it goes too far, for it gives the theory for selves as different from Cavell as he is from everyone else, and who, as persons, thinkers, and talkers, are not like him at all.

This being said, a page or two of Cavell – a paragraph or two in fact – is almost unmistakable. No one would have the slightest difficulty in identifying it as his, even if it illustrates what one might consider the dangerous side of not holding philosophers to the constraints of audition. And in general this is true of the other philosophers I mentioned in my beginning paragraph, whose styles have been allowed to flourish, and even to be appreciated. But that leaves my question still unanswered, if it is not already answered in the negative, namely what is the connection if any between the what and the how of saying? The philosopher may be the writing, so that to discipline the writing is to regiment the philosopher. But is there any internal connection between the writing and the thought? Can, that is, any thought be expressed in any voice, even if not all styles will embody or exemplify it? If the philosopher and the voice are one, do we need to have the philosopher in the writing if we do not need the voice?

Any philosopher with a voice strong enough to be recognized will have a philosophy strong enough to have been commented on, and indeed it will in general be the strength of the philosophy that has allowed the voice to emerge. So each in consequence will have generated a secondary bibliography of articles devoted to his or her philosophy, including, now and again, an article or so by the voiced philosopher on his or her own philosophy. On occasion, one of these is submitted to *The Journal of Philosophy*. Not long ago, for example, we received a paper by a philosopher of world reknown defending his position against criticisms of it made by another philosopher of parallel reputation. Given that the submission was by a philosopher who had made it into the no-audition class, it was somewhat affecting that he had actually submitted a paper to us, and it suggests that there remains a value in philosophical journals after all: it gives someone like him a forum for reaching four thousand or so subscribers who would have a natural interest in a paper by him defending his views, and then the large dilating circle of library readers, recipients of xeroxes, students who may be asked to consider the paper, together with the original critique, in seminars on contemporary philosophy. The editors thought it a valuable paper, since the writer is known to all, and read and discussed wherever philosophy itself is read and discussed. The decision to publish it was uncommonly easy.

At the time, I remember thinking about the difference between his article, and one we might have received from someone who undertook to examine the criticisms of philosopher X of philosopher Y, and who found them wanting in the same way that philosopher Y found them wanting when he undertook to respond, as in the paper he submitted to the *Journal*. Let us imagine such a paper, by someone named Z, and that Z's paper and Y's paper have pretty much the same content: clearly, Z understands Y's philosophy as well as Y himself does. They examine the same criticizing texts of X, find them deficient for just the same reasons, and conclude that Y's philosophy emerges from the ordeal unscathed. We receive a good many papers of this sort and we publish a lot of them as well: the papers that seemed to me breakthroughs in my own tenure as editor are few and far between, and I think I can remember them all. Most of what we publish consists of attacks and defenses and counter-attacks.

Close in their conclusions as I am supposing the papers by Y and Z to be, it is hard to imagine them as indiscernible. I could not really imagine Y referring to himself in the third person, for example. Suppose, though, he did. Having gone to the trouble of submitting a paper, he might have written: I did not know whether or not you have a policy of blind review, so I have arranged the pronouns in such a way that the referee would be unable to tell that the author and the subject were one. Probably there is software for this: you double-click "Blind Review" in the Edit window, and "I" and "my" get replaced by "Y" and "Y's." And now we can imagine, as I always like to do in doing philosophy, that the papers of Y and of Z are indiscernible. There could be no basis for publishing one rather than the other, and so we might toss a coin and publish Z's paper on Y rather than Y's paper on himself, because that is the way the coin falls. Or suppose the coin falls such that when the veils are lowered, it is Y's paper upon which fortune smiled. Then we rejoice that we have – our readers have – Y on Y. Too bad for Z and his publish-or-perish circumstance. He has only the thin cruel satisfaction that he is as good on Y as Y is, for whatever good that does him.

In fact Y's paper was altogether too personal to imagine the blind-review command could regiment it into a state of anonymity. Thus Y might say "I believe, in matters of this sort ..." If the blind-review command transforms this into "Y believes, in matters of this sort ..." – which is exactly what Z writes – we would be reluctant to print it. How does Z know what Y believes? But that question does not arise for Y himself, writing "in his own voice." Recently a hapless biographer of Kennedy was not quite able to exploit certain deconstructionist attitudes that there is no real difference between fiction and history, and ascribe thoughts and feelings to the subject for which there is no documentation, the way a novelist does where the issue of documentation is beside the point. The question was always how the biographer knew. People who bought the book wanted fact and not entertainment, and I for one rejoiced, I am afraid, in the book's failure. In any case, Y, speaking in his own voice, has a right to say what his beliefs are when, were these ascribed to him by some third person, the latter would have to be documented. So the blind-review command would have to be quite sophisticated indeed, and instruct Y to document what, in the first person, he can state with no documentation whatever. But, beyond this, I am uncertain the software exists which could depersonalize a text by Y, irrepressible as he is as a writer and a person, and with the sort of voice everyone in philosophy is sensitive to. On the other hand, it is possible to imagine that Z, Y-ist that he or she has become, has begun to imitate as an inadvertent tribute the voice of Y. There is always a danger in matters of blind review that referees will be taken in by imitations, especially when the model imitated has a strong and identifiable voice. It is an open secret that the judges picked a certain submission for the Paris opera house design at Bastille because they were certain it was Richard Meier, having all the marks. The result was a Meier-like edifice, derivative in style and banal in conception. The danger could be dissipated were judges to employ the criteria of "good architecture," but the difficult truth is that voice is as complicating a factor in architecture as it is in philosophy. It may not be part of good architecture, but there is no good architecture without it. And thinking the building was by Richard Meier gave the judges a good reason to choose it, thinking how important it would be to Paris to have an example of this artist's work. Paris is an architectural museum, after all.

But *The Journal of Philosophy* is not a philosophy museum! And I can at this point hear someone say: what difference does it make? after all – as I myself have argued here – the voice does not really penetrate the philosophy; the philosophy is the arguments; that the question is in the end whether or not X was right about Y, and it does not matter who comes up with the good answer, its goodness being independent of who comes up with it. This is the bottom-line view of philosophy, that philosophy does not vary in any significant way depending upon whose fingers it comes out of or out of whose mouth it issues. The bottom-line view of philosophy is what underlies blind reviewing, and that means suppressing whatever does not on the bottom-line account belong to the philosophy. And that means, as I see it, the suppression of voice. For if the voice is allowed to seep through, the conditions of the blind review have been violated.

"What difference does it make?" is a question I have dealt with in the philosophy of art, where it might arise with the differences, never relevantly visible, between a photograph and an appropriation of that photograph, between a painting and its appropriation. Here one is able to show that even the subject differs, and that all those facts about the artist, the artist's time and place and psychology, make immense differences in how the work is identified and interpreted, and even in aesthetic assessment. If philosophy were literature, the strategies that worked so well in the philosophy of art would work with philosophical writing too. But here we are not dealing with the poetics of philosophy, with philosophy's rhetoric, but with philosophy neat, clean, and simple, where issues of logical consistency and truth trump those that pertain to the expressive dimension of writing. If Wittgenstein held no theories, he would never be falsified, and so the test can never arise as to whether his writing would retain its charm in the face of philosophical falsehood. But, as even Cavell, the great expositor of voice must hold, there are theses – about, among other matters, self, conversation, theses, voice – and so truth or falsity, to the assessment of which voice seems hardly to matter, at least if my arguments have been sound. Once that is allowed, voice may be written off as whatever it was that Kripke alluded to as "caginess," and the theses advanced in what he also calls a "straightforward" way. And why not then go all the way, to the philosophical format that passes the test of the bottom-line, and which answers the question "What difference does it make?" with a curt "None." So I have argued myself into something of a quandary, having incompatible attitudes on voice. I am not sure I know the way out of the quandary, but I will end this essay with a sketch of an exit. It turns on distinguishing voice from self.

The degree to which Y has come to take the privileges which accompany his reputation for granted is testified to by the casualness with which he submitted a paper through which his own familiar and famous voice speaks directly and clearly, with no effort whatsoever to disguise it in the interests of blind review. He has obviously sent his pieces to places for a very long time where the presumption was that they would be printed, subject to minor editing. It is true that *The Journal of Philosophy* has no policy of blind review, but I dare say Y knew nothing of this widely criticized fact. Had he sent his paper to a journal which insists on blind review, the editors, pleased as they would have been to publish Y's article, would have had in consistency to demand that he comply to their strictures of anonymity. This at the very least would mean the elimination of the possessive case from descriptions of his own writings and thoughts, so that there would be no grammatical mark to the effect that he was writing about his own philosophy, and hence no grammatical evidence of the authority he commands regarding what he means and how he sees the implications and consequences (not to speak of his hopes for its future development). He would have to write about himself as if he were a third person, which directly affects the content of what he can consistently describe. The reason voice is relevant to philosophical writing is that philosophical writings by a single person form complex systems and constellations of ideas – they have pasts and futures as well as presents – and the reasons we are interested in voice are those which explain our interest in philosophical creativity. Creative philosophers do not do philosophy by producing atoms of bottom-line "good" philosophy. What they write carries what they have written and what they hope to write as the aura of a total vision.

Now in truth I am uncomfortable with the idea of producing papers from which a zealous enough referee can infer nothing about one's gender, one's race, one's age, one's place, or indeed infer anything that can be elevated into a fulcrum of prejudiced rejection. A well-known art magazine for which I occasionally write does not, of course, insist on blind submission – there are no submissions for the most part but commissions instead – but its publisher insists on a stylistic difference between the articles, where the author is not to speak in his or her own voice, and the columns and departments, where one is expected to speak in one's own voice. One would think that philosophy would have the natural standing of a column, an expression of the writer's views and the writer's philosophical personality. So it is somewhat striking that blind submission should have the effect of transferring writing from the columnist's to the reporter's codes, where the latter complies with the "Just the facts please" of the forensic examiner. At the very least we cannot expect very colorful philosophical personalities to emerge from under that order of regime, nor very colorful philosophy.

Now, of course, as a general rule, all that blind submission amounts to is the suppression of information on the title page in which the name of the author and his/her institutional affiliation is recorded, but I have often pointed out how transparent authorship really is, if only through the fact that the longest number of bibliographical entries is a dead giveaway of who the author is. Anyone anxious to find out who the author is can have scant difficulty, for manuscripts are really strewn with clues. So, strictly speaking, blind reviewing is ritualized suppression of title-page information. But, were the policy really strict, authors should not refer to their bodies in a gender specific way, since that would enable a biased reviewer to turn a manuscript down. Nor in fact should they refer to any of those distinguishing features, for the sake of which blind review was instituted, to insure that there be no prejudiced rejection. This would then have the inadvertent consequence that everyone sounds alike. But we really do experience the world and life as gendered beings, as beings with all the attributes that expose us to the danger of prejudice. This means that suppression of our facticities results in a distorted representation of the world, the world according to Nobody. And this makes bottom-line philosophy abstract and distorted and surrealistic. We talk of Twin Earth, of being connected in some science-fiction way to a violinist who depends upon us not to "abort" him, of veils of ignorance, one important criticism of which is that they presuppose a view of humanity which blind reviewing as a practice institutionalizes. In general we indulge in thought experiments of various kinds where universal intuitions of readers are appealed to, which have nothing to do with the way we are embodied or situated or encultured. And my view is that in detaching writers from their own reality the resulting philosophy is airless and detached, with no tethers to human reality beyond the dubious intuitions alleged to be universal. Yet think of how those who believe in blind review are likely to be critical of Kant for treating human beings as vehicles of pure reason with nothing to connect them to the world save semantics, as though how we decide had nothing to do with our having bodies, or with having to grow up.

Needless to say, all this cannot be blamed on a reasonably benign if innocuous practice meant to secure fairness in the place of publication. Philosophy in its professional practice has loosened itself more and more from the world as we really experience it anyway, in our embodied and historical natures, in its drive to secure something disembodied and timeless. And I think a dreadful price, the price of irrelevance, is paid for this: nobody reads philosophy but philosophers. Here is one philosopher who is privileged to speak in his own voice – Stuart Hampshire – writing about another so privileged – John Rawls – in the pages of *The New York Review of Books*, about Rawls' recent book, *Political Liberalism*. "One tends to be lulled into acquiescence because the noise and muddle of actual politics are altogether absent, and history is scarcely called upon at all." This makes Rawls' analysis too remote, "too gentle and too temperate in tone,"[16] too much finally of the seminar room and not of the negotiating table or the war room. It lacks the teeth of engagement and commitment.

Some years ago, an essay appeared, dispiriting in its title for aestheticians, called "The Dreariness of Aesthetics." These days, I am afraid, I find almost everything in philosophy except aesthetics pretty dreary, and the dreariness has been driven out of aesthetics, it seems to me, in virtue of the fact that it is more and more written by philosophers engaged in the raw world of artistic conflict, far indeed from Twin Earth, and where brains in vats might be things that turn up at the Aperto in Venice or at the Whitney Biennial. Let blind review continue, but blind philosophy might to everyone's profit stop being written. Philosophers should be encouraged to speak in their own voice about the world that means something to them. The freer the voice, the better the philosophy. For now, that is the only connection I see.

Notes

1 An earlier version of this article was presented at a conference called "Philosophy and/as Writing," sponsored by the Greater Philadelphia Philosophy Consortium, October 9, 1993. I am immeasurably grateful to Professor Mette Hjort for her generous and illuminating comments, as well as to Richard Eldridge for *his* generous and illuminating comments and observations in subsequent correspondence.

2 Theodore Kiesel, *The Genesis of Heidegger's Being and Time* (Berkeley: University of California Press, 1993), p. 16.

3 In, of course, Martin Heidegger, "What is Metaphysics?" in *Existence and Being* (Chicago: Henry Regnery Company, 1949.), p. 369: "Nihilation cannot be reckoned in terms of annihilation or negation at all. Nothing

"nihilates" *(nichtet)* itself." The chief finger pointer was Carnap – see especially his "The Elimination of Metaphysics through Logical Analysis of Language," trans. Arthur Pap in *Logical Positivism*, ed. A. J. Ayer (Glencoe, Illinois: The Free Press, 1959), pp. 69–73. In my generation such translations of *"Das Nichts nichet"* as "(Ahem!) 'Nothing noths.' " could always be counted on for a mirthful audience response.

4 Thus in his *A Pitch of Philosophy* (Cambridge University; Harvard University Press, 1993) he praises J. L. Austin for curing "the repression of voice (hence of confession, hence of autobiography)" in philosophy, p. 69.

5 Stanley Cavell, *Conditions Handsome and Unhandsome: The Constitution of Emersonian Perfectionism* (University of Chicago Press, 1990), p. 79.

6 Saul Kripke, *Wittgenstein on Rules and Private Language* (Cambridge University Press, 1982), pp. 70–71.

7 Cavell, *Conditions*, p. 79.

8 Ludwig Wittgenstein, *Philosophical Investigations*, trans. G. E. M. Anscombe (New York: The Macmillan Company, 1955), #217.

9 Cavell, *Conditions*, pp. 81–82.

10 Ludwig Wittgenstein, *Tractatus Logico-Philosophicus* (London: Routledge and Kegan Paul, 1923), 4.1212.

11 Samuel Johnson, "Preface" to *Shakespeare. Works*, Yale edition, vol..7, p. 62.

12 Cavell, *Conditions*, p. xxxvi.

13 *Conditions*, p. 9.

14 Martin Heidegger, *Being and Time*, trans. John Macquarrie and Edward Robinson (New York: Harper & Row, 1962), pp. 377–378.

15 Cavell, *Conditions*, p. 9.

16 Stuart Hampshire, "Review of John Rawls' *Political Liberalism,*" *The New York Review of Books* 40: 14 (August 1993), 46, 47.

5

Poetry and truth-conditions[1]

SAMUEL FLEISCHACKER

Paul Celan writes, in "Tübingen, Jänner": "Should, should a man, should a man come into the world, today, with the shining beard of the patriarchs: he could, if he spoke of this time, he could only babble and babble, over, over, againagain."[2] I am inclined to call this utterance true. What do I mean by this? Do I mean anything like what I mean when I call Einstein's theory of relativity true?

Talk of truth in poetry is liable to upset both philosophers and literary theorists. Literary theorists often feel that to ask whether a poem is "true" or not is seriously to miss its point – that poems are about much *more* than truth, that literature is not bounded by the question, "But is it true?" Philosophers are wary, on the other hand, of the notions of truth that poets are liable to come up with. Valéry suggests that poetry breaks us of our ordinary use of language so we can "confront things as they really are, unmediated as far as possible by the veil of language."[3] One does not have to have done much philosophical thinking about language and concepts to find this notion of a primordial, immediate contact with the things of the world incoherent.

Yet we do say, "that's true," or, "there's a deep truth to that," about lines in poetry; we praise certain poets for their honesty or insight; and we say we have learned from poems and poetic utterances. So what is the relationship between truth in poetry and truth in science? This question may be folly to the scientists and an offense to the poets, but I think it is a good one nonetheless, and that taking it seriously can illuminate both poetry and science.

When I speak of "poetry" and "science," however, I am using the words loosely, and I had better make clear immediately that I am much more interested in the ways of talking associated with those disciplines than in the disciplines themselves. This chapter is primarily concerned with poetic and scientific or literal *utterances*, not with poems and scientific theories. I use the phrase "poetic utterance" in contrast with "literal utterance," such that it is more or less synonymous with a broad use of the term "metaphor."[4] The most ordinary conversation can in this sense contain poetic utterances, while literal utterances may occur in what is otherwise a poem. I use the word "science," on the other hand, not merely to designate the kind of knowledge we seek in physics, biology, and chemistry, but with the connotations it had when it covered anything rightly regarded as knowledge. At the same time, I regard the kind of knowledge we have in physics, biology, etc. – with its emphasis on the building and testing of theories – as a paradigm for all knowledge. Literal utterances then belong characteristically with science because literality belongs – essentially – with theory: we shall see the importance of this point in due course. But, to repeat my methodological warning, the emphasis is on the kind of utterance and not the activity in which it is characteristically made.

Take this emphasis as my excuse for beginning the discussion with utterances to be found neither in poetry collections nor in scientific textbooks: I shall consider how the law interprets what it calls a "frustrated contract." I will then look for analogues to this legal anomaly in ordinary literal discourse, and sketch what I think these cases tell us about the truth in poetry. Section II of the chapter uses Kant and Donald Davidson to suggest how poetry may contribute something to our search for truth that science needs but cannot itself provide.

I

To begin with the legal anomaly, the so-called "doctrine of frustration": A notoriously difficult problem in contract law is what to do when circumstances afford a surprise to both parties to the contract. The coronation of Edward VII was scheduled for June 26, 1902; rooms with a good view of the procession were rented out for that date at inflated prices. Then Edward fell sick and the coronation was put off for two months. Did those who rented the rooms have a right to their money back? When they signed some document declaring, "John Doe agrees to pay Richard Roe so and so much to rent a room on such and such a date," are we to assume that "as long as the coronation procession takes place" was written in between the lines?

Well, there are good arguments for reading in such an implication, and good arguments against it. Legal systems, especially in countries with free markets, have two conflicting impulses as regards the interpretation of contracts. On the one hand, it is widely recognized that a contract may include implied terms. In the United States, not only are all contracts taken to include certain conditions defining the very nature of a legal agreement – the presence of mutual obligations, good faith, etc. – but a court may read into contracts conditions that it thinks the parties ought to meet in "reason and justice" if they are to carry out the purposes they have contracted for.[5] Thus where time is left indefinite, courts have felt free to find an implied "reasonable duration" by which the terms of an agreement ought to be fulfilled. On the other hand, the courts are specifically instructed that they "should not lightly imply additional covenants that enlarge the terms of [a] contract." And the doctrine of frustration is limited to cases of extreme hardship, "so that businessmen, who must make their arrangements in advance, can rely with certainty on their contracts." Indeed the law's general interest in strict construction of contracts is so strong that one is often not excused from performance of a contract even when such performance becomes *impossible*. Thus a mill company was found responsible for carrying out its agreement to build a school even after its mill had burned down. Our legal systems are torn between the principle that people should not be held responsible for conditions they had every right to take for granted and the principle that holding people strictly to their express words allows them the greatest possible freedom to make contracts. As a result, the courts have a hard time knowing what to do when the terms of contracts are overtaken by unexpected events. Of course, there are many easy cases, in which either the contract is clearly null or one party is clearly in breach of it. But there are also interstitial cases, in which courts must debate whether to hold the parties strictly to their words, to declare the contract null and void, or, somehow, to split the difference. What is interesting is that no legal theorist thinks the answer is *clearly* any one of these options: it is not taken as *obvious* that contracts must be interpreted as holding according to their literal terms or failing to hold at all. The ambivalence of the law over such cases comes out in many ways: in disagreements over whether "acts of God" nullify contracts or not; in disagreements over the provenance and legitimacy of the doctrine of frustration; and in the fact that appeal to that doctrine is hedged about with many stringent conditions, plagued by the need to refer to such difficult categories as the "intent" and "reasonable expecta-tions" of the parties, and rarely invoked successfully in the courts.[6]

To avoid some of these specifically legal difficulties for the purposes of our comparison with poetry, let us turn to an analogous phenomenon in non-legal speech. I call you up to find that you are ill; sympathetically, I offer to bring you chicken soup for dinner tomorrow. The next day you tell me you have been to the doctor, and the one thing you definitely may *not* eat is chicken soup. Is it appropriate for me now to say, "Ah well, I said I'd bring you *chicken soup*; if I can't do that, you'll just have to get your own dinner"? Well, it may be appropriate for me to beg off – if I do not know how to make anything else, or do not have the time; if your diet is so restricted that you would do just as well on water and burnt toast – but one thing that does *not* seem right is that the scratching of chicken soup from the agenda immediately voids all commitment I have to you. I may have *said* nothing but "I'll bring you chicken soup," but that sentence alone can imply more generally that I will take care of your dinner, or that I will be over to keep you company, and if you were relying on my getting you dinner, or keeping you company, you would have a right to be disappointed. Furthermore, should I come over with burnt toast, or whatever your doctor allows you to eat, I would certainly not deserve to be berated for failing to keep my word. Although all I said the day before was that I would bring you chicken soup, that word can be quite fully kept, under the circumstances, by an offering of burnt toast.

The point is that, in ordinary life at least, the fulfillment conditions of a promise need not be limited by the literal terms of that promise. In my example, I can fulfill my promise without bringing you chicken soup, and indeed if I do bring you chicken soup after hearing the result of your doctor's visit, it is fair to say I am *not* fulfilling my promise. So the words of my promise provide, in this case, neither a sufficient nor a necessary condition for its fulfillment. There are at least two other morals to the story. First, cases like this arise in exceptional circumstances, when the literal terms of a promise are frustrated by a surprise in the world. The frustration of contracts and promises is necessarily an exception to the rule: otherwise people would build the frustrating circumstances into the terms of their agreements. Second, there seems to be only one literal reading of a contract or promise in normal circumstances, but an indefinite, perhaps even infinite, array of alternative readings once those normal circumstances fail. If I cannot bring you chicken soup, there are any number of things I could do instead to help you out or show you sympathy. Similarly, the disappointed room renters could come to any number of different resolutions with their contractual partner. This does not mean that just anything will count as the fulfillment of a promise or contract once its literal terms fail, but what can fulfill those terms is to a large extent indeterminate, a matter of judgment.[7]

What does all this have to do with poetry? I ask you to bear with me on that, because there remains some work to do on literal utterances before we can say anything useful about poetic ones. One might easily suppose that the distinguishing feature of the utterances we have looked at so far is that they are performative, that it is the *act* of making contracts and promises that somehow allows us to rewrite their terms. I think this is quite wrong, that speech act theory is irrelevant to the doctrine of frustration, so I want at this point to get away from utterances involving a commitment to future actions.[8] Consider therefore the following two cases, neither of which makes any reference to what the speaker plans to do:

(1) I hear yelling upstairs and remark, "Aaron's punching his sister again." In fact Aaron, who usually punches his sister, has today slapped her.

(2) An eighteenth-century biologist writes, "Eye-color gets passed down in the blood."

Prima facie both of these utterances are false. Aaron has varied his usual form of nastiness to his sister, and nothing gets passed down in the blood. But we can also regard both utterances as true – "essentially" true, at least, which may be the best we can say of any utterance. Suppose Aaron tells me that in fact he has not punched his sister. I respond, "But you did something to hurt her, didn't you?" He says, "Yes, but I slapped her, I didn't punch her." I say, "Well, that's what I meant." Is this fair? Is it an accurate account of what I meant? Well, it might be, and it might be regardless of whether "punching" has a conventional meaning, or truth-theoretical meaning in my idiolect, such that it normally cannot refer to slapping. For the purposes of reprimanding or punishing Aaron, certainly, strict construction of my original claim is not essential – as Aaron surely knows. Nor is this a matter of ambiguity in the verb "punching." I simply have license to reinterpret my original remark more broadly should I discover that the facts are somewhat different, but not significantly different, from what I had anticipated.

The same goes for the eighteenth-century biologist. We may well judge correct an eighteenth-century claim that eye-color is passed down in the blood, if it was directed against views that eye-color is a product of the environment. We may presume that if we could bring the biologist back to life today, and teach him about genetic theory and the discovery of DNA, he would say "Well, that's what I meant." And we can easily allow this, even though he surely anticipated nothing quite like modern gene theory when he originally made his remark, and even though "in the blood" does not literally mean "in the genes." We allow for a broad interpretation of the remark, perhaps turning the originally literal language into a metaphor. (If dead metaphors can become literal, why should not literal language be able to become metaphorical? That seems exactly what has happened to words like "melancholic" and "hysterical.") And we can do this for reasons quite analogous to those that create the frustrated contract or promise: the facts have surprised both our biologist and those he was engaging in conversation enough to render the meaning of their debate indeterminate. Whether traits are passed down by blood or by genes was not in question in the debate between our biologist and his opponents; his opponents would have granted that *if* eye-color is passed down, it is passed down in the blood. Hence neither speaker nor hearer would have known what literal language to use in the new circumstances.

This brings out the essential analogy between conversation and contract. Both conversation and contract occur against *background conditions* which all parties share, and the explicit terms of an utterance or agreement concern only what the parties might disagree about. When the background conditions themselves fail, we have a frustrated contract, or an utterance whose literal interpretation no longer captures its meaning.[9] Utterances are surrounded, as it were, by a penumbra of alternative meanings, on which they can fall back when the factual context in which they were made is altered in a surprising way.

I think this is a little noted feature of our speech, but an extremely significant one. If conversations, like contracts, always and necessarily take place against a set of background conditions, which alone provide determinacy to their interpretation but which cannot be spelled out without infinite regress, then we have a way of avoiding such dilemmas as that between Kuhn's claim that scientists across a revolution have entirely different vocabularies, and his opponents' insistence that the reference of scientific terms is fixed independently of their use. Instead we may understand scientific language as becoming more or less metaphorical when its literal interpretation fails as a result of things the speakers in question could not have anticipated. We thereby preserve both enough continuity of language to explain how new discoveries can significantly conflict with old theories, and enough sense of the exceptional or revolutionary to understand why theory change does seem to go with a shift in vocabularies.

Now in what sense is the interpretation of poetry like that of frustrated contracts and literal utterances? I suggest that we consider the conditions making us vulnerable to frustration. It is because we regard a certain amount of human ignorance as eminently excusable that we allow surprising circumstances to rewrite the terms of a promise or contract; we recognize that the practice of pledging oneself to future actions cannot be restricted to those cases in which the circumstances fulfilling the pledge can be completely specified. Similarly, when we allow an exasperated parent to insist that his criticism of one kind of bad behavior was meant to include other kinds of bad behavior, or when we allow a scientist to extend the terms of her theory to cover new and unexpected discoveries, we are acknowledging the common human plight of having to commit ourselves to analyses and evaluations of the world in spite of the fact that we can never know for sure exactly what we might want to commit ourselves to. Of course, sometimes the unexpected circumstances are such as to make us say that the parent or scientist was just plain *wrong*, and sometimes they are such that they fit easily into the original claim. This is like the cases in which circumstances are such as to completely nullify a contract or such that there is no justification for altering its normal, strict construction. But the cases we are interested in, the cases that make frustration of contract a formal legal doctrine, are those which fall in between, where an utterance or contract is not so surprised by circumstances that it lacks all truth or application, but where its truth or application requires some stretching of literal meaning.[10] And if we allow for such cases, then we are making allowances for the general human situation of being limited creatures who must always live beyond their limitations, ignorant creatures who must yet project their actions and beliefs into contexts where their ignorance poses risks. We must stretch the margins of literal meaning when we reach the margins of human knowledge. Poetry, I want to claim, thrives precisely at these margins. It explicitly concentrates on, and derives its power from, the difficult circumstance that we need to live beyond our intellectual means, the fact that we must always project our commitments beyond what, strictly, we know. It plays with, delights in, the uncertainty that we consider frustrating in literal utterance. When reading poetry, we are prepared immediately to delight in the difficulties of interpretation that in science and everyday discourse we would rather avoid.

This delight is the aesthetic joy Kant explained, in his *Critique of Judgment.* I turn next to Kant, therefore, and then offer an account of the exact relationship between scientific and poetic discourse.

II

Kant famously refers the pleasure behind any judgment of beauty to what he calls the "free play of the imagination and the under-standing" (section 9).[11] What exactly is this, and why is it pleasurable? The understanding is the faculty of rules or concepts; the imagination is that which gathers, and places into space and time, the manifold of intuition. According to Kant, the state of mind that leads one to make judgments of beauty is one in which these "cognitive powers ... are ... in free play, because no definite concept limits them to a definite rule of cognition" (section 9). This sentence is often read to elide the word "definite," thus: "the cognitive powers ... are ... in free play, because no ... concept limits them."[12] If this is what Kant had said, he would have expressed the common Romantic view that aesthetic appreciation is wholly an exercise of the imagination. Aesthetic appreciation would then be something independent of the desire to know, the desire to fit things into the concepts, the classificatory structures, of the understanding. But Kant does not say this; he says only that no *definite* concept limits the free play of the faculties.[13] And his account of free play would make no sense if the understanding had no role to play in it. The free play of the faculties is a play not of the imagination alone, but *between* the imagination and the understanding: "the excitement of both faculties (imagination and understanding) to indeterminate but yet ... harmonious activity ... is the sensation ... postulated by the judgment of taste" (section 9).[14] This means that the understanding, the faculty of knowing, cannot be *absent* in judgments of beauty; it must somehow interact with the imagination, albeit differently from the way it does in knowing proper.

114

What might this mean? Well, imagine you are trying to show a friend the beauty in a Jackson Pollock or Anselm Kiefer painting, or in a piece of Debussy's chamber music. The sensory material itself is admittedly confusing, but you feel it has *some* kind of order or point, and you point out to your friend Pollock's ways of questioning the traditional distinction between line and color, or Kiefer's ironic use of myth, or the recurrence of certain motifs and rhythmic structures in the Debussy. These concepts – these organizational tools – help give some coherence to the sensory intuitions, and there is a pleasure in thus using them to bring erstwhile confusion into some kind of focus. But your friend, if she is at all aesthetically sensitive, will not long be satisfied by your remarks, and will complain that there is much *more* in the paintings or music, that your conceptual tools are inadequate. The randomness of Pollock's way of distributing paint, she might say, defeats any thematic reading of his work, or the thickness of the painting's texture is too much left out by a bald contrast between line and color. And there is a pleasure, too, in being able to knock down the conceptual tools of aesthetic criticism, in showing how the sensory manifold overflows the concepts that are supposed to contain it. All the same, having had one interpretation knocked down, you will come back with others, well aware that, if the work is richly interesting, these tools will also prove to be inadequate. This is the free play of the faculties, and your friend will find the work beautiful not if one of the interpretations is finally unanswerable, but if she feels able to continue the play indefinitely. I think this is an accurate, and reasonably familiar, description of aesthetic pleasure. But if so, we should note that just as the play may not be ended by any definite concept, so it also cannot continue unless some concept seems capable of organizing the imagination's material. Aesthetic enjoyment is no more a matter of mindless absorption in a work than of correctly finding the work's "message." If nothing else, the imagination needs intellectual constructs to fight with, to find wanting; it cannot play without some friction.[15]

And why, according to Kant, is all this pleasurable? Because pleasure is the satisfaction of a need, and free play satisfies a cognitive need, a need that any being whose knowledge depends on the organization of sensory material has to have.[16] This need, quite simply, is for the world to be organiz*able*. To have knowledge, we must be able to make what Kant calls "determinant judgments," judgments that apply concepts or rules to particular cases, that determine whether a particular thing is a house or flower or tree. But to make these judgments we need to *have* concepts or rules, and that means we must be able to unify our particular intuitions into concepts in the first place. We need to find general terms that fit the particular sense-data around us. To "fit" is not the same as "to be imposed on," however, so the process of coming up with general terms is as much a matter of trying out a structure on the data as it is one of deciding that that structure does not work and substituting another one for it. We realize that the world is organiz*able*, rather than something upon which we merely *impose* organization, both when we succeed in getting a conceptual framework to apply to the world of our experience and when our experience bucks our frameworks, when we have to repair a framework or start again. Indeed the first part of this process depends on the latter: it is precisely when experience bucks our concepts that we have any reason to regard the application of concepts as something we may succeed or fail in. Someone who understands thoroughly how interpretation works is someone who can say, "This interpretation (this set of concepts) doesn't fit the data – as opposed to that one." Like contracts, concepts must satisfy two conflicting needs: they must protect us against the chaotic "manifold" of raw sensory intuitions, but they must also be responsible *to* the very chaos against which they protect us. It is this two-sided process of developing responsible conceptual frameworks that Kant calls "reflective judgment," and it is this process that requires, perhaps even constitutes, the free play of the faculties. Thus our judgments of beauty are a pre-condition for our judgments of knowledge, and they are pleasurable *because* they show knowledge to be possible. A completely chaotic world would not allow for knowledge; the confusion we feel when we first approach a Jackson Pollock, like the confusion we feel when severely disoriented, is disturbing, because it threatens our entire capacity for making cognitive judgments. Once we begin to interpret the painting, we are relieved, and the relief of this cognitive need is the pleasure on the basis of which we call something beautiful. In addition, the demand on interpretation to be responsible, to "fit" the sensory data in some sense, keeps its pleasure energetic, mentally stimulating, while the potential endlessness of interpretation gives the pleasure that inexhaustible quality, that hint at eternity, traditionally associated with the experience of beauty: "that with which the imagination can play in an unstudied and purposive manner is always new to us, and one does not get tired of looking at it ... We *linger* over the contemplation of the beautiful because this contemplation strengthens and reproduces itself."[17]

I want to add one thing to this picture before applying it to poetry and theories of meaning. Kant thinks that determinant judgment is easy. Once we have rules, he says, fitting particular cases under them is something only stupid people would have trouble with.[18] As Wittgenstein has shown us, this is seriously wrong. Wittgenstein alerts us to the possibility that rules can be interpreted to fit anything or nothing. Even in cases where the application of a rule seems self-evident, the rule, and the case to which it is to be applied, can be interpreted in an indefinite number of conflicting ways. Wittgenstein is not a skeptic about rules – his investigations start from the premise that there *must* be a way to follow a rule[19] – but the questions he asks suggest that every determinant judgment can require a new reflective one and vice versa. Every time we apply a rule, we may need to reinterpret it; indeed, the application itself is sometimes part of the rule's interpretation.[20] We construct general concepts from particular examples, but we also construct them while applying them *to* particular examples. So reflective judgment, and the pleasurable free play that marks it, is only *more* important to knowledge than Kant thought it was.

How does all this apply to poetry? Kant's own account of poetry is, I think, confused. He describes poetry as the highest of the arts, as "set[ting] the imagination free" and offering us "a wealth of thought to which no linguistic expression is completely adequate" (section 53). But it is far from clear how the "imagination," in Kant's sense, can come into poetry at all. What could possibly constitute the sensory material, in poetry, for the imagination to organize and offer to the understanding for unification? The medium of poetry – words – seems to be all a matter of concepts; the raw material seems itself to come from the understanding. At best, Kant owes us an explanation of how the linguistic mode of art could be precisely the one that offers "a wealth of thought to which no linguistic expression is ... adequate"; at worst, he is simply contradicting himself.

So we may be best off explaining poetry by means of an analogy to Kant's general account of beauty rather than trying to apply that account directly. The analogy I have in mind runs roughly as follows: Interpreting an utterance is a matter of being able to bring our intuitions about its grammar together with our intuitions about the conditions that would make it true. Like the imagination and the understanding, these elements of interpretation do not always come together, so it is an occasion for pleasure when they do. When they come together in an attribution of definite truth-conditions, we have an analogue to Kant's "determinant judgment," an interpretation suitable for cognition. When they come together, as they do in poetry, in a play amongst *in*definite attributions of truth conditions, we have an analogue to Kant's "reflective judgment," a mode of indulging in the interpretive process that is useful *for* cognition, but not itself productive of any knowledge. And as, in my Wittgensteinian revision of Kant, determinant judgments can always require new reflective ones, so definitely interpreted – literal – sentences can turn back to the indefinite play of poetry, as in the case of frustration in contract law or theory change in science.

To make these claims clearer, consider how a poem can challenge an entire theory of interpretation. I said in the beginning of this chapter that I am inclined to agree with Celan when he writes, "Should, should a man, should a man come into the world ... he could only babble and babble." What am I agreeing with? Well, to answer that I should first have to interpret the utterance – and according to one influential theory of interpretation, Donald Davidson's, my best shot at doing that depends on my asking first what makes the utterance true or false.

Is this the wrong question? I think it is an essential question. When I interpret a poem, I always in part show what the world would be like if it were true: this is how I attribute ideas to it. I interpret Celan to claim that moral and religious discourse after the Holocaust is broken or incoherent and I defend the truth of that claim. Or I take him to be explaining the reception of Hölderlin's poetry, or I connect his words to the "death of God," or to the experience of madness, and show just why these might be appropriate understandings of the modern condition ... In each case, I understand Celan to be making truth-claims; I understand him to be saying something about the world with which I might agree.

So there is something to Davidson's insistence that meaning be found via truth conditions, even in the interpretation of poetic utterances. On the other hand, what seems inappropriate about demanding of poetry that it yield up truth comes out as soon as we press Davidson a little more closely.

Davidson is known for the claim that we must interpret each utterance on the basis of a theory of meaning for the whole language. This means that we interpret *patterns* of sentences, rather than individual units, and that we assume the sentences to be related to one another in systematic ways. It also means two other things, very important for our present purposes: a theory of meaning will have a determinate, finite base, and it will give a definite answer to the question of what each utterance means. Davidson writes: "An acceptable theory should ... account for the meaning (or conditions of truth) of every sentence by analysing it as composed, in truth-relevant ways, of elements drawn from a finite stock. A second natural demand is that the theory provide a method for deciding, given an arbitrary sentence, what its meaning is. (By satisfying these two conditions a theory may be said to show that the language it describes is *learnable* and *scrutable*)" (*Inquiries*, 56). Davidson famously appeals to Tarski's T-sentences to provide the basis of such a theory: an adequate theory of meaning for a language will be one that proves all sentences of the form " 'Snow is white' is true if and only if snow is white." We need to understand this appeal as part of Davidson's interest in theory, in finitely based and scrutable systems. That we find Tarski's T-sentences trivially true only proves, for Davidson, that a complete set of them would capture "our best intuition as to how the concept of truth is used" – "the totality of such ... sentences uniquely determines the extension of the concept of truth" (*Inquiries*, 194–195). The T-sentences, that is, provide *closure* to a truth-conditional theory of meaning. If we build theories of meaning out of the "truth-relevant" components of sentences, we have a determinate goal at which to aim: we know that at the end of the day truth can be completely characterized by the totality of Tarskian T-sentences.

Now the peculiar thing about the line I have quoted from Celan is that the Tarskian T-sentence for it, far from being trivially true, seems to be *false*. "Should, should a man come, into the world, today, with the shining beard of the patriarchs: he could, if he spoke of this time, he could / only babble and babble over, over againa-gain" is *not* true if and only if should, should a man come, into the world, etc., he could only babble and babble, etc. Should a man with a shining beard, or a man who in some deep way resembles the patriarchs, or even a miraculous reincarnation of Abraham, arrive on earth and babble, it would not prove Celan right; if such a man arrived and spoke "of this time" coherently, it would not prove him wrong.[21] Like the terms of the frustrated promise to bring a friend chicken soup, the literal terms of this utterance provide neither necessary nor sufficient conditions for its truth. We are not sure

119

what the "truth-relevant" components of the utterance are; if there *is* a T-sentence for the utterance, we will not find the premises from which to prove it.[22] To know how to prove the T-sentence for a poetic utterance would be to translate the utterance adequately into literal terms. But that is precisely what eludes us in poetry.

This is to suggest that poetic utterances threaten the completeness of a theory of meaning, and indeed that is what I take to be their point. Davidson's interest in theories of meaning goes together with a hope that we can build up a method of interpretation for a language from the easy sentences whose truth-conditions we know – "it's raining," "snow is white," etc. – and then rely on the systematic connection of sentences to provide us with interpretations of more complex or difficult claims: theological ones, say, or moral ones. Poetic utterances threaten to overthrow this hope altogether: rather than making sense in terms of other, easier utterances, they shed doubt on whether we have understood the easier utterances correctly in the first place. They *challenge* the theories of interpretation we have built up so far: suddenly, we may not be sure that we know what very simple words mean – what "babble" means, or "beard." In the words of a colleague of mine: Poetry *unmakes* sense.[23]

Recently Davidson has himself begun to admit that interpretation of language is a lot more haphazard than his earlier account made it seem. In a paper on convention he writes, "What we cannot expect is that we can formalize the considerations that lead us to adjust our theory to fit the inflow of new information ... in this sense, there is no saying what someone must know who knows the language; for intuition, luck, and skill must play as essential a role here as in devising a new theory in any field; and taste and sympathy a larger role" (*Inquiries*, 279). And in a paper on malapropism, which he now considers endemic to the use of language, he tells us that interpretation depends primarily on "wit, luck, and wisdom," and suggests that, in the sense in which theorists of language use the term, "there is no such thing as a language."[24] This latter suggestion has been greeted with indignation and bewilderment, as an expression of nihilism, a premature concession of defeat, an abandonment of the whole effort to grasp the nature of meaning.[25] Such reactions are based on a misunderstanding. Davidson proposes, not that there is no such thing as communication (let alone meaning), but that *languages* – the finite, static wholes, defined by convention, on which most philosophers and linguists have focused their attempts to understand communication – are misleading and theoretically unwarranted posits. So far, indeed, I agree with him. But implicit in the outraged reactions is a legitimate dissatisfaction with Davidson's conclusion. The thrust of Davidson's argument, in both the articles cited above, is to bring out a tension between theory and language, between formal accounts of how we communicate and how, in fact, we communicate. One expects Davidson to conclude by abandoning the notion of *theory*, or at least diminishing its significance, and the conclusion that we ought to abandon the notion of language instead seems not so much an outrage as a let-down. For, while it may indeed be true that "language" is a tired and artificial construct, there are larger fish to fry here: problems have emerged with the very idea of a theory of communication.

Davidson claims, in this latest work, that we rely on "passing theories" to do the work of communication – theories we constantly and unsystematically take up and reject. But he himself asks, "Why should a passing theory be called a theory at all? For the sort of theory we have in mind is, in its formal structure, suited to be the theory for an entire language, even though its expected field of application is vanishingly small. The answer is that when a word or phrase temporarily or locally takes over the role of some other word or phrase ... the entire burden of that role, with all its implications for logical relations to other words, phrases, and sentences, must be carried along by the passing theory."[26] If all this means is that sentences need to stand in logical relations with one another, and that the contribution of a word to the truth-conditions of a given sentence must be assessed in accordance with its contribution to other sentences in which it might appear, Davidson is surely right. But theories with different and unsystematically related axiom-bases cannot be expected to converge on a *single* theory, with a single and finite axiom base, that gives determinate and accurate interpretations to all sentences of the language. They can thus not fulfill one of the most important features of "theory" as that notion figures in the work of philosophers of science: the ideal of completeness, of a complete explanation that answers all relevant questions in its domain of application.[27]

We may surely conclude from this that theory is not enough for communication, that we need also judgment, the indeterminate, unformalizable process of moving between systematic accounts and the cases to which they apply.[28] And indeed Davidson's call for "intuition, luck, and skill," "taste and sympathy," "wit and wisdom" sounds like a recognition of this point: such terms are traditional synonyms for what Aristotle called *phronesis* and Kant, "reflective judgment." Davidson runs judgment into theory, saying that "wit, luck, and wisdom" are the stuff out of which theories are made.[29] But if Kant is right about the nature of reflective judgment, as I think he is, it is a pre-condition *for* theory but not itself a component *of* theory: reflection plays with the organizational tools of the understanding rather than using them determinately, and it goes on indefinitely rather than having a point of closure. So to give reflective judgment a prime role in the interpretation of language is to diminish the claims of theory, to suggest that theories of meaning are insufficient to account for how we communicate.

As regards Celan's poem, to say that we seek its truth-conditions by means of judgment rather than theory makes eminently good sense. Every time we interpret it, we either attribute truth-conditions to it or show how an earlier such attribution is inadequate. If I make my case for what it means on the basis of its rhythm, you will point out that I have not paid sufficient attention to the imagery of the beard; if I attend to the beard, you will complain that I have said nothing about the earlier reference to blindness; if I talk about Celan's Holocaust experiences, you will object that I need to consider the fact that the poem is a tribute to Hölderlin; if I talk about Celan's relationship to Hölderlin and Heidegger, you can remind me not to be insensitive to his Holocaust experiences. These moves and counter-moves are the stuff of literary criticism. One may therefore be tempted to say there are *no* truth-conditions for a poetic utterance, but I think this is wrong. We argue fiercely over whether it is true that Celan's Holocaust experiences are central to his poetry, over whether the formal structure of his poem truly has a particular historical or conventional or perceptual resonance, over what kinds of beliefs about the world are true, and truly interesting, enough to be attributed to him; and we agree, at least, that some interpretations are wildly false. So it is not that our interpretations of poetry simply *bypass* issues of truth, but that they never satisfactorily *grasp* it: our dissatisfaction with the truth of each interpretation is precisely what allows us to go on with the process.

I want therefore to ring a change on Davidson's account of literal meaning: poetic utterances have truth-conditions, and have meaning by virtue of their truth-conditions, but they do not have any definite set of truth conditions. Since their Tarskian T-sentence may be literally false, since they fail, that is, to show their truth-conditions on their face, we have no clear limit to the sentences that might express those conditions. That is the point of the analogy to frustrated contracts: as with frustrated contracts, for which we must find fulfillment conditions elsewhere than in their explicit terms, in the case of poetic utterances we cannot determine their truth-conditions by looking to their explicit contents alone. Not the utterance itself but *other* utterances – some unspecified set of them – will best express the appropriate truth-conditions. Frustrated contracts remind us that the explicit terms of a contract are not all it contains, and force us to rethink what leads us to make contracts. Poetic utterances remind us that the explicit terms of a sentence do not always express what the sentence is committed to, and force us to rethink what allows us to communicate, to utter sentences and interpret them.

And what does allow us to communicate? I have argued that in certain circumstances a literal utterance can require a completely new reading, one that is not at all evident on the face of that utterance. I think it is plausible to suppose all utterances to be vulnerable to such treatment, to suppose that we may rewrite the truth-conditions for any utterance in the context of interpreting a wider body of evidence about the language of the utterance and the world to which it applies. But the flip-side of this claim is that it makes sense to see truth-conditions as slipping way from an utterance only if the utterance had those truth-conditions in the first place. We could never rewrite what an utterance meant unless we had earlier taken it to mean something else. To deny that there is a definite set of truth-conditions enabling us to interpret an utterance is thus not to say that the utterance has *no* truth-conditions. Rather, it is to claim the possibility of always opening up again the particular set of truth-conditions by which we have at any point interpreted the utterance. We communicate by attributing truth-conditions to utterances and by rewriting our attributions, by means of both the determinacy of concepts of truth and their vulnerability to revision.

What accounts for this interrelationship of fixed interpretations and their reworking is that, just as contract law is governed by two conflicting impulses, communication has to satisfy two conflicting needs. We need to claim some finality in our interpretations in order to go forward in our theorizing and decision-making, but we need also some flexibility, some allowance for uncertainty, if we are to have any idea what to do when the world shows our theories and decisions to be misguided. For the purposes of a *theory* of meaning, therefore, and indeed for any theory, any scientific account of the world, we need to draw limits to the truth-conditions an utterance can have; ultimately we need one set of truth-conditions for each utterance. But when we are surprised by ignorance and error, when we find we have been tripped up by the limits on our knowledge, we need to be able to open our theories again, and redistribute the truth-conditions of our earlier claims. To hold our background judgments open to a possibility of such radical revision is an accommodation *we* make in our theory-building, but we make it precisely *because* we do not want to be simply coherentists. Only if the world can frustrate our terms of justification are those terms truly responsive to something beyond our control. Truth-claims, to be both "claims" and claims of "truth", must be simultaneously intelligible and objective. We preserve intelligibility by keeping our background judgments under strict construction, by insisting on incorporating all evidence under classificatory categories and means of explanation established in advance. But we preserve objectivity by allowing those judgments as much flexibility as we can to respond to the unexpected.[30]

Thus poetry and science make each other possible. Scientific theories cannot survive without the possibilities of reinterpretation that poetry keeps open for them, while poetry thrives precisely by contrast with the apparent determinacy of scientific language. Poetry, and the reflective judgment by which we interpret it, occur precisely where ordinary and literal language gets frustrated. They are thereby parasitic on the literal even as they simultaneously provide it with its condition of possibility. On the account I have offered, we make the definite judgments that allow us to *have* an ordinary, literal way of speaking out of an indefinite array of alternative possibilities and concepts, and on the condition that those judgments can be opened up again at a later date should the way we are constructing come to grief. What is this but a claim that poetry provides the ground (in Heidegger's terminology, the "origin") for truth-conditional theories of interpretation? But it is also a claim that truth-conditional theories of interpretation are essential *to* poetry: there is no overturning ordinary ways of determining truth without ordinary ways of determining truth to overturn.

It follows that we have a cognitive need for finding that definite and indefinite attributions of truth-conditions can belong together, for ensuring that the same utterance can be given one fixed meaning *and* have that meaning ripped open again in the presence of new circumstances. It is this cognitive need that poetry fills; thereby does it give us pleasure. Poetic utterance, when successful, allows us to give a sentence a definite meaning, but also to replace that meaning with a new one as often as we like. It allows for free play between ascriptions of truth-conditions and their challenge by new insights into the utterance's syntax or semantics. I am not at all sure this harmony of indefinite and definite interpretations is included in what Kant meant by the harmony between the intuitive and the conceptual, but it is at least not far from it: we can, I think, legitimately rework Kant's terms to include this type of cognitive pleasure. Minimally, the account I have given is Kantian in the sense that it locates the cognitive significance of linguistic beauty in a *condition* for knowledge rather than a special *kind* of knowledge. Poetry is cognitively valuable, not by giving us access to a world different from the one of literal utterance and scientific theory – the "pre-conceptual" world of Valéry – but by making us attend to the conditions for all interpretation and theory in this, our familiar and only world.[31]

Notes

1 This essay is a somewhat revised version of my "Frustrated Contracts, Poetry, and Truth," which appeared in *Raritan* 13: 4 (Spring 1994). I thank the editors of *Raritan* for permission to reprint it.

2 Translated by Michael Hamburger, in *Poems of Paul Celan* (New York: Persea Books, 1988), p. 177.

3 Quoted in David Cooper, *Metaphor*, (New York: Basil Blackwell, 1986), p. 150.

4 Cooper (*Metaphor*, pp. 7–23) points out that contemporary theory has tended, for good reasons, to assimilate all kinds of figurative speech (synecdoche, hyperbole, etc.) to metaphor, drawing a sharp line between figurative and literal language rather than among kinds of figurative language. (There are, on the other hand, those who want also or instead to blur this latter line: see below, note 9.)

5 Francis Ludes and Harold Gilbert, *Corpus Juris Secundum*, (West Publishing Co., Saint Paul 1963), vol. 17A, p. 284. All quotations in this paragraph come from this volume – pp. 285n40, 286n42.5, and 619 respectively. The case of the mill company appears at p. 614n31.

6 See *Corpus Juris*, pp. 286–289, 614ff., 617–619.

7 The hornbook on the Uniform Commercial Code (James White and Robert Summers, *Uniform Commercial Code*, 2nd edn. [West Publishing Co., Saint Paul 1980]) writes that the remedies for frustration are varied and in

principle indeterminate: "One should note that a direction to allocate
prorata is far from an explicit and rigid set of allocation rules. Seller may
choose to pro-rate based upon historic deliveries, historic contract
amounts, historic needs, current deliveries, current needs, current contract amounts and possibly other grounds" (p. 136).

8 Traditionally, utterances like this have had their interpretations sorted
into speaker-meaning and sentence-meaning, but I think the relevant
distinction is rather between theory, of any kind, and judgment. If we
formalize speaker-meaning, what "I'll bring you chicken soup" means
will still not be literally and normally equivalent to what "I'll bring you
burnt toast" means. Nor is this a case in which we get to the "occasion-
meaning" of the utterance by *virtue* of the falsehood of the sentence-
meaning (cf. Davidson, *Inquiries into Truth and Interpretation*, [Oxford:
Clarendon Press, 1984], pp. 271–273, and "A Nice Derangement of
Epitaphs," in *Truth and Interpretation*, ed. E. LePore, [Oxford: Basil
Blackwell, 1986], pp. 439ff.): neither truth-theoretical formalizations nor
conventionalist ones will be of any help. What *does* lead us to its
significance? Well, I am suggesting that there are implications in every
utterance, built partly into context, partly into social conventions, and
partly into the theories about the nature of the world against the background of which the utterance is made, that do not usually appear but
surface to provide fallback conditions for truth in those exceptional
cases in which conventionalist, truth-theoretical, and other formal readings of an utterance wildly conflict. If I am right that such cases exist,
they necessarily constitute an exception to *all* theories of meaning,
whether based on the intentions of particular speakers or the structure of
a language as a whole. Finding the meaning and truth of these utterances
requires judgment, not theory – what Kant calls reflective judgment –
and what gives judgment legitimacy is only the transcendental argument
that without it theory would be impossible. (See below.)

9 As my examples I think have shown, this does not mean the utterances
were originally non-literal. My view here dovetails with Davidson's
intimation that there is no sharp line between metaphorical and literal
discourse (see the "floor" example and the discussion of dead metaphors
in *Inquiries,* pp. 251–253), and David Cooper's suggestion that the
interpretation of an utterance *as* metaphorical is as much a part of
drawing the distinction as any feature of the utterance itself (*Metaphor*,
pp. 242–243).

10 Jonathan Berg, of Haifa University, has asked me whether the law could
not subsume all such cases under the doctrine of implied conditions. If
so, he argued, we could analogously treat "frustrated utterances" as a
strict subset of conversational implicature – and subsume the whole area
under a theory of pragmatics. Now, the doctrine of frustration is indeed
said, by some legal authorities, to be derived from the doctrine of
implied conditions (*Corpus Juris*, p. 617), but I think it worth emphasizing that the law is on the whole *not satisfied* with the latter doctrine

alone; it adds the notion of frustration precisely in order to deny that the significance of a contract in unforeseen circumstances can be adequately read off from the implications of the contract as it was originally entered into. Analogously, I think we need more than theories of speech – which, whether semantic or pragmatic, must draw their evidential base from normal and predictable cases – to deal with how utterances are to be interpreted in circumstances quite abnormal and unexpected.

11 All references in the text are to Kant, *Critique of Judgment*, trans. J. H. Bernard (New York: Hafner Publishing Co., 1951).

12 I take this as a common reading of Kant primarily from discussions with friends and from an impression that both Romantic artists and neo-Romantic literary critics (Harold Bloom *et al.*) view Kant as vindicating their endorsement of the imagination over against the understanding, but it turns out also to be widely held by commentators on the third *Critique*. Donald Crawford, for instance, says that "In the case of the experience of the beautiful ... no concept is forthcoming" and strongly implies that "free play" is an activity *of* the imagination, rather than between the imagination and the understanding (*Kant's Aesthetic Theory*, [Madison: University of Wisconsin Press, 1974], p. 89). Paul Guyer, wrestling explicitly with this issue, concludes that the word "definite" or "determinate" does no work in Kant's theory. Commenting on a passage that speaks of the imagination's work having to agree with the understanding's "presentation of a concept ... (regardless of which concept)", he writes: "This somewhat inept wording might suggest the idea of a concept which is no concept in particular, much like the idea of a triangle that is 'neither oblique, nor rectangle, equilateral, equicrural, nor scalenon' to which Berkeley so vigorously objected. But it is surely more charitably interpreted as describing a state in which the ordinary condition for the application of a concept ... obtains without the application of any concept at all ... Reflective judgment, it turns out, leads to aesthetic response not by finding a *possible concept* for a given particular, but by discovering that a given object fulfills the *general condition for the possibility of the application of concepts* without having any concept at all applied to it." In a footnote to this discussion, Guyer rebuts Mary Warnock's attempt to interpret Kant as supposing that the understanding provides an "indeterminate concept" to the imagination; he notes that Kant never uses any such phrase (Guyer, *Kant and the Claims of Taste*, [Cambridge MA: Harvard University Press, 1979], pp. 88–89 and note 60 on pp. 408–409. See also Guyer, p. 251: "It is clear that any actual occurrence of the harmony of the faculties requires the presentation of a manifold which is unifiable without concepts.")

Guyer is right to refuse Warnock's interpretation, but not to ignore Kant's repeated emphasis on the word "definite" or "determinate." To think without a determinate concept is not, indeed, to think *with* an *inde*terminate concept – the phrase would be an oxymoron for Kant – but to use concepts without allowing any single concept to determine one's thought. "Without a determinate concept" might perhaps best be understood as "without a determin*ing* concept"; to think without a determining concept is then to allow a range or array of concepts (each quite "definite" in and of itself) to play with the contents of one's imagination instead of using one of them to fix the interpretation of that content. I note briefly here that Guyer raises a series of problems for his own reading of the *Critique of Judgment* – that it conflicts with the first *Critique*'s insistence that there is no thought without concepts (pp. 96ff.), that it makes no sense of the fact that aesthetic pleasure and reflection extend indefinitely over time (pp. 94–95), that it allows no active role to the understanding in the harmony of the faculties (p. 86) – none of which arise for the reading I shall offer here.

13 The word "definite" or "determinate" appears again and again in similar passages of the *Critique*. "Flowers, free delineations, outlines intertwined with one another without design ... have no meaning, depend on no *definite* concept, and yet they please. The satisfaction in the beautiful must depend on the reflection upon an object, leading to any concept (however *indefinite*), and it is thus distinguished from the pleasant, which rests entirely upon sensation" (section 4). See also section 12 (p. 58), section 22 (p. 78), and "First Introduction," section VII, p. 408, in Kant, *Critique of Judgment*, trans. W.S. Pluhar (Indianapolis: Hackett Publishing, 1987).

14 See also "First Introduction", section VII (*ibid.*, pp. 408–409): "So if the form of an object given in empirical intuition is of such a character that the *apprehension*, in the imagination, of the object's manifold agrees with the *exhibition* of a concept of the understanding (which concept this is being indeterminate), then imagination and understanding are – in mere reflection – in mutual harmony, a harmony that furthers the task of these powers."

15 Kant might say that the search for harmony between the faculties presupposes both that the understanding does not simply dictate terms to the imagination, and that the imagination sets as its goal something that can satisfy the understanding. This suggests that there is some kind of order to intuitions before they get unified by concepts, as well as that the application of concepts to the manifold of intuition is not purely arbitrary. Our intuitions, at least once they have come through the imagination, are not mere chaos: they can fit or fail to fit into the order of concepts we have at any given point developed. The imagination constitutes a pre-conceptual organization to which the understanding must be responsible: we cannot impose just any concepts on the world of our sensations. At the same time, this pre-conceptual organization is structured by the fact that its purpose is to allow for an organization by concepts; it must borrow from the understanding at least the general conditions for the application of a concept, if not, in part, some of the actual concepts in play, in order to arrange even preliminary groupings of the intuitions it has received.

16 See the *Critique of Judgment*, Introduction, section V (p. 20 in the Bernard translation).

17 Ibid, sections 22, 12 (pp. 80, 58).

18 "Deficiency in judgment is just what is ordinarily called stupidity, and for such a failing there is no remedy." *Critique of Pure Reason*, trans. N. K. Smith (New York: St. Martin's Press, 1965), p. A134n=B173n.

19 "This was our paradox: no course of action could be determined by a rule, because every course of action can be made out to accord with the rule ... It can be seen that there is a misunderstanding here from the mere fact that in the course of our argument we give one interpretation after another; as if each one contented us at least for a moment, until we thought of yet another standing behind it. What this shows is that there is a way of grasping a rule which is *not* an *interpretation*, but which is exhibited in what we call 'obeying the rule' and 'going against it' in actual cases" (*Philosophical Investigations*, trans. G. E. M. Anscombe [New York: Macmillan, 1958], section 201). That Wittgenstein is not, *pace* Kripke, a skeptic about rule-following should be clear from this passage. But the account at which he here gestures of how we do follow rules is not, I think, fully satisfactory. The almost mystical superiority of practice to argument is not a happy feature of *PI*. It is quite unclear to me why, moreover, as Wittgenstein insists in the paragraph immediately following the quotation above, actions in accordance with a rule should not be regarded as themselves a kind of interpretation. At any rate, when I describe rule-following as an implicit or explicit interaction between reflective and determinant judgment, or claim, as part of such a view, that the application of a rule can itself be regarded as part of the rule's interpretation, I am aware that I am not in agreement with Wittgenstein's own position in *PI*; I do not think I am as far, however, from what he says in *On Certainty*, where "judgment" becomes perhaps his most important term, and legal interpretation, with its movement back and forth between specific and general, serves as a model for how judgment is carried out.

20 A version of this claim which fits more precisely with Wittgenstein's argument about rule-following in *PI* would be: "If a rule is stripped of the context(s) in which it is ordinarily used, any single application of it may require us to re-interpret that rule, and that abstract possibility translates in practice into a possible need for re-interpretation in an unpredictable number of cases."

21 Mary Mothersill has pointed out to me that the subjunctive mood of the Celan line muddies the waters here: Davidson has not claimed to solve the vexed question of how one finds truth-conditions for counterfactuals. This is correct, but I doubt the mood of the line is particularly relevant to the issues I am raising. For consider an indicative version of the same sentence: "Men, men, who come into the world, today, with the shining beards of the patriarchs ... only babble and babble, etc." I do not think the difficulty of finding a truth-conditional interpretation for such a line would be a whit less severe than they are for the line Celan actually uses;

I stick with the subjunctive version for the simple reason that it is incomparably more beautiful.

22 Davidson admits that there are many cases in which the right branch of a T-sentence is not simply a disquotation of the left branch (see *Inquiries*, pp. 33–35 on demonstratives, and his essays on quotation and imperatives, *Inquiries*, pp. 79–92, 109–121); to construct the correct T-sentence, in these cases, is a matter of picking out the semantic element causing the problem and finding a formal interpretation of its use. But if poetry works at all the way we normally suppose it does – if it provides endless play of interpretation even to expert linguists and philosophers of language – then we cannot expect to find an adequate way of defining, much less formally interpreting, the semantic element that confuses us when trying to construct a T-sentence for a line of poetry. Which elements of the Celan line are relevant to its truth? Well, that depends on what Celan is trying to do. If he is simply making a comment about ancient prophets or patriarchs, the repetitions of "should, should," "over, over," "againagain" are irrelevant, mere stylistic froth. On the other hand, perhaps the word "beard" and the temporal connotations of "patriarch" are the stylistic froth and the repetitions go to make the essential point: like the man with the shining beard of the patriarchs, Celan is himself babbling and babbling, over and over, undermining himself along with all other contemporary prophets. So I can't say for certain what elements have semantic relevance until I know what truth is being claimed – although, of course, I try to determine what truth is being claimed on the basis of how I understand the semantic relevance of each element. The notion that *formalizing* the semantic relevance of any of these elements would help me here – constructing a theory of their relevance that will hold across the language – is thus misguided; the process of interpretation goes on indefinitely in poetry precisely because it is possible for meaningful utterances to resist any such formalization.

23 I owe this wonderful phrase to Jim Mahon (Political Science, Williams College).

24 "Nice Derangement..." (see note 8 above), p. 446.

25 See especially Ian Hacking's "The parody of conversation," in *Truth and Interpretation*. I would like to thank Josef Stern for pushing me to clarify the issues raised by Davidson's claim here.

26 "Nice Derangement...," p. 443.

27 See Charles Taylor's "Rationality," in *Rationality and Relativism* M. Hollis and S. Lukes (Cambridge, MA: The MIT Press, 1982), or Bernard Williams' writings on what he calls "the absolute conception of the world": *Descartes: The Project of Pure Enquiry* (Harmondsworth: Penguin Books, 1978), pp. 65–67, 211–212, 239, 245–249, 301–303, and *Ethics and the Limits of Philosophy*, (Cambridge, MA: Harvard University Press, 1985), pp.135–140. For Davidson's own adherence to this ideal, see "On the Very Idea of a Conceptual Scheme," in *Inquiries*.

28 The transcendental argument for the importance of judgment to which I
    refer in note 8 above would be simply a more formal version of the
    claims in this paragraph. Roughly: To construct any theory, let us say of
    communication, we must work from an evidential base of cases which
    we can accept as examples of successful or unsuccessful communica-
    tion. Then the theory consists in giving criteria that mark off the
    successful from the unsuccessful cases and (correctly) predict how to
    distinguish cases in untested parts of the domain. But how do we know
    that the original cases are successful or unsuccessful? If on the basis of
    our theory, then our distinction is mere stipulation, not something
    drawn from the evidence. If on the basis of *another* theory, then we must
    ask the same question of it, and regress to the evidential base from which
    it began. And if we suppose the distinction somehow "speaks for itself,"
    apart from any theoretical apparatus, then it is quite unclear that we
    retain any grip on a general distinction between successful and unsuc-
    cessful communication: enough of a grip, for instance, to make sense of
    how we might make *mistakes* about determining the distinction in the
    original cases. So there must be some process *between* theory and
    immersion in particular cases that makes theories responsible to cases
    and cases responsible to general criteria of truth and error.
29 "Nice Derangement . . .," p. 446, and *Inquiries*, p. 279.
30 How exactly does this translate into practice, during, say, a major
    scientific revolution? I confess I am not sure. One thing that is certainly
    not true is that interpretive ingenuity itself brings on radical scientific
    change. Quite the opposite: those communities most adept at showing
    how the terms they already have can be reinterpreted to accommodate
    any unexpected datum are precisely the ones that tend above all to resist
    change. Brilliant hermeneutical stretching of the Ptolemaic system long
    kept the threatening ideas of Copernicus and Galileo at bay. It may well
    take a certain bull-headed literalism, an insistence that an existing
    theory means precisely what it seems to mean and is *wrong*, for paradigm
    shifts to be possible. But this cannot be the whole story either. The most
    bull-headed of scientific literalists themselves want to insist that new
    paradigms *correct* old ones, and this cannot be the case unless the new
    and the old have something in common, a talking-point on which the
    new one can establish its superiority. To get to such a talking-point,
    however, reflective judgment will have to be at work, bridging the gaps
    left by many a now frustrated scientific "contract" about what counts as
    justification in the relevant field. (The analogy is strong here: from the
    time they are graduate students, budding scientists are introduced to a
    network of agreements about what moves are permissible, what exam-
    ples should be emulated, and what principles can be taken for granted.
    When these agreements are threatened, a situation arises much resem-
    bling breach of contract. The question then becomes, was the breach
    merely apparent, something unjustifiable, or something, like a frustrated
    contract, about which no one knows quite what to say?) Ordinarily

scientists determine correctness according to the coherence of a new truth-claim with background beliefs whose truth they regard as well established. When a significant portion of those background beliefs fall into question, so too do the very standards by which they measure truth. Reflective judgment is always present in science to some degree or other, but it now comes to the fore. Whether the particular, startlingly new data or the body of older theory should give, and how, in either case, to interpret or reinterpret both data and theory, become central and explicit rather than mere background concerns of scientific practice itself. But how this interpretive work comes together with a decision about which side has the truth is a bit of a mystery.

It does follow from my account that the question of whether different scientific paradigms are incommensurable or not is unsettleable. Post-revolutionary scientists may reinterpret the terminology of their predecessors as capturing in a partial, confused, or metaphorical way the same general aims for research that they themselves maintain: thus can they uphold the regulative ideal that science pursue a unified and univocal truth. But philosophers and intellectual historians need not share such a concern for unity. We may learn, once again, from the analogy with art. I said, about the Pollock or Debussy, that we come to regard the work as beautiful *if* we can *feel* that the process of interpretation may go on indefinitely; I could not prove that it *will* go on indefinitely. Whether a work is in fact open to indefinitely many interpretations is a matter that itself cannot be definitely settled. To prove indeterminacy would already require capturing the work conceptually. Something similar holds for the nodes of radical change in science. Exactly how to bring together the vocabularies from before and after such a change may seem to many a matter for endless interpretation, but such incommensurability can never be proven: that itself would defeat the linguistic openness that allows a scientific paradigm to be frustrated. And this inability to *prove* indeterminacy gives the scientist a right to proceed on the absolutist stance that insists on an ultimate possibility of commensurating all truth claims, while legitimating equally an intellectual historian's assumption that no adequate reconciliation of the pre- and post-revolutionary language will ever be found. Resolution of the very debate over conceptual "absolutism" and "relativism" cannot be given definitively, nor can there be anything more than endless interpretation as to what properly belongs between the two.

31 In addition to those already mentioned, I would like to thank Amy Reichert, Jacob Meskin, Sarah Buss, Dan O'Connor, David Frum, Charles Altieri, Eva Kittay, Richard Eldridge, and an anonymous reviewer for Cambridge University Press, for their many helpful comments on drafts of this chapter.

6

Fractal contours: chaos and system in the Romantic fragment

AZADE SEYHAN

Ist nicht System die Form der Wissenschaft Chaos der Stoff? (Is it not the case that system constitutes the form of knowledge [and] chaos its material?)
Friedrich Schlegel, *Philosophische Lehrjahre*

Where chaos begins, classical science stops. For as long as the world has had physicists inquiring into the laws of nature, it had suffered a special ignorance about disorder in the atmosphere, in the turbulent sea, in the fluctuations of wildlife populations, in the oscillations of the heart and the brain. The irregular side of nature, the discontinuous and erratic side – these have been puzzles to science, or worse, monstrosities.
James Gleick, *Chaos: Making a New Science*

As a visual and conceptual metaphor, chaos represents a recurrent term in the critical writings of early German Romantics. Both Friedrich Schlegel and Novalis (Friedrich von Hardenberg), two prominent theorists of German Romanticism, define chaos as the condition for the possibility of all knowledge. Like a mirror-image that is neither essence nor representation, but an intangible and elusive form suspended in-between, a form necessary for self-(re)-cognition, chaos is an uncontainable and unrepresentable presence that is a precondition of any form of human cognition. Schlegel speculates that chaos may be the first, unconditional principle of system construction, a possible nickname for Fichte's "Ich" (self): "Self [*Ich*] and not-self [*Nicht-Ich*] perhaps identical with chaos and system and with spirit and letter."[1] In other words, chaos designates a higher metaphysics, an originary consciousness prior to systematic thought. In Schlegel's analogic formula, then, chaos corresponds to the first proposition of Fichte's analytic philosophy. As an absolute (spirit), chaos is unrepresentable and suprasensible. In order to be made present to sense perception, it has to be represented through a formal medium, as letter (*Buchstabe*), script, or formula. Thus, chaos invades the world of experience in forms that can represent its essence only in fragmented parts.

In *The Postmodern Condition*, Jean-François Lyotard envisions the post-modern consciousness as one which "puts forward the unpresentable in presentation itself ... [one] which searches for new presentations, not in order to enjoy them but in order to impart a stronger sense of the unrepresentable."[2] Such freedom from referential constraints points to the possibility of the ongoing corrective transformation of all signifiers, but also motivates profound fears that the world is nothing but an unrepresentable chaos. Caught up in these linguistic tranformations and pulled in various directions by them, the agent comes to have a split subjectivity, situated at the intersections of competing and conflicting cultural discourses and representations.

In *The Subject of Modernity*, Anthony Cascardi argues that although "the invention of subjectivity" depends on the rejection of an inherently orderly universe, "it remains difficult for the subject to accept its place within a contingent order of events. In response the subject attempts to transform contingency into necessity."[3] One strategy for recuperating meaning and order out of contingency, but without denying the open-ended conflicts of language and culture, lies in the political and ethical uses of what we term aesthetic judgments. Reinterpreting Kant's critique of aesthetic judgment, Cascardi develops an aesthetic liberalism, wherein the antinomies between necessity and freedom, individual and society, and reason and desire are not resolved in the creation of a totalizing narrative but retain their force, as each interest realigns its spheres of culture against the others. Exercising "aesthetic judgment" is the condition for the possibility of the subject's self-transformation which, in turn, can preserve and promote ethical principles under siege by the disintegrative forces of modern capital.

In a similar vein, I would like to illustrate how contingencies of knowledge and value, time and space, and selfhood and community are negotiated in the Romantic and modern representations of chaos. The reinvention of the fragment in the discourse of early Romanticism answers to the necessity for creating a form through which the future (re)cognitions inherent in the Romantic concept of "infinite perfectibility" could be achieved. The form of the Romantic fragment, as a mode of inquiry and self-questioning, preserves the tensions and paradoxes of modern discourses. Fragments are symbolic markers of a "chaotic" progression that strives toward the cognition of an "infinite reality." Their open resistances to redemptive attempts at final restorations of unity and harmony embody an impetus for self-transformation.

In an attempt to conceptualize mythical notions of disorder, pre-Socratic philosophers like Thales, Anaximander, and Anaxagoras argued that the structures of the phenomenal world had developed from a specific substance – such as water or air – which had been in an original state of chaotic disorder. In his Jena lectures on *Transzendentalphilosophie*, Friedrich Schlegel subscribes to the notion of chaos as the generative source of the structure of experience: "It is the characteristic of chaos that nothing can be distinguished within it; and what cannot be distinguished cannot access consciousness. Only form comes into empirical consciousness" (*KA*, 12: 38). In the critical lexicon of Romanticism, form (in particular, the representational form of the work of art) is the manifestation of reality. The conception of chaos struck a seductive chord in Romantic sensibility, since it pointed to the shifting, unstable nature of reality. As a regulative metaphor of its time, chaos represented the world of experience in terms of the strangely fractured myths of modernity, those of reason, enlightenment, and progress. In an age of violent political and intellectual births, when even the energy of the concept of crisis was threatened by collapse, the guiding models of rational and ethical life seemed hopelessly frayed. In one *Athenäum* fragment, Schlegel describes the French Revolution as "the most frightful grotesque of the age where the most deep-seated prejudices and their most brutal punishments are joined in a gruesome chaos and interwoven as bizarrely as possible with a colossal human tragicomedy" (*KA*, 2: 248, no. 424).

In Romantic poetics, the fractured reality of the world found its coincidental form of expression in the fragment. As a formal and figural representation of the unrepresentable, fragment became the progeny of generative chaos, for it implied the infinity of the forms of aesthetic expression. "Fragmentation is not ... a dissemination, but is rather the dispersal that leads to fertilization ... The genre of the fragment is the genre of generation."[4] I would also add that the frequent occurrences of the terms *chaos*, *form*, and *fragment* in early German Romantic criticism is not coincidental, but rather indicates an idiosyncratic critical stance positioned against the representationalist project of philosophy. The Romantics implicated the stubbornness of this project in the malaise of the age. Thus, their strategies of writing ideas self-consciously oppose "the image of philosophical thought as atemporal and undramatic ... [which] has been very much taken for granted in the historiography of philosophy since the nineteenth century."[5] The indirect, allegorical, and ironic character of the Romantic fragment controls the reading and interpretation of the philosophical ideas it contains, for it emphasizes the status of philosophy as writing, "a condition that, not alone but also, makes philosophy possible."[6]

The early Romantics often valued and endorsed unexpected alliances of misalliances. Novalis, for instance, maintained that a genuinely philosophical stance necessitated the introduction of systemlessness (*Systemlosigkeit*) into a system. Only this self-interrupting gesture could avoid the shortcomings of the system, while resisting the anarchy of systemlessness.[7] "The co-presence of the fragmentary and the systematic has a double and decisive significance," write Philippe Lacoue-Labarthe and Jean-Luc Nancy in *The Literary Absolute*. "It implies both the one and the other are established in Jena within the same horizon, and that this horizon is the very horizon of the System, whose exigency is inherited and revived by romanticism."[8] Is it possible, then, that in this conceptual model of systematic systemlessness, the seemingly disparate and motley categories of chaos, fragment, representation, knowledge, and reflection are joined in an arabesque – to use a favored Romantic figure – performance of critical readings? Schlegel locates the intuition of the infinite in the space of the indirect, non-mimetic representations of Romantic *Poesie*. Poetry yields not concepts but intuitions, and strives to represent the chaos of ideas, that is, endlessness, in beautiful and meaningful form (*KA*, 11: 114).

This form as an aesthetic construct can only represent the necessarily uncontainable nature of chaos in figural and discontinuous installments. The structuring or controlling of originary chaos in formal segments is the first stage in the generation of knowledge. On the other hand, the practice of critical philosophy as an act of self-reflexive praxis tests the limits of this knowledge. The post-structuralist debates of the 80s have further shown us that the choice of a formal vehicle for the expression of philosophical thought itself states a philosophical stance. The valorization of the fragment, aphorism, letter, and dialogue in Romantic writing has strong implications for philosophical thought. As Berel Lang rightfully observes, "To speak of philosophical texts as literary artifacts, then, whatever difficulties it encounters in the way of literary analysis, forces philosophy to an awareness of its historical character

– a necessary step if philosophy is to follow its own advice of knowing itself."[9] Lacoue-Labarthe and Nancy single out the fragment as "the romantic genre *par excellence*."[10] Of course, we need to remember that in early Romanticism works in almost every genre – including novels, novellas, letters, dialogues, and philosophical treatises – took on the mask of the fragment. This choice of genre is closely tied to Romantic views on representation and to a conception of philosophical inquiry as deeply implicated in literary collaboration.

The fact that certain tropes and topoi become dominant modes of expression in some ages strongly suggests that form and style are intimately linked to movements and speculations in the history of ideas. In Romantic writing, the terms chaos, fragment, irony, and *Witz* are linked through feedback loops; that is, they create the conceptual fields within which each term is generated and reciprocally reconfigures the others. The common denominator of these terms is the question of representability. In the aftermath of the French and Kantian revolutions, that were to alter the political and intellectual landscapes of eighteenth-century Europe radically, the question of representation acquired renewed currency. The political, social, moral, and intellectual crises of the age were deeply felt on the German soil, a fragmented land consisting of numerous separate politically oppressed states. Since writers and intellectuals felt hopelessly inadequate in attempting directly to envision solutions to the political chaos, they sought refuge in intellectual speculations by reformulating questions of necessity and freedom, truth and appearance, and right and wrong. Representation came to be seen as mediated truth and presence, a re-presentation of a lost presence, an implication of identity through non-identity. This heightened awareness of the crisis of representation and a consequent determination to respond to it constitute the context of the Romantic will to refashion paradigms of understanding and revalorize certain forms of writing. The new textual models of understanding that result from this will are informed by a powerful consciousness of their necessarily indirect, figural, and interpretive nature.

How do chaos, fragment, irony, *Witz*, and criticism figure in the complex reconceptualization of representation? Schlegel's many references to chaos cast it as a metaphor for an unrepresentable and unreflected essence. Fragment, in turn, is the vehicle of an ironic inquiry about the reliability of representation and, therefore, a mode of critical self-reflection. This non-linear and self-interrupting form that establishes the very nature of Romantic poetry introduces breaks and gaps into the representation of the world. As such, it implies a dialectic of order and disorder, an "eternal alternation" that matches the undecidability of the forces that inform human experience:

This artificially ordered confusion, this attractive symmetry of contradictions, this wonderful, eternal alternation of enthusiam and irony, which lives even in the smallest units of the whole, appear to me to be an indirect mythology ... [T]his is the beginning of all poetry, to cancel the course and laws of rationally thinking reason and transport us once more into the beautiful confusion of fantasy, into the original chaos of human nature.

(*KA*, 2: 318–319)

The site of disappearing reason metamorphosing from its illusory home in a coherent and objective self into an impartial, paradoxical otherness, is taken over by an originary chaos where imagination exults in the sublime. The endless and the unfathomable can only be captured in aesthetic form. In his Jena lectures on transcendental philosophy, Schlegel asks how the formless endlessness which he had designated as chaos is cast into individual structures accessible to consciousness:

Actually we avail ourselves of the concepts, *an endless substance* [chaos] – and *particulars*. If we wish to explain the movement from one to the other, we can only do this by introducing another term between the two, that is, the concept of *the picture* or *representation* [*Darstellung*], *allegory*. In other words, the particular is *a picture* of *an endless substance*. (*KA*, 12: 39)

Like allegory, Romantic irony constitutes an indirect and self-reflexive middle term. Irony mediates between system and chaos. In the presence of irony, system and chaos reflect on and relativize one another. In one of his many definitions of Romantic irony, Schlegel writes: "*Irony* is clear chaos in agility, an intellectual intuition of an eternal chaos, one that is endless, full, brilliant, and eternally cyclical" (*KA*, 18: 228, no. 411). In every form of mediation in language there remains an irreducible absence, where representation represents its own impossibility and yields to chaos as irony. For Schlegel, the realization of this paradox, that is, the ability to place oneself in the "sphere of incomprehensibility and confusion," constitutes "a sublime and perhaps the final stage of intellectual formation. A true understanding of chaos derives from this acknowledgment" (*KA*, 18: 227, no. 396). It follows from this that acknowledging chaos is also the condition of critical thought. Schlegel argues that the welfare of humanity depends upon this acknowledgment of an irreducible chaos underlying the inception of the subject and language:

But is incomprehensibility really something so thoroughly contemptible and evil? I think the salvation of families and nations rests on it ... Even the most precious thing a human being has, inner happiness itself, depends ... in the last analysis on some such point that must be left in the dark, but that nonetheless carries and supports the whole and would lose this strength the moment it were subjected to reason ... And isn't this endless world itself formed by the understanding out of incomprehensibility or chaos?

(*KA*, 2: 370)

Thus understanding as a mode of representation is a derivative of chaos. Understanding and chaos, therefore, are not opposed but rather dialectical or successive terms. "Chaos and system (in philosophical works) each must constitute itself – or only after this, should chaos be deduced from the system. All chaos emerges from *Witz*" (*KA*, 18: 285, no. 1068) writes Schlegel. Elsewhere Schlegel refers to *Witz* as "the appearance, the outer lightning of fantasy" (*KA*, 2: 258, no. 26). Pointing to the close alliance of fragment and *Witz*, Lacoue-Labarthe and Nancy state that *Witz* incorporates "the entire fragmentary, dialogical and dialectical structure"[11] of the fragment and shares its tendency for spontaneity. Like the fragment, *Witz* synthesizes an order out of chaos; it is "ars combinatoria, criticism, art of invention" (*KA*, 18: 124, no. 20). Like the other popular Romantic forms and tropes such as fragment, arabesque, irony, and allegory, *Witz* is also a synthetic formal expression of the originary chaos. In its resistance to, and fracturing of, analytic thought, *Witz* is allied with fragment and chaos. It constitutes "the other name and the other 'concept' of knowledge, or rather the name and 'concept' of knowledge that is other: of knowledge that is other than the knowledge of analytic and predicative discursivity."[12]

The Romantic project undertakes the task of showing that the bold gestures of poetic language are well prepared to challenge the restricted protocols of analytic inquiry and to urge philosophy toward a more profound undertaking of conscious self-knowledge. Within this effort, criticism reduplicates the work of poetry. The Romantic ideal posits criticism as the representation of the work of art, better still, its critically informed aesthetic equal, a metafiction that comments on the condition of its self–other. As an analytic of representation, Romantic criticism is willfully reinvented by Schlegel and Novalis in the form of rhetoric. For self-consciously rhetorical Romantic criticism, then, the only possible response to a poem would be a poem: "One cannot really speak of poetry save in the language of poetry" (*KA*, 2: 285). Thus criticism, like poetry, is itself a synthetic operation that reflects on the coming into being of representation, that is the birth of (aesthetic) form from chaos, and on the conditions for the production or generation of form. If truth is only accessible to human consciousness as fractured, partial, incomplete, and infinite, then the Romantic imagination will strive to incorporate domains that the light of reason obscures and to retrieve occluded knowledges and marginal forms. The reconceptualization of such figural forms as the fragment, ellipsis, arabesque, and grotesque enacts a critical position that underlines the non-coincidence of the object or concept with representation; it is an eloquent interrogation of claims to certainty. As a mode of articulation, fragment implies an elusive approximation of facticity, truth, and concepts. As a result it emerged as the overarching literary form of the early German Romantics' speculations on questions of knowledge and history, understanding and interpretation, and logic and rhetoric. These questions were exhaustively and dialogically pursued in the pages of the journal *Athenäum*, published by Friedrich Schlegel and his brother August Wilhelm in the very concentrated time span of 1798–1800 in Jena. Several important literary figures of the time contributed regularly to the journal, along with critics and philosophers.

The contributions of the editorial collective consisted mostly of fragments which were intended later to become part of a universal encyclopedia project – which, of course, true to Romantic form never came into being. Nevertheless, *Athenäum* included a good number of longer narrative texts such as essays, reviews, and dialogues. The apparently random ordering and presentation of the fragments and the absence of the author's name defy the classification of texts according to author, genre, and œuvre – or what Michel Foucault has called the discursive unities. In this way, the significance of any published submission was established only in the context of its relationship to other forms of discourse such as philosophical and scientific inquiry, literary conventions and history, social mores and customs, and religious and political practices. In this sense, the fragment displayed an episodic structure wherein each segment could be complete in itself but was also linked to the others in an infinite framework.

The fragment was neither invented nor first consciously employed as a genre by the members of the *Athäneum* collective. Lacoue-

Labarthe and Nancy state that Schlegel was inspired to experiment with the form after the posthumous publication of Chamfort's *Pensées, Maximes et Anecdotes* in 1795.[13] The Romantics inherit a tradition with a long genealogy and then allow that tradition to fulfill its potential as a formal innovation in critical discourse. The pre-ferred genre of the Romantics was the Romantic novel, a *"Mischge-dicht,"* synthesized from fragments of other genres, and itself a long fragment that resisted formal closure. What differentiates the use of fragment in the Jena circle from the history of its former employ-ments is the presentation of a collection, often published as *Frag-ments*, an ensemble of an apparently disconnected series of critical insights, historical accounts, and philosophical musings, anon-ymously composed by several authors. The Romantics reinvent the fragment not only as a prolonged prologue and an incomplete postscript, but also as a performative vehicle of theory. Like the novel, the fragment in writing itself writes its own theory of compo-sition. The novels and novellas of Romanticism, in their complex uses of narrative conventions such as frames, multiple narrators, shifting narrative perspectives, and embedded genres – poems in novellas, novellas in novels – remain maxi-fragments. By raising the fragment to the status of a fully-fledged literary genre, the editors resist a desire for non-contingent systematization and emphasize that truths can only be intimated or alluded to in an indirect and discontinuous fashion. The fragment sustains a series of ruptures, variable terms, and spontaneous ideas which are experienced by the reader as disorder irreducible to authorial intention. In this way, the writer of the fragment constructs an implied reader who is an agent of generative interpretations:

The analytic writer observes the reader as he is; he then makes his calcula-tions and sets up his machines in order to make up the proper impression on him. The synthetic writer constructs and creates a reader as he should be; he doesn't imagine him calm and dead but alive and responsive. He lets whatever he has created take shape gradually before the reader's eyes, or he urges the reader to discover it himself. He does not try to make any particular impression on the reader, but enters with him into the sacred relationship of the most profound symphilosophy or sympoetry.   (*KA*, 2: 161, no. 112)

This "sympoetic" bonding of the writer and reader enables both to transcend the need for propositions that express certainties. The act of reading synthesizes order from disorder, and then fragments that order into further disorder, thus destabilizing any prospect of attri-buting a systematic plan to the text. Since for Romanticism the world is an infinite text and our interpretations of it derive from our sympoetic readings of the world as a text, the fragment becomes a performative mode of understanding and knowledge. If "the phenomenal world itself is chaotic, infinitely self-replicating, and fractally ordered,"[14] the fragment then shares in the characteristics of this world, not by mimetically representing them, but by enacting them or rather by structuring itself in such a way that it partakes in this chaos. Self-generative critical readings multiply strategies for reconfiguring disorder as order.

The fragment, then, mediates between system and systemlessness, attempts to function as a critical instrument for the review of apperceptual regimes, and renegotiates the status of the poetic in the anatomy of philosophical discourse. It implies identity and totality by means of the non-identity and incompletion that inform its formal gestures; it constitutes the immediate experience of what it "incompletes"[15] in infinite generations. And it duplicates fractured time, a sense that history and memory are always incomplete yet always in unending pursuit of completion as their fictional telos. Most important of all, fragment dialogizes itself, so that the writer assumes the position of both writer and reader. In the dialogue structure that the fragment sets up, the writer posits an ideal reader whose response revises the authorial propositions, thereby generating a field of interactive pedagogics.

Metaphors of chaos inform discourses of crisis. And in the Romantic imagination, crisis remains a creative force whose dynamics of conflict and contradiction should never be traded in for bland reassurances of apparent resolutions. "At times, in crazy moments, it seems to me that humanity itself made a mess of chaos and was too eager to establish order," laments the night-watchman Kreuzgang in Bonaventura's fragmentary Romantic novel *Nachtwachen*: "[t]hat's why nothing is in its proper place and the creator thus has to cross out and destroy the world like a failed system."[16] Bonaventura implies that what is repressed in history returns with a vengeance. And, indeed, Romanticism's speculations on chaos have emerged once again, in reconfigured form, in modern chaos science which, like Romantic theory, aims to understand and come to terms with the non-linear, unpredictable, and fractal dimensions of nature and human experience.

It is not my purpose either to employ concepts of chaos science as a convenient metaphor for a further exploration of Romantic theories of representation or to use it as another vocabulary through which to speak of Romanticism's critical concepts. Nevertheless, whenever a new cultural discourse emerges, "it is not only the present that is changed; the past is also reinterpreted."[17] Let me reiterate that the poetics of Romantic philosophy were an inquiry into an alternative mode of reading and writing the world of experience. The dynamics and philosophy of the Romantic fragment display characteristics typical of what science terms chaos. Moreover, the Romantic validation of the fragment is indicative of cultural factors which we consider today to be important constituents of scientific inquiry. As Katherine Hayles has convincingly argued, one of the most important of these factors is language. For the most part, scientific discourse has considered language a merely instrumental tool and "adopts as its ideal univocality – one word, one meaning."[18] Recent debates in literary criticism and theory have shown us that language dictates thought as it expresses it, and much recent research has confirmed that metaphors, rhetorical strategies, and even largely anecdotal evidence affect the constructive protocols of scientific inquiry. "The science of chaos is new not in the sense of having no antecedents in the scientific tradition," writes Hayles, "but of having only recently coalesced sufficiently to articulate a new vision of the world."[19] A wealth of prescient metaphors regulated Romanticism's understanding of the world, and these metaphors reappear in the terms through which chaotic systems are perceived today.

Chaos, the interdisciplinary science, covers two interrelated fields, fractal geometry and random dynamical systems, systems that are vulnerable to instances of unpredictable chaotic disorder. After the publication of Benoit Mandelbrot's book *The Fractal Geometry of Nature* in 1983, many visual and literary artists of the post-modern persuasion became aware of fractals as a predominant feature of their art. The word comes from the Latin *fractus* meaning irregular, but, in fact, fractals represent irregularity through regularity, for they "are generated by a simple act of repetition or iteration, so that they are at one and the same time both highly complex and yet ordered in a simple way."[20] Thus, fractals provide a vision of endless complexity and detail and, like the Romantic work of art, represent an infinity of forms in nature. A quantity such as length is replaced by the qualitative measure of effective fractal dimensions which gauge the relative degree of complexity of an object. Mandelbrot posed questions like "what is the essence of a coastline?" to which Euclidian geometry offered no answers. His fractal geometry takes cognizance of pitted, ruptured, and broken surfaces. It does not represent an abstract, orderly world, because orderly abstraction is inadequate for describing the complexity and diversity that characterize such natural formations as coastlines, mountains, galaxies, clouds, weather patterns, and the brain. Just as a fragment states a resistance to system-building and totalizing theories, fractals implicate traditional geometry in glossing over differences that are crucial to an understanding of global and local differences. Fractals are replications of similar patterns at smaller scales which are able to draw out ever finer distinctions in repeated patterns. They conceive of nature as mirroring itself in endless forms, such as when a pattern repeats itself on a tree, branch, and twig. In a sense, then, fractals fracture the unity of concepts as abstractions and create expansion, differentiation, and concretization in models of understanding.

In "On Truth and Lie in an Extra-Moral Sense," a brilliant essay on the metaphorical origins of philosophical thought, Nietzsche had argued along similar lines against the totalizing tendencies of abstract concepts:

Every concept arises from equating non-equals (*durch Gleichsetzen des Nichtgleichen*). Just as surely as no one leaf is exactly the same as another, the concept leaf is surely formed by an arbitrary omission of individual differences and a forgetting of distinguishing factors. This creates the illusion that there is such a thing as the "leaf" in nature besides leaves, that is, an *Urform* according to which all leaves are supposedly woven, drawn, measured, colored, crinkled, painted but by clumsy hands, so that no sample would appear as accurate and authentic as the true image of the *Urform*.[21]

In the oft-quoted *Athenäum* fragment 116, a fragmentary manifesto of the Romantic program, Schlegel calls Romantic poetry (*romantische Poesie*) "a progressive universal poesy." It "floats in the middle between the represented and the representing, free from all real and ideal interest, on the wings of poetic reflection; it constantly potentiates this reflection and multiplies it as if in a series of endless mirrors" (*KA*, 2: 182–183). Like the reflections of Romantic poetry, fractals are characterized by recursive symmetries – complex systems of nature that reproduce themselves on finer and finer scales, in infinite divisions, replications, generations of form. Fractals reflect the irregularity of the real world, the shifting grounds of reality. However, like all symbolic forms they can do so only indirectly. "Fractal geometry isn't meant to be an exact representation of complexity. In fact, that's the point."[22] Like Romantic poetics or the imaginary numbers, modern chaos theory, in effect, is or attempts to be a representation of unrepresentability. Romantic poetics inscribed a transition from mimesis to critical *poiesis*. Similarly, properties such as constant self-renewal in chaotic systems are called autopoietic structures and considered highly paradoxical. Briggs and Peat state that autopoietic structures, ranging from simple systems such as whirlpools to the complexities of human anatomy, are self-generating and thus autonomous. On the other hand, they are also embedded in a larger environmental context and are intricately linked to its fluctuations. Because they are self-renewing, they remain highly autonomous, yet because they occupy the space of open systems in nature, they are inextricably linked with their environment. To sum up the paradox:

Each autopoietic structure has a unique history, but its history is tied to the history of the larger environment and other autopoietic structures: an interwovenness of time's arrows. Autopoietic structures have definite boundaries, such as a semipermeable membrane, but the boundaries are open and connect the system with almost unimaginable complexity to the world around it.[23]

Fragment, as the textual site of the dialectic of system and chaos, incorporates the operations of a highly complex autopoietic structure, renegotiating transitions between different histories of totality and individuality. The life-force of Romantic poetry resides in the generative field of its "open systems" or in its *poietical* nature. As Lacoue-Labarthe and Nancy describe it:

The poetic is not so much the work as that which works, not so much the organon as that which organizes. This is where romanticism aims at the heart and inmost depths – that "most profound intimacy" scattered throughout the texts, which it would be a mistake to reduce to a sentimental interiority – of the individual and the System: always *poiesis* or, to give at least an equivalent, always *production*. What makes an individual, what makes an individual's holding-together, is the 'systasis' that produces it. What makes its individuality is its capacity to produce, and to produce itself, first of all, by means of its internal 'formative force' – the *bildende Kraft* inherited from the organism of Kant, which romanticism transcribes into a *vis poetica*.[24]

Called the "paradigm shift of paradigm shifts," chaos theory, like Romantic poetics, envisions and enforces a shift in the ground of representation. Its concepts are couched in metaphors of unpredictability, unrepresentability, and randomness masquerading as order. Like all recurrences of the problematic of representation, it is poised on the threshold of a revolutionary change in our perception of the world, following a meteoric rise in the importance of new physics. "In our world, complexity flourishes," writes Gleick, "and those looking to science for a general understanding of nature's habits will be better served by the laws of chaos."[25] Just as modern literary criticism has challenged the epistemological certainties of philosophy by its analysis of language that always threatens the stability of the philosophical idea, so chaos theory has emphasized the need for sharpened self-reflexivity in the understanding and employment of scientific methods. Chaos theory turns on the metaphor of elusive approximations of reality. Nevertheless, the effort of chaos scientists is focused on taming turbulence by trying to bring it within the scope of mathematical modeling, in other words to contain it in form – this is perhaps not too far a cry from the Romantic desire to channel chaos to consciousness in form, even if that form were destined to remain forever fragmented. Thus, chaos science is positioned at the interstices of the search for certainty and a critique of the possibility of that certainty. As such, across time and space, the notions of chaos, fragment, fractals, and irony form feedback loops.

In Romantic criticism, both poetry and commentary operate by rules of discontinuity, yet discontinuity paradoxically implies a syncretic and synthetic operation, a reconciliation of the linear with the fractal, of the grotesque with the aesthetic, of the disorderly with the orderly. Chaos functions as the regulative concept of productivity and syncretism. For Schlegel, all systems are derived from chaos and have to refer to it. In his version of Romantic algebra, the various square-roots of chaos are the multiplicity of forms. Consequently, endlessness or chaos is the nth power of poetic form. Romantic poetry and criticism assume the patterns of fractal geometry. Poetic reflection is endlessly multiplied in refracted form – as infinitely reduplicated reflection. "In the mind's eye, a fractal is a way of seeing infinity,"[26] reaffirms Gleick.

Chaos theory looks afresh at the categories of order and disorder to assert that traditional perspectives fail to suggest the rich and complex interplay between them. It has introduced a vision of irony into modern science. The appropriation of chaos by literary theory marks a renewed celebration of irony as an indispensable trope of modern literature and criticism. In *Criticism and Truth*, Roland Barthes argues that the irreducible and unquantifiable distance between criticism and its object (language) "allows criticism to develop precisely what is lacking in science ... *irony*. Irony is nothing other than the question which language puts to language ...

146

perhaps the only serious form of discourse which remains available to criticism so long as the status of science and language is not clearly established."[27] This recalls Schlegel's prescient insight that "irony is the duty of all philosophy that is not yet history or system" (*KA*, 8: 86, no. 678). Romantic irony is informed by an interlocking series of statements which vacillate between the differences of the terms they articulate. Likewise, chaos portrays a world that is vaster, more fluid, less secure, less foundationalist than that portrayed by previous scientific paradigms. Romantic poetics sees derivative forms of chaos, such as fragment, rupture, and ellipsis as artistic constructs of mediating reality. The choice of genre and form is intimately related to the syntax of their larger cultural philosophy. The "status of genre," as Lang eloquently argues, "is much like that of history itself: contingent in each appearance but unavoidable as a kind."[28] In the final analysis, the most significant objective of Romantic forms of writing may be the "aesthetic education of man," to invoke Schiller's famous "letters" on the topic. "The true reader has to be the extended writer,"[29] Novalis writes. In the dialogue between reader and writer, whether in fragments or letters, expanded and diversified accounts of the world of human experience are generated. These accounts are not aimed at an explanation of the world, but rather, in the true hermeneutic spirit which the fragmentary form enables, at a differentiated understanding wherein the whole is derived from the parts and the parts imply the whole.

German Romanticism's metaphors of chaos, of the chaotic sublime, and of the representation of unrepresentability provide a literary historical reference-point in a new interdisciplinary critical adventure. The new chaos science deploys fractional dimensions to measure qualities that have no definition, such as the degree of roughness, brokenness, irregularity, or non-linearity of an object. These also take into consideration the different scales on which objects are measured. Similarly, the Romantic fragment valorized contingency as the condition of system. The critical praxis of the early Romanticism demonstrates that only what we may now call "fractal" criticism could negotiate the rough curves of opposing disciplinary discourses that are, in the final analysis, products of different and not necessarily comparable cultural positions and scientific heritages. Just as fractal mathematics does more justice to mapping the jagged edges of the landscapes it represents than does traditional geometry, so too the Romantic fragment maps the potentialities of intellectual life in a more open-ended fashion than does more traditional, treatise-inspired theoretical discourse. In one of the most famous statements of the *Athenäum,* fragment 116, Schlegel states that "[t]he Romantic art of poetry is still in becoming; in fact, that is its true nature that it can only become and never be completed" (*KA,* 2: 183). Almost two centuries later, in *Chaos: Making a New Science,* a bestseller that alerted popular culture to the significance of a major scientific breakthrough, James Gleick echoes Schlegel: "To some physicists chaos is a science of process rather than state, of becoming rather than being."[30]

Understanding and coming to terms with complexity and unpredictability need not indicate a search for objective or absolute truth, but rather the realization that truth is multidimensional and culturally situated – a poietical form – and that so-called objectivity is a heuristic fiction. Returning to my initial observations on the condition of the modern subject, who in Cascardi's words "tends on the one hand to accept the principles of science as reflecting the indisputable truths of reason, while on the other hand ... assents to the proposition that disputes about value and desires cannot be resolved according to the standards of rational truth,"[31] I suggest that the chaotic sublime of the Romantic fragment offers the subject the venue to negotiate multiple truths in the quest of self-transformation. "Germany is probably such a favorite subject for the general essayist," writes Schlegel, "because the less finished a nation is, the more it is a subject for criticism and not for history" (*KA,* 2: no. 26). Germany, as the subject of the essayist, the writer of fragments, is allowed the privilege of transformation and the reinterpretation of its fate. "[T]he language of history, which speaks in terms of necessity," writes Cascardi, "will lead us to deny the possibility of transformation and to interpret our inherited modern identity as fate ... the lure of theory will by contrast tempt us to imagine recognition as taking place within the framework of a purely speculative and ideal whole."[32] The representations of a world in flux captured in the aesthetic gesture of the Romantic fragment suggest an interlinkage of the contesting languages of history and theory.

The many post-"ism"s of our age now find their strange attractor in the post-Euclidian geometry of chaos theory, just as, at the height of the German Romantic age, poetics was mesmerized by chaotics.[33] Scientific discourse has, since the Enlightenment, successfully colonized the epistemological territory believed to have direct access to the facticity of the physical world. Now, however, like that brief and glorious moment in Jena, art has been issued the heady challenge of fractally inscribing the digressions and deflections of a fast-paced cultural history. In this quest, art reaches out to chaos theory which, through its wider implications in various disciplines, has offered a certain freedom from representational certainty. Perhaps this liberation will dispel the shroud of mystification that is both the glory and burden of all religions, including the religion of science.

Notes

1 Friedrich Schlegel, *Kritische Ausgabe*, ed. Ernst Behler (Paderborn: Ferdinand Schöningh, 1958–) 18: 277, no. 995. Further references to Schlegel's work are cited from this edition (abbreviated *KA*) and indicated in the text with volume, page, and, when given, fragment number. All translations from the German are mine.
2 Jean-François Lyotard, *The Postmodern Condition: A Report on Knowledge*, trans. Geoff Bennington and Brian Massumi (Minneapolis: University of Minnesota Press, 1984), p. 81.
3 Anthony J. Cascardi, *The Subject of Modernity* (Cambridge University Press, 1992), p. 5.
4 Philippe Lacoue-Labarthe and Jean-Luc Nancy, *The Literary Absolute: The Theory of Literature in German Romanticism*, trans. Philip Barnard and Cheryl Lester (Albany: State University of New York Press, 1988), p. 49.
5 Berel Lang, *The Anatomy of Philosophical Style* (Oxford and Cambridge, Mass.: Basil Blackwell, 1990), p. 22.
6 *Ibid.*,, p. 23.
7 Novalis (Friedrich von Hardenberg), *Schriften*, ed. Paul Kluckhohn and Richard Samuel (Stuttgart: Kohlhammer, 1960) 2: 289, no. 648.
8 Lacoue-Labarthe and Nancy, *The Literary Absolute*, p. 42.
9 Lang, *Anatomy*, p. 22.
10 Lacoue-Labarthe and Nancy, *The Literary Absolute*, p. 40.
11 *Ibid.*, p. 52.
12 *Ibid.*, p. 53.
13 *Ibid.*, p. 40. For a more detailed explanation of the genealogy of the fragment in its reception by the Jena critics, see, in addition to Lacoue-Labarthe and Nancy, Ernst Behler's very thorough introduction to volume two of the Schlegel *Kritische Ausgabe*, the volume that includes the *Athenäum*.
14 Peter Stoicheff, "The Chaos of Metafiction," in *Chaos and Disorder: Complex Dynamics in Literature and Science*, ed. N. Katherine Hayles (Chicago and London: University of Chicago Press, 1991), pp. 83–99, 94.
15 Lacoue-Labarthe and Nancy, *The Literary Absolute*, p. 43.
16 Bonaventura, *Nachtwachen*, ed. Wolfgang Paulsen (Stuttgart: Reclam, 1964), p. 48. Published in 1804 anonymously under the title *Nachtwa-*

chen des Bonaventura, this novel is a performance in reading chaos. Speculations about the authorship of this madcap narrative have long been a staple of literary historical scholarship. It has been attributed to Clemens, Brentano, Schelling, his wife Karoline, and even E. T. A. Hoffmann. True to Romantic form and the spirit of the *Athenäum*, *Nachtwachen* defies any authorial program, subverts narrative order, and ruthlessly parodies philosophical presuppositions. Written as sixteen loosely connected fragments, called night watches and an entry from the devil's notebook, *Nachtwachen* is a poetic metanarrative that provides incisive musings about critical philosophy, Romantic poetics, identity, language, and madness. It is an eloquent testimony to Romanticism's endorsement of the dialectics of chaos and order, imagination and understanding, and the sublime and the rational.

17 N. Katherine Hayles, "Introduction: Complex Dynamics in Literature and Science," in *Chaos and Order: Complex Dynamics in Literature and Science*, ed. Hayles, pp. 1–33, 22.
18 *Ibid.*, p. 5.
19 *Ibid.*
20 John Briggs and F. David Peat, *Turbulent Mirror* (New York: Harper & Row, 1989), p. 171.
21 Friedrich Nietzsche, *Werke*, ed. Karl Schlechta (Munich: Karl Hanser, 1956) 3: 313.
22 Briggs and Peat, *Turbulent Mirror*, p. 110.
23 *Ibid.*, p. 154.
24 Lacoue-Labarthe and Nancy, *The Literary Absolute*, pp. 48–49.
25 James Gleick, *Chaos: Making a New Science* (New York and London: Penguin, 1987), p. 308.
26 *Ibid.*, p. 98.
27 Roland Barthes, *Criticism and Truth*, trans. and ed. Katrine Pilcher Keunemann (Minneapolis: University of Minnesota Press, 1987), pp. 89–90.
28 Lang, *Anatomy*, p. 42.
29 Novalis *Schriften*, 2: 470; no. 125.
30 Gleick, *Chaos,* p. 5.
31 Cascardi, *The Subject of Modernity*, p. 11.
32 *Ibid.*, p. 301.
33 Hayles (*Chaos and Order*, p. 7) uses this term suggested to her by Ihab Hassan to include cultural areas informed by the principles of chaos theory (7).

7

The mind's horizon

STANLEY BATES

In Philippe Lacoue-Labarthe and Jean-Luc Nancy's brilliant study of early German Romanticism, *The Literary Absolute*, the authors establish that a crucial element of the matrix of influences out of which this Romanticism developed was Kant's critical philosophy. The translators of the book write, "What *The Literary Absolute* demonstrates is first of all that the concept of literature arises as a response to the problems posed by Kant's critical enterprise."[1] Lacoue-Labarthe and Nancy themselves write, "Philosophy, then, controls romanticism. In this context, and crudely translated, this means that Kant opens up the possibility of romanticism ... The romantics have no predecessors. Especially not in what the eighteenth century insistently held up under the name of *aesthetics*. On the contrary, it is because an entirely new and unforeseeable relation between aesthetics and philosophy will be articulated in Kant that a 'passage' to romanticism will become possible."[2]

Their book traces a particular track of Romanticism as it develops in the circle associated with the journal, the *Athenaeum* – a track for whose importance they argue. In this chapter, I want to go back to the problematic in Kant which they identify as crucial – "the problematic of the subject unpresentable to itself"[3] in order to clarify the issue that it presented to Hegel and to subsequent philosophers who are not a part of their sharply focused discussion of early German Romanticism. I am inclined to regard this issue involving, as it does, the relations among self, world, and representation, as, perhaps, the best around which to try to organize a view of nineteenth- and twentieth-century philosophy, but I shall not attempt any such far-reaching synthesis in this chapter. Rather I shall, after a brief general discussion of Kant's critical enterprise, focus on some specific moments in his texts when that enterprise seems to come to a breaking point. These moments seem to me "blind spots" in the text, in Paul de Man's sense of the term. I shall then turn to Hegel – to his critique of Kant, and to what I consider *his* own blind spots.

The chief discovery of the philosophical revolution of the seventeenth and eighteenth centuries seemed to be of the mediated nature of the self's relationship to the world. Once our representations of the world, whether as *cogitationes* or ideas, were recognized as distinct from the world, the whole dialectic of skepticism ensued with the "rationalist" and "empiricist" responses to it – or so Kant thought, for he was the first to summarize his predecessors in this way. Kant attempted to undermine an earlier mode of thought, in which the world (of things as they are, apart from our representation of them) was conceived as a set of stable entities, the self was also conceived to be a stable entity, and the central issue for philosophy was then the relationship between the world and our representation of it (including our representation of our own "self.") We shall look below at Kant's "Copernican revolution" in reconceiving the relationship of "self" to "world" and try to understand the inherent instability of his attempted settlement of the fundamental questions of philosophy.

Kant's Copernican revolution in philosophy attempted to establish a "limit to knowledge" and, hence, to bring to an end one strand of Enlightenment philosophizing which had ambitions for an unlimited extension of reason. Simultaneously, he attempted to end the skepticism which he viewed as the outcome of Enlightenment empiricism, by providing an account of, and justification for, knowledge within the limits of reason. The Kantian critical philosophy is the crucial hinge of modern philosophy. Kant is a figure in the history of philosophy who might be thought of as comparable to his contemporary, Beethoven, in the history of music – someone whose work both brings to an end an era and a way of doing things, and, simultaneously, opens up a whole new set of issues and a new way of going on with a discipline. The comparison is particularly apt when one thinks of the complex role of Beethoven in the transition from the classical to the Romantic in music. No matter how rough these terms of historical periodization may seem, that particular transition seems to take place not only in Beethoven's works over a lifetime, but even in a single work.

Near the conclusion of the *Critique of Pure Reason*, Kant writes,

"All the interests of my reason, speculative as well as practical, combine in the three following questions:

1. What can I know?
2. What ought I to do?
3. What may I hope?"[4]

Famously, Kant provided answers for these questions in his major works, but, equally famously, these answers both determine, and are determined by, his answer, partly implicit and partly explicit, to a more basic question – who (or, what) am I? Here, I would like to explore some of the implications of certain passages from Kant's critical philosophy for his understanding of the role of the self (or, in his terminology the transcendental ego) in the constitution of the world, and why this relation between self and world was so crucially problematic for subsequent thinkers.

I

Let us begin with a well-known passage which occurs in the first edition of the *Critique of Pure Reason* in the section known as the Transcendental Deduction of the Categories. It will be remembered that this is one of those sections of the first *Critique* which was completely revised for the second edition, possibly because of Kant's fear that it gave some grounds to those who accused him of advocating what he called empirical idealism. The passage goes:

Now, also, we are in a position to determine more adequately our concept of an *object* in general. All representations have, as representations, their object, and can themselves in turn become objects of other representations. Appearances are the sole objects which can be given to us immediately, and that in them which relates immediately to the object is called intuition. But these appearances are not things in themselves; they are only representations, which in turn have their object – an object which cannot itself be intuited by us, and which may, therefore, be named the non-empirical, that is, transcendental object=x.[5]

Kant goes on to say a bit more about the concept of the transcendental object, "This concept cannot contain any determinate intuition and therefore refers only to that unity which must be met with in any manifold of knowledge which stands in relation to an object. This relation is nothing but the necessary unity of consciousness." If we return for a moment to a general characterization of Kant's "Copernican revolution" in philosophy, we can see both how the above passage on the transcendental object is an inevitable consequence of it, and how problematic this passage is.

The crucial move of Kant's critical philosophy is to explore the possibility that "objects must conform to our knowledge" in opposition to earlier modes of thought which all assume that "knowledge must conform to objects."[6] This is the move which he likened to the "primary hypothesis" of Copernicus in which the observed movements of heavenly bodies become a function of the observer's viewpoint. (Of course, Kant thought that, in the first *Critique*, he had done more than explore this possibility; he claimed to have proved it "apodeictically.") That aspect of our knowledge of objects which is a priori certain is so because the world of objects (the phenomenal world) is, partially, constituted by the self. (I continue to use the term "self" for what Kant calls the transcendental ego, and I shall write "the self represented to itself" for what he calls the empirical ego.) In other words, the self is an active maker of the world, rather than a passive recipient of either rational inputs or empirical data. The world is a product of the activity of the self working on inputs (things-in-themselves.)

One cannot stress too much how radical, and how brilliant, this move is. Because we are accustomed to a history of philosophy partially created by Kant himself, in which his work looms so large, it is hard now for us to perceive the magnitude of this change in philosophy's history. What had been the central problems of philosophy for almost two centuries are all completely reformulated. Nonetheless, Kant's perspective in the first *Critique* seems to share the Enlightenment perspective that the basic issue of philosophy is about the status of knowledge – and it seems to be an implication of this that the fundamental feature of human existence is that the human being is a potential knower. This perspective is increasingly altered as Kant develops the whole of the critical philosophy in the second and third *Critiques*, and in his other writing, and this alteration is a consequence of the distinction – between things as they appear to us and things as they are in themselves – which makes such a vivid appearance in the passage quoted above from the first version of the transcendental deduction of the categories.

It is a consequence of the distinction between things as they appear to us and things in themselves, that the latter are *not* available in experience. When a teacher comes to explicate the *Critique of Pure Reason*, it is almost inevitable that she or he will represent the world of experience (the phenomenal world of things as they appear to us) by drawing a circle, and by noting that what is excluded from that circle of experience includes both things in themselves and the subject of the experience. The subject's relationship to its experience has often been analogized to the relationship between a physical eye, and its field of vision. Whatever else appears in that field of vision, it cannot include the eye which is doing the seeing. Similarly the self is not ultimately available to itself, though, of course, it can represent itself to itself, as the eye can see itself in a mirror. (This feature of Kant's philosophy amounts to a denial of the possibility of a totally reflective self-consciousness.) Hence, Kant is in the position of asserting the existence both of absolutely incognizable objects (things in themselves) and of an unknowable self (transcendental ego). Kant himself writes:

The division of objects into phenomena and noumena and the world into a world of the senses and a world of understanding, is therefore quite inadmissible in the positive sense ... What our understanding acquires through this concept of a noumenon, is a negative extension; that is to say, understanding is not limited through sensibility; on the contrary it itself limits sensibility by applying the term noumena to things in themselves (things not regarded as appearances). But in so doing it at the same time sets limits to itself, recognizing that it cannot know these noumena through any of the categories, and that it must therefore think them only under the title of an unknown something.[7]

This passage, like that referring to "the transcendental object=x," shows the incredible internal strains of a position like Kant's. From what perspective could one be in a position to say what Kant says in these passages? The attractiveness of drawing a line to represent the limits of possible experience, can hide from us that the obvious consequence of such limits would be the impossibility of drawing such a line. Unfortunately for Kant's aspirations, his version of the *via negativa* proved as difficult to sustain in philosophy as an earlier one had in theology. It is extremely difficult to make any sense at all of a completely negative concept. (I shall discuss briefly below Kant's attempt to distinguish concepts from Ideas.) Given Kant's account of concepts, how can we so much as have the "concept of a noumenon." Concepts are of objects of possible experience; the defining characteristic of a "noumenon" is that it cannot possibly be experienced. Moreover, both "object" and "possibility" are a priori concepts of the Understanding according to Kant, inapplicable beyond the bounds of possible experience. Indeed, how can we even make sense of the notion of "bounds" of possible experience. We seem to need to be both within and beyond our own experience, simultaneously.

Hegel was one of the first to raise these obvious questions. He writes, in the *Encyclopaedia*:

The Thing-in-Itself [and under "thing" is embraced even Mind and God] expresses the object when we leave out of sight all that consciousness makes of it, all its emotional aspects, and all specific thoughts of it. It is easy to see what is left, – utter abstraction, total emptiness only described still as an "other-world" – the negative of every image, feeling and definite thought. Nor does it require much penetration to see that this *caput mortuum* is still only a product of thought, such as accrues when thought is carried on to abstraction unalloyed: that it is the work of the empty "Ego," which makes an object out of this empty self-identity of its own. The *negative* character-istic which this abstract identity receives as an *object*, is also enumerated among the categories of Kant, and is no less familiar than the empty identity aforesaid. Hence one can only read with surprise the perpetual remark that we do not know the Thing-in-itself. On the contrary there is nothing we can know so easily.[8]

One way to think of this attack by Hegel on the central conception of Kant's critical philosophy is that it is an accusation of *incoherence*. If what Kant is asserting were true, it would follow that Kant could not be in a position to assert it. A more recent critical vocabulary might find these moments in Kant's works to be examples of textual self-deconstruction. (Perhaps it should be noted that, for this latter characterization to be illuminating, or revelatory about *this* text, it must not be the case that this characterization fits all texts.) Hegel does go on to state:

This ... will show how a limit or imperfection in knowledge comes to be termed a limit or imperfection, only when it is compared with the actually-present Idea of the universal, of a total and perfect. A very little considera-tion might show, that to call a thing finite or limited proves by implication the very presence of the infinite and unlimited, and that our knowledge of a limit can only be when the unlimited is *on this side* in consciousness.[9]

Our question later will be whether Hegel can work out a coherent alternative to the Kantian view that he here criticizes.

Kant, of course, does attempt to work out an account of how we can have concepts whose application goes beyond the bounds of possible experience. Such concepts are crucially necessary for his entire project in the critical philosophy of denying *knowledge* in order to make room for *faith*. If Kant is to be in the position of asserting that, for example, the existence of God, or the existence of human freedom is *possible*, at the same time that he is asserting that knowledge of the existence of God, or of the existence of human freedom is *impossible*, then there must be some way that he can make sense of the concept of "God" or the concept of "freedom." He attempts this in the "Transcendental Dialectic" in the chapter called "The Transcendental Ideas." I will not attempt to discuss this attempt in any detail, but I do want to quote a passage from it which, once again, I believe shows the internal strains of the position Kant is attempting to hold.

I understand by idea a necessary concept of reason to which no corresponding object can be given in sense-experience. Thus the pure concepts of reason, now under consideration, are *transcendental ideas.* They are concepts of pure reason, in that they view all knowledge gained in experience as being determined through an absolute totality of conditions. They are not arbitrarily invented; they are imposed by the very nature of reason itself, and therefore stand in necessary relation to the whole employment of the understanding. Finally, they are transcendent and overstep the limits of all experience; no object adequate to the transcendental idea can ever be found within experience. If I speak of an idea, then as regards its object, viewed as an object of pure understanding, I am saying a *great deal*, but as regards its relation to the subject, that is, in respect of its actuality under empirical conditions, I am for the same reasons saying *very little* ... The absolute whole of all appearances – we might thus say – *is only an idea*; since we can never represent it in image, it remains a *problem* to which there is no solution.[10]

One can, perhaps, sympathize with Hegel's impatience with Kant when reading such a quotation. This may be one of the points at which Kant's vast Baroque architectonic, inherited from the rationalist metaphysical tradition, is at odds with his critique of that tradition. Certainly this passage is, on the face of it, extremely difficult to reconcile with the conclusions of the Transcendental Analytic. Speaking of a transcendental idea one is simultaneously saying both a great deal and very little; the transcendental idea of the whole of all appearances is both crucially important and "only an idea"; it is a problem, but one without a solution. Kant hopes to justify this doublespeak by reference to his distinction between phenomena and noumena, but that is the very issue at question – whether we can make sense of *that* distinction.

Now, perhaps, we can trace the connection between these moments in the first *Critique* and their consequences for issues crucial in the development of Romanticism. If we turn to Kant's treatment of issues that we call "aesthetic," we find it primarily in the *Critique of Judgment*, in the "First Part" of that work. We shall find our connection to the issue of the transcendent in his discussion of the "sublime," and before we look at that discussion we should recall the absolutely central role that this concept plays in Romanticism in all the arts. Here again Kant is reformulating an older philosophical issue (especially as it had been discussed by Edmund Burke) to create another "Copernican revolution" in philosophy. It is not surprising that there should have been a proliferation of accounts of the sublime in England given the background of introspective empiricism there. What was wanted, by that tradition, was an account of the conditions under which the feeling of the sublime was experienced, and an account of the feeling itself. The sublime shared with beauty the newly established distinguishing feature of aesthetic response, *viz.* disinterestedness, but it was the *difference* between beauty and the sublime which was of interest to the earlier theorists. Beauty was generally thought of as gentle and harmonious while more powerful emotions were thought to be evoked by the sublime. Edmund Burke associated the sublime with pain, danger, and terror. All of this is, of course, familiar to students of Romanticism, as is the fact that it was left to Kant to attempt to provide a philosophical understanding of the sublime within the framework of his critical philosophy.

Kant's initial characterization of the sublime as different from the beautiful is, "The beautiful in nature is connected with the form of the object which consists in having [definite] boundaries. The sublime, on the other hand, is to be found in a formless object, so far as in it or by occasion of it *boundlessness* is represented, and yet its totality is also present to thought."[11] This passage immediately connects Kant's discussion of the sublime to the problems of those passages from the first *Critique* quoted above. Already we see involved in the notion of the sublime "boundlessness" or lack of form, and totality. There seems to be an obvious problem here of the possible coherence of these terms – how can the boundless achieve totality? We can also recall the passage about the transcendental ideas, quoted above, in which Kant characterizes them as, "concepts of pure reason ... [which] view all knowledge gained in experience as being determined through an absolute totality of conditions ... [and which are] transcendent and overstep the limits of all experience." The issue of "totality" shows that the theme of a limit to reason from the first *Critique*, which raised the question of from what point of view such a limit can be drawn, is relevant to what Kant wants to say about the sublime.

The problem of the coherence of "boundlessness" and "totality" becomes especially obvious in Kant's account of the mathematical sublime which he begins by stating, "We call that *sublime* which is *absolutely great*."[12] The term "absolutely great," however, must be an oxymoron, for all that is great is great by comparison to something else. Kant, of course, understands this perfectly well, and, hence, attempts throughout section 25 of the *Critique of Judgment* to distinguish the "absolutely great" of the sublime from the "great" which is a term always applied relative to some norm of a particular class, or concept. Hence of the former term he writes, "we soon see that it is not permissible to seek for an adequate standard of this outside itself, but merely in itself. It is a magnitude which is like itself alone. It follows hence that the sublime is not to be sought in the things of nature, but only in our ideas."[13] (Again, it should be noted that the concept of "a magnitude which is like itself alone" ought to be recognized as self-contradictory by Kant.) Here Kant marks the crucial step taken by his discussion of the sublime as compared to previous theorizing on the subject. What is important for us is that he has changed the concept of the sublime from being a property of certain kinds of grand or terrifying scenes in nature (and, secondarily, of being a property represented or evoked by objects imitative of such scenes) to its being a property of the way in which human consciousness relates to some of its objects:

Nature is therefore sublime in those of its phenomena whose intuition brings with it the idea of its infinity ... As this, however, is great beyond all standards of sense, it makes us judge as *sublime*, not so much the object, as our own state of mind in the estimation of it ... We hence see also that true sublimity must be sought only in the mind of the [subject] judging, not in the natural object the judgment upon which occasions this state.[14]

When we experience the sublime, our imagination must, inevitably, fail to represent what we seek to represent, since that is without form, and is limitless. Hence there is according to Kant an inevitable conflict between imagination and reason, and our awareness of this conflict is at the heart of the feeling of the sublime. It is this that constitutes our awareness that something transcends our mind's capacity to grasp it. All that we can imagine or know is conditioned, but the concept of the conditioned seems to require the concept of the unconditional. We, of course, can never *experience* the unconditional according to Kant, but we can become aware that we are *not* experiencing the unconditional. Curiously, in this account, the feeling of the sublime is engendered by our awareness of the limitation of our faculties. "The feeling of our incapacity to attain to an idea *which is a law for us* is *respect* ... the feeling of the sublime in nature is respect for our own destination, which by a certain subreption, we attribute to an object of nature (conversion of respect for the idea of humanity in our own subject into respect for the object)."[15] Here we see again the essential step of Kant's Copernican revolution in philosophy – the assertion of the constitutive activity of the mind in the production of a phenomenon (in this case, the feeling of the sublime) which we mistakenly ("by a certain subreption") take to be something (a thing in itself) which is totally independent of us. It is the incapacity which is inherent in human faculties which paradoxically provokes our awareness of what lies beyond our capacities. The idea of the absolutely incognizable object, (the thing in itself, and the transcendental ego) with its corollary of the impossibility of a totally reflective self-consciousness lies at the heart of the sublime.

Before turning to Hegel, let me briefly summarize what seems to me the core difficulty of the Kantian position. When we focus on his central distinction between phenomenon and noumenon, and the limitation of possible knowledge to phenomena, it becomes very difficult to see how a mind with this limitation could have ever formulated the distinction; the very formulation, it seems, must have escaped the limitation. This seems to me the essence of the Hegelian objections, quoted above, to Kant. This issue now is whether Hegel, having made this criticism, can formulate a coherent alternative to Kant, having accepted that the fundamental mode of human existence is knowing.

II

The aspects of the unknowable transcendental ego – the self – that Kant most stresses in the early part of the *Critique of Pure Reason* are its unity, and its limitation by the horizon of possible experience. He conceives of the forms of apperception (space and time) and the a priori principles of the understanding as fixed and unchanging. In other parts of his philosophical work, he acknowledges the power of culture and education in the formation of the individual human being, but we can know of the effects of these forces only on the self as represented to ourselves – in our own case or in the cases of others.[16] Hence, while Kant holds that there is an unavoidable duality of the self and the self-as-represented-to-itself (between the transcendental unity of apperception and the phenomenal self), he also holds that the a priori forms of consciousness hold unchangingly of the unitary self. If the development of the critical philosophy can be taken as a clue, these synthetic a priori forms of consciousness constitute our most fundamental mode of being toward the world. (They cannot quite be our fundamental mode of being-*in*-the-world according to Kant.) No doubt a full account of Kant would have to modify this claim in the light of the second and third *Critiques*, but we shall now turn to Hegel to consider the ways in which the concept of the self as it is developed in his philosophy differs from the Kantian notions we have been exploring, and whether his conclusions about the possibility of knowledge constitute a viable alternative to Kant's.

In discussing Hegel's general position on these issues, I shall concentrate on some passages from the *Phenomenology of Spirit* and ignore the general exegetical and philosophical questions about the place of this work in his philosophy as a whole. Perhaps it would be best to begin with a brief characterization of some differences between Kant's and Hegel's conceptions of their philosophical projects as well as of their philosophical views. Hegel's own description of the *Phenomenology* begins, "This volume deals with the *becoming of knowledge*. The phenomenology of the spirit is to replace psychological explanations as well as the more abstract discussions of the foundation of knowledge."[17] This already provides a significant contrast with Kant, for although there might be a "becoming" of empirical knowledge for Kant, there can be no "becoming" of synthetic *a priori* knowledge. One of the crucial features of Hegel's opposition to Kant in the *Phenomenology of Spirit* is his addition of the notion of dialectical development to the concepts and categories of human self-understanding. That book constitutes Hegel's first attempt to write the history of the human spirit coming to self-consciousness. Kant had attempted to set a limit to the power of reason to know – a limit beyond which lay the absolutely incognizable object which reason could never know, and beyond which lay the self (transcendental ego) which could never know itself. An alternative to this Kantian position would be to claim the possibility of a perfect coincidence of reflection and reality – something which might be phrased as "the real is the rational." This, of course, is the alternative which Hegel explores throughout his mature philosophy. However, what I describe as a "possibility" must be, for Hegel, the product of a process – the process of the history of spirit coming to self-consciousness mentioned above. This is a notoriously difficult process to describe, for the description can only be given from the point of view which results from the process. The phenomenologist, at each point of the *Phenomenology*, must have already reached the end of the process which is in progress at that point. Hegel deals with this difficulty in the "Preface":

The True is the whole. But the whole is nothing other than the essence consummating itself through its development. Of the Absolute it must be said that it is essentially a *result*, that only in the *end* is it what it truly is: and that precisely in this consists its nature, viz. to be actual subject, the spontaneous becoming of itself.[18]

Hegel immediately considers the offense which will be caused by the notion that the Absolute is a *result*, since this seems to be radically opposed, for example, to both any traditional theistic view, and also to something like a Kantian transcendentalism, but he suggests that the offense rests on a mistaken notion of mediation which assumes that the process of development must be different from the result. Hegel, however, claims that:

mediation is nothing beyond self-moving selfsameness . . . It is reflection that makes the True a result, but it is equally reflection that overcomes the antithesis between the process of its becoming and the result, for this becoming is also simple, and therefore not different from the form of the True which shows itself as *simple* in its result; the process of becoming is rather just this return into simplicity. Though the embryo is indeed *in itself* a human being, it is not so *for itself*; this it only is as cultivated Reason, which has *made* itself into what it is *in itself*. And that is when it for the first time is actual. But this result is itself a simple immediacy, it is self-conscious freedom at peace with itself, which has not set the antithesis on one side and left it lying there, but has been reconciled with it.[19]

I have quoted this passage at length because it seems to me to set the problematic of the whole Hegelian philosophy in the *Phenomenology*. On the one hand, there is an end-state, or a result, which is the Absolute actualized. On the other, self-consciousness at every stage of this process prior to the final reconciliation necessarily fails to know itself. Hegel's official position on the self – that it can reach a state of total self-reflection – is indeed the antithesis of Kant's position in the critical philosophy. For Hegel, there is no incognizable object – no Kantian thing in itself – nor is there an aspect of the self which necessarily transcends all the self's efforts to bring it into consciousness. However, at every historical moment prior to that final resolution, the self is alienated from itself. The dialectical movement of this process occurs, because at each stage there arises an awareness that the current forms of thought are inadequate; that they generate questions which cannot be answered by accepting them as they are. Thus at each stage there is a skepticism about current ideas and opinions which leads to their negation:

The scepticism that is directed against the whole range of phenomenal consciousness on the other hand, renders the Spirit for the first time competent to examine what truth is. For it brings about a state of despair about all the so-called natural ideas, thoughts, and opinions, regardless of whether they are called one's own or someone else's ... The necessary progression and interconnection of the forms of the unreal consciousness will by itself bring to pass the *completion* of the series ... the *goal* is as necessarily fixed for knowledge as the serial progression; it is the point where knowledge no longer needs to go beyond itself, where knowledge finds itself, where Notion corresponds to object and object to Notion. Hence the progress towards this goal is also unhalting, and short of it no satisfaction is to be found at any of the stations on the way.[20]

It is only because of this goal that the movement through these stages of skeptical despair by the spirit is progressive. Short of the goal, however, every movement is partial and brings the spirit to a new form of alienation (a form which may be judged to be *higher* by its relation to the goal.)

The obvious question at this stage is: how is the stage of Absolute knowing to be distinguished by the consciousness experiencing it from all the states of partial knowing? From the perspective of Absolute knowing, every (previous) historical moment and conceptual scheme is partial, but may possess a false consciousness that does not know itself as partial. If this is so, it is difficult to see how the supposed "Absolute knowing" can avoid the historicist fate of all other historically arrived at intellectual positions, namely that it is *its* period's form of self-understanding, but that it will in turn be overcome. (That this was the fate of Hegel's system is not exactly established by the fact of post-Hegelian philosophical history [which Hegel would have had to have believed had been foreclosed by his work; hence, such philosophical "history" would have to be based on misunderstandings of his thought] but such must seem its fate to any non-Hegelian.) Hegel could, of course, claim that there is something intrinsic to the state of Absolute knowing which allows it to be self-verifying which no other state of consciousness, according to him, can be. However, it is hard to see how such a claim could be more than what Kant calls dogmatism. (As a brief aside, I might mention that this problem seems to me to be the essence of what Kierkegaard, through the pseudonym Johannes Climacus, urges against Hegel in the *Concluding Unscientific Postscript.*[21])

However, if we question the possibility of a state of Absolute knowing within the Hegelian schema of the "becoming of knowledge" a new problem arises. The alternative seems to be some form of historicism – the option known to some historians of this era as "dialectics without the system." What I mean by "historicism" in this case involves a thoroughgoing relativism such as that espoused by Karl Mannheim. This would accept the Hegelian notion that all of our categories and concepts, along with our social practices and institutions, are historically conditioned – changeable and changing – but deny that there is a *result* of this process, a privileged end-state. While we have seen the possible problems for the notion of a state of Absolute knowing, this historicist alternative seems to have its own problems. Historicism itself, formulated as I have done above, seems to face the charge of incoherence. Either it is itself a historically conditioned thesis, or it is not. (1) If it is, then it is merely an expression of our present state of self-understanding about the possibility of knowledge. Such "present states" have always been, and continue to be, liable to revision, and to being surpassed. (2) However, if it is not itself a historically conditioned thesis, then it is self-refuting. The historicist thesis itself would escape historicism.

To put this latter argument in terms of the "self," historicism seems to accept the claim that alienation of the self from itself is inevitable at every historical stage. However, if the thesis of historicism is true and known to be true, then the self would have achieved complete self-consciousness about its possibility for knowledge and have overcome its self-alienation. In this form, the argument looks rather like Hegel's argument quoted above against the Kantian notions of a limitation to reason, and the thing-in-itself. That too seemed to amount to the charge that these positions of Kant are self-refuting.

I do not want here to commit myself to the claim that these arguments against historicism, as I have characterized it, are successful. These issues are complex, but I do want to use these thoughts to characterize the reciprocal dialectic between a Kantian and a Hegelian position on the possibility, and extent, of knowledge in order to understand the matrix of issues out of which both Romanticism in the arts, and philosophy in the nineteenth century (and the twentieth) develop. What has emerged from the discussion so far looks suspiciously like a Kantian antinomy. Either one opts for the absolutely incognizable object, and the self which cannot know itself, as Kant did, or one opts for Absolute knowing and the totally self-reflective self, as Hegel did. One emblematic expression of this radical disagreement between Kant and Hegel can be seen in their responses to the night sky. Kant famously wrote, "Two things fill the mind with ever new and increasing admiration and awe, the oftener and more steadily we reflect on them: the starry heavens above me and the moral law within me."[22] Hegel, perhaps less famously, was standing at a window next to Heine on a beautiful starry evening and responded to a remark of the young poet about the beauty of the heavens by saying, "The stars, hum! hum! the stars are only a gleaming leprosy in the sky."[23] For Kant, the starry sky above both represents what can be known, and leads the mind to what lies beyond knowledge. It is the quintessential experience of the sublime. For Hegel, the view of the heavens represents the end-lessness of what he called the "bad infinite." Indeed, in the anecdote retold by Heine, Hegel goes on immediately to disparage Heine's hope for an afterlife of moral reward which had been evoked by the poet's view of the stars – a reminder that the core of Kant's project of limiting knowledge was in order to make room for faith, and that for Hegel (as Kierkegaard aptly claimed) there simply was no room for faith at all.[24]

III

I have suggested that the difference between Kant and Hegel on the issues we have been discussing looks like a Kantian antinomy. Let me now make that explicit. On the one hand, we have Kant's position asserting the existence of an absolutely incognizable object. We have explored the problematic of this position at length; can the very idea of a "thing-in-itself" be coherently formulated from within Kant's philosophy? It would seem that Kant's account of the limita-tion of *knowledge* to possible experience ought to limit *meaning* to possible experience. On the other hand, we have Hegel's denial of an absolutely incognizable object, but this too seems to be an inherently unstable position if we work within the Hegelian dialectic – whether we believe that there can be a position of absolute knowing or not.[25] However, these two positions appear to be exhaustive. The normal Kantian procedure in attempting to resolve an antinomy is to show that both of the positions which are opposed to each other share something in common, which can be rejected, and that they are, thus, not exhaustive. (Of course, Kant in the resolution of the antinomies which he discusses deploys the very noumenal/phenomenal distinction which is here at issue.) Perhaps what is problematic here is the concept of "absolute knowledge" – which is denied by Kant, and asserted by Hegel. What seems to be needed is a new conception of knowledge, or perhaps, of the role that knowledge, and knowing, play in the structure of the self. From the time of Descartes' philosophy, most of the philosophers of the enlightenment sought foundations of knowledge, and sought to extend the scope of reason. Kant wrote, *"Sapere aude!* 'Have courage to use your own reason!' – that is the motto of enlightenment."[26] Both Kant and Hegel, however, severely altered the foundational project. Kant, in a sense, provided foundations for empirical knowledge, but that was only a part of his project, for the very form of his foundations for empirical knowledge set a limit to knowledge while showing us that there was a reality beyond the empirical which we could not know. Hegel thought that one reached the functional equivalent of foundations only at the end of the process of knowing, not at the beginning; it was only from the perspective reached in the end-state that Absolute knowing was possible. Nonetheless both of them seem to be implicated in the Enlightenment project to the extent that they were committed to a concept of "pure" reason. (I mean here not just Kant's technical conception of "pure reason," but more generally any notion of a reason apart from, and not irrevocably embedded in, our physical and cultural existence – any notion of an "absolute" reason.) Clearly any reconception of reason, and its place in human existence, is simultaneously a reconception of the self. Stanley Cavell has written of Kant's

> effort to make room for faith by, so to speak, limiting faith; to deny that you can experience the world as world, things as things, face to face as it were, call this the life of things. About the victory Kant declared over skepticism by negotiating away the possibility of knowing the thing in itself, one will sometimes feel: Thanks for nothing ... If experiencing the life of things is another expression for a feeling for what Kant calls the unconditioned then it is an experience, in Kant's terms, of the sublime.[27]

Here, I believe, Cavell comes close to the heart of many of the responses to Kant. We have already looked at Hegel's response in some detail, but even a figure as radically different in metaphysics from Hegel as Schopenhauer also could not abide the idea of the Kantian limit: rather than a triumph over skepticism, it seemed a surrender to it. What I want to do now is to look briefly at some examples of the convergence of a number of themes which we have considered which emerge after the impasse of reason reached in what I have called the reciprocal dialectic of the Kantian and Hegelian positions. The themes that I have in mind are: (1) the idea that reason is not the most fundamental mode of human being in the world but that something else, variously characterized as practice, doing, passion, feeling, etc., is; (2) the idea that there is a kind of division in the self, so that one may not know oneself fully (an idea something like that of the unconscious); (3) the idea that the individual self is not a given entity, but a goal to be sought in a process, potentially progressive, in which the self constitutes itself (an idea expressed in the subtitle of Nietzsche's *Ecce Homo* – "How One Becomes What One Is"); (4) the idea that certain experiences, which might be described as moments when the self-as-it-would-be transcends the self-as-it-is, provide intimations of the directionality of this process – and that these experiences fit comfortably under the rubric of the sublime; (5) the fact that many of the subsequent authors who express these themes do so, not in traditional (Descartes to Hegel) philosophical forms, but in other literary genres – essays, fictions, parables, polemics, pseudo-scriptures, etc. I shall not attempt an exhaustive account of any of this convergence in even a single post-Kantian/Hegelian thinker, but I would like at least to gesture toward this constellation of issues in certain moments of Emerson's texts, and to suggest that it can also be found in Kierkegaard and Nietzsche. To appropriate Nietzsche's terminology, the question for each of these thinkers when confronted with the impasse of reason is: how can nihilism be avoided?

Before discussing the Emersonian examples, I should clarify one point of vocabulary. I have classified Emerson as one of those thinkers who hold that "reason is not the most fundamental mode of human being in the world," even though Emerson places tremendous emphasis on "Reason" in *Nature* and other texts. We can see Emerson's use of the term "Reason" explained in a letter he wrote to his brother on May 31, 1834:

Do you draw the distinction of Milton, Coleridge, and the Germans between Reason and Understanding? I think it a philosophy itself, and like all truth, very practical. Reason is the highest faculty of the soul, what we mean often by the soul itself: it never *reasons*, never proves; it simply perceives, it is vision.[28]

The key here is that Reason never reasons. What is fundamental for Emerson is not what achieves knowledge, in the ordinary sense of "knowledge," nor is it reason in the ordinary sense of "reason." It is conceived as underlying "reason" in the ordinary sense. Perhaps what Emerson conceived it to be will become clearer as we turn to some passages from his work.

My first example is from Emerson's *Nature*, and may be the most famous passage of all the famous passages in his writing. I begin, however, as Emerson began his essay, with a reminder of what he means by "nature." This reminder locates us squarely in the problematic of German Idealism which we have been investigating. "Philosophically considered, the universe is composed of Nature and the Soul. Strictly speaking, therefore, all that is separate from us, all which Philosophy distinguishes as the NOT ME, that is both nature and art, all other men and my own body, must be ranked under this name, NATURE."[29] Well, strict speaking of this kind was never very appealing to Emerson, and he does not remain long within the boundaries of this definition. It is clear, however, from this comment that he is using the term "nature" for what Kant calls the phenomenal world, which includes the self-as-represented-to-the-self. But Emerson seeks to transcend the Kantian limit. Here is the key passage:

> In the woods, we return to reason and faith. There I feel that nothing can befall me in life – no disgrace, no calamity (leaving me my eyes), which nature cannot repair. Standing on the bare ground – my head bathed by blithe air and uplifted into infinite space – all mean egotism vanishes. I become a transparent eyeball; I am nothing; I see all; the currents of the Universal Being circulate through me; I am part or parcel of God.[30]

Surely we have here the experience of the sublime (of Reason with a capital "R"); perhaps we might even charge Emerson with exemplifying the Egotistical Sublime, but this is a charge he explicitly rejects. It is worth noting that, in this exaltation, the "eyeball" which is transparent becomes the "I" which is both "nothing" and also at the same time sees. The passage reminds us of the end-point of the Hegelian dialectic since it suggests a coincidence of subject and object which for Hegel would be the state of absolute knowing. However, for Emerson, this moment of the most extreme self-awareness is not a moment of knowing (in the ordinary sense) at all; it is a moment of feeling.

I want to try to work out Emerson's view of the relationship between self and world in terms of one of his favorite concepts –

that of the "horizon" – in order to continue the comparison of his view to Kant's and Hegel's. Shortly after the passage quoted above, Emerson writes, "In the tranquil landscape, and especially in the distant line of the horizon, man beholds somewhat as beautiful as his own nature."[31] Of course, the infusion of self into landscape is a topos of Romantic thought, but I believe something more than a standard version of this is going on here. I would like to follow out Emerson's invocation of the "line of the horizon" and its relationship to the human being's "own nature." A horizon has a number of features worth contemplating. First, and perhaps most obvious, when I do contemplate "the" horizon, what I contemplate is a function of my own placement in the world; it literally marks the limits of my present vision. The notion of the horizon as an idea of the mind has long been a popular one. A second feature of the "line of the horizon" is less often remarked; this is that the horizon line is not present in a great deal of our visual experience. One needs to attain a position of a certain visually unobstructed distance from what is seen in order to become visually aware of the limit to vision. (This distance can, normally, only be attained outdoors, or, perhaps by contemplating the outdoors from within a building.) Finally, though a horizon marks a limit, and though our visual field when extended to its maximum must have a horizon (so that there *must* be something which lies beyond my present visual field), it does not follow that there is any particular something which must always be beyond our vision. We are capable of changing our placement in the world. To adapt a phrase of Stanley Cavell's, the necessary limitations of vision are not failures of it. Why is the line of the horizon a figure for Emerson of the mind's horizon? Perhaps this is because the horizon permits the closure required by individual finitude, while at the same time permitting the awareness that even the potentially infinite movement of the horizon will always leave something beyond it.

Return for a moment to the "transparent eyeball" passage. In its claimed coincidence of subject and object it seemed to offer a non-epistemological version of Hegel's absolute knowing, but the figure of the line of the horizon modifies this. In fact, Emerson is not just interested in the exaltation of "Reason," but in the dialectic of exaltation and ordinariness, and the possibility of finding exaltation in ordinariness. He writes of this at length in his essay, "The Transcendentalist," which presents itself as an attempt to make known to his fellow New Englanders the views of those known as transcendentalists. Emerson does *not* claim that name for himself, but rather expresses his own characterization of some young people known to him, who, he believes, are commonly misunderstood. (It is impossible not to think that Emerson is describing Thoreau when one reads this essay.) The essay begins with a little sketch of the two "sects" into which mankind as thinkers have ever been divided as "Materialists and Idealists."[32] Not surprisingly, this is his version of that Kantian view of *his* predecessors which we have considered above. Emerson argues that the dialectic of the relationship of materialism to idealism (idealism here under the name of "transcendentalism") is such that "there is no pure Transcendentalist."[33] What the transcendentalist cannot avoid are her or his own doubts and objections to idealism. The moments of exalted awareness, such as Emerson himself had described, cannot be sustained. "These two states of thought diverge every moment, and stand in wild contrast. To him who looks at his life from these moments of illumination it will seem that he skulks and plays a mean, shiftless and subaltern part in the world."[34] He goes on to discuss the back and forth movement of these states of consciousness:

The worst feature of this double consciousness is, that the two lives, of the understanding and of the soul, which we lead, really show very little relation to each other: never meet and measure each other; one prevails now, all buzz and din; and the other prevails then, all infinitude and paradise; and with the progress of life the two discover no greater disposition to reconcile themselves.[35]

This "double consciousness" seems to me to be Emerson's way of characterizing the continuing process of becoming what one is; the unity of the process is the unity of the self but that very unity is constituted by continuing alteration so that what we have are relations of self-succession.[36] The self continually constitutes and reconstitutes itself. The issue is whether Emerson – having neither the notion of the Kantian stable, though unknowable, self nor the Hegelian confidence in the necessity of the process reaching a result which is embryonically present in it from the beginning – can avoid a total skepticism about values. Is it possible, with this conception of the unfinished self, to find a value which can guide, or evaluate, this process? Emerson claimed in "Self-Reliance," "I have my own stern claims and perfect circle. It denies the name of duty to many offices that are called duties. But if I can discharge its debts it enables me to dispense with the popular code. If any one imagines that this law is lax, let him keep its commandment one day."[37] But of course this "law" is essentially unstateable. What Emerson is indicating is the unendingness of the dialectic of the "double consciousness" which incorporates both our particular finitude-now, and the always present possibility of transcending *that* particular finitude-now. The acknowledgment of human finitude must also recognize that a mode of the activity of that finitude has involved the attempt to transcend itself. (The denial of the human is a characteristic feature of the human.) I think that Emerson is getting at this when he writes of a new picture of life and duty that it "will comprise the skepticisms as well as the faiths of society, and out of unbeliefs a creed shall be formed. For skepticisms are not gratuitous or lawless, but are limitations of the affirmative statement, and the new philosophy must take them in and make affirmations outside of them, just as much as it must include the oldest belief."[38]

Both Kierkegaard and Nietzsche seem to me to be illuminatingly categorizable with Emerson in this project, though I have no space to attempt to work that out in detail here. They all are recognizable as a part of the broad current of anti-foundationalism in post-Hegelian philosophy – a current wide enough to include Kierkegaard and Marx, Nietzsche and Peirce, Heidegger and Wittgenstein, Quine and Derrida. All of these very disparate thinkers face a similar problem: how, consistent with their various rejections of the tradition of Western philosophy, to be in a position to formulate and state their own views consistently. Kierkegaard and Nietzsche are particularly striking in the variety of literary forms in which they choose to present their views. One might choose to say that what these post-Hegelian thinkers are criticizing is a particular conception of reason which developed in Western philosophy in the Enlightenment and which came to grief in Kant and Hegel in the ways I have described. They agree that an *intellectual* response to the impasse of reason is inadequate. What is needed is not just a better concept of reason, but rather an acknowledgment of what it is to be a human being. This may suggest why Emerson, Kierkegaard, and Nietzsche do not write philosophical treatises, or dissertations, but work in journals, essays, stories, sermons, poems, aphorisms, or in an unclassifiable form like that of *Also Sprach Zarathustra*.

Jacques Derrida mentions a number of the major critiques of the concepts of the philosophical tradition – Nietzsche's of metaphysics, Freud's of self-presence, and Heidegger's of the determination of Being as presence – and writes of them:

171

all these destructive discourses and all their analogues are trapped in a kind of circle. This circle is unique. It describes the form of the relation between the history of metaphysics, and the destruction of the history of metaphysics. There is no sense in doing without the concepts of metaphysics in order to shake metaphysics. We have no language – no syntax and no lexicon – which is foreign to this history; we can pronounce not a single destructive proposition which has not already had to slip into the form, the logic and the implicit postulation of precisely what it seeks to contest.[39]

Derrida seem to me to be here describing what I have earlier called the impasse of reason which I have characterized by reference to the Kantian and the Hegelian critiques of the philosophical tradition. It is exactly the search for that language which Derrida says is impossible that unites the projects of Emerson and Kierkegaard and Nietzsche. In each case this involves the complex reconciliation of a number of themes about the self – that knowing is not the most basic mode of human being; that human being is finite and limited; that nonetheless it involves a continuing process of self-overcoming, and that this process while not infinite is itself without a limit. The representation of the self to itself always fails to achieve total self-comprehension, but there is no particular stage of the self which cannot be represented to itself. The mind's horizon is essential for the existence of *a* self. This is what Nietzsche is saying in the following which shall be the final word here:

let us be on guard against the dangerous old conceptual fiction that posited a "pure, will-less, painless, timeless knowing subject"; let us guard against the snares of such contradictory concepts as "pure Reason," "absolute spirituality," "knowledge in itself" ... There is *only* a perspective seeing, *only* a perspective "knowing"; and the *more* affects we allow to speak about one thing, the *more*, eyes, different eyes, we can use to observe one thing, the more complete will our "concept" of this thing, our "objectivity," be. But to eliminate the will altogether, to suspend each and every affect, supposing we were capable of this – what would that mean but to *castrate* the intellect?[40,41]

Notes

1 Philip Lacoue-Labarthe and Jean-Luc Nancy, *The Literary Absolute*, (Albany: State University of New York Press), p. xiv.
2 *Ibid.*, p. 29.
3 *Ibid.*, p. 30.
4 Immanuel Kant, *Critique of Pure Reason*, trans. Norman Kemp Smith (London: Macmillan & Co., 1961), p. 635.

5 *Ibid.*, p. 137.
6 *Ibid.*, p. 22.
7 *Ibid.*, pp. 272–273.
8 *The Logic of Hegel*, William Wallace trans. (Oxford University Press, 2nd edn) p. 72.
9 *Ibid.*, p. 92.
10 Kant, *Critique of Pure Reason*, pp. 318–319.
11 Immanuel Kant, *Critique of Judgment* (New York and London: Hafner Publishing Co., 1966), p. 82.
12 *Ibid.*, p. 86.
13 *Ibid.*, p. 88.
14 *Ibid.*, pp. 94 and 96.
15 *Ibid.*, p. 96.
16 For a fine discussion of Kant on culture see: Salim Kemal, *Kant and Fine Art* (Oxford: Clarendon Press, 1986), chapter 3.
17 Walter Kaufmann, *Hegel: Texts and Commentary* (Garden City, NY: Doubleday Anchor, 1966), p. 4.
18 G. W. F. Hegel, *Phenomenology of Spirit*, trans. A. V. Miller (Oxford University Press, 1977), p. 11.
19 *Ibid.*, pp. 11–12.
20 *Ibid.*, pp. 50–51.
21 S. Kierkegaard, *Concluding Unscientific Postscript* (Princeton University Press, 1941), especially in the section "An Existential System is Impossible," pp. 107ff.
22 Immanuel Kant, *Critique of Practical Reason*, trans. Lewis White Beck (Indianapolis: Bobbs-Merrill, Library of Liberal Arts, 1956), p. 166.
23 Walter Kaufmann, *Hegel: A Reinterpretation* (Garden City, NY: Doubleday Anchor, 1966), pp. 366–367.
24 Kierkegaard, of course, writes in this vein in many places in many works. One such reference is in S. Kierkegaard, *Fear and Trembling*, translated by Alastair Hannay, (London: Penguin Books, 1985), pp. 96–97.
25 There is a nice brief discussion of the inherent instability of the Hegelian concepts in Alasdair MacIntyre, "Existentialism," reprinted in *Sartre: A Collection of Critical Essays*, ed. Mary Warnock (Garden City, NY: Doubleday Anchor, 1971,) pp. 11–12.
26 Immanuel Kant, *Foundations of the Metaphysics of Morals* and *What is Enlightenment?*, trans. Lewis White Beck (Indianapolis: Bobbs-Merrill, Library of Liberal Arts, 1959), p. 85.
27 Stanley Cavell, *In Quest of the Ordinary* (University of Chicago Press, 1988), p. 53.
28 Quoted in Paul E. Boller, Jr., *American Transcendentalism, 1830–1860: An Intellectual Inquiry* (New York: G. P. Putnam's Sons, 1974), p. 50.
29 *Selections from Ralph Waldo Emerson*, ed. Stephen E. Wicher (Boston: Houghton Mifflin, 1957), p. 22.
30 *Ibid.*, p. 24.
31 *Ibid.*, p. 24.

32 *Ibid.*, p. 193.
33 *Ibid.*, p. 196.
34 *Ibid.*, p. 203.
35 *Ibid.*, p. 204.
36 This topic is discussed under the heading of "Emersonian Perfectionism" in Stanley Cavell, *Conditions Handsome and Unhandsome* (University of Chicago Press, 1990), especially in the Introduction and in chapter 1.
37 Wicher, *Selections*, p. 161.
38 *Ibid.*, p. 269.
39 Jacques Derrida, *Writing and Difference* (University of Chicago Press, 1978), pp. 280–281.
40 Friedrich Nietzsche, *Genealogy of Morals*, in *Basic Writings of Nietzsche*, ed. Walter Kaufmann (New York: Random House, The Modern Library, 1968), p. 555.
41 Certain passages in this paper are based on an earlier paper of mine, "The Lined Horizon: the Sublime as Figure," delivered at the conference, *Romantic Revolutions* at Indiana University in 1988. I hope that in the revision of those passages I have profited from the sympathetic and helpful remarks made on that occasion by my commentator, Richard Eldridge.

8

Kant, Hölderlin, and the experience of longing

RICHARD ELDRIDGE

There is a natural and reasonable temptation to try to find or ground morality within common human life. If moral commandments cannot be lived out there, then what good are they, and why ought we to allow ourselves to be tyrannized by them? So either, it seems, we must show how a culture of justice or freedom or respect is achievable in accordance with one of these high ideals, or we must give them up in favor of more modest balancings of values that are not so categorical. Does not "ought" imply "can"?

Yet it may be not so easy quite to do what seems so natural and reasonable. Is it possible not reasonably to care about freedom or justice or respect, and not also to regard this care as higher or deeper, more woven into our humanity, than a liking for pistachio ice-cream? Our sense of the pull of certain high ideals on us, a pull that involves our humanity, may be not so easily stilled. But then it is not so obvious either how to achieve a culture of justice or freedom or respect, particularly in advanced technological cultures with significant divisions of labors and class antagonisms. What pieces of institutional design or state policy or individual habitual action could possibly lead to universal justice, freedom, or respect?

It is this sense of the human person as caught between an aspiration toward the ideal and also the standing defeat of that aspiration that is expressed or released in the texts of Kant and Hölderlin, as well as in other major Romantic writers, German and English. Within major Romantic and Idealist texts, literary and philosophical, German and English, the struggles of protagonists, real and implied, to come to terms with both the categorical appeal of high ideals and the difficulties of achieving them are traced. The activity imagined for these protagonists itself emerges as a kind of *poiesis*, an effort imaginatively to take up present routes of cultural

activity and to redirect or resignify them in at least partial further-
ance of the ideal. Or so, at any rate, it may emerge when Kant and
Hölderlin are read through or against one another.

I

It is nowadays little realized and less appreciated first that Kant's
philosophical project was essentially *descriptive*, and second that in
his descriptions Kant dwells above all on human reason's difficulties
and perplexities, as though reason were at odds with itself and as
though our lives, in which we exercise our rational capacities, were
opaque to us, tangled. But that is, mostly, what Kant says. "Human
reason," he famously tells us in launching his project of critique, in
the *Critique of Pure Reason*'s first sentence, "is burdened by questions which, as prescribed by the very nature of reason itself, it is not
able to ignore, but which, as transcending all its powers, it is also not
able to answer" (Avii).[1] Thus "human reason precipitates itself into
darkness and contradictions" (Aviii).

The project of critique, to be sure, aims at undoing these contradictions and illuminating the darkness. The critique of pure reason
is to serve as "a tribunal which will assure to reason its lawful
claims, and dismiss all groundless pretensions, not by despotic
decrees, but in accordance with its own eternal and unalterable
laws" (Axi–xii). That is, the critique of pure reason will sort out the
principles that we are entitled to assert – "All events have a cause;"
"An unchanging quantum of substance underlies all changes of
appearance;" "As beings with practical reason we must treat all
beings with practical reason not as means only, but always also as
ends" – from speculative claims that are empty, that are *not*
ineluctably woven through our lives as conscious and self-conscious
beings – claims such as "God is the providential first cause and
orderer of nature;" or "My soul is a self-identical, simple, and
indestructible substance." In this way, by sorting principles into
"lawful claims," on the one hand, and "groundless pretensions," on
the other, the critique of pure reason will enable us to escape from
both *despotic dogmatism* and *anarchic skepticism* (Aix) into self-
assured self-responsibility in our practices, as we live by the principles that have survived critique.

This, at any rate, is the ambition of the Critical Philosophy. We are
to become reasonably responsible under and to contentful and
secure principles we cannot help but have in our cognitive, moral,

and aesthetic practices, freed alike from attachment to false idols, empty principles, and overmastery by an anarchic, arbitrary otherness. This same image of the *task* of reason or its criticism in aiming at reasonable self-responsibility betweeen empty idolatry and anarchic skepticism also massively informs the English philosophic and poetic traditions, as it figures centrally in the texts of both Hume and Wordsworth.[2]

Is this ambition fulfilled? Are our perplexities and contradictions undone by critique's tribunal in sorting principles? It is not so clear. Certain anxieties or worries about human responsibilities persist in Kant's texts. Instead of being resolved, they are continually rearticulated. Problems supposedly solved in the *Critique of Pure Reason* or the *Foundations of the Metaphysics of Morals* recur, particularly in the *Critique of Judgment*. Principles supposedly justified and woven into our practices as self-conscious beings are re-queried. What is my place in the world of nature as a rational, moral being? How can I express in action in nature my nature as a free, rational, noumenal being standing under moral principle? If I can't do that, or can't do so stably and securely, so that every act I undertake is a test of my rational nature, of whether it can sustain itself in the world and whether the world will allow this, then do I really know myself as a free, rational, noumenal being, possessed of a form of continuous, apperceptive self-consciousness rooted in noumenal activity? Is the world of phenomena that appears to my apperceptively unified consciousness really there for me, stably ordered under causal laws no matter what, if the consciousness to which that world appears might fail to sustain itself in coherent action? What awareness of the apperceptive unity of my consciousness enabled me to follow out the threads of transcendental logic? Can that awareness falter? Can apperceptive unity falter? How was or is critique possible at all?[3]

These questions are raised in the *Critique of Judgment* as Kant attempts to put the parts of his system – phenomena and noumena, nature and freedom – back together again, to find, as he puts it, "a ground of the *unity* of the supersensible that lies at the basis of nature, with what the concept of freedom contains in a practical way."[4] That is, there must be something behind or under natural phenomena and also behind or under my rational free will. There must be a unity between these supersensible somethings that enables and guarantees all at once my continuing, apperceptively unified consciousness and self-consciousness, the presentation to that consciousness of a stably ordered phenomenal world under a system of laws that is not a hodgepodge, and, most importantly and directly, my ability to act as a rational being, commanded by moral principle, *in that world*: causality by freedom "is to take effect in the world" (*CJ*, 37). How?

It may seem that this characterization of Kant's project runs together topics that ought to be kept apart. What do the problems of my own self-consciousness and of knowledge have to do with the problems of the formula and requirements of the moral law, or with the problem of the justification of judgments of taste? Kant, after all, devoted three separate *Critiques* to these problems. Surely his main insight is that we just are as self-conscious beings committed to certain principles of understanding that describe an order among phenomena present to us, and we just do regard ourselves as free insofar as we stand under a moral law. Surely it would be better, and more in the Kantian spirit, simply to explicate and elucidate these separate epistemological and moral principles, avoiding all this nonsense about freedom in the world. As Kant notoriously said in his open letter on Fichte's *Wissenschaftslehre*, in response to Fichte's effort to develop a metaphysical system upholding freedom in the world, "May God protect us from our friends, and we shall watch out for our enemies ourselves."[5] Why not back to description, explication, and critique, away from the metaphysics of freedom in nature?

The trouble with this anti-metaphysical line of thought – dominant in Kant's contemporary Anglo-American reception – is that it is belied by certain passages in Kant's major texts, where Kant himself connects the topic of apperceptively unified self-consciousness with that of standing under the moral law, as he worries about the place of the rational subject in the natural world. Here are two such passages:

Man, however, who knows all the rest of nature solely through the senses, knows himself also through pure apperception; and this, indeed, in acts and inner determinations which he cannot regard as impressions of the senses. He is thus to himself, on the one hand, phenomenon, and on the other hand, in respect of certain faculties the action of which cannot be ascribed to the receptivity of sensibility, a purely intelligible object. We entitle these faculties understanding and reason. The latter, in particular, we distinguish in a quite peculiar and especial way from all empirically conditioned powers. For it views its objects exclusively in the light of ideas ... Reason does not here follow the order of things as they present themselves in appearance, but frames for itself with perfect spontaneity an order of its own according to ideas, to which it adapts the empirical conditions, and according to which it declares actions to be necessary, even although they have never taken place, and perhaps never will take place ...

Now in view of these considerations, let us take our stand, and regard it as at least possible for reason to have causality with respect to appearances.

(A546–7=B574–5; A548=B576)

In this passage we see a characteristic Kantian transition from claims about self-consciousness to claims about our powers as moral beings. I must regard myself as an intelligible object, as spontaneously and transparently able to formulate and apply certain rules, for example to say "this is a chair." My seeing of objects is rule-governed in a way that is transparent to my consciousness. I not only have chair-stimuli, as it were, I am also aware of myself as seeing a chair, as subsuming that object under certain sortal rules freely and transparently.[6] And it is this very freedom or spontaneity, evident in the transparently rule-governed empirical judgments of a self-conscious being and constitutive of its apperceptive unity, that at the same time is the source of the moral law. This spontaneity "frames an order of its own according to ideas," responding to or instancing something higher than the ways of the natural, phenomenal world and legislating for action in that world. Thus, as the *Critique of Practical Reason* continues, "I have this right [to accept the existence in me of noumenal causality, a causality of freedom with the moral law as its determining ground], by virtue of the pure nonempirical origin of the concept of cause."[7]

To be sure, I can regard myself as a noumenal cause only insofar as I deliberate about how I ought to act. I cannot understand theoretically what in nature or ultimate reality makes me such a being. "We have thought of ... man as belonging to a pure intelligible world, though in this relation man is unknown to us."[8] But there is at least this much. I transparently follow rules in making empirical judgments. Certain rules – the concepts of events as caused, of qualities as pertaining to substances – are necessary for there to be any empirical judgments at all. Adherence to these rules brings it about that my consciousness is judgmental and apperceptively unified. These rules are themselves freely created: there is no experience of causality or substance. And whatever freely creates those rules – reason, or spontaneity, or pure understanding stimulated by reason – distinguishes me from all merely natural beings and legislates for my actions in the world, yet in ways that are ultimately mysterious to me. I do not know how or why I am both a free, noumenal agent and an embodied, natural being.

So can I really sustain these beliefs about myself that apparently force themselves on me? What if physiological psychology advances in tracing the motions of my body back to complicated neurochemical causes? What if my culture does not make sense, so that nothing I do seems readily to evince or express freedom and practical rationality? Suppose things seem just to happen. How is freedom to "take effect in the world"? My awareness of myself as a unified self-consciousness, possessed of a moral dignity born of reason's spontaneity, seems to fade. Maybe it is all just an illusion.

This is, I think, the deep anxiety that is latent in Kant's extraordinary wanderings back and forth between claims about what we must presuppose (we have apperceptively unified consciousnesses; we are free) and claims about ultimate and impenetrable mysteries (the interaction of phenomena and noumena, nature and freedom; our opacity to ourselves as both natural and freely rational beings). And it is this deep anxiety that comes to the fore in the *Critique of Judgment* and in the historical and anthropological essays. It is the presence of this anxiety in Kant's texts, his mode of responding to it, though never quite stilling it, and its refiguration in his successors – English and German, philosophical and poetic – that launches and defines Romanticism. This anxiety, together with certain ways of responding to it, is as definitive of human life as anything is, according to these texts. We are beings who are caught between aspirations to realize our dignity and free rationality in a transparent, harmonious culture, aspirations we can't it seems, give up, and the defeat of these aspirations by nature and culture as they stand, even as we can imagine recasting them. So we are caught in anxiety. Are our aspirations, capacities, and possibilities genuine, or not? How might we make sense of ourselves as having something to live up to?

Kant's way of responding to these questions is exemplary. When he came in the *Critique of Judgment* and in the historical and anthropological essays explicitly to confront the problem of *how*, in what manner, self-conscious self-identity, morality, and freedom could be expressed in a stable, receptive world, what Kant mostly did was to produce imaginative narratives of the past and future of human culture. The function of these narratives is to uncover the existence of a human capacity, practical reason, as that capacity has been dimly, partially, exercised in practice, thence to suggest that the full, self-conscious exercise of that capacity may inaugurate a perfected culture, a kingdom of ends, in which all human beings reciprocally respect, attend to, and practically love all human beings, without coercion.

Roughly, Kant's imaginative narrative of humanity's progressive development and realization of its capacities goes like this.[9] Originally human beings are creatures of sensation and animal instinct. They then begin to use their reason to make comparisons among things, perhaps preferring some foods to others, and further acquiring new, artificial desires through imagining satisfactions, rather than merely pursuing them instinctively. Having these artificial desires and no longer being dominated by instinct, human beings "become aware of what it means to choose,"[10] become conscious of their negative freedom. Arising out of this consciousness of freedom comes an awareness of one's life in time and of a need to work and to plan. Human beings become aware of, and come to fear, their own death, and they take rational pains to avoid it. But this is not the end of the story. Through the use of reason, "the human being becomes aware, however obscurely, that he is the end of nature."[11] This awareness of oneself as an end, and of all rational beings as ends, is then imagined to drive two further developments. Initially we are to establish a rational state, "a universal civic society which administers law among men."[12] This civil society is not, however, the final end of our development. It is rather the necessary framework and precondition for our further development of a kingdom of ends, a rational community in which our ends "are brought systematically into harmony by reason as reciprocal end and means, like the interdependent organs of a living thing."[13] Achieving this harmonious culture of rational freedom, a moral culture beyond politics and the enforcement of rights within competition, is the work of Enlightenment, "man's release from his self-incurred tutelage."[14] Kant regards his own philosophical writing as advancing this work, helping to free us from tutelage or service to our animal nature so as to achieve collective rational freedom. His articulation of the principle of morality is to help to move us first to found a liberal state and then further, through culture, to bring our ends into rational harmony with one another.

This advance toward freedom first through politics and then through culture is not, however, the work of philosophy alone. Art has a crucial role to play in this development. "Fine art ...," Kant writes, "has the effect of advancing the culture of the mental powers in the interests of social communication" (*CJ*, 166). The work of art, in blending sublime, natural *originality*, the "primary property" of genius, "the innate mental aptitude *through which* nature gives the rule to art" (*CJ*, 168) with sense, intelligibility, and the crafting of material serves as an exemplar of embodied freedom in the world and a spur to its further development. In taking up "something of a compulsory character ... or, as it is called, a *mechanism*," that is, the demand to craft material intelligibly, original artists embody the soul, which otherwise "would be body-less and evanescent" (*CJ*, 164) ("gar keinen Körper haben und ganzlich verdunsten würde").[15] "The poet essays the task of inter-preting to sense the rational ideas of invisible beings, the kingdom of the blessed, hell, eternity, creation, & c. Or, again, as to things of which examples occur in experience, e.g. death, envy, and all vices, as also love, fame, and the like, transgressing the limits of experi-ence he attempts with the aid of an imagination which emulates the display of reason in its attainment of a maximum, to body them forth to sense with a completeness of which nature affords no parallel" (*CJ*, 176–177) ("in einer Vollständigkeit sinnlich zu machen, für die sich in der Natur kein Beispiel findet").[16] The poet's work thus shows us that the embodiment of rational ideas, including the idea of freedom, is possible. The poet's work thus both locates us as beings for whom the project of constructing a culture that fully embodies rational freedom is possible and ad-vances that very project. It embodies, expresses, and advances our aspirations as rational beings, and in doing so it "binds up language, which otherwise would be mere letters, with spirit" (*CJ* 179, modified) ("mit der Sprache, als bloßem Buchstaben, Geist ver-bindet").[17] The poet's work, one might say, makes our sayings and doings intelligible as ours. Rather than standing as mere material happenstances, they become legible to us in the poet's high achievement as vehicles of our possibilities for freedom, rooted in our rational humanity or Spirit. We can, as it were, see our humanity in them.

This is in many ways a wonderful story. But how much reassur-ance about our capacities and possibilities does it provide? Do we now know ourselves as possessors of rational freedom, able to manifest that freedom in a harmonious moral culture? As thus rehearsed, this story smacks of what Dostoyevsky stigmatized as Schillerizing – blathering about the achievement of moral culture through artistic activity. (In fairness to Schiller, the essays on the sublime and on naive and sentimental poetry are a lot tougher than the *Letters*, show more awareness than the *Letters* of the tendency of art in modernity to deepen antagonisms rather than to smooth things over;[18] and even in the *Letters* there is a crucial incoherence that undoes Schiller's imagination of progress, as he wavers between saying that artistic activity is merely instrumental to the emergence of a moral culture and saying that it is rather an end it itself, as though he can't quite really envision a definite path to the end of history.) What is wrong with Schillerizing?

In the first place, it scarcely requires much perceptiveness to notice that Kant's narrative of our realization of our capacities has not in fact come true. Bitterness, antagonism, envy, competitiveness, violence, and domination are conspicuously more the stuff of our lives than reciprocity and harmonious rational freedom. Nor did Kant fail to notice this. The imaginative narrative of our progress in realizing our capacities that he produces is merely conjectural in its treatment of the past. With regard to the present it is merely an ideal that should govern the writing of more specific histories and inform our present political efforts. "Conjectures cannot make too high a claim on one's assent. They cannot announce themselves as serious business, but at best only as a permissible exercise of the imagination guided by reason."[19] Conjectural narrative is not intended by Kant to be evidently true as things stand, nor to provide any *justification* of our ascription to ourselves of rational capacities and self-legislated moral principles. Officially, those ascriptions are secured by the arguments of the first two *Critiques*, and the remarks about freedom in history and art are mere playings out of possibilities established elsewhere.

Unofficially, Kant's argumentative itinerary suggests, these later narratives *are* epistemically crucial. In taking up the topic of *how* freedom is to appear in the world, they literalize and develop an anxiety about our capacities that was already latent in earlier swerves between claims about our awareness of a noumenal spontaneity and its deliverances in us and claims about what we must presuppose in so far as we already accept the idea that we have overriding, categorical obligations.

But this reading scarcely makes things better. If we have no secure prior warrant for ascribing certain capacities and possibilities to ourselves, but instead need the imaginative historical narratives in order to make such ascriptions plausible, then why narrate the history that way, with that ideal, in the face of the obvious facts of misery and domination? Just who do we think we are?

Kant himself, to repeat, was aware of the obvious facts of history. Recall that the imaginative historical narrative of our progress is a story of the progressive development of our rational nature out of our animal nature – a kind of second birth – through the setting up of competitive, artificial desires. The birth pangs here are considerable. Kant's general name for the energy or power that drives this development and shapes all of culture is *antagonism*:

The means employed by Nature to bring about the development of all the capacities of men is their antagonism in society, so far as this is, in the end, the cause of a lawful order among men. By "antagonism" I mean the unsocial sociability of men, i.e. their propensity to enter into society, together with a mutual opposition which constantly threatens to break up the society ... This opposition it is which awakens all [man's] powers, brings him to conquer his inclination to laziness, and, propelled by vainglory, lust for power, and avarice, to achieve a rank among his fellows whom he cannot tolerate but from whom he cannot withdraw.[20]

Thus art, while embodying our soul and rational freedom, will also embody conflict, vainglory, lust for power, and avarice. The ideal narrative of our possible achievement is a narrative also of the struggle of our nature against itself. The picture of human nature as it expresses itself in history is neither naturalistic, despairing, and Hobbesian–Nietzschean, nor optimistic, blandly utopian, and apolitical, as certain strains in Rousseau and Marx are. It is rather what Allen Wood calls a "deeply moralistic conception of the human condition, which makes it axiomatic that human beings are capable of living with one another on decent terms only when their natural desires and dispositions are under quite strict constraint (if not forcible external constraint, then rational self-constraint)."[21] Every exercise of power or virtue, every act of originality or courage or kindness or justice or love that we might look to as advancing our culture, will be at the same time marked by vainglory and antagonism. The virtues, the powers that might advance culture, are not clearly harmoniously compossible among us. History is the record of their exercise under and often contributing to relations of domination. Yet it makes sense to hope for their compossibility, to struggle against our own vainglory in the hope of achieving a harmonious kingdom of ends, even if we can't see how. "Nature," Kant tells us, "reveals something, but very little"[22] of the path toward a kingdom of ends. And yet we are also drawn toward it. Or so, at least, Kant's story would have it.

II

Here then are two beliefs that seem inescapable. We do not live in a moral culture or kingdom of ends, but instead in a world of antagonism, vainglory, and domination, without any clear sense of how to inaugurate a moral culture. Yet we also believe – something in us, something that among other things expresses itself in art, seems to make us believe – in the dim possibility of a kingdom of ends, believe that things will ultimately make sense, that the virtues are compossible, that all things might express their natures harmoniously, that life is not all and only power against power, nature against nature.

Narratives, or at least rich ones, explore how it is that we live with both beliefs, in the space, one might say, of tragedy, not self-sufficient in our power to inaugurate a moral culture, but not dispossessed of the aspiration to do so either. As Jean-Pierre Vernant and Pierre Vidal Naquet put it,

The tragic sense of responsibility arises when human action becomes the subject of a reflection, a debate, but has not yet acquired a status autonomous enough to be self-sufficient. The proper domain of tragedy is situated in a frontier zone where human actions come to be articulated with divine power, and it is in that zone that they reveal their true sense, a sense not known to the agents themselves, who, in taking on their responsibility, insert themselves into an order between men and gods which surpasses the understanding of man.[23]

The working out of this tragic sense of responsibility, as we are caught between the demands of rational freedom and the difficulties of antagonistic historical life, is tracked or traced in narrative, which investigates *how* these demands and difficulties might be reconciled. Narrative will be, one might say, the necessary scrutiny of our powers and possibilities of rational freedom and moral culture as they bump up against the facts of antagonism in history, those powers and possibilities never quite disappearing, but never quite receiving full realization either.

What is it like to live in such a way, to inhabit such a narrative or to hold together narratively one's sense of possibilities of rational freedom in a moral culture with one's sense of the immediate and standing ways of the world? It is this sense of human life that is powerfully expressed in Hölderlin's elegies and in particular in "Dichterberuf," "The Poet's Vocation."[24] Many of Hölderlin's lyrics center around the persistence of longing, as the poet simultaneously seeks to envision a transfigured, moral culture of freedom and reciprocity emerging out of the ashes of the old and confronts the non-emergence in fact of such a culture. His sense of himself as a bearer of rational humanity, one who has a soul to be materially embodied in culture, is tied to his ability to envision narratively a transfigured culture, so that when that envisioning falters in the face of the ways of the world, so does the poet's sense of his own identity and power. Yet the faltering is never quite complete, never quite a collapse into complacency either, never quite a rejection of aspiration and a sense of possible power in favor of the naturalist, Humean thought that all we can do is act on the basis of desires and projects that we happen naturally to have, so that we would do well to break with high aspirations and become honest eaters, drinkers, and compromisers with the world. Hölderlin never rests in such a thought. Instead the lyrics close only in ambiguous, highly charged ways, with a sense still of possible powers not yet housed in, or attached to, any definite course of culture. "And let me say at once / That I approached to see the Heavenly, / And they themselves cast me down, deep down /Below the living, into the dark cast down / The false priest that I am, to sing / For those who have ears to hear, the warning song. / There"[25] "As on a holiday ..." ends. The poet's sense of power, identity, and cultural possibility is further bound up with a sense of obscure divinity in or around us, waiting to be realized, but never quite present here, so that the poet's investigation of genuine but blocked possibilities of poetic power and moral culture in history is at the same time an investigation of the possibility of a religious human life, a possibility never definitely heralded, but always longed for. Hölderlin is thus pre-eminently the poet of what Schiller called "*elegy* in the narrower sense," wherein nature and the ideal are an object of sadness," as nature "is treated as lost" and the ideal "as unattained."[26] The persistence of the elegiac tone in Hölderlin's texts produces a peculiarly intense strangeness in them, a kind of inexplicable unparaphrasability. His work is, as Eric Santner puts it, "a site where the contradictions, stresses, longings, and disenchantments that scar our own modern selves are passionately rehearsed."[27]

Hölderlin's peculiarly intense elegiac tone or manner or substance has been submitted to a number of explanations in literary history. Santner suggests that Hölderlin's thought might be explained in Oedipal terms as stemming from the lack of a "successfully internalized ... father as idealized totemic figure."[28] For Santner, building on Lacan, it may be that only "identification with the figure in whose names these [Oedipal] taboos were instituted in the first place"[29] can enable one to work through grief and mourning at the loss of the mother, so as to achieve an integrated self and reasonable desire. Since Hölderlin lacked such a father-figure – his father died when Hölderlin was two; his stepfather when he was seven – he is condemned to an eternal "search for viable paternal totems"[30] throughout his life and work.

Or, following Weber and Benjamin, it may be modernity's fault. In dividing life up into separate spheres of knowing through science, acting morally and politically, attending aesthetically to art, working for a wage, and consuming, the self is torn apart by the incoherence of the routines of life offered in modernity. J. M. Bernstein, drawing on Weber and Habermas, suggests that the modern art object expresses mourning for a lost integrated society and longing for its recovery. This mourning and longing result, he claims, from "a double isolation": first, "the diremption of the question of moral value from questions of truth and falsity – the fact/value distinction – that resulted from the growth of modern science and its methodological self-understanding; and secondly, the separation of artistic worth from moral worth – the inscribing of art within the autonomous domain of the 'aesthetic'."[31] Hölderlin's work is here cast as a symptom of modernity's political pathology, in contrast with the comparative healthy integrity of premodern societies then ruptured by science and technology.

Or it may be that Hölderlin's elegiac longing stems from a simultaneous covert awareness of and repression of the agonies of political life that is typical of the bourgeoise.[32] What the bourgeoisie, which generally does *not* suffer much under a market economy, prefers to see as individual longing or alienation that is open to aesthetic suasion is really a retrogressive attempt to displace and deny a material anger rooted in class oppression of agricultural and industrial laborers. On this reading too, Hölderlinian longing would disappear were class consciousness and politics to develop explicitly, and this longing is itself a bourgeois indulgence that inhibits that development.

Or it may be that Hölderlin's longing itself contains or intimates its own cure, as Heidegger suggests. "The poet," Heidegger writes in considering Hölderlin, "names the gods and names all things in that which they are. This naming does not consist in something already known being supplied with a name; it is rather when the poet speaks the essential word, the existent is by this naming nominated as what it is ... The essence of poetry is the establishing of being by means of the word.''[33] For Heidegger, the experience of longing that is expressed in Hölderlin's poetry is open to cure through a more attentive, patient, poetry that hearkens to Being in such a way that it can point to the refiguration of culture and its existents. And indeed Heidegger sees this hearkening and pointing as already underway in Hölderlin's work. Resoluteness in this hearkening and pointing is all that is needful.

Or it may be that Hölderlin's longing expresses the inextricable entanglement of human consciousness with language, something in its essence conventional and hence barred from satisfactory engagement with the natural, as de Man suggests in his radically anti-Heideggerian reading:

> Poetic language seems to originate in the desire to grow closer and closer to the ontological status of the object, and its growth and development are determined by this inclination. We saw that this movement is essentially paradoxical and condemned in advance to failure ... The word is always a free presence to the mind, the means by which the permanence of natural entities can be put into question and thus negated, time and again, in the endlessly widening spiral of the dialectic.[34]

For de Man, the entanglement of human consciousness and desire in the conventionality of language that is always exterior to Being casts human subjects as *êtres pour soi* always vainly seeking to be also *êtres en soi*, and Hölderlinian Romantic longing is the exemplary expression of this unavoidable desire.

Each of these explanations has considerable interest and plausibility. Yet Hölderlinian longing in fact encompasses and synthesizes each of these cruder reductions of it. Would it help to cure us of such longing if we all somehow had happy relationships with our fathers or father-figures? Were pre-modern societies in fact free of alienation and fragmentation, or are these phenomena, as Marx suggests, already primordially present with the rudest forms of division of labor and simply exacerbated in modern society? Could we return to or inaugurate an integrated society beyond the antagonisms that seem fearfully part of the stuffs of our identities? Would we even want to? Would a class politics help to do this? Or will class politics itself be an activity in part of individuals responding competitively to shared conditions? Would we be better off politically to conceive of our aspirations as divergently determined by various class experiences, rather than as shaped in part by our nature's struggle with itself?

So the reductive psychological and political readings of Hölderlinian longing seem too optimistic, seem not to see how much this longing runs through what we are. Heideggerian resoluteness seems no more likely to cure this condition than do psychoanalytic therapy or class politics. But de Man's reading of our ontological exteriority to reality as conscious *êtres pour soi* entangled with language seems to cast us as victims of something, to counsel quietude, and to deny the political and psychoanalytic dimensions of our condition that we might address. If the political cannot cure us, then neither ought we to flee from or deny it. What then is the character of our longing, and how ought we to come to terms with it?

Here we may dwell on just how Hölderlin expresses it. It is clear that Hölderlinian longing, for all that it also has psychoanalytic, political, and ontological dimensions, directly expresses a moral aspiration and anxiety: a sense of the possibility of a moral culture, and of finding one's own identity and power in prophesying and contributing to its inauguration, coupled with a sense of being blocked by culture as it stands from any immediate route toward this cultural transfiguration. Hölderlin has this to say about his aspirations in a letter of 1793 to his half-brother Karl Gok:

My affections are now less directed toward particular individuals. The object of my love is the entire human race, though not, of course, as we so often find it, namely in a condition of corruption, servility, and inertia ... I love the race of coming centuries. For this is my deepest hope, the faith that keeps me strong and vital: our grandchildren will have it better than we, freedom must finally come, and virtue will better flourish in the warmth of freedom's sacred light than in the ice-cold zone of despotism ... This is the sacred purpose of my wishes and my activity: that I might stir the seeds of change that will ripen in a future age.[35]

And here is what he has to say two years later, in a letter to Schiller, about his frustration in his hopes. "I am frozen and numb in the winter that is all around me. The heavens are as iron, and I am as stone."[36] These remarks are expressions of Kantian–Schillerian aspirations to realize one's rational dignity and freedom in a transfigured moral culture, to secure one's identity in contributing as a poet to the transfiguration of culture, and of awareness of the deadness and inertia of culture as it stands in embodying antagonisms. This aspiration and this awareness are all at once ontological, political, psychological, moral, and quasi-religious.

We can trace how these dimensions of aspiration and frustration are woven together in "The Poet's Vocation," "Dichterberuf," as a

189

Richard Eldridge

Romantic elegy. What picture of our halting progress and of the poet's role in it does it develop?

The poem opens with the sense that once, in prehistory, nature and the divine interacted, preparing a place for a humanity not yet on the scene. "Shores of Ganges heard the paean for the god / Of joy when Bacchus came, conquering all, / Young, from the Indus" (1–3). There is, in nature's reception of the god, as it were a second, higher nature within nature. It is the task of the god to rouse humanity from its merely instinctive, natural existence, into an awareness of some- thing higher, an awareness that is dimly embedded in its nascent self-consciousness. Bacchus came "with holy wine / Rousing the people from their slumber" (3–4). This arousal or first awakening to self-consciousness takes place, the reference to Bacchus suggests, through ritual, not just because we have intentionality somehow wired into our minds one by one.

This first arousal through ritual to self-consciousness is not, however, complete. An "angel of our time" is needed to arouse us further,[37] to "Give the laws, / Give life to us" (6–7), to enable us now fully to realize our higher nature in a moral culture of free, reciprocal recognition and attention under moral law. The appearance that is needed of the angel of our time is to take place neither through ritual nor through the ordinary routines of farming, hunting, and house- keeping, in which we reason, and are aware of ourselves as reasoning, but only instrumentally. "Not the thing that is man's care and skill / Inside a house or underneath the sky" (9–10) shall now further awaken us, albeit that these cultural routines are more than animal activities: "a man fends and feeds more nobly / Than animals do" (11–12). Nor will it help simply to love and care for others, unless we first learn what it is to love and care for a human being, and for human beings with opposed interests, rather than for a pet.

It is instead poets who are suited for the highest, "Der Höchste, der ists, dem wir geeignet sind" (14). Dedicated to care and service of the highest, poets are ever anew through their singing to enable friendly hearts to take it in, "Daß näher, immerneu besungen / Ihn die befreun- dete Brust vernehme" (15–16), thus enabling the higher birth throughout the people of a transfigured culture that is responsive to the highest.

So far, in stanzas 1 to 4, this is the optimistic side of the more or less standard Kantian–Schillerian story of the development of a fully human culture out of nature through a first birth of the human in ritual and a second birth through the poet's work in expressing the highest. There now occurs, however, a complicated extended

190

apostrophe, occupying all of stanzas 5 to 7, as the poet addresses successively "you heavenly gods / And all you streams and shores / hilltops and woods" (17–18) and "You deeds rampaging out in the wide world / You days of destiny, fast and furious" (25–26). The substance of this apostrophe, the independent clause asking a question of all the things addressed, does not begin until the first line of the eighth stanza. The effect of this extended, multiple, jumbled apostrophe, with all its images of violence –"by the hair one of you / Seized us" (19–20); "dumbfounding / the mind" ("stumm / Der Sinn uns wards") (22–23); "as if struck by lightning" (24); "rampaging out in the wide world" (25) – is to interrupt and block the imagination of the smooth completion of the poet's task. Something, it seems, is violently in the world, and perhaps in us, that the poets, for all their dedication and appointed work, cannot take up, engage with, and make use of as material to be transfigured into the life of a moral culture. If the gods come in this way – multiply, violently, rage-drunk, loosing deeds that cannot be held or gathered ("ruhelosen Thaten") – then what now is to be done? Should the poets then conceal, repress, or deny this violent way-wardness of the ways of the gods in the world? "Should we *not* speak of you?" "Euch sollten wir verschweigen?" (29). There seems in the face of the ways of the world no way to go on with the task of the poet. Art threatens to collapse into something idly aesthetic. The harmonies that poets are capable of seem condemned to idleness and impotence, seem destined only "to ring as if in idle caprice" ("Muthig und müßig" – brazenly and idly)/ Some child had dared to touch for fun ("im Scherz") / The master's consecrated and pure strings" (31–33).

This violent, incoherent culture in which art is reduced to the aesthetic is further a culture dominated by thankless consumptive-ness: "Too long all things divine have been put to use / Heavenly powers trifled away, mercies / Squandered for sport, thankless, a / Generation of schemers" (45–47). In the service of thankless, compe-titive consumptiveness, we name and number what is higher, thinking to make use of it by quantifying it, but therein missing its meaning. "The telescope scans and quantifies / And names with names the heaven's stars" (51–52). We make "the good ... / Play for a fee like a beast captive" (38, 40).

In a culture under the sway of entertainment, consumption, and instrumental reason, what place is there then for the poet? The poet's identity and sense of himself falter. The narrative shifts fully out of the envisioning of the poet's work and into the interrogation of present despair at an apparently impossible vocation. "Was it for this" ("darum hast du") (34), this present condition of impotent dejection, that the poet "heard the prophets of the East / And Greek song and lately ... / Voices of thunder" (34–36)? "Was it for this?" – the very question that launches Wordsworth's *Prelude* on its course when in Book I, line 273, Wordsworth turns from an overwhelming sense of failure and self-betrayal in his inability to find a high theme that will lend his poetry a serious life in culture, therein establishing his own poetic identity, to the activity of recollecting his halting growth in nature and culture.

And here too, as partly in Wordsworth, there is a partial recovery of a more modest sense of poetic power, rooted in gratitude and remembrance and in the abandonment of the wish to transfigure the entire culture in accordance with one's vision. After one has been left "unsouled" ("entseelt") (44) by the failure of the highest ambition to transfigure the whole of culture now by bringing forth the word, it is possible to close one's eyes, or have them covered with night, giving up one's highest hieratic ambitions. "And yet with holy night the father will veil / Our eyes, that still we may not perish" (53–54). An expansive, puffed up power can never force heaven. "Doch es zwinget / Nimmer die weite Gewalt den Himmel" (55–56). "Nor is it good to be too knowing" (57). Yet the submission of our wills and vision to the mysteries of nature, holy night, and the father, now letting culture to some extent go as our wills are chastened by our lack of clarity and vision, is not a lapse or reduction back into mere animality either. There is a work of thankfulness still to be undertaken, a preserving and containing (behält) (58) of what is higher in a more muted form. This work is not easily undertaken alone. "Yet to keep and contain it alone is a hard burden" (58–59). When alone, the poet's envisionings may become too grandiose and lead to madness. So "others the poet / Gladly joins who help under-standing" (59–60), thus ratifying and reinforcing one another's now muted powers and identities as those who respond more dimly and receptively, in gratitude not excessive pride, to what is higher. Yet even such pleas or prayers for joint work and understanding are, as pleas or prayers, reminders of present antagonisms. "Man stands ... lonely / Before God" (61–62). Hölderlin's highly charged, difficult, and ambiguous syntax further reminds us of his difference from us, making the poem an object that is resistant to any moralizing appropriation to some form of cultural work. His work is informed not by secure possession of divine power and knowledge of how to spread it through culture, but by God's fault or absence or lack ("Gottes Fehl" [64]).

Not then as prophets and installers of an accomplished moral culture, not in secure possession of an apocalyptic knowledge of last things, but protected by simplicity ("es schüzet die Einfalt ihn") (62), with neither weapons nor subterfuges (62), we may stand or persist, possessed of human identities, powers, and possibilities that are dimly responsive to what is higher, but veiled, and are not themselves divine. Thus we may stand, so long as God's being, but not being present, helps us in our human works, "so lange, bis Gottes Fehl hilft" (64). There[38]

Notes

1 Immanuel Kant, *Critique of Pure Reason*, 2nd edn., trans. Norman Kemp Smith (London: The Macmillan Press, Ltd., 1933), Avii, p. 7. All subsequent references to this work will be to this edition and will be given in the text by page numbers of 1781 first German edition [A] and 1787 second edition [B], given in the margins of Kemp Smith's English translation.

2 For a discussion of this image of the task of reason in English letters, and of the refiguration of reason away from deduction in the service of this task by Coleridge and Wordsworth, see my *On Moral Personhood: Philosophy, Literature, Criticism, and Self-Understanding* (University of Chicago Press, 1989), pp. 128–131; 106–116.

3 Frederick Beiser, in *The Fate of Reason: German Philosophy from Kant to Fichte* (Cambridge, MA: Harvard University Press, 1987), usefully takes this last question and the general problem of a "meta-criticism of reason" (p. 6) as his organizing theme in surveying Kant's various receptions from 1781 to 1793.

4 Kant, *The Critique of Judgment*, trans. James Creed Meredith (Oxford: Clarendon Press, 1928), p. 14. Subsequent references to the *Critique of Judgment* will be to this edition and will be given in the text by page number following "*CJ*."

5 Kant, "Open Letter on Fichte's *Wissenschaftslehre*, August 6, 1799," *Public Declarations*, 12, 6, 370–371; reprinted in Kant, *Philosophical Correspondence, 1759–99*, ed. and trans. Arnulf Zweig (University of Chicago Press, 1967), p. 254.

6 Robert Pippin, in *Hegel's Idealism: The Satisfactions of Self-Consciousness* (Cambridge University Press, 1989), pp. 16–24, usefully and lucidly discusses the connection between apperceptive self-consciousness and taking oneself to follow certain rules in making empirical judgments.

7 Kant, *Critique of Practical Reason*, trans. Lewis White Beck, (Indianpolis: The Bobbs-Merrill Company, Inc., 1956), pp. 57–58.

8 *Ibid.*, p. 52.

9 In rehearsing Kant's narrative of history, I draw not only on Kant's essays "Idea for a Universal History from a Cosmopolitan Point of View" (1784), trans. Lewis White Beck, and "Conjectural Beginning of Human History" (1786), trans. Emil L. Fackenheim, both in Kant, *On History*, ed. Lewis White Beck (Indianapolis: The Bobbs-Merrill Company, Inc., 1963), but also on Allen Wood's elegant and insightful reading of Kant's anthropological and historical works in his "Unsociable Sociability: The Anthropological Basis of Kantian Ethics," *Philosophical Topics* 19: 1 (Spring 1991), 325–351.

10 Wood, "Unsociable Sociability," p. 330.

11 Wood, "Unsociable Sociability," p. 330; citing Kant, "Conjectural Beginning," p. 59.

12 Kant, "Idea for a Universal History," Fifth Thesis, p. 16.

13 Wood, "Unsociable Sociability," p. 343.

14 Kant, "What is Enlightenment?" (1784); in Beck, ed. *On History*, p. 3.

15 Kant, *Kritik der Urteilskraft* (Frankfurt: Suhrkamp, 1974), p. 238.

16 *Ibid.*, p. 251.

17 *Ibid.*, p. 253.

18 "This leads me to a very remarkable psychological antagonism among men in a century that is civilizing itself: an antagonism that because it is radical and based on inner mental dispositions is the cause of a worse division among men than any fortuitious clash of interests could ever provoke; one that deprives the artist and poet of all hope of pleasing and affecting universally, as is their task; which makes it impossible for the philosopher, even when he has done his utmost, to convince universally: yet the very concept of philosophy demands this; which, finally, will never permit a man in practical life to see his course of action universally approved – in a word, an antithesis that is to blame that no work of the spirit and no action of the heart can decisively satisfy one class without for that very reason bringing upon itself the damning judgment of the other. This antithesis is without doubt as old as the beginnings of civilisation and is scarcely to be overcome before its end other than in a few rare individuals who, it is to be hoped, always existed and always will; but among its effects is also this one, that it defeats every effort to overcome it because neither side can be induced to admit that there is any shortcoming on its part and any reality on the other; despite this, it still remains profitable to pursue so important a division back to its ultimate source and thereby to reduce the actual point of the conflict at least to a simpler formulation." Friedrich Schiller, "On Naive and Sentimental Poetry," trans. Julias A. Elias, in *The Origins of Modern Critical Thought*, ed. David Simpson (Cambridge University Press, 1988), p. 171.

19 Kant, "Conjectural Beginning," p. 53.

20 Kant, "Idea for a Universal History," p. 15.
21 Wood, "Unsociable Sociability," p. 346. Though his general theme of
Kant's emphasis on our need to struggle with ourselves is surely right,
Wood may put the point slightly too strongly. Just as Kant pictures the
growth of culture as involving antagonisms that are slowly overcome as
we move toward rational harmony, it is possible to picture the development toward rational harmony within the person's set of desires as a
matter not simply of constraint or coercion, though not a matter of pre-
established harmony either, but rather as occurring through the tension-
laden but harmony-tending *education* or *Bildung* of desire by reason.
See the discussion of the relations of reason and desire in Kant's moral
psychology in my *On Moral Personhood*, pp. 41–47.
22 Kant, "Idea for a Universal History," p. 22.
23 Jean-Pierre Vernant and Pierre Vidal Naquet, *Mythe et tragédie en Grèce
ancienne*, vol. 1, cited in Bernard Williams, *Shame and Necessity*
(Berkeley: University of California Press, 1993); Williams' translation.
Like Williams, I reject Vernant and Naquet's progressivism and think
that we do *not* outgrow this sense of responsibility. All human life,
ancient and modern, is situated in this frontier zone. I would regard the
"debate" about how to "articulate" our actions "with divine power," a
debate in which no one can ever be a self-sufficient master, as a debate in
which we are caught up, here and now. See my "How Can Tragedy
Matter for Us?" *The Journal of Aesthetics and Art Criticism*, 52: 3
(Summer 1994), 287–298.
24 Friedrich Hölderlin, "Dichterberuf," "The Poet's Vocation," in Friedrich Hölderlin, *Hyperion and Selected Poems*, ed. Eric L. Santner,
trans. Christopher Middleton, (New York: Continuum, 1990),
pp. 152–157. All references to this poem, presented in both German
and English on facing pages in the Santner edition, will be given in the
text by line number.
25 Hölderlin, "Wie wenn am Feiertage …," "As on a holiday …," trans.
Michael Hamburger, in *Hyperion and Selected Poems*, pp. 195–196.
26 Schiller, "On Naive and Sentimental Poetry," p. 163.
27 Eric L. Santner, "Introduction," in Hölderlin, *Hyperion and Selected
Poems*, p. xxiv.
28 *Ibid.*, p. xxxiv.
29 *Ibid.*
30 *Ibid.*
31 J. M. Bernstein, *The Fate of Art: Aesthetic Alienation from Kant to
Derrida and Adorno* (University Park, PA: The Pennsylvania State
University Press, 1992), p. 2. Santner suggests a similar reading,
Hölderlin, pp. xxiii–xxiv, xxxv.
32 I have in mind here the kind of New Historicist criticism of English
Romanticism that has recently been produced by Marjorie Levinson and
John Barrell.
33 Martin Heidegger, "Hölderlin and the Essence of Poetry," trans. Douglas

Scott, in Heidegger, *Existence and Being: "The Four Essays"*, ed. Werner Brock (South Bend, IN: Henry Regnery Company, 1949), pp. 281–282.

34 Paul de Man, "Intentional Structure of the Romantic Image," *Revue internationale de philosophie* 51 (1960); reprinted in English, trans. de Man, in *Romanticism and Consciousness: Essays in Criticism*, ed. Harold Bloom (New York: W. W. Norton and Company, Inc., 1970), pp. 69, 70.

35 Hölderlin, "Letter, 1793, to Karl Gok," cited in Santner, "Chronology," in Hölderlin, *Hyperion and Selected Poems*, pp. xi–xii. Compare a letter of 1797: "I believe in a coming revolution in the way we think, feel, and imagine, which will make the world as we have known it till now grow red with shame" (p. xv).

36 Hölderlin, "Letter, 1795, to Schiller," *ibid.*, p. xiii.

37 Compare Wordsworth's similar usage of the image of arousal from sleep in outlining his own ambitions and sense of vocation in the "Prospectus" to *The Recluse*. "– and, by words / Which speak of nothing more than what we are, / Would I arouse the sensual from their sleep / Of Death, and win the vacant and the vain / To noble raptures;" from *The Recluse*, in Wordsworth, *Selected Poems and Prefaces* ed. Jack Stillinger (Boston: Houghton Mifflin Company, 1965), p. 46, lines 811–815.

38 Much of the thinking for this paper emerged out of teaching together with my colleague Hans-Jakob Werlen, to whom I am grateful for stimulation, encouragement, and conversation. An earlier draft was presented to the members of a 1993 NEH Summer Institute on Ethics and Aesthetics, directed by Charles Altieri and Anthony J. Cascardi; the discussion there led to significant improvements.

9

Wordsworth and the reception of poetry

MICHAEL FISCHER

Many contemporary literary critics distrust universals. By "universals," I mean here claims that something is necessary, natural, desirable, or reasonable for all people. Among the several developments contributing to this suspicion of universals, feminist criticism has played a major role. Feminist criticism first began making an impact on academic literary criticism in the 1970s partly because critics like Elaine Showalter, Sandra Gilbert, and Susan Gubar successfully argued that seemingly universal definitions of knowledge and aesthetic value were in fact slanted to fit the point of view and reward the social privileges of men. Debunking fraudulent universals went hand in hand with affirming the differences that these universals had kept in check. Anne Phillips describes the suspicion resulting from "these moves against transcultural, transhistorical, transcendent rationality":

after so many sightings of the "man" in humanity, many have come to view such abstractions as beyond redemption, and to regard any claims to universality as therefore and inevitably a fraud. Each candidate for universal status has presented itself in sharp contrast to the peculiarities and particularities of local identity, something that delves behind our specificity and difference and can therefore stand in for us all. But the "individual" turns out again and again to be a male household head, the "citizen" a man of arms, the "worker" an assembly line slave. Each gender-neutral abstraction ends up as suspiciously male.[1]

From this point of view, universals invariably function as smokescreens for male domination.

In my opinion, this assault on universals has enabled advances and brought problems. Among the advances, I would count broadening the canon to include writing denigrated by supposedly disinterested aesthetic criteria (such as the ambiguity, complexity, and irony championed by the New Criticism). Some of the problems, however, center around the loss of authority that the disenchantment with universals has left in its wake. Interestingly enough, this loss of authority first appeared as a problem when some women began applying to mainstream feminist criticism the same reasoning that feminist critics had been applying to the dominant culture. African-American writers in particular started challenging the right of white academic critics to speak for all women, even women of a different race and class, and lesbians similarly began contesting the right of heterosexual women to represent them. Much as pioneering critics like Showalter had smoked out the "man" concealed in humanity, African-American writers like bell hooks and lesbian critics like Barbara Smith suspected that white, middle-class, heterosexual women were controlling the definition of what it means to be a woman. Mainstream feminism began to seem as exclusionary and unrepresentative as the traditionalist criticism it was attacking. The political problem for feminists has subsequently become one of keeping together a movement in danger of imploding into different factions. Can any group – never mind any person – now presume to have the authority to represent women? How can solidarity among women be achieved without shortchanging their diversity? Has politically effective sisterhood collapsed into endless internal bickering?

The more general problem here is what Richard Rorty has called "the problem of how to overcome authority without claiming authority."[2] Although I have used feminist criticism to pose this problem, I agree with Rorty that it is endemic in contemporary literary theory, from deconstruction to the New Historicism. This problem arises when contemporary theorists demystify the seemingly universal positions of their adversaries by exposing the ideological basis of all putatively universal claims. The very argument that enables these critics to challenge authority, however, makes them reluctant to claim authority for themselves. More exactly, they can only claim to be speaking for themselves because they distrust the disinterestedness of all viewpoints, their own necessarily included. They become reluctant to impose their views on others or to speak on behalf of them.

In part, this reluctance results from a laudable wish to let others express themselves, but it becomes disabling when we start to couch all claims in terms of our own experience, or the experience of our group, questioning their extension to others. It is as if the otherwise praiseworthy commitment to difference goes too far, leaving us no basis (or only very localized bases) for community. We begin to feel that there is something coercive about all universals – even universals we might favor – as they inevitably interfere with the autonomy of others.

For help with the issues I have been raising, I want to turn to an unlikely source: William Wordsworth's Preface to the *Lyrical Ballads*. Wordsworth is an unlikely source because he is apparently enamored of the univeralist claims contemporary theory teaches us to distrust. The poet, he says famously, "is a man speaking to men" – *all* men, he emphasizes, not just a coterie of fellow poets.[3] Along similar lines, he insists that "the Poet writes under one restriction only, namely, the necessity of giving immediate pleasure to a human Being possessed of that information which may be expected from him, not as a lawyer, a physician, a mariner, an astronomer, or a natural philosopher, but as a Man" (325). Unlike the scientist, whom Wordsworth pictures seeking truth as "a remote and unknown benefactor" (326), cherishing and loving science in his Frankenstein-like solitude, the poet sings "a song in which all human beings join with him" (326), a song that necessarily connects him with his fellow beings.

More generally, Wordsworth attaches great importance to the reception of his work. In an 1807 letter, he even goes so far as to say that to be dead to poetry "is to be without love of human nature and reverence for God."[4] Wordsworth knows what he likes, expects others to share his values, and reads considerable significance into the acceptance – or rejection – of his aesthetic judgments and literary practice. Yet, as we will see, he is also conspicuously reluctant to impose his judgments or even to argue for them. He is uncomfortable, for example, even writing a preface to the *Lyrical Ballads*, suspecting that readers will look coldly upon any attempt to persuade them into approving of his poems. And he repeatedly urges readers to make up their own minds about his work, to "decide by [their] own feelings genuinely, and not by reflection upon what will probably be the judgment of others" (330) – Wordsworth himself included.

In what follows I examine the tension between Wordsworth's confidence in the value of his poetry and his wish that readers arrive at their own judgments of his work. Wordsworth wants his readers to change their minds about poetry – and change their lives – without feeling pushed onto the path he would like them to take. I want to argue that how Wordsworth does this – how he affects readers without coercing them – can help us with the problem of authority and representation in contemporary theory that I have been describing. Before turning to Wordsworth, I accordingly pose this problem in a more specific way, this time as it plays itself out in feminist teaching. With this classroom scenario in mind, I then take up Wordsworth's very ambivalent and vexed attempt to influence the reception of his poetry through his Preface and I conclude by briefly commenting on what Wordsworth's example has to say to politically motivated contemporary critics.

I

In "Empowering Otherness," Barbara Ewell forcefully restates the critique of authority that I cited at the outset, arguing that appeals to objectivity, truth, and universal values only underwrite masculinist bias and male privilege. According to Ewell, these appeals are especially congenial to the university and shore up the oppressive hierarchies that she thinks prevail there. In her view,

> as in the society it serves, every dimension of the academy's organization assumes the priority and priorities of men: from the cluster of mostly male administrators and faculty at the top to the mostly female students and clerical and janitorial workers at the bottom; from the fragmentation of knowledge into discrete disciplines to the favoring of researchers – and particular kinds of research – over teachers – and particular styles of teaching; from the hierarchies of rank and tenure to the professional societies and our impanelled pronouncements; from the lecterns and podia in front of orderly rows of student desks to the promotion and protection of organized competition as sport.[5]

As Ewell realizes, this wholesale indictment of university education poses difficult problems for the feminist teacher. The first is how to avoid being implicated in the system that Ewell wants to challenge. Specific feminist pedagogical strategies – fostering student participation by dividing the class into small groups, encouraging ungraded journal writing, rearranging the classroom by putting the chairs in a circle and thus decentering the professor's prominence – these specific measures, while perhaps helpful, in my opinion do not go far enough. Although meant to empower students, they still leave the teacher's authority intact because, as Nina Baym has pointed out, that authority comes with our being in a classroom, however set up. By a "classroom" I mean not so much a physical structure as a teaching relationship. As Baym puts it, "An imbalance of power in the form of an imbalance of knowledge is what makes teaching necessary ... [W]herever there is teaching, there is a power relationship."[6]

Even more important than the difficulty of avoiding authority, however, is the problem of relinquishing the influence that authority can bring. Baym notes that most feminists experience power as oppression and hence their own desire for power "is frequently disavowed" (66). Yet, Baym goes on to argue, "insofar as power is the energy and control that gets things done, it is not only an ineluctable dimension of any situation, it is something that feminists require" (66). The problem for the feminist teacher becomes how to exercise power in the classroom without claiming it – how to get things done, make something happen, without resorting to the hierachical heavy-handedness that dissatisfies her.

A recent essay by Deborah Bowen, "Reading the Decentered Class-room: or, If There Is Such a Thing as Misreading, Who Am I to Say So?," brings home the dilemma I have described. Bowen reports her reluctance to be the deciding voice in the classroom, even when students are gravitating toward what she thinks is the wrong reading of a text. As she puts it, "my concern for plurivocality, and for the nurturing of students who 'make meaning rather than just receive meaning' constrains me to keep quiet."[7] Bowen's reluctance to speak for her students, to settle the question for them, becomes her reluctance even to speak to them, because she knows they will turn whatever she says into support for a particular reading. As a teacher in a classroom responsible for the grades of her students, her comments are never regarded as innocent, but always decoded as clues to the right answer (hence the familiar scene of students only taking notes when the teacher, not when a fellow student, talks). Even as Bowen restrains herself, however, she is restless with her own passivity. Her silence feels at odds with her desire – her responsibility – to influence and educate her students. Her problem is thus how to get her students to participate in the production of readings she can endorse – how to get them to do this without manipulating them (because manipulating the students undermines their power as free co-creators or collaborators).

I will be describing in my next section how Wordsworth encounters a similar problem in his Preface, when he worries about even appearing to manage the reception of his poems. Ewell provides an especially vivid formulation of the problem I have been describing when she notes how "feminist classrooms often struggle against diffusion, degeneration into rap sessions, and the loss of critical thought. Evaluation becomes tangled in the mire of subjectivity: how can 'standards' be applied when their distorted perspective has been deliberately exposed?" (55). Contemporary theory (in this case, feminist criticism) thus lands us in what may feel like a vicious circle, searching for a non-hierarchical yet still effective challenge to oppressive hierarchies. The reluctance to claim authority seems in tension with the wish to achieve change. As Ewell asks, "How can the teacher exert authority when its deconstruction is in process?" (55).

II

At first glance, it would appear as if Wordsworth, unlike the feminist critics I have been discussing, is very confident about his authority – in this case, his authority as a poet entitled to make all kinds of magisterial pronouncements on the purpose of poetry, the make-up of the canon, and the unquestionable value of his own poems. The Preface abounds with seemingly confident (not to say arrogant) claims. Some of them I have already mentioned: the poet is a man speaking to men and (judging from the monologues we get in Wordsworth's own poetry) apparently not doing much listening. In addition to addressing everybody, the poet speaks on their behalf, for them, as if he were authorized to safeguard their better interests. The poet, Wordsworth says, "is the rock of defence for human nature"; the poet "binds together by passion and knowledge the vast empire of human society, as it is spread over the whole earth, and over all time" (326). We all apparently need poetry to be human: "the knowledge of the [poet] cleaves to us as a necessary part of our existence, our natural and unalienable inheritance" (326). Poetry communicates with us naturally, with no prerequisites to be met, except the precondition that the poet must respect that "information" which any human being possesses "not as a lawyer, a physician, a mariner, an astronomer, or a natural philosopher, but as a Man" (325).

I take Wordsworth to be saying that the knowledge required to understand poetry is the opposite of expertise. It is something we already have, not something we may or may not acquire. By "we," Wordsworth adamantly means every single one of us, "all human beings" (326). When Wordsworth speaks of readers already having the requisite "information" for appreciating poetry, "information" may not be quite the word. He is referring to something more rudimentary or fundamental, in his words the "immediate" (as opposed to the eventually learned) knowledge that we all carry about with us "without any other discipline than that of our daily life" (326). The discipline of daily life is here contrasted to an academic discipline like astronomy or medicine. In Book Thirteenth of *The Prelude* Wordsworth accordingly speaks of his poetry origi- nating outside educational institutions in his daily walks, which brought him into contact with "the wanderers of the earth" (l. 155):

> When I began to enquire,
> To watch and question those I met, and speak
> Without reserve to them, the lonely roads
> Were open schools in which I daily read
> With most delight the passions of mankind.   (lines 160–164)

A poetry responsive to what we get from everyday life with others is inherently social, not the elitist product of specialized expertise.

Wordsworth sounds very sure of himself in the pronouncements I have been reviewing. In these passages, there are few signs of his second-guessing his authority as a poet, his right to speak *the* truth to and for his readers, who, as we have seen, apparently include everyone. This image of the poet as everyman, as spokesman for us all, is, however, hard to square with the isolation that characterizes Wordsworth's own poetry. In his poetic practice, Wordsworth may be a man speaking to men, but he is most often heard, or overheard, by one or two people, usually his sister or his closest friend Coleridge. To put it mildly, he is not the popular poet that his claims for poetry might predict. As he puts it elsewhere, "It is an awful truth, that there neither is, nor can be, any genuine enjoyment of Poetry [his own included] among nineteen out of twenty of those persons who live, or wish to live, in the broad light of the world – among those who either are, or are striving to make themselves, people of consideration in society."[8]

Wordsworth's awareness of his own solitude surfaces in the Preface to the *Lyrical Ballads* when he says that although the object of poetry is general truth, it is truth "not standing upon external testimony, but carried alive into the heart by passion; truth which is its own testimony" (325). The poet here resembles a witness on the stand alone, backed up not by experts or independent observers, but somehow still convincing others by his very words, or, more exactly, by the passion that validates them. One serious problem with this picture is that it eliminates the need for a preface helping the poet's words reach others. After all, Wordsworth's own poems are carried into the heart of his readers not just by passion but by additional words – the words of the preface that precedes and makes clear their way.

Wordsworth is very uneasy about writing the Preface to *Lyrical Ballads* and his discomfort will return me to the problems I started out discussing. Much as Bowen, in the classroom described earlier, is uncomfortable intervening in her students' discussion (even as they drift toward what she regards as a wrong reading), Wordsworth feels the need for a preface but he is not happy about it. He needs to write a preface because without one he fears that readers will "have to struggle with feelings of strangeness and awkwardness: they will look round for poetry, and will be induced to inquire by what species of courtesy these attempts can be permitted to assume that title" (321). In his view, "a practical faith in the opinions which I am wishing to establish is almost unknown" (324). He is uncomfortable writing a preface, however, partly because writing one suggests the inability of his poems to reach readers on their own and partly because he does not want to force or even coax his readers into liking his poems. As he says, "I was unwilling to undertake the task [of writing a preface], knowing that on this occasion the Reader would look coldly upon my arguments, since I might be suspected of having been principally influenced by the selfish and foolish hope of *reasoning* him into an approbation of these particular Poems" (320). Wordsworth cannot do without a preface, lest his readers fail to grasp his poems; but he also cannot do with a preface what he wants, namely, let his readers come to an appreciation of his work on their own.

Wordsworth's aspirations for his poetry are every bit as ambitious as the goals of more recent politically minded writers. He wants nothing less than to overcome the authority and hierarchies of eighteenth-century neoclassical poetry, which means that he wants to create a taste for his poetry, to rearrange the canon, and to redefine what counts as serious literature. In his words,

If my conclusions are admitted, and carried as far as they must be carried if admitted at all, our judgments concerning the works of the greatest Poets both ancient and modern will be far different from what they are at present, both when we praise, and when we censure; and our moral feelings influencing and influenced by these judgments will, I believe, be corrected and purified. (324)

By intertwining moral feelings and aesthetic judgments, Wordsworth contests what eighteenth-century theorists such as Joseph Addison and Immanuel Kant called the purity, innocence, or disinterested-ness of taste. Wordsworth's own term here is "indifference": he rebukes, as the "language of men who speak of what they do not understand," those "who talk of Poetry as of a matter of amusement and idle pleasure; who will converse with us as gravely about a *taste* for Poetry, as they express it, as if it were a thing as indifferent as a taste for rope-dancing, or Frontiniac or Sherry" (325). The judgment of poetry is not a thing "indifferent" but something consequential, bound up as it is with our moral feelings and relationships with one another.

All of this is to say that for Wordsworth more is at stake in the reception of poetry than the reputation of a handful of writers. Wordsworth wants to redefine poetry and reshape the canon for political, not just aesthetic, reasons. "The subject [of his poetry] is indeed important!" (322), he thunders: he aims not only at making room for his own writing but (by so doing) shaking his readers out of their debilitating "savage torpor" (322).

For the human mind is capable of being excited without the application of gross and violent stimulants; and he must have a very faint perception of its beauty and dignity who does not know this, and who does not further know, that one being is elevated above another in proportion as he possesses this capability. It has therefore appeared to me, that to endeavor to produce or enlarge this capability is one of the best services in which, at any period, a Writer can be engaged; but this service, excellent at all times, is especially so at the present day. (322)

Wordsworth elsewhere calls this capability of response "imagina-tion." According to him, one person is "elevated above another in proportion as he possesses this [internal] capability," not in proportion to wealth, social position, or educational credentials.

Wordsworth, of course, means morally elevated here. For him, the capacity to love depends on imagination, which overcomes estrange-ment and sees through alienating differences, thereby connecting us to others. In the Preface Wordsworth calls this "the perception of similitude in dissimilitude" and argues:

This principle is the great spring of the activity [as opposed to torpid passivity] of our minds, and their chief feeder. From this principle the direction of the sexual appetite, and all the passions connected with it, take their origin: it is the life of our ordinary conversation; and upon the accuracy with which similitude in dissimilitude, and dissimilitude in similitude are perceived, depend our taste and our moral feelings. (328)

205

Book Fourteenth of *The Prelude* offers a more lyrical explanation of the indissoluble link between imagination and love and the importance of love in elevating human beings:

> By love subsists
> All lasting grandeur, by pervading love;
> That gone, we are as dust ...
> This spiritual Love acts not nor can exist
> Without Imagination.   (lines 169–170, 188–189)

Taste and moral feelings come together in imagination, their source: hence Wordsworth's claim that the poet carries everywhere with him "relationship and love" (326), cutting across the vocational, class, generational, and other kinds of divisions tearing apart society. "In spite of difference of soil and climate, of language and manners, of laws and customs; in spite of things silently gone out of mind, and things violently destroyed" (326), the poet binds people together.

Wordsworth thus intends his deliberately prosaic, minimalistic poems to activate his readers' imagination, not to overpower them and cater to their morally enervating passivity, their craving for outrageous stimulation. By calling Wordsworth's poems deliberately prosaic and minimalistic, I mean to invoke not only his well-known alignment of poetry with prose, but also his claim that what distinguishes his poems "from the popular Poetry of the day" is that "the feeling therein developed gives importance to the action and situation, and not the action and situation to the feeling" (322). Elsewhere, offering another version of his "savage torpor" thesis, Wordsworth laments that the imagination of his readers "has slept; and the voice which is the voice of my Poetry without Imagination cannot be heard."[9] Here is Wordsworth's variant of the vicious circle noted earlier: how to get readers to wake themselves up. The problem, in Wordsworth's terms, would seem to be finding the right level of stimulation. Too much stimulation, and his poetry becomes another melodramatic spectacle, dazzling happily passive readers. Too little stimulation, however, and his poetry does not make any impact at all – gets written off as too prosaic, too dull.

In "Simon Lee," one of the poems in *Lyrical Ballads*, Wordsworth grapples with this dilemma by directly addressing the reader. Wordsworth pauses after the first sixty lines of his poem, which conclude with another description of Simon Lee's weak ankles (the more the poor old man works, the more they swell). Suspecting his

reader's impatience, as if this last homely detail might be the straw
that broke the reader's interest in the poem, Wordsworth writes,

> My gentle Reader, I perceive
> How patiently you've waited,
> And now I fear that you expect
> Some tale will be related.
>
> O Reader! had you in your mind
> Such stores as silent thought can bring,
> O gentle Reader! you would find
> A tale in every thing.   (lines 61–68)

Here the reader's threatened rejection of the poem becomes the
reader's problem – a sign of his (morally culpable) lack of imagination. The difficulty with Wordsworth's move here is that if the reader
could find "a tale in every thing," what would be the responsibility
of the writer? How could he go wrong? The problem for the writer
remains, despite Wordsworth's attempt to evade it here. It is the
problem of doing enough to quicken the reader's imagination but not
too much, lest the reader only sit back and marvel at the external
excitement.

Wordsworth discourages a passive response to his poetry because,
as we have seen, he wants readers to tap in themselves the imaginative energy that he himself has employed in writing the poem. From
Wordsworth's point of view, the reception of poetry, in other words,
should be as creative as the writing of poetry. Wordsworth is trying
to prevent the reader from merely admiring what someone else (in
this case Wordsworth) has done, much as Coleridge notes that the
poet, "described in *ideal* perfection," subordinates "our admiration
of the poet to our sympathy with the poetry."[10] Wordsworth wants
credit for his work – I do not want to downplay his much-discussed
egotism – but he also wants to phase himself out of a job: his job, that
is, as a special person writing in a special language only a select few
can understand, let alone create themselves. Unless, he says, we
poets "are advocates for that admiration which subsists upon ignorance, and that pleasure which arises from hearing what we do not
understand, the Poet must descend from this supposed height" (327)
and inspire, not stun, his readers – inspire them to go and do
likewise, to create for themselves.[11]

In short, Wordsworth wants to revolutionize society and literature,
but in an insidious, almost imperceptible way, without browbeating,
arguing or otherwise forcing readers into agreeing with him. The

universal claims that I mentioned earlier – the poet as a man speaking to all people, singing a song all readers sing with him – these claims are consequently best understood as what I would call conditional or provisional universals. They become universals, in other words, if and when readers subscribe to them or make them come true. I would compare them to the curious kinds of claims Kant says we make when, in making aesthetic judgments, we speak with "a universal voice." These claims are curious because even though we act as if we have a rightful claim upon everyone's assent, our aesthetic judgments are not (strictly speaking) cognitive, at least not for Kant. We cannot compel agreement with aesthetic judgments, although we do have ways of arguing for them. Not all claims to speak with a universal voice are thus as coercive or absolutist as they first appear: I would argue that Wordsworth's are a case in point.[12]

What I have been describing as Wordsworth's wish to change the world gently results in the conflict that destabilizes the Preface's conclusion. One last request I must make of my reader, Wordsworth says in concluding, is "that in judging these Poems he would decide by his own feelings genuinely, and not by reflection upon what will probably be the judgment of others ... let the Reader then abide, independently, by his own feelings, and if he find himself affected" (330), he should not let public opinion interfere with his pleasure. But, Wordsworth continues, if readers do not find themselves affected by his poetry, if they are displeased, they should remember that "an *accurate* taste in poetry, and in all other arts, as Sir Joshua Reynolds has observed, is an *acquired* talent, which can only be produced by thought and a long-continued intercourse with the best models of composition" (330).

Wordsworth's appealing to the authority of Reynolds should come as a surprise. Earlier in the Preface, commenting on the truth of poetry, Wordsworth had written, "Aristotle, I have been told, has said that Poetry is the most philosophic of writing: it is so: its object is truth, not individual and local, but general and operative" (325). Wordsworth's lack of concern to check his sources here, to see (like a good student) whether Aristotle actually said what Wordsworth has been told he said, makes the citation seem casual, even optional. (Wordsworth's nonchalance also fits in with his account in *The Prelude* of his carefree student days at Cambridge.) Wordsworth apparently does not need the authority of Aristotle to make his point, the truth of poetry again being something so natural or obvious that readers can verify it on their own.

Wordsworth's much more earnest, cautionary appeal to Reynolds, by contrast, speaks to deeper need than the offhand citation of Aristotle. At this late point in the Preface, the embattled reception of Wordsworth's own poems is still at stake, not just the truth of poetry in general. It is an additional sign of stress in Wordsworth that Reynolds is the critic he calls on – that idiot Reynolds, William Blake would say, or did say in his acerbic annotations to Reynolds' *Discourses*. As Blake makes clear, Reynolds, in the eyes of some Romantics, epitomized the kind of upper-class refinement and delicacy that Wordsworth elsewhere opposes. Blake also annotated Wordsworth's Preface and suspected a latent conservativism in Wordsworth's theory of poetry at odds with the imaginative power of the poems themselves, which is why in his annotations to Wordsworth's *Poems* (1815), he professes not to "know who wrote these Prefaces they are very mischievous & direct contrary to Wordsworths own Practise."[13] Wordsworth's calling on Blake's nemesis Reynolds lends weight to Blake's fear that Wordsworth is of the mistaken opinion that "Genius May be Taught" (632), preferably, Blake fears, in an institution like the Royal Academy Reynolds directed, where the inquiry "is not whether a Man has Talents. & Genius? But whether he is Passive & Polite & a Virtuous Ass: & obedient to Nobelmens Opinions in Art & Science" (632).

By invoking Reynolds, Wordsworth does begin to sound like one of the people he has been warning us about, one of those "gentlemen, persons of fortune, professional men, ladies, persons who can afford to buy, or can easily procure, books of half-a-guinea price, hot-pressed, and printed upon superfine paper."[14] By citing Reynolds, Wordsworth begins to sound like a cautionary expert, contradicting his earlier wish to distinguish poetry from specialized knowledge and to let poetry achieve its effects on its own, like a witness who does not need any corroboration. As if aware that he is sounding like the neoclassical connoisseurs he has been cautioning us about, Wordsworth hastens to add that he still is encouraging readers to make up their own minds about his poems. From his point of view, by recommending "long-continued intercourse with the best models of composition," he is only tempering the rashness of his readers' decision, not tampering with their right to decide. Nevertheless, Wordsworth's nervousness about entrusting this decision to his readers recalls his uneasiness about his poems working on their own – the very uneasiness that inspired his writing the Preface in the first place. Instead of dispelling Wordsworth's doubts about the efficacy of his poetry, the Preface thus concludes with them.

III

I have been picturing Wordsworth torn between trusting his poems and his readers and anxiously wanting to make sure that his readers will at once appreciate his poems and change their lives. His mood swings between despair and hope. In less confident moments, he understandably worries that what he calls "the feeble endeavour" (322) of his poems will be defeated by the powerful cultural obstacles that they are up against. By calling his poems a "feeble endeavour," he is not just being modest but is acknowledging the non-coercive path he has chosen. He anticipates a comment by William Butler Yeats, who in a similarly apprehensive mood also wondered whether the poet is just "a trifling, impertinent, vexatious thing, a tumbler who has unrolled his carpet in the way of a marching army."[15] Nevertheless, although Wordsworth has good reason to fear failure, he still can hope that his project will succeed, and "that the time is approaching when the evil will be system-atically opposed, by men of greater powers, and with far more distinguished success" (322).

I would argue that the non-coercive path Wordsworth has chosen is the path of education. I have already mentioned his regarding the lonely roads of his daily walks as "open schools" where he read the passions of mankind. Along similar lines, he concludes *The Prelude* (Book Fourteenth) picturing himself and Coleridge as

> joint labourers in the work
> (Should Providence such grace to us vouchsafe)
> Of their [nations'] deliverance, surely yet to come.
> Prophets of Nature, we to them will speak
> A lasting inspiration, sanctified
> By reason, blest by faith: what we have loved,
> Others will love, and we will teach them how.   (lines 444–450)

We will teach them how, Wordsworth says, through our writing. He is entrusting his hopes and values to his poems.

"Entrusting" is a key word here because Wordsworth is acutely aware of what I would call the contingency of education, or the lack of any guarantee that teaching will work, that, in Wordsworth's particular case, his writing will "take" with his readers. Wordsworth often expresses hope in the ultimate success of his teachings, but it is a long-range hope that he refers to. In the short term, he does not see himself making an immediate impact. Speaking of the current neglect of his poems, he tells Lady Beaumont:

trouble not yourself upon their present reception; of what moment is that compared with what I trust is their destiny, to console the afflicted, to add sunshine to daylight by making the happy happier, to teach the young and the gracious of every age, to see, to think and feel, and therefore to become more actively and securely virtuous; this is their office, which I trust they will faithfully perform long after we (that is, all that is mortal of us) are mouldered in our graves.[16]

"Trust" – repeated twice – is exactly the right word here, because Wordsworth cannot be sure that his work will have the eventual effect that he wants it to have.

As we have seen, Wordsworth is more anxious about the reception of his writing than he lets on to Lady Beaumont. I can think of only one time when he is unequivocally optimistic about the future, when he believes that his values are going to triumph, sooner rather than later. This is during the early days of the French Revolution, as recorded in Book Eleventh of *The Prelude*:

> O pleasant exercise of hope and joy!
> For mighty were the auxiliars which then stood
> Upon our side, we who were strong in love!
> Bliss was it in that dawn to be alive,
> But to be young was very Heaven! O times,
> In which the meagre, stale, forbidding ways
> Of custom, law, and statute, took at once
> The attraction of a country in romance!
> ... The inert
> Were roused, and lively natures rapt away!
> (lines 105–112, 124–125)

Significantly, this time is not only short-lived, but a time when Wordsworth is not yet writing his major poetry. As already shown, when he is writing the *Lyrical Ballads* and other poems, he is not nearly so confident about rousing the inert, sunk as they are in their savage torpor. Society does not seem so malleable to him, so much like a country in romance where wishes always come true. In the absence of political "auxiliars" on Wordsworth's side, writing is not so much a "pleasant exercise of hope and joy" as it is a worrisome project, with triumphs and setbacks, whose overall success one can never gauge with any certainty.

Many critics have noticed that Wordsworth's major poetry often turns on anxiety about the future. Most read this anxiety, however, in personal terms, with Wordsworth worrying about the dulling of his senses or loss of his capacity to write. These personal fears are definitely there but, in light of the concerns I have been discussing, I also see Wordsworth worrying about the inheritability of his work, or its being taken up and carried on by later generations. Nowhere is this concern more apparent than in the otherwise strange meditation on books in *The Prelude*, Book Fifth, where Wordsworth speculates about what would happen

> Should the whole frame of earth by inward throes
> Be wrenched, or fire come down far to scorch
> Her pleasant habitations, and dry up
> Old Ocean, in his bed left singed and bare. (lines 30–34)

Brooding on this unlikely prospect is really a pretext for worrying about the fragility of books and asking

> why hath not the Mind
> Some element to stamp her image on
> In nature somewhat nearer to her own?
> Why, gifted with such powers to send abroad
> Her spirit, must it lodge in shrines so frail? (lines 45–49)

I see Wordsworth pondering not so much the specific fate of books as the transmissibility of culture itself, "all the meditations of mankind" (line 38), among them his own. This doubt about the future echoes Wordsworth's more immediate uncertainty about whether his work is getting through to readers here and now, the concern we have seen him struggling with in the Preface.

Sometimes Wordsworth gives up hope of influencing the future – the reception of his work feels so much a matter of chance, so out of his control. Such pessimism overtakes him in *The Prelude*, Book Eleventh, when he recalls losing "all feeling of conviction" and "[yielding] up moral questions in despair" (ll. 303, 305). He even occasionally fantasizes about taking more active control over the future, eliminating his uncertainty through force. I have in mind Book Tenth of *The Prelude*. In these lines the French Revolution is starting to sputter, to put it mildly, thanks to the atrocities of Robespierre. It is beginning to look as if Wordsworth is going to be disappointed in its outcome, despite his initial enthusiasm. He reports

> Yet did I grieve, nor only griev'd, but thought
> Of opposition and of remedies

An insignificant stranger, and obscure,
And one, moreover, little graced with power
Of eloquence even in my native speech,
And all unfit for tumult or intrigue,
Yet would I at this time with willing heart
Have undertaken for a cause so great
Service however dangerous. I revolved,
How much the destiny of Man had still
Hung upon single persons ...
That objects, even as they are great; thereby
Do come within the reach of humblest eyes.

(lines 146–156, 159–160)

Nothing comes of this apparent willingness to lie humbly in wait, unnoticed, for Robespierre and then to assassinate him and save the Revolution. The improbability of Wordsworth killing Robespierre is less important, however, than his readiness even to imagine himself doing such a thing. This readiness shows one common reaction to intolerable uncertainty over the future: sieze control through force; make something happen instead of waiting for it; put an end to ambiguity by oversimplifying things, in this case by making one person responsible for the outcome of history, one conveniently vulnerable person.

Even though Wordsworth feels the allure of the violence he is contemplating, he rejects this option, turning instead to writing (as his mode of intervention in history): one last comment from the Preface helps explain why. Throughout much of his work Wordsworth thinks about how he, as a writer, is affecting his readers, how they are taking his words. But toward the end of the Preface he trades places with his readers and imagines himself the recipient, not the giver, of instruction. He speaks as an author asked by others to revise his work, and he cautions

It is dangerous to make these alterations on the simple authority of a few individuals, or even of certain classes of men; for where the understanding of an Author is not convinced, or his feelings altered, this cannot be done without great injury to himself: for his own feelings are his stay and support; and, if he set them aside in one instance, he may be induced to repeat this act till his mind shall lose all confidence in itself, and become utterly debilitated. (329)

Wordsworth knows how it feels to make changes – in one's writing or life – that one does not really consent to. He acknowledges the pain and loss of confidence that forced compliance can bring. Wordsworth's uneasiness about writing the Preface springs from this admirable sense that the feelings and understanding of others must be convinced, not manhandled, for real growth to occur. Compelled assent is not assent at all, but only substitutes one form of debilitating conformity or torpor for another. If loss of authority remains a problem for Wordsworth, authoritarian manipulation – not to mention force – is not the answer.

Wordsworth has his shortcomings. Most prominently among them I would place his often-noticed self-absorption. He is adept at speaking for and to others, not so good at listening to their voices. He is consequently too quick to think that his poetry can cut through the cultural, vocational, and other kinds of differences he wants to transcend (lacking independent expression, these differences offer little resistance to Wordsworth's subsuming them in his presumably all-encompassing vision). Nevertheless, in his restraint, his repudiation of violence, I read an important lesson for contemporary literary critics, in particular the feminist critics I discuss at the outset. I do not imagine these critics fantasizing about killing the Robespierres in their lives, but force can take many forms, from curtailing certain kinds of unwelcome speech to discouraging pleasure in the "wrong" kinds of literary works, and we all are vulnerable to its appeal. I take these examples of force from Nina Baym, who goes on to conclude that "the teacher needs to encourage her women students to say what she does not expect them to say and perhaps would rather not hear. Otherwise, the only real reader in the class will be the teacher, whether she is a feminist or not" (75). This is excellent advice, very much in the spirit of Wordsworth's discomfort with coercion in the Preface. Wordsworth reminds us that coercion, far from insuring genuine change, sabotages it. The letting go of control that makes change uncertain also may make it possible.

Notes

1 Anne Phillips, "Universal Pretensions in Political Thought," in *Destabilizing Theory: Contemporary Feminist Debates*, eds. Michele Barrett and Anne Phillips (Stanford University Press, 1992), p. 11.
2 Richard Rorty, *Contingency, Irony, and Solidarity* (Cambridge University Press, 1989), p. 105.
3 William Wordsworth, "Preface to the Second Edition of the *Lyrical Ballads* (1800)," in *English Romantic Writers*, ed. David Perkins (New York: Harcourt Brace Jovanovich, 1967), p. 324. Subsequent references are inserted in the text. References to *The Prelude* are also inserted in the text

and are to the 1850 edition, as reprinted in *The Prelude 1799, 1805, 1850*, eds. Jonathan Wordsworth, M. H. Abrams, and Stephen Gill (New York: W. W. Norton, 1979).

4 To Lady Beaumont, May 21, 1807, *English Romantic Writers*, p. 355.
5 Barbara C. Ewell, "Empowering Otherness: Feminist Criticism and the Academy," in *Reorientations: Critical Theories and Pedagogies*, eds. Bruce Henricksen and Thaïs E. Morgan (Urbana and Chicago: University of Illinois Press, 1990), pp. 44–45.
6 Nina Baym, "The Feminist Teacher of Literature: Feminist or Teacher?" in *Gender in the Classroom*, eds. Susan L. Gabriel and Isaiah Smithson (Urbana and Chicago: University of Illinois Press, 1990), p. 66.
7 Deborah Bowen, "Reading the Decentered Classroom: or, If There Is Such Thing as Misreading, Who Am I to Say So?" *ADE Bulletin* (Fall 1993), 28.
8 To Lady Beaumont, May 21, 1807, p. 355.
9 *Ibid.*, p. 356.
10 Samuel Taylor Coleridge, *Biographia Literaria*, *English Romantic Writers*, p. 455.
11 In saying that Wordsworth encourages his readers to go and do likewise, I am implying he seeks disciples. On discipleship as a (desired) response to Romantic writing, see my "Accepting the Romantics as Philosophers," *Philosophy and Literature* 12 (October 1988), 179–189.
12 Stanley Cavell notes a parallel between the "subjective universality" at work in aesthetic judgments (as characterized by Kant) and J. L. Austin's claims about what we ordinarily say. See *Must We Mean What We Say?* (1969; reprinted Cambridge University Press, 1976), p. 94. I think this point helps us understand the universal claims of two other Romantics: Samuel Coleridge and Henry David Thoreau. See my "Coleridge and the Authority of Ordinary Language," *Soundings* 65 (Winter 1992), 555–569, and "*Walden* and the Politics of Contemporary Criticism," in *New Essays on Walden*, ed. Robert F. Sayre (Cambridge University Press, 1992), pp. 95–113.
13 David Erdman, ed., *The Poetry and Prose of William Blake* (Garden City, New York: Doubleday, 1970), p. 655.
14 To John Wilson [June, 1802], *English Romantic Writers*, p. 351.
15 William Butler Yeats, *Essays and Introductions* (New York: Collier Books, 1961), p. 318.
16 To Lady Beaumont, p. 355.

10

Self-consciousness, social guilt, and Romantic poetry: Coleridge's Ancient Mariner and Wordworth's Old Pedlar

KENNETH R. JOHNSTON

For a brief space in March of 1798, perhaps no more than a weekend, a two-poem book was envisaged by William Wordsworth and Samuel Taylor Coleridge that could have changed the course of English poetry, and perhaps of English moral philosophy as well. Since the volume they finally did publish in September of that year, the first edition of *Lyrical Ballads*, also changed the course of English poetry, we need not regret that they did not pursue their temporary notion of publishing Coleridge's "The Rime of the Ancient Mariner" together with Wordsworth's "The Ruined Cottage." But if these two poems had appeared together then, the moral-philosophical dimension of their enterprise would have been much clearer than it is in *Lyrical Ballads*, either in its anonymous first edition, whose brief "Advertisement" presents the poems mainly as a language experiment, or in its still more famous second edition. The latter has Wordsworth's name alone on the title-page, and contains a long preface, at once aggressive and defensive, that does indeed raise many points about the relation of *poiesis* to morals, asserting that poetry is more centrally concerned with representing feelings than actions. But it does this in language that is rarely straightforward, because it uses the rhetoric of poetics to discuss – and disguise – its authors' motives of political doubt and social guilt.

All editions of *Lyrical Ballads* contain "The Rime of the Ancient Mariner," but none contains "The Ruined Cottage," which was not published until 1814, as Book I ("The Wanderer") of *The Excursion*, a heavily revised version that substitutes Christian categories of explanation for the radically open-ended explorations of human moral responsibility that Wordsworth was willing to pursue some fifteen years earlier. "The Ruined Cottage" as a separate poem was not published in any form until 1949, as an appendix in Ernest de Selincourt's final volume of Wordsworth *Poetical Works*, and was not available to more general (though still largely academic) audiences until 1968, when one of its two quite distinct manuscript versions was printed in the second edition of volume two of *The Norton Anthology of English Literature*. Hence the originary relation of these two poems at the beginnings of English Romanticism (as traditionally understood) has been largely lost. But it is worth recovering for the light it sheds on the moral dimension of one important episode in the history of *poiesis*, an episode in which the two authors found themselves uncomfortably situated between strong claims to political action on the one hand, and very attractive calls to a reflective, idealist philosophy on the other.

The intellectual situation in which Wordsworth and Coleridge found themselves in 1797–98 illustrates with exemplary clarity both the attractions of construing human beings as subjects of representations and the problems of doing so. On the one hand, both young men had, during the preceding five years, attached their considerable imaginative and intellectual powers to a critical theory of human representations – the Enlightenment theory of free-standing individual subjects joining together in free will to form *representative* governments – that had been established by violent revolution, first in Britain's American colonies and more recently in France, where the *Declaration of the Rights of Man* was first promulgated in 1789. Wordsworth's later lines on the enthusiasm of this period are the second most famous lines, in English, on the world-wide historical significance of the French Revolution: "Bliss was it in that dawn to be alive, / But to be young was very heaven!" (1805 *Prelude*, X.692–693). But – on the other hand – by 1797–8 flaws in this theory of the representational subject were becoming woefully evident, both in theory and in practice. For this situation, the *most* famous lines in English on the Revolution were more appropriate, though they would not be written for another sixty years, by Charles Dickens in *A Tale of Two Cities* (1859): "It was the best of times, it was the worst of times, it was the age of wisdom, it was the age of foolishness, it was the epoch of belief, it was the epoch of incredulity, it was the season of Light, it was the season of Darkness, it was the spring of hope, it was the winter of despair." 1798 was, in short, a time of intense moral ambiguity. The 1790s had been a decade when everyday actions had metaphysical implications that were clear to almost everyone. By the end of the decade, as wide cracks appeared in the political foundations of the philosophical concept of the representational subject, the impending crisis was dreaded as likely to be far worse than the fall of the Bastille, since by 1798 the sense of what was going to be *lost* was much clearer than the blissful but inchoate sense of human possibility that had dawned on astonished Europe in 1789.

In this situation, Wordsworth and Coleridge did not "retreat" into poetry, as is sometimes glibly assumed: they were already poets, among other things. But they did begin to retreat, in effect, from the engaged political activity – writing, publishing and speaking – that Coleridge had been most actively involved in, especially in Bristol since 1795, when he had been one of the most notable and articulate proponents of social reform outside of London. Wordsworth, for his part, had in 1793 written, but not published, a republican tract against "renegades" to the revolutionary cause (*A Letter to the Bishop of Llandaff*), aimed at the liberal Whig bishop, Richard Watson, and in 1795 had more likely than not been involved in radical journalism before he mysteriously left London in August, never to reside there again.[1] All his major compositions between 1793 and 1797 were, though also unpublished, on socially engaged topics, especially the condition of the lower classes displaced by the ruinous economic fallout from Pitt's war policy against France.

Wordsworth and Coleridge in effect became poets twice: once conventionally and once radically or "Romantically." Their first poetical coming-of-age was characterized by a relatively benign liberal attitude toward socio-political progress, as exemplified by Wordsworth's optimistic and typically neo-classical praise of "Freedom" in the concluding passages of *Descriptive Sketches* (1793), or many of Coleridge's early occasional poems of 1790–5 ("Destruction of the Bastille," "To a Young Lady with a Poem on the French Revolution," *The Fall of Robespierre*, etc.). Their second coming-of-age was characterized by a much more complex and problematic series of textual efforts to disengage themselves imaginatively from the intense and radical political commitments they had made after 1793, and a sense of guilt is powerfully at work in their self-transformation. This disengagement can by no means be simply characterized as a rejection of or "apostasy" from political engagement, but their *feeling* of being renegades or turncoats was particularly strong, since both had flung such charges against others who abandoned the French cause earlier. As Seamus Deane has observed, "Those who – like Sir James Mackintosh, Wordsworth, Coleridge, and Southey – had changed their allegiances were particularly vulnerable to the charge of betrayal, not only from others but from themselves. The remorse which was often a consequence of this conflict was understood as a punishment for the initial 'crime'" [of supporting revolution in the first place].[2] Mackintosh (1765–1832) is an interesting point of reference, since his *Vindiciae Gallicae* (1791) was the most closely reasoned of all responses to Burke's *Reflections on the French Revolution*, and has been called "the ablest ideological defence of the French Revolution ever written."[3] But in 1799 he delivered a series of lectures on "The Laws of Nature and of Nations," attacking the ideological foundations of the Revolution, which systematically refuted the arguments of his own earlier pamphlet. Coleridge attended the first five in the series, but then quit in disgust.[4] Mackintosh was no reactionary, and remained throughout his career a liberal Whig, but these lectures became the public symbol of liberal intellectuals abandoning all hope of gaining anything for their goals from the example of France, and Mackintosh "became the whipping boy for his generation's remorse and disillusion" because he "embodied the new phenomenon of betrayal in an ideological war."[5] It was a fate that Coleridge and Wordsworth intuited for themselves (i.e., they saw correctly that their changes in opinion might be characterized in this way), and one that they were determined to avoid.

Instead of seeing this first stage of English Romanticism as an escape from politics, I would argue that the key ingredient in Wordsworth's and Coleridge's new – i.e., Romantic – poetry is the strong trace we can read in it of their profoundly troubled commitment to the cause of human possibility, democratically defined. Its most distinguishing mark, at this juncture, was a turn that we usually identify as an "inward" one, meaning away from society, away from social action – and, as it all too often seems, away from social responsibility, effectiveness and relevance, toward self-conscious reflection on states of mind and emotion. But my view is closely related to that of E. P. Thompson's (among others) on Wordsworth's poetry, that it is at its best when it holds social responsibility and individual vision in creative tension.[6]

Coleridge's political commitments were more extreme and public than Wordsworth's, and his reaction against them was correspondingly more shrill. His letter to his conservative clergyman brother,

George, *c.* March 10, 1798, within days of the window-of-opportunity in which a volume combining "The Ancient Mariner" and "The Ruined Cottage" momentarily appeared, captures the mood of European liberals following the news of Napoleon's invasion of Switzerland in February, which dashed almost all hopes that he might yet be the embodiment of the French Revolution's promise of universal freedom. Coleridge says he has "snapped my squeaking baby-trumpet of Sedition," and tries to distance himself from every radical, or liberal, political position available to him: "I am no Whig, no Reformist, no Republican" – but "a good man & a Christian." He then goes on to say, "Of GUILT I say nothing."[7] In the letter's context, the guilt may be that of the British government (for its provocative policies toward France), or, more likely, of Coleridge himself. But in either case, we can say, from a late twentieth century, post-structuralist perspective, that insistently saying one will say "nothing" about guilt – capitalized – is in fact to indicate quite a lot about it – if not its content, certainly its effective presence in the text and situation at hand.

Guilt is not the usual psychological or moral category in which to consider Romantic literature. Indeed, the traditional criticism of Romanticism has been precisely the *lack* of an adequate sense of guilt (or evil) that defines its characteristic excesses of height and depth, its odes to Joy and its odes to Dejection. For Matthew Arnold, the poets of the first quarter of the nineteenth century "did not know enough" – evidence for their inadequate knowledge being provided by their too hasty or enthusiastic embrace of the principles of the French Revolution.[8] But all the Romantic poets, and especially the young Wordsworth and Coleridge, knew a great deal about the possibilities – for good and for evil – of the principles of the French Revolution, and their sense of the guilt accruing from embracing *or abandoning* those principles contributed much to the creation of the first characteristically English Romantic poetry – i.e., the *Lyrical Ballads* of 1798. But these issues are even clearer in a volume that could have become, but did not quite, the foundational document of English Romanticism: a two-poem package that the two poets dangled briefly before the eyes of their earnest evangelical Bristol publisher, Joseph Cottle, in the early spring of 1798: *"The Rime of the Ancient Mariner" and "The Ruined Cottage,"* by S. T. Coleridge and W. Wordsworth.

Just before they completed these two poems, both poets were very busy polishing two other works, Wordsworth's *The Borderers* and

Coleridge's *Osorio*: classic five-act historical tragedies that try to represent directly the question of human responsibility for very powerful, conflicted occasions of guilt. They provide an illuminating prologue to the double-drama of "The Ancient Mariner" and "The Ruined Cottage," in that both explore – more discursively than dramatically – the issue of guilt that the poets pursued more successfully in their two narrative poems. Neither play presents the issue in contemporary terms, though Wordsworth's hero, Mortimer, is the leader of a band of outlaw "borderers" at the time of the Barons' War (thirteenth century) between Scotland and England. Instead, the issue of guilt and (ir)responsibility for human suffering is presented in smaller, more manageable terms: i.e., is Mortimer justified in killing the blind, old, disinherited Baron Herbert if – as it seems to Mortimer – Herbert has been raising up from infancy a little girl (whom he pretends is his daughter), intending to deliver her to the obscene concubinage of the rich, powerful Baron Clifford? This melodrama is further displaced onto the quasi-Satanic temptations of another character, the villain Rivers, to get Mortimer to commit this act of vengeance: all of the preceding "facts" are actually fictions created as lies by Rivers. Rivers is an ex-Crusader who was tricked by his ship's crew into marooning its captain to certain death on a stony isle because he believed the crew's story that the captain had designs against him. He felt hugely remorseful when he learned the truth, but after a three-day mental struggle and purgation of himself (fittingly, in the Wilderness of the Holy Land), he went beyond normal categories of human responsibility to become a kind of ideological missionary for the new, existential freedom he discovered:

> [I] have obeyed the only law that wisdom
> Can ever recognize: the immediate law
> Flashed from the light of circumstances
> Upon an independent intellect.   (III.v.30–33)

This is the freedom he now offers Mortimer, which Mortimer's role as hero raises back up to its contemporary (1797) political form: immediately, as the "savior" of Herbert's daughter (who happens to be his beloved), and, by extension, as the leader of the band of outlaws protecting the defenceless poor people of their Border region: "Henceforth we are fellow-labourers – to enlarge / The intellectual empire of mankind" (IV.ii.188–189). The close applicability of this promise to Wordsworth's sense of himself is indicated by the similar language with which he addressed Coleridge at the conclusion of *The Prelude*: they were to be "United helpers forward of a day / Of firmer trust, joint labourers in the work" of man's redemption. (1805 *Prelude*, XIII.438–439).

Coleridge's *Osorio* is not so complicated, but as its later title, *Remorse*, clearly indicates, it too is fascinated by the intellectual possibilities of remorse. The slight but significant difference between guilt and remorse has much to do with the large step forward that "The Ancient Mariner" and "The Ruined Cottage" take from these dramas. Essentially, one feels remorse for having committed an *action*, whereas one can feel guilty whether or not one has committed an action – whether, indeed, one is guilty *in fact* or not. The first two definitions of guilt in the *OED* concern failures to act: neglect of duty, or delinquency. Guilt, by its very lack of specificity, is deeper and longer-lasting than remorse. Both Osorio and Mortimer feel guilty for crimes they only *think* they have committed.

In "The Ancient Mariner" and "The Ruined Cottage," Coleridge and Wordsworth explore guilty *feelings*, instead of guilty actions, whose expiation is not a matter of law or justice – of action – but of seeking the sympathy and understanding of others, in the kind of temporary human community that is created by listening to another person's story: the space of art or *poiesis*. The Ancient Mariner and the Old Pedlar are, as characters, transformations of the evil personages of Osorio and Rivers into the good angels of the consciences of their auditors, the Wedding Guest of "The Ancient Mariner" and the young Poet-narrator of "The Ruined Cottage." But they are also human beings, not angels, and they both *have* committed some (vaguely) guilty actions, into which they must initiate the Wedding Guest and the Poet, who have not done anything at all, in order to create a broader and more human community of feeling. This element of initiation, and the story-telling art by which they get their auditors to share in their guilt, is the key aspect of the two poems' moral significance. It is what makes them go beyond, even as they subsume, the age-old tale of human suffering (in "The Ruined Cottage") and the fantastic exfoliations of human guilt (in "The Ancient Mariner").

My attempt to draw out, by drawing together, the moral significance of these two basic Romantic texts is framed in terms of practical literary criticism, and is founded on two basic contentions. First, that Wordsworth's "The Ruined Cottage" was part of the inspiration for Coleridge's "Rime of the Ancient Mariner": that

Coleridge, in effect, rewrote Wordsworth's poem, not merely in a supernatural mode, but in such a way as to bring out dramatically the issue of guilt which Coleridge saw buried, or hidden, in Wordsworth's text. Second, that Coleridge's "Ancient Mariner" was, in turn, a source of inspiration for Wordsworth's subsequent work on "The Ruined Cottage." Wordsworth took from Coleridge's poem, and dramatically brought to the foreground of his own poem, a more articulated and effective use of the narrative framework, so that the relations between the Pedlar and the young narrator in "The Ruined Cottage" form an even more important part of the meaning of that poem than do the relations between the Ancient Mariner and the Wedding Guest in Coleridge's poem. In short, with all due allowances for oversimplification, I am proposing a revisionary intertextual relation between these two poems: Coleridge reinterpreting Wordsworth's text in terms of *content*, Wordsworth reinterpreting Coleridge's in terms of *form*.[9]

Several points of contact in the intricate compositional sequence of the two poems are well known. First, Wordsworth wrote the bare narrative of "the Tale of Margaret" between March and June of 1797; it was the first poem he read to Coleridge on that famous day in June, 1797, when Coleridge came to visit the Wordsworths at Racedown in Dorsetshire and the *annus mirabilis* of English Romanticism began. We are not sure precisely what form of the poem Coleridge heard, but we know that Coleridge never forgot the poem's effect upon him, and that late in life he could still regret that Wordsworth had never published it as a free-standing poem in its own right. Indeed, it was very likely hearing "The Ruined Cottage" that led Coleridge to recognize in Wordsworth the successor to Milton, and to propose that Wordsworth write the epic "on Man, on Nature, and on Human Life" – *The Recluse* – that was to establish Wordsworth's right of succession by displacing *Paradise Lost* as "the first great philosophic [i.e., not religious] poem" in English. Second, Wordsworth did little or no writing on it or any other new poem between July '97 and January '98, being preoccupied with revising *The Borderers*, as Coleridge was with *Osorio*. Third, Wordsworth and Coleridge began composing "The Ancient Mariner" in November, 1797, and at this very earliest stage, between November 12 and 20, they were to be *co-authors* of "The Rime."[10] Wordsworth suggested the shooting of the albatross as the act which would motivate the guilt and penance of the Mariner, and perhaps a half a dozen other lines and images in the poem originated with him, including the idea of the "ghastly crew" of dead men working the ropes and sails of the ship. But he soon withdrew from the project because, as he said, "our respective manners proved so widely different."[11] By January of 1798 Coleridge had composed about 300 lines of it, or roughly one half its length in the *Lyrical Ballads* of 1798. Fourth, Wordsworth began revising and expanding "The Ruined Cottage" in late January of '98, working from MS. B, which at that point contained 528 lines. By early March he had completed another version of the poem, running to more than 900 lines. Most of the expansions concern the biography, character, and philosophy of the Pedlar, and, more generally, the articulation of the poem's narrative framework: the elaborate opening landscape description, the interlude between Parts I and II concerning moral *vs.* immoral tale-telling, and various versions of the "reconciling addendum," or moral, which the Pedlar delivers at the end.[12] Fifth, Coleridge came over to Alfoxden (where the Wordsworths had moved in July of '97 to be closer to him) on March 23 with a completed version of "The Ancient Mariner." In sum, we can say that the two poems reached their conclusions together, and that much of the actual final composing of both must devolve upon February and March of 1798 – the time of Napoleon's invasion of Switzerland, when English liberals were forced to abandon all hopes of a regenerative politics emerging from France, and a period during which the two poets were in almost daily contact: 25 out of 40 days, between February 11 and March 23, according to Mark Reed.[13]

Their internal similarities are quite obvious, once we decide to think about them together. In both, we have a narrative situation in which an old and formally uneducated man tells a story of intense suffering to a young man, probably better educated and of higher class, which fundamentally shatters the young man's immediate preoccupations and seems likely to change his life forever after. The Wedding Guest, stunned, turns *from* the bridegroom's door, and rises, the morrow morn, "A sadder and a wiser man." The young narrator of "The Ruined Cottage" (whom I will often call "the Poet", from the name he is given in *The Excursion*), is almost unmanned by his grief at hearing of Margaret's decline and death, so much so that in all versions of the poem written after Wordsworth's resumption of it in 1798, the narrator must be rescued from an excess of grief by the Pedlar's calming words of wisdom – which parallel, *in function if not in doctrine*, the Mariner's moral to his tale. In two early attempts at a conclusion, Wordsworth has the young Poet reflect on the tale's meaning for him. One is self-reflective ("and to myself / I seem'd a better and a wiser man"); the other is directed toward the Pedlar ("And for the tale which you have told I think / I am a better and a wiser man").[14] These phrases naturally draw the ending of "The Ancient Mariner" back into the picture, though Paul Magnuson cautions that it is impossible to say whether Wordsworth took them from Coleridge or vice versa.[15] Also, we should note that the two old wise men are portrayed as notably *un*wise and *in*effective during the course of the main action which they narrate to their young auditors. Evidently, to a greater or lesser degree, it is these specific experiences of ineffectiveness which have made them wise.

Beyond this, there are other general similarities: (1) a derelict structure (cottage or ship) in the midst (2) of a wide, bare natural expanse (common or ocean) which becomes (3) the scene of moral instruction. Fourthly, there is the symbolic function of ugly or grotesque natural objects (weeds or water snakes) which are both signs of the sufferer's agony yet also become the focus of his or her redemption. The mariner blesses the water snakes, "unawares," and finds that he can pray at last; the Pedlar, passing the deceased Margaret's cottage with troubled thoughts, suddenly sees the weeds and spear grass "silver'd o'er" with mist, an "image of tranquillity" so persuasive that he can "walk along [his] road in happiness."[16]

Finally, both the Mariner and the Pedlar have the advantage, as narrators of tales, that they get around a lot. The great majority of Wordsworth's poems in the 1790s are "road poems," or narratives set in the framework of casual wayfaring encounters. Coleridge rarely wrote such poems, but his most famous poem clearly owes something to the Wordsworthian model.[17] The Mariner goes half way round the world and comes back again to the normal world, where he will be forever, to an "uncertain" degree, a stranger ("at an an uncertain hour ... / That anguish comes and makes me tell / My ghastly adventure," lines 615–619). And of course the Pedlar's recurring seasonal rounds past Margaret's cottage are crucial to one of Wordsworth's masterful effects: the sort of stop-action or time-lapse photography, through which we gradually and with exquisitely slow painfulness see the signs of Margaret's decay and decline.

One could go further in detailing and dove-tailing the ways in which these two poems "fit" together.[18] But I want to move on to the more important question, which is how useful these similarities are in interpreting the poems and assessing their significance as texts of moral philosophy. We should not, of course, ignore the poems' very obvious differences. Coleridge's is a highly stylized imitation of the folk-ballad narrative, especially in its 1798 version, which arouses very different expectations in readers than Wordsworth's blank-verse narrative. Wordsworth's elevated diction furthermore leads us to expect a serious poem, and would have done so for his contemporary audiences too, but they would have expected its lower class, marginalized characters to be treated in ballad form, as Wordsworth consistently did deal with such characters in his *Lyrical Ballads* poems, most of which he composed immediately following his completion of "The Ruined Cottage".

But the biggest difference, for the terms of my comparison, is the simple fact that in Coleridge's poem the Mariner himself undergoes the torments he describes, for which he himself is responsible, if we accept that everything that befalls him after the shooting of the albatross has been caused by that shooting. Whereas, in "The Ruined Cottage," the Pedlar only narrates a story that happened to somebody else, to Margaret, and for which he has no *apparent* responsibility other than that of by-passing observer. Apparently: for though Margaret herself is partly the cause of her own suffering, and though we may say that the war policies of the Pitt administration in 1797–8 are also causes at fault, it is on the question of the narrator's implication, or guilt, in the tale he tells – and his justifiable projection of this guilt onto his auditor – that we can begin to interpret the two poems' strong intertextual relationship. In summary, the two poems appear almost as templates for each other, or as the die and cast of the same basic conception. But Wordsworth's raises issues of human suffering, and questions of human guilt, not in some fantastic ocean, heaven knows where, but in the world which is the world of all of us, and was certainly the two poets' world of rapidly narrowing political and poetical options, *circa* 1798.

It is no news that "The Ancient Mariner" concerns guilt: the obviousness of guilt in the poem is underscored by its arbitrariness. The Mariner shoots the albatross, for no very apparent reason. Disaster follows. Then, later on, after everyone else on the ship is dead, he blesses the gruesome water snakes, again for no reason: "I blessed them unawares." Success follows. In abstract terms of guilt and redemption, it is clear that we have a situation of arbitrary violation roughly analogous to Original Sin, followed by an equally arbitrary act of atonement, roughly analogous to Amazing Grace. But if we ask whence this guilt arises, we find no easy answers in the poem, though many have been suggested. But we find an abundance of sources if we consider the source – i.e., the author – since

Coleridge was a veritable connoisseur of guilt, theological, political, and psychological. So we may feel we need look no further than Coleridge and Christian tradition for the sources of the guilt in "The Rime of the Ancient Mariner." The legend of the Wandering Jew, who taunted Jesus on his way to Golgotha, is part of this source: "our Saviour sayd, / I sure will rest, but thou shalt walke, / And have no journey stayed."[19] Coleridge did not like an illustrated version of his poem which showed the Mariner on board ship, preferring to stress his endless wanderings on land. "He is in my mind the everlasting Wandering Jew — had told this story ten thousand times since the voyage, which was in his early youth and fifty years before."[20] Wordsworth also wrote a very-little-known poem, "Song for the Wandering Jew," on the same theme, but it associated the Jew with Jesus since, like the Son of Man, he can find no place to lay his head: "day and night my toils redouble! / Never nearer to the goal, / Night and day, I feel the trouble, / Of the Wanderer in my soul."[21]

But where, it may well be asked, is the guilt in "The Ruined Cottage"? Everybody has something to say about the Mariner's guilt, but few commentators have said much about the Pedlar's guilt. Indeed, the subject is hardly ever broached; it seems scandalously bad taste to do so. But there are several things in the story of Margaret, even as he tells it, that might make the Pedlar feel guilty — more than just sad — and give him a rationale (call it a program) for retelling her story as an expiation for these feelings. The responses of fresh, first-time readers, like students, can help us here. Part of their uneasiness with "The Ruined Cottage," as with Wordsworth's similar "Old Cumberland Beggar," arises from a naive sense that somebody could have done something for Margaret, despite her fixation on her absent husband. This may be, partly, the feeling of the young narrator as well. In educating students away from this "inappropriate" response, I have also come to appreciate its justice.[22]

There are several places in which we can find reasons for the Pedlar's feeling guilty about his role in Margaret's tale — certain cracks or inconsistences in its presentation that Marxist critics call "contradictions," or that Marx-influenced critics like Jerome McGann and Marjorie Levinson refer to as "incommensurables".[23] The overdetermined quality of these passages constitutes problems that the text creates for itself, by giving answers to questions it has not raised explicitly. Here, then, is a point at which post-structuralist or deconstructive reading can come into play, and, in conjunction with detailed historical, contextual research, produce the kind of results that the New Historicism claims for itself. Levinson's claim that a materialist deconstructive method can represent "the literary work as that which speaks of one thing because it cannot articulate another" is applicable to the hidden presence of guilt in "The Ruined Cottage," and to what might be called its overexposed masquerade in "The Ancient Mariner." In such texts' "allegory of absence ... the signified is indicated by an identifiably absented signifier." The method is especially valuable in texts where the rhetorical contradictions are so deep as to be imperceptible to readers who share the work's field of vision – as is the case when Wordsworth is read by devout Wordsworthians.[24]

I am speaking of the Pedlar's guilt not as cause, but as an *effect* – or perhaps an *affekt* – of Margaret's situation: not what the Pedlar did to worsen her situation, but what he failed to do to alleviate it. These evidences of the Pedlar's guilt fall into two groups: first, the incidences of his failure to help comfort Margaret; and second, the repetitions of his obtuseness in recognizing the signs of her misery. Although the Pedlar appears to the young narrator as the very mouthpiece of "natural wisdom," and although Wordsworth's long revisions of his background and character are largely concerned with giving plausibility to his philosophic utterances, he is, in the story he tells, notably unwise and ineffectual – just as the Mariner is in his "rime." Although he can offer effective consolation to the young narrator, that is precisely what he cannot offer to Margaret. Each time he attempts to do so, he fails. On the first of the four return visits described in Part II, Margaret weeps bitterly instead of giving her usual friendly greeting, and the Pedlar says, "I wist not what to do / Or how to speak to her" (309–310). A "strange surprize and fear" comes over him when Margaret asks about her husband, "And I could make no answer" (316). After she tells her tale, "with many tears," he comments, "I had little power / To give her words of comfort," and not only that, *he* "was glad to take / Such words of hope from her own mouth as served / To chear us both" (333–337). And so it goes, more or less, with each visit. At the end of his second visit, he "left her then / With the best hope and comfort I could give; / She thanked me for my will, but for my hope / It seemed she did not thank me" (428–431). The Pedlar's powerlessness before the ostensible object of his aid and pity anticipates his young auditor's weakness after hearing the tale: "nor had [I] power / To thank him for the tale which he had told" (MS. D, 495–496) – one of the many ways which, I suggest, the narrative situation *in* the poem recapitulates or anticipates the reading situation *of* the poem.

Of course, we will want to say, in response to this, that Margaret is a hopeless case: fixated on her love for Robert, she has no other object in life but news of him. Or, as in the case of Wordsworth's earlier "The Female Vagrant," we might say that he is not, here, interested in remedies for human suffering but in its effects. Yet this explanation from the pyschopathology of economic deprivation does little to comfort the Pedlar. Indeed, he hardly even raises its possibility: certainly much less so than my modern twentieth century students, especially women, who are amazingly hard on Margaret for being so unhealthily dependent on her husband and for failing to be, as they put it, an autonomous, self-actualizing individual.

The Pedlar's unhelpful words of wisdom and comfort during the primary action are reinforced by the slow deliberation with which he only very gradually recognizes the signs of decay in her cottage on each return visit, and his even slower readiness to connect these signs to similar evidences in Margaret's person and family. On his second visit, it takes more than thirty lines for him to draw the proper conclusion. The cottage seemed "in any shew / Of neatness little changed, but I thought / The honeysuckle crowded round the door" (364–366). Then he strolls into the garden and realizes "it was changed" (371). And finally, after a couple of hours' wait of "sad impatience," hearing "her solitary infant" cry aloud from inside the cottage (but not doing anything about it), he begins to feel what is happening: "The spot though fair seemed very desolate, / The longer I remained more desolate" (386–387). And only then does he notice on "the corner stones, / Till then unmarked" (388–389), the blood stains and tufts of wool from the sheep that have started to use the cottage as their nighttime "couching-place." These slow perceptions may be explained as Wordsworth's effective drawing-out of Margaret's decline, parallel to the Pedlar's widely spaced return visits, but they also indicate that, for one whose message and mission is to tell the young narrator, "I see around me here / Things which you cannot see" (129–130), he was a long time coming to see them himself.

These two kinds of evidence, of the Pedlar's inability to comfort Margaret and his relatively slow perception of her decline, are reinforced by two other qualities, one of tone and one of language. It is important to recognize that the Pedlar is still upset over Margaret's pathos, even as he tells her tale, and is not a neutrally impassive dispenser of a sort of Lucretian cold comfort, nor of a stoicism like that of Ecclesiastes, that all flesh withereth as the grass (though there is an allusion to the book of Ecclesiastes [12:6] in Margaret's broken bowl). When he asks, at the end of Part I, "Why should a tear be in an old Man's eye?" (250), it is not a rhetorical question. There *is* a tear in his eye, as is indicated by his saying, "Why should we *thus* with an untoward mind / And in the weakness of humanity / From natural wisdom turn our hearts away?" (251–253; italics added). The "natural wisdom" and "natural comfort" he has achieved have not insulated him from his emotions; he still feels for Margaret. Similarly, the famous "image of tranquillity" he describes at the end of the poem is not a cold icon. It appeared to him "as once I passed," but perhaps not always, and was addressed to "the uneasy thoughts which filled my mind" – uneasy thoughts, it appears, which still come over him in thinking, or telling, about Margaret.

Finally, as evidence of the Pedlar's residual guilt feelings, we have the oddly inappropriate language in which he twice summarizes Margaret's experience, which is echoed in the language of the young narrator's penultimate response to her tale. It is surprisingly sexual or sensual language, and hard to know whether to attribute it to the characters or to their author directly, as a subliminal way of heightening the anguished empathy the story commands. In his very first summary of her story – she was once here but now she is dead – he uses the same weeds and spear grass of the later "image of tranquillity" to suggest that the death of Margaret is something like Nature's rape or violation of scenes of human affection. Margaret was a friend to every passer-by:

> no one came
> But he was welcome, no one went away
> But that it seemed she loved him. She is dead,
> The worm is on her cheek, and this poor hut,
[his synecdoche for her]
> Stripped of its outward garb of household flowers,
> Of rose and jasmine, offers to the wind
> A cold bare wall whose earthy top is tricked
> With weeds and the rank spear-grass. She is dead,
> And nettles rot and adders sun themselves
> Where we have sat together while she nursed
> Her infant at her bosom.   (155–165)

Since Margaret's initial generosity to wayfarers is later paralleled by her pathetic questioning of any man who passes by for news of her husband, one might see a certain promiscuity in the off-the-shoulder *déshabillé* of this imagery, as though her ruined cottage is a symbol of the fate she provoked. But raising up the sensual connotations of these words seems so inappropriate to the context that one almost feels guilty for noticing it. Even the Pedlar seems embarrassed, as he says, "You will forgive me, Sir, / I feel I play the truant with my tale" (170–171). To what is he "truant," that is, not attending? To its moral respectability? Perhaps so, for such language is reinforced twice over, both at crucial summarizing moments. At the beginning of Part II, before the Pedlar accedes to the Poet's request that he "resume" his story, the Pedlar warns that he should not tell it, nor the Poet hear it, inappropriately; that is, sensationally:

> It were a wantonness, and would demand
> Severe reproof, if we were men whose hearts
> Could hold vain dalliance
[the "dalliaunce" of courtly and Cavalier love poetry]
>   with the misery
> Even of the dead, contented thence to draw
> A momentary pleasure never marked
> By reason, barren of all future good.   (280–85)

This connotes a warning against promiscuity in literature, which is to say, against pornography – a possibility so foreign to the evident intention of the poem that we tend, I think, to block or efface the suggestion altogether. And yet it appears again at the end, when the young narrator turns aside "in weakness," "and leaning o'er the garden-gate / Reviewed that Woman's suff'rings, and it seemed / To comfort me while with a brother's love / I blessed her in the impotence of grief" (495–500). And the mention of "a brother's love" reminds us that Margaret gave the Pedlar "a daughter's welcome ... and I loved her / As my own child" (149–150). A wealth of very intimate human relationships are invoked here, metaphorically, in ways that can make us very uncomfortable when we attend to them.

There are plenty of suggestive signs of guilt here, but they are signs which seem at odds with, inappropriate to, the obvious moral burden of the narrative, and which force us – if we are not going to dismiss them as "mere" metaphors, or "just" details – to recognize a certain deconstructive disjunction between the direction of the message and the direction of the metaphors. In sum, a close examination of the "originary textual moments"[25] of these two texts, plus some fairly restrained deconstructive probing, raises two or three important possibilities for explaining "The Ruined Cottage's" extraordinary emotional power: (1) a suggestion of the Pedlar's feeling of guilty implication in Margaret's decline, and (2) a suggestion that he is manipulating his young auditor into a similar feeling of guilt-*cum*-sympathy – which manipulation extends, implicitly, to (3) Wordsworth's manipulation of us as his readers.[26]

The parallel between the poetic acts of both the Pedlar and the Mariner, as manipulations of their audience, can profitably be extended, by analogy, to Wordsworth's and Coleridge's probing of their own self-conscious problems, as projected onto *their* presumed audiences. Successive displacements of the hard core of the story (from Robert to Margaret to Pedlar to narrator to reader) enact the endlessness of *poiesis* as a continuous story-telling that feeds the human need for constant testing and reinforcement of our moral investments. Insofar as Wordsworth and Coleridge felt themselves being forced out of a politics that would alleviate human suffering (i.e., beyond what they might do as local individuals), they were thrown back on the need to test, or re-assess, the basic grounds of any active human sympathy. They wanted to know if there was, in England, any kind of readership for poems that explored questions of human sympathy and community without entailing revolutionary programs of dictatorily enforced human rights on the one hand, or for the increasingly inadequate system of *status quo* parish relief (supplemented by individual charitable acts) on the other. In their explorations for a readership like this (which was of course simultaneously an attempt to *create* such an audience), they were testing the tenability of their own new commitment to the enlargement of human freedom through enlarging human sympathy. If there were no such sympathetic readers, perhaps they were fooling themselves: perhaps their own commitments to a sense of self – and of poetic vocation – based on such an ideal of sympathy was illusory, and politically gratuitous. If so, then even writing this kind of poetry was an additional reason to feel guilty. How then might such a poetics of sympathy work, in and of itself, to assuage this potential guilt? In this regard, the extremely stripped-down narrative situation of both poems might be regarded as the laboratory condition necessary for experiments in human kindness, and the reactive effect of the stories on their auditors as the experiments' moral "yield."

It was just these potential disjunctions between message and metaphor, I suggest, that Coleridge read carefully and seized on in writing his tale of guilt and redemption, "The Rime of the Ancient Mariner," recognizing the buried burden – the "weary load," as the Pedlar calls it (394) – of Wordsworth's "Ruined Cottage." He brought them to the fore with stark symbolic simplicity in the apparently arbitrary shooting of the albatross, an act which many critics have claimed derives its special brilliance precisely from its quality of arbitrary violence. Once we bring out, or at least bring up, the possibility of the Pedlar's guilt in the Tale of Margaret – not so much any actual definable guilt as a nagging, residual feeling of guilt – we can put it in the balance with Coleridge's poem and see a moral dove-tailing with Wordsworth's that helps to explain why Coleridge's remains, for all its supposed terrors, so popular and attractive, while Wordsworth's remains, for all its supposed natural wisdom and consolation, so powerfully upsetting and troubling. The wide allegorical possibilities of guilt in "The Ancient Mariner" do not interfere with our pleasure in reading it also as an enjoyable adventure story, but we cannot read "The Ruined Cottage" that way.

Here we come to that albatross hanging about the neck of all interpretations of "The Ancient Mariner," the shooting of the albatross. Is the shooting of the albatross in any way an act of personal guilt, such as may be operating in the Pedlar's narration of the death of Margaret? I simply mention the suggestion of John Livingston Lowes, the dean of Coleridge source-hunters, that he "really knew of no better short-cut to the comprehension of the poem's unique art than to imagine ... the substitution of a human being, as the victim, for the bird."[27] This fits well with the poem's use of the Wandering Jew legend, whereby any sufffering person becomes a type of the crucified Christ. Personal guilt can also appear in the fact that the Mariner has shot "the bird that lov'd" him (409), just as the Pedlar has let die she whom he loved "as my own child." In this line of interpretation, I am following Stanley Cavell, in his project of using the philosophic claims of literary Romanticism as ammunition in his dispute with the pervasive – he might say, endemic – conditions of skepticism in modern life. In Cavell's reading of the "Rime," the Mariner kills the bird to remove a claim of otherness or community which he feels impinging upon him: or, in Cavell's paradoxical idiom, to establish a connection "closer, as it were, than his caring for it: a connection beyond the force of his human responsibilities."[28] That is, the killing aims to assert or re-establish the conditions of radically "free" individualism which is the supposedly necessary or inevitable condition of human knowing and being in the skeptical view of the world. Although the information that "the bird lov'd the man / Who shot him with his bow" (409–410) comes rather late in the poem, it is indisputably there. Furthermore, it is sworn to be true by the voice of the First Spirit, in an oath which links this skeptical "sacrifice" contrastively to the most radically "romantic" sacrifice – and victim – of all:

> By him who died on the cross,
> With his cruel bow he lay'd full low
> The harmless Albatross. (404–406)

In "The Ancient Mariner," the guilty act seems very small, compared with the weight of punishment and penance that flows from it. In "The Ruined Cottage," there seems to be no specifically guilty act at all, until we identify it in the Pedlar's language and behavior, and then it appears as a much greater guilt than the Mariner's – being unable to do anything, even to offer any comfort, in the face of the decline and death of another human being. Whereupon, the punishment and penance flowing from it seem altogether too "mild" and "cheerful" (as the Pedlar's face appears to the Poet), except as we may come to see that the Pedlar's 'existential' penance is parallel to the Mariner's. That is, beyond the similar moral each attaches to his tale, there is the fact that the Mariner must wander from land to land, *teaching* his tale to the persons that he knows as soon as he sees them, and the Pedlar may have condemned himself to tell Margaret's tale to whomever stumbles upon her ruined cottage. When the narrator comes upon him, he is lying there with his "weary load" pillowing his head, and seems to have "no thought / Of his way-wandering life" (106–108). Or perhaps, though this suggestion is developed in only some versions of the text, he may be lying in wait for this one person in particular, this young poetical person whom he had seen the day before and knew to be in the neighborhood, hiking in search of the picturesque.[29] The Mariner wanders, the Pedlar waits; the one searches out, the other entraps, his chosen auditor.

But, granting that we may have found some guilt lurking at the heart of "The Ruined Cottage," from whence does it arise? Who is guilty, and of what? Margaret, her husband Robert, and Prime Minister William Pitt are as likely candidates as the Pedlar, to say nothing of the young narrator, who was just passing by, looking for some shade and refreshment. Margaret's guilt was seized on by that arch-conservative master of psychologically manipulative tales, Thomas DeQuincey. She was guilty, he said (indicting her creator in the same charge), of an irresponsible habit of gadding about the countryside, neglecting her children, and incredibly ignoring the most obvious sources of likely information about her husband, such as the local army post and the town magistrate, "the rector, the curate, or the parish-clerk ... the schoolmaster, the doctor, the attorney, the innkeeper, or the exciseman." "To have overlooked a point of policy so broadly apparent as this vitiates and nullifies the very basis of the story."[30] DeQuincey's response is a contextual, historicist interpretation that would match up quite well with those of McGann, James Chandler, and Levinson, even though its political stance is almost diametrically opposed to theirs. They fault Wordsworth's inadequate vision of the system(s) that cause such suffering, whereas DeQuincey faults his inadequate representation of the systems – the human communities – already in place to help alleviate it.

Or, to turn the charge around, is anybody guilty here? Need anyone be? It is one thing to wonder what our best human response should be to a "street person" asking for help or manifesting need. It is another, more mediated question to ask about the proper response to a story describing the hardships that led to such a person's plight, or death. The later eighteenth century specialized in philosophical arguments for the rights of man, and in reaction to the most optimistic of these, which posited an essential compassion (Rousseau) or benevolence (Godwin) as part of man's elemental nature, there arose a small but persistent line of rationalist argument *against* feelings of remorse or guilt in the face of widespread social evils.[31]

The young narrator would seem to be the least likely suspect of all, since all the poem's narrated events transpired ten years before he ever showed up at the scene of the ... crime? What crime? Robert's lack of feeling? Margaret's pathological romanticism? Pitt's domestic policies? And yet, in the poem as we have it, he feels the worst of all. So bad, in fact, that it is precisely to rescue him from his excessive over-reaction to Margaret's tale that the Pedlar must employ his "natural wisdom" in the reconciling addendum. Like the feckless Wedding Guest of the "Ancient Mariner," the narrator must become a sadder and a wiser man. Or rather, in the more violent paradoxes of Wordsworth's humanistic nature myth, he must become a sadder and a *happier* man. Before hearing the story he was, so far as we can infer, merely superficial, not guilty. But now he has been moved to ask, Am I my brother's keeper? Or, in this case, his sister's, since that is the relationship he adopts toward Margaret, when, "with a brother's love / I blessed her in the impotence of grief" (MS. D, 498–500).

And what of the Pedlar, who assuages his guilt? Why has he made the narrator feel guilty in the first place? Perhaps, as in so many classic guilt trips, to make someone else share in his own sense of guilt. If the Pedlar loved Margaret like a daughter, could he not have done more to "keep" her? Or rather, since I do not really find much to blame the Pedlar for, we should put the question this way: Given the Pedlar's love for Margaret, is it not likely, indeed inevitable in some terms of common humanity, that he should feel guilty precisely for his inability to help her? It is an education in these human terms, set in an enabling context of "natural wisdom" and "natural comfort," that he now seeks to convey to the Poet, by way of expiation. The issue is not only guilt, but also, as David Miall has said, in a psychoanalytic context, guilt *for death*. These are survivors' tales: two hundred sailors died in one, and in the other, "many [of the poor] did cease to be," Margaret being but one among the many.[32]

As lessons about the necessity for human love, responsibility, and community, both poems proceed largely by negative instruction. In strictly literal human terms, "The Ruined Cottage" presents the harsher evidence, but its final outcome is more optimistic, after Wordsworth added the Pedlar's moral. The Poet is calmed by the Pedlar, the setting sun shines with a new "mellow radiance," the mild air of this "sweet hour" is specifically "peopled" (MS. D, 533) with the songs of birds, and, "Together casting then a farewell look / Upon those silent walls" (535–536), the two men leave the shady spot, "And ere the stars were visible attained / A rustic inn, our evening resting-place" (537–538). This is very like a moment in the middle of the "The Ancient Mariner" when, after the first lifting of the curse and a fearsome night of storm when the "ghastly crew" works the ship's ropes and sails, the spirits leave their bodies and fly up to the sun, with sweet sounds issuing from their mouths that the Mariner compares to a similar kind of speaking Nature:

> Sometimes all little birds that are
> How they seem'd to fill the sea and air
> With their sweet jargoning.   (349–351)

But of course the Mariner does not get off so easy, and his pious moral, that "He prayeth best who loveth best, / All things both great and small" (647–648), is always qualified by the return of that "uncertain hour" when his "anguish comes and makes me tell / My

236

ghastly adventure" (615–618). Nor does the Wedding Guest find such an easy resting-place, when he turns away, "stunned," from "the bridegroom's door" and wakes "the morrow morn" with the permanent moral legacy, or hangover, of his new life, "A sadder and a wiser man" (658).

But, negative or positive instruction aside, Wordsworth's narrative framework is more crucial to conveying his lesson than Coleridge's. Clearly the Pedlar and the Poet are rounder, more realistic characters than the Mariner and the Wedding Guest. Wordsworth's more detailed narrative framework and more rounded characters enable him to blur the question of guilt because, to the extent that he makes his narrator seem wiser and wiser (as he was always doing, in subsequent revisions), our perception of his guilt fades: his improved telling helps him to "manage" his guilt – his expiation – better and better. This kind of managing-by-telling, by *making*, is, these two poems suggest, something we must all always be doing, caught as we inevitably are in the double-bind of being: between a dim but strong sense of human possibility, and an equally strong but "dimming" awareness of present suffering and cultural and political contradictions.

But what Wordsworth's frame does, that it is not necessary for Coleridge's to do (because of the obviously literary, balladic nature of the "Rime"), is to enable him to raise an issue that was, I think, very much in both poets' minds at the time. Namely, how is it possible – that is, what is a possibly effective way – to write tales of human suffering? Or, more starkly: can ordinary, unrelieved human suffering be made the stuff of poetry, of art, and still avoid the sensationalism of sentimentality on the one hand, or of pornography on the other? Minutely detailed accounts of variously ruined women were, after all, one of the great staples of eighteenth-century literature, from *Roxana* to *Pamela* and *Shamela*, and thence to the *Memoirs of a Woman of Pleasure* and the sub-literary genre known as whore biographies. (The contemporaneous rise and rapid development of opera as an art form shares the same constitutive feature.) James Averill has studied Wordsworth's poetry of this period as a search "for an adequate, non-exploitative literature responsive to human suffering."[33] This is as much the theme of "The Ruined Cottage" as the theme of suffering itself, and is the one the Pedlar specifically raises at the end of Part I when, having whetted the Poet's appetite for Margaret's story he proceeds to retell it, now for the first time in direct response to the Poet's request. Following the warning against "vain dalliance" cited earlier, he continues, suddenly embracing his auditor in a plural pronoun,

> But we have known that there is often found
> In *mournful thoughts*, and always might be found,
> A power to virtue friendly; were't not so,
> I am a dreamer among men – indeed
> An idle dreamer. 'Tis a common tale,
> By moving accidents uncharactered,
> A tale of silent suffering, hardly clothed
> In bodily form, and to the grosser sense
> But ill adapted, *scarcely palpable*
> *To him who does not think*. But at your bidding
> I will proceed. (286–296; italics added)

Much of Wordsworth's aesthetic is contained in these lines (partly cribbed from *Othello*), from "Simon Lee's," "but should you *think*, / Perhaps a tale you'll make it," to the Intimations Ode's "soothing *thoughts* that spring from human suffering."

Both of these issues impinge directly on the poetical and political composition situation of spring, 1798, as both poets were moving, consciously and deliberately, from overtly political writings to writing that was much less so. They were by this shift gaining immensely in poetical power, not only in strictly artistic terms, but also from the extent to which their friendship was based upon a mutual recognition that their poems should move in this less political direction. And I think they were feeling a great deal of guilt and anguish as they made the move – the move, as we might say, that made them famous. It was the guilt of not *doing something*, just as the Pedlar may feel guilty for not having done something. And it is a guilt which is both caused and expiated by the telling of stories, in two ways: first, for telling stories about the Margarets of this world instead of helping them more directly; but then, telling stories about them as a means of self-recovery, a way of expiating the guilt of not having been able to help them – or, in Wordsworth's case, not being able to address the cause of suffering poor people more actively and directly. This is the sense of guilt and anguish which is present but obscured in both poems. It is hidden in "The Ancient Mariner" by being translated into the safer literary register of the traditional ballad, which allows Coleridge to use the "purloined letter" strategy of foregrounding his sense of guilt until it stares us in the face, apparently arbitrary and without need of explanation or motivation. It is hidden in "The Ruined Cottage" by the still more radical "strategy" of Wordsworth's not publishing the poem at all for seventeen years – and then, as the first book of *The Excursion* (1814), in a much more conventional moral framework which further blunts our sense of the narrator's anguish over his tale.

This sense of anguish is largely neglected in recent – and otherwise powerfully illuminating – New Historicist readings of these poems and these poets, such as James Chandler's stern devaluing of "The Ruined Cottage," relative to the "Adventures on Salisbury Plain," because the latter is more explicit about the socio-political causes of suffering. Chandler has no patience with the Pedlar's moral because the change from "sorrow" to "happiness" "takes place in the absence of any change in material circumstance ... in a region where natural and human history alike are debarred from entry ... in which grief itself becomes the occasion of a feeling happier far than what might result from the effort to discover and elminate the cause of grief."[34] And when he says "there is no need in *The Ruined Cottage* for those final stages in which sorrow issues in enlightenment and enlightenment produces reform," he is not making a statement about the poem's self-sufficiency, but a strongly negative judgment on it. The difficulty in disagreeing with such judgments is that one sounds, in their face, socially retrograde. But what are "those final stages" so confidently denominated by that demonstrative adjective? I wish that we, or Wordsworth, or any writer dealing with wide-spread social problems (Dickens, for example) knew them with such assurance. But they might range from a Paineite revolution to a Malthusian policy of *laissez faire* starvation. Setting aside all the failures, disappointments, and downright errors that one finds in the course of discovering and eliminating the causes of human grief, it is simply too easy to make strong political judgments like this in all the beauty of hindsight.

McGann's criticism of the ideology of "The Ruined Cottage" is even balder, for failing to make explanatory use of the contemporary socio-political references it introduces, such as the war, unemployment, and Robert's leaving Margaret to gain the government's three guinea enlistment bounty.[35] Wordsworth is simply the wrong poet to be telling such a story, because "an Enlightenment mind like Diderot's or Godwin's or Crabbe's would study this poem's events in social and economic terms, but Wordsworth is precisely interested in preventing – in actively countering – such a focus of concentration."[36] Indeed, it would seem that "The Ruined Cottage" is just a "wrong" poem for failing to treat its events in social or economic terms. But McGann overrates Crabbe's powers of socio-economic analysis. *The Village* (1783) concludes by recommending that the poor of the parish pray for a local aristocrat who will be as good as he is great: "If such there be, then let your murmurs cease, / Think, think of him, and take your lot in peace" (Book II, ll. 113–114).[37]

I prefer Nicholas Roe's account of the case, in the most thorough account we have of Wordsworth's and Coleridge's radical years: that Wordsworth's poetry does indeed move "as an inverse ratio of its explicit political purpose" from 1795 to 1798.[38] If finding and eliminating causes along Enlightenment lines is the New Historical desideratum, relative to Romantic interiorizing or universalizing of human suffering, we can find other candidates for that job presenting themselves in 1798: Napoleon, invading Switzerland as part of his plan to unify Europe, or, closer to home, Thomas Malthus' *Essay on the Principle of Population*. Those who prefer these alternatives are welcome to them. The choice of one's champions, even among "Enlightenment minds," is never easy. DeQuincey's reaction to Margaret's story is also a political one; we feel its inadequacy, but we cannot set aside completely its aptness as a response to the poem. Wordsworth's insight may be still more radical, and difficult, politically: not all poor people will avail themselves of such help as is available (DeQuincey's complaint), and what should we do about that?[39]

Marjorie Levinson develops a more supple reading of the poem by setting its "myth of production" over against its "myth of reception." By demystifying the former – refusing to take the poem's "wisdom" for "truth" – she discovers in it "a human quality" that "enable[s] an experience no less profound" than the one evidently intended by Wordsworth. I find this persuasive, since it fits well with the way I (like many readers) take the Mariner's moral in Coleridge's tale: i.e., appropriate to him, but not necessarily to be taken as a full account of the significance of the events he has recounted. Though based on McGann's historicist critique of the poem, Levinson's analysis in this instance is a generic one, based on the forms and strategies of the Romantic Fragment Poem. The fragment in this case is not the poem but its central symbol, the ruined cottage. Yet Levinson also feels that poetry bought at this cost is too dear: "It is the entire want of anyone's practical interest in Margaret's house and grounds that so hugely increases the value of her home. This act, *a failure to act*, transforms the cottage from a directly and privately or locally utilitarian value – practical and emotional – into a symbolic, indirect, and generally available and readily commutable value."[40] Margaret in her suffering is "the producer of this value," and, in her "spiritually generative passivity, [a] type of the Romantic poet, or … of the ideology that defines the poet as a maker of this kind." And the young narrator is finally the Pedlar's dupe, because, "rather than focus the terrible – that is, historical – absences the ruin inscribes, [he] contemplates the reassuring presences, natural and supernatural, that the cottage quietly impresses upon the fond eye." But this is to conflate the narrator's response with the Pedlar's exordium, and thus Levinson also ends, like Chandler and McGann, by glossing over or rejecting the anguish that the poem produces, and which produced it.

I do not, of course, propose that political disillusionment and retrenchment is the only source of the guilt and despair Wordsworth and Coleridge express and explore in these two seminal poems of English Romanticism. (Or their "Guilt and Sorrow," as Wordsworth retitled his Salisbury Plain/Female Vagrant poem when he finally published it in 1842, thus foregrounding its moral feelings over its social action.) Both had plenty of other reasons for feeling guilty at the time, and the sources of human guilt are anyway inexhaustible. D. W. Harding's summation of "The Ancient Mariner" is apt for both poems: "The essence of the poem is a private sense of guilt, intense out of all proportion to public rational standards."[41] George Whalley proposed that "The Ancient Mariner" embodied one of Coleridge's many epic proposals of this period, to be called *The Origin of Evil*.[42] Coleridge's steady, though radical, Christian faith (unique among the major English Romantics), and his justified sense of having let down both his families (i.e., as son and as father), made him a veritable connoisseur of guilt all his life. Wordsworth was less troubled by having disappointed his guardian-uncles, but he still had, unresolved, his own version of the Margaret–Robert situation in his relationship with Annette Vallon. He had, moreover, been working since 1793 on almost nothing but a whole series of poems in which the relation between suffering, sorrow, and guilt was the overriding issue, especially the Salisbury Plain poems and *The Borderers*. (Roe points out how the Mariner's lifelong penance parallels that of Mortimer, the traduced young hero of *The Borderers*, who becomes a self-condemned "wanderer on the earth," forever crossing and recrossing the Border wastes where he mistakenly abandoned old Baron Herbert to his fate.) His handling of guilt in these poems had, moreover, become increasingly complex and obscure, or, as in "The Ruined Cottage," disguised.

But for these poets at this moment, *poiesis* or art-making provided a space for thinking – and for action, since writing is an action, with or without publication – when all other available spaces or options seemed, to them, closed. The efforts at self-definition which they worked out in two powerful poems *about* powerful tellers-of-tales (meta-poems, if you will) were for them more humanly valuable than any body of doctrine, political, religious, or critical, they knew of – and they had both had direct and active experience in seeking out, and identifying themselves with, the most advanced bodies of social thought of their day: what Wordsworth would later self-censoriously refer to as the "wild theories" that were then afloat, referring most immediately to Godwinian perfectibilianism. Their defense against the charge of apostasy and renegadism, which they had raised against others and which as a result they felt particularly vulnerable to, or guilty about, could be that of Theodor Adorno's defense for "open thinking," when he was charged that his interest in art and philosophical criticism was evidence of a dangerous *a*politicality: "The uncompromisingly critical thinker, who neither subordinates his conscience nor permits himself to be terrorized into action, is in truth the one who does not give up ... Open thinking points beyond itself. For its part, such thinking takes a position as *a figuration of praxis* which is more closely related to a praxis truly involved in change than is a position of mere obedience for the sake of praxis."[43] Such a defense stands firmly against triumphal privilegings of the political at all times or places, where undoubted social suffering gives moral weight to any doctrine which proposes to address it, or represent it, most adequately and effectively. But which doctrine, which representation? Paine, Pitt, or Robespierre? Watson, Malthus, or Mackintosh? Yet it also stands firmly against a subtle, subsidiary form of intellectual privileging – namely, the assumption that we *have* to choose between politics and poetics so finally or irrevocably. That Wordsworth pursues neither the line of interpretations proposed by DeQuincey or McGann in telling the tale of Margaret does not mean he has given up on, or opted for, either a "conservative" or a "radical" view of her situation and that of millions like her.

What "The Ruined Cottage" *means*, rather, before any position is taken, is that the question of the *representation* of human suffering must be attended to very carefully, with attention to as many as possible of its various nuances, mistakes, partial truths, and personal inadequacies. The very vagueness or uncertainty of both the nature and the placement of guilt in both poems, including its apparent arbitrariness in "The Ancient Mariner," works to implicate us *as readers* in the complexities of the stories, just as the two young auditors are implicated by their crafty narrators – whose craftiness, in turn, derives largely from their own naiveté when they confronted directly the events that form the narrative heart of their tales. Each thus presents, not a metaphysical explanation for human suffering, but a meta-poetical situation that literally *articulates* the need for constant telling (including revising) of tales of human suffering. The endless (re)telling effect of the two poems can thus be seen as a particularly clear and illuminating example of the work of *poiesis* in going "beyond representation," or perhaps more accurately *away from*, temporarily, the double-bind of cultural representation and its historically inevitable critiques as being either (a) effective but dogmatic, or (b) reflective but inefficient. Their double-edged narratives allow them to explore the question of *why* we should be *interested* in the suffering of others not known to us personally ("Why should a tear be in an old man's eye?"), not as moral preachments (the least effective part of both old mens' stories) but rather as identity-ratifying responses to our own reflections on suffering. This identity strives toward rational freedom and solidarity, but it also recognizes that its aspirations will always be blocked or compromised by cultural antagonisms. Any realization of this identity is thus always only partial. Hence the need for constant retelling of such stories (the paradigmatic implication of both poems): *not* as a cure or solution for cultural contradictions, but to help to establish a drift or tendency in their auditors toward similar states of reflexivity, thus achieving (however fleetingly) a larger human solidarity. It is in this respect essential that neither the Wedding Guest nor the Poet-narrator know anything at all about the person whose suffering they come to participate in so movingly. Suffering blocks reflection, and reflection blocks attention to suffering, yet we need both – unless of course we are saints and saviours, and assume everybody else should be like us. (Not a temptation that Wordsworth could always avoid: "what we have loved / Others will love, and we may [*1850*: "will"] teach them how"; 1805 *Prelude*, XIII, 444–45.) In the face of the omnipresence of human suffering, we need constant self-education about both it and ourselves. The continual, penitential, and *other-implicating* retelling that Wordsworth and Coleridge devised for their narrators, and their auditors as "reader's representatives," is a particularly strong and clear example of the work of *poiesis* in a time of peculiarly strong socio-political binds. The ensnaring-for-virtue that the Mariner and the Pedlar work upon the Wedding Guest and the Poet-narrator is thus much more effective than the ensnaring-for-evil that Rivers and Osorio tried to work upon their intended victims, all the more so as it extends very directly and effectively to every reader of either poem, with far more "dramatic" impact than either poet was able to achieve in his preliminary effort to represent this, the philosophic dilemma of their moment, in their stage dramas.

Guilt will out, and it does come out in both these poems, not only as theme or content, but also in terms of form, including the artist's forming, creative power. As Coleridge raises up guilt to view, to show that it is at issue, so Wordsworth raises up narration to view, to show that guilt-by-narration, by poetry, is also at issue, formally speaking. And, if we are sympathetic to their plight, we might say that better narratives might lead to a more persuasive recognition of the problem, that the personages in these poems, by deserving serious literary treatment, might be seen to deserve serious social and political treatment. In Coleridge's extraordinary letter to his brother, he defends himself against his brother's warning of dangerous involvement in politics by bidding farewell to any hope that the Lord's work of redemption might be found in the French Revolution: it is the earthquake, not the still, small voice. He also bids farewell to the view, dear to the heart of historicists new or old, that governments are the determining causes of human happiness or unhappiness, rather than their inevitable effects. And when he says, "Of GUILT I say nothing," I take him to be saying everything, or saying nothing because there is too much to say. Coleridge is raising the issue of both the morality and agency of art, especially the new "philosophic" poetry in which he has been instructing Wordsworth, that we now call "Romantic."

Notes

1 K. R. Johnston, "Philanthropy or Treason? Wordsworth as 'Active Partisan,'" *Studies in Romanticism*, 25 (1986), 371–409.
2 Seamus Deane, *The French Revolution and Enlightenment in England, 1789–1832* (Harvard University Press, 1988), p. 2.

3 Melvin Lasky; cited in *Biographical Dictionary of Modern British Radicals*, vol. 1, p. 306.

4 *Notebooks of Samuel Taylor Coleridge*, ed. Kathleen Coburn (Princeton University Press, 1957), vol. 1, entry 634.

5 Deane, *The French Revolution*, p. 46.

6 E. P. Thompson, "Disenchantment or Default? A Lay Sermon," in *Power and Consciousness*, ed. W. Vanech and C. C. O'Brien (New York: New York University Press, 1969).

7 *Selected Letters of Samuel Taylor Coleridge*, ed. H. J. Jackson (Oxford University Press, 1987), pp. 70–71.

8 Matthew Arnold, "The Function of Criticism at the Present Time" (1865).

9 I assume that readers know the story of Coleridge's poem, but Wordsworth's may need some summary. Its "plot" is very simple: Margaret and her husband Robert were poor but self-sufficient weavers until the economic dislocations of the war threw them out of work, and bad harvests reduced the food supply for them and their two children. Eventually Robert enlisted in the army to get a three guinea bounty, and stole away one morning, leaving the money on the window-sill. Margaret waits for him for five years (nine, in one version), neglecting her house, her garden, her children, and herself. One child is taken by the parish authorities, the other dies, as does Margaret herself, finally. All this "action" is over when the poem commences, as the young narrator stumbles upon the old Pedlar resting in the shade of the elms around Margaret's ruined cottage. The narrator asks for a drink of water, the Pedlar directs him to the well, and then, rising up and solemnly intoning, "I see around me here / Things which you cannot see," commences telling the Tale of Margaret to him. The poem is thus as much (if not more) about the *telling* of such stories as about their events and personages.

10 Mark Reed, *Wordsworth: The Chronology of the Early Years, 1770–1799* (Harvard University Press, 1967), p. 210.

11 Isabella Fenwick Notes. *The Prose Works of William Wordsworth*, ed. Alexander Grosart (London: Moxon, 1876), vol. 3, p. 17.

12 James Butler, ed. *"The Ruined Cottage" and "The Pedlar"* (Ithaca: Cornell University Press, 1978), pp. 7–22.

13 Reed, *CEY*, pp. 218–288.

14 Dove Cottage MS. Verse 33; *Poetical Works*, V.400.

15 *Coleridge and Wordsworth: A Lyrical Dialogue* (Princeton University Press, 1988), pp. 112–113. It seems to me unlikely that Wordsworth would adopt such phrases from an effective and memorable ending of a substantially finished version poem by Coleridge. But he may have been experimenting with them in trying to draft an ending to his own poem – an ending which clearly caused him a great deal of trouble.

16 Jonathan Wordsworth has compared the Mariner's blessing of the water snakes, "unawares," to the young narrator's blessing Margaret, "in the

impotence of grief." (*The Music of Humanity* [Edinburgh: Thomas Nelson, 1967], p. 98.)

17 Paul Magnuson makes a number of apt comparisons between "The Ancient Mariner" and Wordsworth's Salisbury Plain poems and "The Discharged Veteran" passage (published as the conclusion of Book IV of *The Prelude*), but he does not draw "The Ruined Cottage" into the comparison, reserving it for comparison to "Christabel" (Magnuson, *Coleridge and Wordsworth*, chapter 3.)

18 For example, among more or less literal parallels: (1) the Mariner's "glittering" eye and the Pedlar's "active countenance" and "busy" eye; (2) Margaret's uncanny tears and sighs (which seem to have no physical cause), and the unnatural winds and breezes in "The Ancient Mariner" (which blow without effect); (3) the apocalyptic, technicolor confusion of the elements in Coleridge's poem *vs.* the simple, domestic confusion of "unprofitable" weeds with useful plants and flowers in Wordsworth's; (4) the general impressiveness of both narrators: the solemn Pedlar and the scary Mariner. Among more fancy figurative parallels, one might compare Margaret's "look / That seemed to hang upon" the Pedlar to the albatross hung round the Mariner's neck.

19 "The Wandering Jew," in Thomas Percy, *Reliques of Ancient English Poetry*, ed. Edward Walford (London: Warne, 1887), p. 253.

20 *Notebooks*, I.45n.

21 *Lyrical Ballads* (1800), lines 17–20.

22 I acknowledge especially the insistence of Jonathan Barron, which led to our co-authoring the arguments in the case: "'A Power to Virtue Friendly': the Pedlar's Guilt in *The Ruined Cottage*," in *Romantic Revisions*, ed. R. Brinkley and K. Hanley (Cambridge University Press, 1991), pp. 64–86. My evidence for the signs of the Pedlar's guilt is here summarized from that essay.

23 McGann, "Lord Byron's Twin Opposites of Truth," in *Towards a Literature of Knowledge* (University of Chicago Press, 1989); "The Dawn of the Incommensurate," in *Social Values and Poetic Acts: The Historical Judgment of Literary Work* (Cambridge, Harvard University Press, 1988); Marjorie Levinson, *Wordsworth's Great Period Poems* (Cambridge University Press, 1986).

24 Levinson, *Wordsworth's Great Period Poems*, p. 9.

25 McGann, "Keats and the Historical Method in Literary Criticism," in *The Beauty of Inflections: Literary Investigations in Historical Method and Theory* (Oxford: Clarendon Press, 1985), pp. 17–65.

26 A further indication of the deep resonance of the theme of guilt in "The Ruined Cottage" is its "cultural intertext": the many biblical echoes in the language and situation of the poem, especially from the Genesis story of the Garden of Eden. If Wordsworth had chosen to call his poem "The Ruined Garden," these echoes would be much stronger – perhaps too strong, he may have felt. Most of the poem's evidence of Margaret's decline is taken from her garden rather than her cottage. Her garden is

now a "fallen" paradise, and she is an abandoned Eve. In other ways, the narrator and the Pedlar are figured as "Satanic" interlopers, in the physical action of their climbing a wall to get into Margaret's garden (there must be an easier way), and, on the moral plane, in their efforts to tell – and hear – her story without prurience, or guilt. There are also such smaller but still consistent details as the "young apple-tree" (MS. D, 421), which will evidently not survive her carelessness. I am grateful to Professor Sharon Setzer for suggesting these parallels, in a paper delivered at the 1988 Wordsworth Summer Conference in Grasmere.

27 *The Road to Xanadu* (1927), pp. 302–303.

28 Stanley Cavell, "In Quest of the Ordinary: Texts of Recovery," in *Romanticism and Contemporary Criticism*, eds. Morris Eaves and Michael Fischer (Cornell University Press, 1986), pp. 197, 193.

29 Reeve Parker speaks of "elective affinities" between the narrator and the Pedlar, in discussing the version of the poem in which their previous knowledge of each other is most fully developed – the Pedlar having known the narrator as a child, when he "singled [him] out" for his serious manner. ("'Finer Distance': The Narrative Art of Wordsworth's 'The Wanderer,'" *ELH*, 39 (1972), 97.)

30 *Collected Writings*, ed. David Masson (Edinburgh: Black, 1890), vol. 11, pp. 306–307.

31 Deane, *The French Revolution*, pp. 8–9, 15, 50–51, and *passim*.

32 David Miall, "Guilt and Death: The Predicament of *The Ancient Mariner*," *Studies in English Literature*, 24 (1984), 633–653. Miall discusses survivors' tales in the context of Robert Lifton's *Death in Life: The Survivors of Hiroshima*.

33 James Averill, *Wordsworth and the Poetry of Human Suffering* (Cornell University Press, 1980). The summary quotation is from Kroeber and Jones, *Wordsworth Scholarship, 1973–1984* (New York: Garland, 1985), p. 179.

34 James Chandler, *Wordsworth's Second Nature: A Study of the Poetry and the Politics* (University of Chicago Press, 1984), p. 138.

35 McGann, *The Romantic Ideology* (University of Chicago Press, 1983), pp. 81–86.

36 *Romantic Ideology*, p. 84.

37 McGann has generalized this specific interpretative crux into a challenge to all contemporary interpretations of Romanticism, and, by direct extension, to all literary and cultural work in the contemporary American academy: "The ground thesis of this study is that the scholarship and criticism of Romanticism and its works are dominated by a Romantic Ideology, by an uncritical absorption in Romanticism's own self-representations." And again: "When critics perpetuate and maintain older ideas and attitudes in continuities and progressive traditions they typically serve only the most reactionary purposes of their societies, though they may not be aware of this; for the cooptive powers of a vigorous culture like our own are very great."

38 *Coleridge and Wordsworth: The Radical Years* (Oxford University Press, 1988), p. 132.

39 For similar arguments in more theoretical discourse, cf. Alan Liu, "The Power of Formalism: the New Historicism," *ELH* (1989), 721–771; "Local Transcendence: Cultural Criticism, Postmodernism, and the Romanticism of Detail," *Representations* 32 (Fall 1990), 75–113; Mark Edmundson, "Criticism Now: the Case of Wordsworth," *Raritan* (Fall 1990), 120–141. Liu speaks of a certain "nostalgia for 1968" or some other era which the historicist critic construes as being politically and culturally more integrated than his or her present moment. He finds this tendency more marked in the practice of Renaissance New Historicists, feeling that Romantic New Historicism has been protected from such sentimentalism by the bracing example of McGann's ideological polemic.

40 Marjorie Levinson, *The Romantic Fragment Poem* (Chapel Hill: University of North Carolina Press, 1986), p. 222.

41 "The theme of 'The Ancient Mariner,'" in *Experience into Words* (Penguin Books, 1974), p. 59, cited by Miall, 639, note 11.

42 *Notebooks*, vol. 1, entry 161 (c), and note.

43 "Resignation," reprinted in *Telos* 35 (Spring 1978), 168; italics added. I thank Richard Eldridge for drawing my attention to this essay.

11

Her blood and his mirror: Mary Coleridge, Luce Irigaray, and the female self

CHRISTINE BATTERSBY

What is it to write as a woman? It is not just opponents of feminism who have argued against trying to find specific features in texts by female authors that represent either "the existence of a specifically feminine psychology," or a "feminine" form of discourse that must always and necessarily undermine the authority of a "masculine" symbolic language. Thus, for example, Rita Felski has urged fellow feminists to move *beyond* "any theoretical position which argues a necessary or privileged relationship between female gender and a particular kind of literary structure, style, or form." Writing by women is, she claims, "a social and historical problem rather than a purely theoretical one." What is required is not feminist aesthetics, but "a sociologically based analysis of the reception of artworks in relation to specific audiences."[1]

There are many virtues in Felski's critique of those who treat the "feminine" in ahistorical and context-blind ways. It is, however, not necessary to conclude that sociological analysis is the only legitimate means of focusing on the relationships between being female and particular forms of artistic expression. What I wish to do in this essay is to work towards a non-essentialist and more historically specific account of *female* writing: one that does not, I believe, fall victim to Felski's critique of "feminine" psychology. Indeed, as this argument will illustrate, "feminine" is very much the wrong word to describe what is specific to the female authorial predicament from the Romantics on.

My argument will suggest (against Felski) that in modern Western culture there are characteristic features of the female subject-position which are likely to reveal themselves in texts. These features are not

249

to be equated with a shared female "experience." But neither can the female subject-position be easily located in terms of the "feminine." Instead, I will suggest with Luce Irigaray that the female subject-position is one that is characterised by opposition and reversal. However, this "reversal" should not be conceptualized as a purely deconstructive move. Taking some hints from early Irigaray (but drawing back from her ahistoricism and some of her later conclusions), I will locate the female subject in terms of specific negations that operate with respect to mind/body and self/other relationships: negations that do not simply serve to "transcend" ego in the manner of the feminine, but which work to construct a different characteristically "female" subject-position.

My own position is closer to that of (early) Irigaray (whom I read as constructing a *female* subject-position) than to Hélène Cixous or Julia Kristeva, who are more interested in a form of femininity that involves a move "beyond" or "before" the Oedipalised self. However, the distinction that I have just made between the "feminine" and the "female" is hard to make in the French language since the word *féminin* encompasses both the English-language "female" and "feminine." There is a term *"femelle"*; but since it is normally used only of animals and plants, it is generally avoided in analyses of human sexuality. *Féminin* is consequently used both for biological sex (English-language "female") and for behavioural characteristics associated with that sex (English-language "feminine").

In English-language feminist theory, it was traditional to suggest that the term "female" refers to sex (the biologically given) and the term "feminine" refers to gender (the culturally constructed). However, in recent feminist theory in English-language cultures, the sex/gender distinction has (quite properly) come under question as it has been registered that the body (and hence also "sex") is not simply a primitive, non-mediated "given." The way bodies are ascribed to one of two sexual categories itself has a history; biology itself is socially constructed. This does not, however, affect the point of differentiating "female" from "feminine." To be "female" is to be allocated to one of two sexes on the basis of the way one's body is perceived. To be "feminine" is to possess characteristics of mind, behavior, comportment, or expression that are, in our culture, more standardly associated with females than males. As such, there is no contradiction at all in being a "feminine" male. However, a "female" male involves a category mistake.

As the argument of *Gender and Genius* showed, in Romanticism (and post-Romanticism) certain privileged *males* – the "geniuses" – were valued for their passivity, their feminine androgyny and for their ability to transcend normal masculine selfhood. Thus according to Otto Weininger, "genius is simply perfectly developed, universally conscious maleness" – but his "universal" maleness was also taken by him to include "feminine" characteristics.[2] In saying this Weininger was not atypical, since "masculine" and "feminine" are non-reversible terms.

Whereas the male genius retained his maleness whilst encompassing bisexual characteristics, the female genius was regarded as de-sexed by her supposed "masculinity." "Genius" involved a transcendence of the normal subject-position: a position that is "masculine." The "masculine" woman was returned to normality (as measured against the norms of male subjects), not pushed towards transcendence. Indeed, because "femininity" was *expected* of women, for them there was no easy position of transcendence. Masculine women were men; feminine males were super-men; feminine women were inferior men. It is for this reason that, during the nineteenth century, it became a kind of cliché to say: "there are no women of genius; the women of genius are men."[3]

Indeed, this last remark of Cesare Lombroso's positions women geniuses not as androgynes, but as hermaphrodites – to employ a distinction adopted by William Blake.[4] The hermaphrodite has ambiguous sexual organs, or the primary characteristics of *both* sexes. The hermaphrodite is monstrous and creatively sterile. The *androgyne*, by contrast, has clearly defined physical sexuality, but psychic bisexuality. When post-Romantic writers described the genius as an androgyne, they thought of this in terms of a male with a "feminine" psyche. In male androgynes artistic creativity was *dis*placed sexual energy; in female hermaphrodites, by contrast, genius was a form of *mis*placed (male) sexual energies. It is a question of the difference between noble and ignoble monsters.

In what follows I will use the non-reversible logic of androgyny to contextualize a particular poem by Mary Elizabeth Coleridge – "The Other Side of a Mirror" (written 1882; see Appendix).[5] I will then go on to make links between the *female* (not merely "feminine") subject-position adopted by Coleridge and similar (though also much more sophisticated) moves made by Luce Irigaray in *Speculum of the Other Woman* (1974).[6] As we will see, both female writers position themselves in terms of a "master" – and a dis-

251

course that valorises feminine males. Indeed, each of these "masters" draws on a metaphysics that mixes Kant and Plato.

I will be arguing that Mary Coleridge's poem has to be read in terms of her alliance with the Romantic androgyne – and her incapacity as a female to occupy the "feminine" subject-position that is associated with androgyny. What underlies Irigaray's text is a similarly impossible alliance with the *féminin* within the Lacanian system. Via mimicry and mirror-imagery, the two women writers construct a fluid *female* subject-position which necessitates ditching "femininity" and rethinking the self/other relationship. Neither woman can be described as either simply reversing – or extending – Platonic and Romantic "truths" about the self. However, the new subject-position emerges only via the two women's strategic attempts to explore the impossibilities for *women* in that form of femininity that is "beyond" (and that constitutes the edges of) the masculinized self.

Both Mary Coleridge and Luce Irigaray have (quite notoriously) been read as offering an essentialist vision of a female subject-position. There are already substantive refutations of this reading of Irigaray; but, so far, the only analysis of the Coleridge text that exists interprets it as reifying and reporting a universal and primitive "female experience." The comparison between Coleridge and Irigaray will thus only open up after working through a critique of this more standard reading of Coleridge. Although I have not got time in this chapter fully to refute the parallel reading of Luce Irigaray's text, I would also suggest that a similar mistake has been made. There has been a tendency to read Irigaray as describing in a straightforward, experiential way her feelings about her body, instead of recognizing that – like "The Other Side of a Mirror" – *Speculum* works dialectically to *reconstruct* (not just deconstruct) a female subject-position. Both texts turn inside out a metaphysics that makes monstrous female embodiment and self.

Coleridge's poem is quoted in full in the opening chapter of Sandra Gilbert and Susan Gubar's *The Madwoman in the Attic*: a book heavily (and legitimately) criticised by Felski for having reified an essential (trans-historical) "femininity." Since the poem is described by Gilbert and Gubar as "central to the feminist poetics" that they are seeking to construct, how one reads this poem raises important meta-theoretical issues.[7] My account of the historical background from which the poem emerges enables a different reading of the poem, and this opens up new possibilities for understanding the specificity of the female subject-position – a specificity that is historically and metaphysically (not experientially) based.

Gilbert and Gubar's comments on "The Other Side of a Mirror" suggest that this poem acts as a mirror in which the author looks deep into male-inscribed literary tradition. At first, all the poet can see is "a 'perfect' image of herself": "those eternal lineaments fixed on her like a mask to conceal her dreadful and bloody link to nature." But then – gradually – another image emerges: "an enraged prisoner: herself." At that point Coleridge breaks free of the voiceless dread and "speechless woe" imposed on her by patriarchal tradition. It is "the authority of her own experience" and "an invincible sense of her own autonomy, her own interiority" that she sees as she looks deep into the mirror.[8] Thus, Gilbert and Gubar do not only claim that Coleridge's text represents that of a woman who refuses to see herself in the male-defined terms, they also interpret this poem as expressive of a particular, historical and experiential act: one of looking in the mirror and seeing behind the surface image a true, authorial, female, angry self.

But this model is far too simplistic, and is particularly weak in the way it locates an "authentic" female self as surviving within Romanticism – a Romanticism which, as Felski points out, they depict as a "monolithic unified totality."[9] Significantly enough, Gilbert and Gubar get the title of Coleridge's poem wrong, calling it "The Other Side of *the* Mirror," instead of "The Other Side of *a* Mirror." For Coleridge is not just writing about what she sees in her own mirror, but is trying – and failing – to construct her authorial self by adopting (and reversing) the persona of "Anodos": the hero of George MacDonald's *Phantastes: A Faerie Romance for Men and Women*, first published 1858. Attention to MacDonald's text will show that, far from asserting an authentic autonomy and interiority, as Gilbert and Gubar suppose, Mary Coleridge fails to mark out a stable subject-position. Indeed, she seems only to be able to sense her own interiority via an elaborate alignment of her body against the male gaze. Understood in this way "The Other Side of a Mirror" complicates both the account offered in *Madwoman* of the way in which female authors resist patriarchal structures, and also the account of those structures.

Gilbert and Gubar argue (it seems to me conclusively) that for the Romantics creativity was an act bound up with male procreativity. What they do not adequately explore, however, is the notion of androgyny that was equally important to Romanticism. Had they looked more closely at Mary Coleridge's history they would have seen that this woman poet was not primarily interested in owning (or proclaiming) her female sexuality or her self. On the contrary, her choice of pseudonym indicates an interest in *renouncing* sexuality in a way similar to MacDonald: an ideal that left Mary Coleridge with severe problems, since MacDonald's androgyne was a feminine male and his women were represented as *naturally* sexless and as lacking any real personality or will of their own.

Mary Elizabeth Coleridge's decision to publish her poetry under the name of Anodos was in part motivated by an inability to think of herself as a genius, and an unwillingness to defile the surname made famous by her great-great-uncle. Her poetry was written for a small circle of friends, and was not designed for public consumption. In 1891, for a Christmas present, Mary Coleridge gave one of her closest women-friends a little white notebook half-filled with poems written in "an odd, laborious lettering of her own invention."[10] The poet added to this notebook until spring 1894, when the book became full. Without telling Coleridge what she was doing, her friend then left these anonymous "Verses by Verspertilio" ("Bat") lying around where Robert Bridges would see them. His enthusiasm for the poems was immediate, and Mary Coleridge was eventually persuaded to own herself as the author. She was even bullied into publishing a selection of the verses, but only under a new pseudonym – "Anodos." This name was retained until her death, aged forty five, in 1907, although her novels, short-stories, and essays were published under the name of Coleridge.

The first pseudonym – "Bat" – provides clues to the meaning of the later "Anodos," since for the Neoplatonists and alchemists the bat represented the androgyne. Mary Coleridge was a classical scholar, and also read extensively in non-classical sources of mythical quests. We can be sure that she knew the significance of this dual-natured creature: between bird and mouse, appearing between night and day, often seen as the symbol of melancholy. Indeed, her second pseudonym, "Anodos" also points us to the role of the androgyne in the alchemical quest for perfect form and for a Neoplatonic purity of being. For although in most common non-Platonic contexts "*anodos*" means "on no path" and is glossed by Coleridge herself as "wanderer," it is MacDonald's self-consciously philosophical novel of a mystical (male) quest for Platonic perfection that provides the rationale for the choice of pseudonym. Indeed, in the myth of the cave in Plato's *Republic* "*anodos*" is the term used by Plato (at 517 b5) to denote the movement of the psyche towards the intelligible realm as it emerges from the cave into the world of sunlight.

Plato asks us to imagine prisoners trapped underground and

chained so that their eyes confront only the back wall of the cave, deceived by their senses into supposing the shadow-images that they see projected on the back wall of the cave are real. Plato uses this imagery to suggest the necessary delusion of embodiment. But the myth also goes on to explore a form of enlightenment open to one of the prisoners who clambers out of the cave, up into sunlight, thus escaping the prison of the senses and of the bodily self. After passing through *"anodos"* (the passage of rebirth into pure being), the escaped philosopher realises that all sense impressions are merely faint mirror-images of a perfect and unchanging world of pure form. And it is this Greek term *"anodos"* that George MacDonald appropriates for the hero of his novel, *Phantastes* – and that Coleridge also later takes up as the name for herself.

MacDonald's *Phantastes* start on Anodos' twenty-first birthday, as the hero embarks on a metaphysical quest for completeness of being. The quest starts as the young hero enters his father's study and penetrates the blackness that clung "bat-like" to its walls.[11] As Anodos rummages amongst the withered rose leaves and letters concealed in a secret cubby-hole at the back of his father's desk, a tiny statuette of a woman comes to life and "in a voice that strangely recalled a sensation of twilight" promises to grant Anodos whatever he would wish. Mocking Anodos' belief that small size implies impotence, the Greek figurine makes herself the same size as Anodos and, in so doing, becomes irresistibly beautiful and incomprehensibly attractive to him. But she warns Anodos not to fall in love with her, since she might be one of his forgotten foremothers: "a man must not fall in love with his grandmother, you know." But as Anodos looks into her eyes he is filled with "an unknown longing" which makes him remember that his mother died when he was a baby (pp. 4–5).

Anodos is offered a trip to another purer reality – fairyland – which he then enters via sleep. Thus, from the start of *Phantastes*, the hero allies himself explicitly with his mother, grandmother, and all his matrilineal predecessors: it is his father – and male sexuality – that is the foe that must be conquered. Thus, at various points during his adventures Anodos is protected by a series of older women, including one who cuddled him and fed him from a spoon "like a baby" and who made him feel "like a boy who has got home from school" (p. 165).

The themes of incest – and conquering male sexuality – are fairly obviously continued as Anodos quests through fairyland after a series of white women and marble women who remind him of his mother. Adult male sexuality is always presented as a threat to the mystical quest. Sometimes, this threat comes in the form of an older male: the hungry Ash Tree with "ghoul eyes" and "ghastly face" who tries to "bury" Anodos in the "hole in his heart" that he is always trying to fill (pp. 56, 35). Sometimes, the threat of sexual need is attached to Anodos himself. Thus, Anodos opens a door that he should not open and gains a shadow that makes him do evil things. One particularly perverse act is the breaking of a delicate, crystal bowl which was "the greatest treasure" of a child who seemed "almost a woman." Anodos first touches the globe gently "with a finger" so that a "slight vibratory motion arose in it"; but then, ignoring the girl's struggles and her "prayers" and "tears," he seized the globe with both hands, so that it "trembled and quivered, and throbbed ... till at last it burst in our hands, and a black vapour broke upwards from out of it" (pp. 76–77).

From within fairyland Anodos enters a library in a magic palace and reads books which become real to him. In one of these alternative realities, he enters a world in which babies are found by their mothers under bushes, and youths and maidens who look too deeply into each other's eyes "wander away, each alone, into solitary places, and die of their desire." In this reality women have delicately coloured wings, instead of arms. When Anodos tells them that earthly women do not, this is thought "too bold and masculine" to be credible; when he makes them understand how babies are born on earth, their wings become folded in horror – one of the winged women even dies of sadness (pp. 102–103). The imagery of *Phantastes* is heavily sexual, for the shadow that accompanies Anodos and spoils the magic of fairyland is male lust. It is not, however, until the end of the novel that Anodos will transcend lust via a transcendence of ego.

Mary Coleridge would have recognized the Christian Platonist moral barely concealed in MacDonald's fantasy. Since she read Plato in the Greek, there is also little doubt that she would have known that in Plato's *Republic* the word denotes the way out of the cave that represents bodily form. Moreover, since Coleridge was also for many years one of a devoted circle of women who read Plato under the tutelage of the disgraced classicist William Cory (dismissed from Eton under a cloud of suspected homosexuality), there is also no doubt but that she would have recognized the way that *Phantastes* reworks the myth of androgyne from Plato's *Symposium* (see 190 b–193 e). For in the Christian and alchemical take-up of Plato's work it was the myth of the androgyne that came to represent *anodos* – and to substitute for Plato's own account of the nobility of chaste (male) homosexual desire as a means of transcendence.

Through the character of Aristophanes in *Symposium*, Plato provides a mythical account of the origins of love. In the beginning selves were rounded and whole: with four arms, four legs, and two faces and sets of genital organs. The gods were jealous of these self-sufficient and too-complete beings and cut them in two. Love is a search for one's lost other half; and it is also a journey towards a higher, hidden reality that can only be mirrored in a pale kind of way by this life on earth. Some of these original beings comprised two male or two female halves. Others were androgynes: with a combination of male and female sides in the original state of primal perfection. For Plato, the noblest love was that of a male for another male: it was (chaste) male homosexuality which made a male most resemble a god. However, for MacDonald – as for other writers in the Christian and alchemical traditions who took up this imagery – the search remains a male quest, but the searched-for other must be a woman. The lover becomes an androgyne in search of his feminine "other half" in ways that point to a mystical (not sexual) completion of self through transcendence of desire and through merging with the other.

In *Phantastes* we learn that "it is by loving, and not by being loved, that one can come nearest the soul of another" (pp. 232–233). Indeed, in *Phantastes* it is the quest for a pure white woman that becomes Anodos' search for a lost feminine other half – and is explicitly positioned in terms of a loss of primal bonding with the mother. By contrast, a male search for another male is represented – via the hideous shadow of the Ash Tree – as a form of vicious perversion. The female Beech Tree (who guards Anodos from the "touch" of the "dreadful Ash") wonders whether the Ash with the hole in his heart will ever be a man: "If he is, I hope they will kill him" (pp. 34–35).

At the end of *Phantastes* Anodos loses his shadow, having turned his back on the evil tower, at the centre of which is the girl whose globe he broke. He transcends sexuality; but only via a process of taking "revenge" upon the self which had "fooled" him so long (p. 228). After the self is annihilated, there is a form of rebirth. But when MacDonald's hero is reborn after merging with "the great heart of the mother" which is "the whole earth," he remains bound to

Plato's timeless world of being in which there are only eternal truths and neither change nor desire. Indeed, since death (and lack of passion) is presented as the perfect state (and characteristic of angels), it is only by preserving this lack of desire that Anodos can keep in touch with the "ideal bliss" of death (pp. 230–234). Anodos is the perfect androgyne who attains a (mystical) union with his female "other," in ways that recall the lack of identity in the womb and in early infancy. The self is reborn – a purer self, free of (male) lusts – and the girl in the tower sings of a better (fairyland) type of happiness as Anodos sheds his shadow.

In this context, Coleridge's decision to publish her poetry under the name "Anodos" is highly revealing. This metamorphosis of self – of affirming self through slaying self and sexual desire – is open only to males. Since there are no flesh-and-blood women in *Phantastes*, and MacDonald's female figures are but ciphers of male desire, the quest for androgyny remains a male quest. However much Mary Coleridge might have wished to embark on a similar journey towards a perfect Neoplatonic completion of being, MacDonald's narrative and philosophical frame leaves no room for female questing – or female selves. As we will see from their very different usage of mirror-imagery, Coleridge could neither identify with one of George MacDonald's female love-objects, nor ally herself with the lover who sublimates physical lust into mystical bliss.

MacDonald makes extensive use of the mirror motif within one of the fictions that Anodos reads in the fairyland library. Anodos reads about/becomes a student of alchemy who buys a magic mirror, looks in it and fails to see in it his own image, but only that of his ideal other. He falls in love with the "exquisite lady-form," clothed in white on the other side. Her "unutterable loveliness" is allied by description with marble and the eternal, rather than with living, breathing women. Despite the tears that well from behind her eyes, her face and form betray few emotions. There is faint sorrow, disdain, and once a blush. But even when she cries she remains "still as death, save for the convulsive motion of her bosom" (p. 114). It transpires that this pale lady is sad because she is under the spell of an old woman who has imprisoned her in the mirror. Thus, although MacDonald's hero can watch her in the room, he cannot touch her, or even hear her sigh. And neither can she hear his words of love.

The absent mirror-presence of Princess von Hohenweiss – "High white princess" – renders the student of alchemy/Anodos "passive, without assertion, or speculation, or even conscious astonishment"

(p. 116). Eventually, however, Anodos' delirium leads him to cast a spell on this princess, to summon her into his reality. As he casts the spell, his voice penetrates the mirror; but she pleads for her freedom from the mirror, and also from him: "if thou lovest me, set me free, even from thyself; break the mirror." Fearing never to see her again, the lover hesitates before annihilating "the one window that looks into the paradise of love" (pp. 125–126). A clap of thunder and subsequent brain fever means that it is many months before he can return to the magic mirror and sacrifice his life to his love to free the white lady.

The chapters of MacDonald's novel start with quotations from Samuel Taylor Coleridge, Goethe, Heine, Jean Paul, Novalis, Schiller, Schleiermacher, Wordsworth *et al.* As such, MacDonald signals in no uncertain terms his own allegiance to Romanticism and to an eclectic synthesis of Romantic views of the relation of art and reality with Plato's metaphysics. For Plato, art (and the imagination) offered only a faint imitation of reality that is itself only an imitation of the eternal and universal world of forms. For MacDonald, by contrast, the art-work is not less – but *more* – perfect than phenomenal reality. Art provides direct access to the higher reality: a reality in which desires, passions and sensual fulfilment have no place. Again, this point is made quite explicitly in the "magic library" episode of *Phantastes*. Here we are told that a "wondrous affinity" exists between a mirror and a man's imagination (p. 112). In the mirror, everyday reality "is the same, and yet not the same":

All its commonness has disappeared. The mirror has lifted it out of the region of fact into the realm of art; and the very representing of it to me has clothed with interest that which was otherwise hard and bare ... [A]rt rescues nature from the weary and sated regards of the senses, and ... appealing to the imagination, which dwells apart, reveals Nature in some degree as she really is, and as she represents herself to the eye of the child. (p. 113)

The analogies – and contrasts – with Mary Coleridge's poem are striking. Like MacDonald's Anodos, the "I" in Coleridge's poem looks through a mirror to a woman trapped in a glassy prison of silence. However, unlike MacDonald's white mirror-princess, the woman in Mary Coleridge's mirror is marked by harsh signs of red – "the parted lines of red." There is the same "speechless woe"; but the mirror-image of the female gazer is "bereft" of the "loveliness" that was the distinguishing feature of MacDonald's high-white lady. Indeed, whereas MacDonald's magic mirror transforms hard bare reality into eternal beauty, it is in her glass that Coleridge "conjured up a vision bare." Despite the apparent alliance with MacDonald that is signified by the appropriation of the name (and imagery) of *Phantastes*, Coleridge does not use the magic mirror of Romantic art to reverse the hierarchies of illusion and reality. Instead, Coleridge reverses MacDonald's mirror back upon itself (implicitly denying that art is more truthful than the phenomenal world of the senses).

The woman in the female poet's glass is no exquisite, pale, passionless, love-object, but a lover herself: envious, jealous, vengeful, bleeding, wounded. Her "wild" and "more than womanly despair" is very different to that of the sorrowful "pale" and "marble" ladies that Anodos pursues. Indeed, since all George MacDonald's female love objects are naturally sexless (and ideally have wings instead of sexual parts), the "feminine" subject-position is closed off to a female who calls herself Anodos. Although the woman in Coleridge's text is (like Anodos) "Made mad" with emotion, there is not the same celebration of passivity, of changelessness or of a delirium that will eventually lead beyond desire. Instead, the eyes of the woman in the poem are "lurid" as they shine with the "dying flames of life's desire." Indeed, via a series of contraries that typify the movement of the poem, it becomes impossible to tell whether desire will or won't die out. The desire is positioned as indeterminate: linked both to the "dying flame" and to the "leaping fire."

The contraries continue as the poetic voice moves through a (paradoxical) affirmation of the "hideous wound" of the female body, female desire, emotion and sensuality before it goes on to deny them by willing the vision to "Pass – as the fairer visions pass," and to be no more than "The ghost of a distracted hour." The aureole (or redeeming halo) of the poet's mirror image is not that of a marble, sexless, bloodless image; but "unsanctified" passion. Its "thorniness" is suggestive of a crucified, bleeding Christ. However, the wound is not stigmata; but something unnameable – indefinite – as "secret" and shameful as the hole in the Ash Tree's heart. The phrasing – the gaping lips, and the strong suggestion of sexual bleeding (rape, loss of virginity, the female "curse") – positions women along with MacDonald's Ash Tree. They are incomplete – as are all lovers in Plato's *Symposium* – but in ways that cannot be redeemed via entrance to MacDonald's otherworldly "paradise of love."

Retaining the shadow of imagery that is resonant of Platonism and a metaphysics that negates the flesh, the female poet retains the horror of flesh whilst simultaneously blocking traditional models of spiritual transcendence. The "vision," the "hope" and the "despair" in the poem are not directed out towards a love-object (an "other" which was once lost and must now be regained), as in the magic mirror of MacDonald's Anodos. Instead, the female poet seems entirely caught up with the paradoxes and the contraries of the other within. As such, her distress remains "unsanctified": abstract, despite the nouns ("jealousy," "revenge") that suggest a beloved. Hypnotised by her own image, the female gazer remains locked in a model of self/other relationships in which the "other" is also the self and hence blocks off the MacDonald/Platonic path to "slaying self" via the mystical/spiritual finding of the (lost) other.

Coleridge's text still carries with it traces of the Christian transmutation of Plato: not all wounded androgynes are holy. Male homosexuals – and females – have wounds in their bodies that prevent a higher, more transcendent wound in their souls. Trapped by the position of monster and hermaphrodite, Coleridge cannot position herself alongside Macdonald's Anodos; but neither can she see herself as the high-white princess who acts as the object of the lover's quest. The poet uses a non-idealised image of a female flesh-and-blood body as a counter to a metaphysical tradition that finds truth in art, and in the deathly whiteness and purity of unchanging Platonic universals or forms. The woman in Coleridge's glass is not even a "shadow" (the evil attendant of sexual desire in MacDonald's novel), but the "shade of a shadow." Indeterminate to the end, she remains caught between desiring desire and Platonic negation.

Thus, it is not the bloody prisoner, but the "crystal surface" of the glass that the poem would set free. The poet privileges the reflective surface – the cusp between the "I" and the "she" – and seems to will a position that falls outside the alternatives offered by MacDonald's Neoplatonic metaphysics of transcendence. The poem offers neither a sense of the gazer's autonomy, nor a consciousness of interiority based on "the authority of her own experience," as Gilbert and Gubar would seem to imply. Thus, the ultimate "I am she!" is not even affirmed; but is refused – whilst also given a position of finality which means that it is not simply negated.

As a female poet, Coleridge was faced with an impossible either/or, since what is blocked off to her is the position of the "I" that reaches transcendence via reaching for the pure, white (perfect) woman that is the substitute for the lost m/other. Unable to identify either with the "ghost" revealed in her glass or with the "fairer vision" of MacDonald's mirror, Coleridge's own "I" disappears in the play of mirror-images. The female poet situates herself on both sides of the mirror, and on neither side of the mirror: she can't align herself with the mirror at all, and moves in and out. In some ways, Mary Coleridge's original "Bat" pseudonym turns out to be more fitting than the Platonic "Anodos." Instead of questing for a way out of the Platonic cave of illusion in the manner of MacDonald's hero, she positions herself like a bat at the entrance to the cave of shadows. She makes forays out into the moonlight, but she lives in the twilight. She could not occupy the position of MacDonald's androgynous Anodos or "wanderer" who used his longing to clamber from sensual illusion up towards truth. As such, Coleridge positions herself in much the same way as Luce Irigaray in *Speculum*, that much more recent female response to Plato and to Lacan's appropriation of the Platonic myth of the androgyne.

Irigaray's text is itself structured like a curved mirror: a "speculum." This instrument was developed to see into the most distant reaches of the heavens, but was then employed as a gynecological instrument to probe inside the bodies of women. *Speculum* as a whole reverses the direction of gaze, using woman's body as the apparatus through which to regard the philosophers' accounts of being. *Speculum* divides into three roughly equal sections: the first on Freud and psychoanalysis; the third on Plato (primarily the myth of the cave from the *Republic*); and the middle section a series of shorter essays designed to reveal the continuities in the tradition of Western metaphysics running from Plato to Freud and Lacan. Jacques Lacan's name is never explicitly mentioned in Irigaray's book. However, it is his methods and assumptions that are mimicked – but also implicitly under critique.

Like Plato, Lacan constructs a divide between a "real" and the world that is presented via the optics of sensual desire. It is, however, not the body as such that is the illusion for Lacan; rather it is the notion of a "self" that is autonomous and whole. To see our selves – and even our bodies – as complete, we block off "otherness" and the infinite that persists at the edges of vision. Furthermore, Lacan takes from Kant the notion that self is only constructed via a "cut" from its "other" – the not-self. As in Kant, the notion of a transcendental ego becomes a form of necessary illusion. But in Lacan, "woman" represents the mother/that Other against which the

Oedipalised/masculinised self constructs itself as self. "Woman" does not exist – except in so far as she acts as the necessary limit to the Oedipalised self. Women are not "woman."

In *Speculum* Irigaray used the topology of an impossible (curved and shifting) mirror to show how women cannot position themselves either side of this self/other divide. In the final section on Plato's *Republic* Irigaray moves in and out of the philosopher's cave, examining what is (and is not) made visible via this myth of bodily transcendence. For Plato *anodos* represents both "the way back" (towards an eternal reality that exists before birth) and "the way up" (towards the truth, beauty and goodness that remain as real and as essential to the soul as the sun). Irigaray does not use the term *anodos*, but it is *anodos* that she examines as she brings out the womb and vagina imagery that runs through the myth of rebirth. But birth is precisely what Plato – and Lacan – do not discuss in their accounts of the real. As she says, in order to understand what is not representable in the history of philosophy: "It would be necessary to knock down the field of optics whilst at the same time keeping it the same."[12] Only by this double move would it be possible to see/ represent as a woman, given that woman is the blind spot of man's gaze.

In the most densely philosophical essays in the middle part of the book Irigaray reverses the mirror imagery employed by Plato and Lacan back on itself, as she works to produce a "burning point" that would reflect back and destroy the metaphysical past. Here also, alongside the metaphors of birth, topology and mirroring, Irigaray introduces the language of bonding by blood. She opens up a division between "sang rouge" (red blood, that is linked to matrilineal descent) and "sang blanc" (white blood/anaemic blood which links with white sperm and patrilineality and is also homophonous with *le semblant* or semblance).[13] "Whiteness" is the language of purity, and a dead, static, *specularised* nature. Against this whiteness, "redness" is used to suggest a form of identity that bleeds onto otherness. Irigaray is not providing an experiential report, nor an appeal to "nature" as unmediated access to the body. Instead what is offered is a new (blurry) image of a female subject-position that (she claims) has remained unrepresented in the history of the West.

Via an engagement with their philosophical "masters," Irigaray and Coleridge thus end up employing a number of common themes. Both women implicitly take up two Platonic myths: that of the prisoners in the cave of illusion and that of the holy androgyne who has attained *anodos*. Both use tricks with mirrors as they implicitly discover that neither Plato nor their more immediate "masters" can think identity from the perspective of a body that bleeds. Indeed, just as both Irigaray and Coleridge employ the language of mirrors to reflect patriarchal images of womanhood back on each other in order to mark out a subject-position that is at the cusp between "I" and "she" (ego and "other"), so also do the two women set up a similar tension between the red and the white. On the one hand, there is the flesh that bleeds with a "hideous wound": the kind of wound that cannot simply be reincorporated within the body of the androgyne. On the other hand, there is female flesh whitened into an unnatural purity – which is that of MacDonald's women and, according to Irigaray, also that of woman as represented in the history of metaphysics from Plato to Lacan.

Although I think Irigaray is wrong to construct the history of metaphysics as a seamlessly "white" imaginary, both MacDonald and Lacan are similarly positioned at the juncture of Platonism and of Kantianism. For Lacan, as in Kant, the self is not given as an immediate certainty based on introspection (in the manner of Descartes). Instead, the self both acts as the centre of the self/time reality, and is only positioned as such via an act of separation which cuts self from not-self (other/mother). The process of establishing a distinction between subject and object starts with the infant synthesizing a whole body out of the manifold of limbs and body-parts that appear in the mirror, and proceeds only gradually as language confirms the syntheses and separations of the mirror stage. As such, the self is fragile and, in the moment of the sublime, comes up against its (potential) limitations. For a fleeting moment the "I" comes face to face with that infinite otherness that has the potential to undo the self and its world.

For Kant the moment of the sublime was explicitly gendered.[14] Only males were credited with the full personhood that is necessary for the transcendence of fear. But Romantic aesthetics and metaphysics explicitly built on this transcendent moment to suggest a way of contacting "otherness" and the "beyond self" that Kant himself had denied. Furthermore, in the *Ethics of Psychoanalysis*, Lacan implicitly links woman – personified by Sophocles' Antigone – not only with the Kantian beautiful, but also with the Kantian sublime.[15] "Woman" is symbolically bonded to the death drive, *jouissance* and to that which threatens the self. This is the logic of the link that Irigaray establishes between the Lacanian "woman" and the "white" symbolic which symbolizes self only via an act of vampirism that drains real *women* of red blood.

Like MacDonald's Anodos, Lacan operates from a position that is that of a male, not a female. Asserting the normality of the male subject-position to what we call sanity, he flirts with the feminine whilst denying the female. Lacan can operate safely within the field of the *féminin* because as a male subject he is historically aligned with an ego strong and firm enough to be broken down and transcended. When MacDonald's Anodos looks in the mirror in fairyland that reveals "truth," there is no self: only the feminine "other" that substitutes for the mother. Lacan, analogously, allies himself with the *féminin*, psychosis, hysteria, madness and that which would show the illusoriness of ego. Of course, this is also very different from MacDonald in that Lacan idealises not male control of sexuality, but "feminine" lack of control. Lacan also adopts a very different – less Victorian – attitude to female desire. His "woman" experiences orgasm or *jouissance*; she does not just have delicately coloured angel's wings. But Lacan's "woman" is also as abstract a creature as the white and marble femininities that inhabit Anodos' world. Indeed, intriguingly, it is the *marble* statue of Bernini's St. Theresa that comes to represent the *féminin* and *jouissance* in Lacan's texts.[16] Lacan's "woman" is *frozen* in a position of writhing ecstasy that represents the polar opposite (and the necessary counterpart) to the male self.

When Luce Irigaray looks in the mirror, what do we see? A new subject-position? Or the breakdown of all subject-positions? It is precisely because in post-Kantian metaphysics self has been defined in opposition to otherness that it is so hard to answer this question. It is also because women have been denied access to the "beyond self" that constitutes the transcendence of the self. Irigaray's new female subject-position can only be constructed via a denial of the oppositional nature of the self/other relationship. Indeed, it is precisely the radicality of the metaphysical solution that Irigaray proposes that makes it problematic to see that what Irigaray wants is not just another frozen, marble gesture of reaching out towards an unattainable "other." Irigaray's "red" gesture works more dialectically to construct a subject that is always already wounded – and in which otherness extrudes out of (and into) self.

Intriguingly, there is another meaning for the Greek word *anodos*. In the ancient festivities of the Thesmophoria – the all-female festivities that were the precursors of the Eleusinian Mysteries –

anodos was the name of one day in the three-day rites of burial and rebirth which were celebrated each autumn.[17] On this day a procession of women from all over Attika climbed up a hill in procession, heavily laden with sacrificial food (phallic-shaped cakes) and animals (pigs), as well as a variety of other objects. The point of the festivities was to reinforce "the laws of Demeter" and ensure the fertility of the land and of the women themselves. What was symbolically restaged (with much rowdiness and "shameless" lewdness) was the rebirth of Kore (Persephone) after her abduction and rape in the underworld kingdom of Hades.[18] The women re-enacted the "bringing up" of the remains of pigs and the phallic cakes that had been thrown to snakes in a chasm in the ground during the previous year. To ensure a good harvest they then mixed these rotten remains with seed which was thus prepared for sowing. In the laughter and revelry of these rites of female fertility, the women celebrated the re-uniting of the daughter (Kore/Persephone) with the mother (Demeter/Ceres).

In the Thesmophoria, *anodos* meant (as also in Plato's *Republic*) "the way up" and the way out of the underworld. In *The Republic* (at 514–515) there is a marked similarity between Plato's account of the procession of figures going past the mouth of the cave – laden with objects whose shadows deceive the prisoners – and contemporaneous accounts of the all-female processions. But the forms of *anodos* – or spiritual "going up" – were very different in so far as the women celebrated flesh and (male and) female sexuality, whereas Plato opted for transcendence of flesh. Furthermore, Plato equated the good with the unchanging world of being, whereas for the women what was celebrated was change and becoming. Since the very first sentences of *The Republic* (at 327 a) start with Socrates "going down" to Piraeus to observe the ritual celebration of the introduction of a new goddess into the city state of Athens, it seems possible that Plato would have expected his audience to read his own account of spiritual rebirth and the way out of the cave of bodily form as displacing the traditional female celebrations that negated neither fertility nor desire.

In the Kore/Demeter myths that were so central to the Thesmophoria, the figure of the daughter and the figure of the mother coalesce, so that one becomes an offshoot of the other. What is celebrated is not simply a narrative of transcendence (the way out of the cave of bodily form). Instead, these female rites re-enact (with uproar and excess) the cycles of repetition whereby the daughter (spring) is birthed by the mother (the period of sowing) and then takes the mother back into herself (ripening, harvest). What was celebrated was not a (Christian/Platonic) narrative of transcendence of flesh, nor a Dionysian breakdown of identity, nor even the eternal recurrence of the same. Instead, what was celebrated in these all-female spaces was a form of identity in which self was relational, and in which otherness extruded out of (and was then reincorporated within) the female self via relationships of gift, birth, ripening and (productive) decay.

Anodos is not a term that Irigaray uses in *Speculum*. But when she first introduces the subject of Plato and that which is forgotten or blocked out via his account of vision and mirrors in that text, she plays with the word *kore* which (when capitalised) means Persephone; but which otherwise signifies "virgin," "pupil of the eye," "doll," and "daughter" (of some particular mother).[19] Elsewhere Irigaray mentions Kore/Demeter as she complains about the way that the mother/daughter bond has been displaced by the father/son bond in the religions of modernity.[20] Her general point is that neither psychoanalysis, Western metaphysics nor Christianity (which also re-stages and spiritualises the three-day ceremony of burial and rebirth) offer women models that think maturation, growth and transcendence in female terms.

Although it was historically possible that Mary Coleridge could have known of the ancient Greek rituals of *anodos*, we have no evidence of this. On the contrary, it is MacDonald that Coleridge mentions in a diary as the source for her name:

lest this *I* should grow troublesome and importunate, I will christen myself over again, make George MacDonald my godfather, and name myself after my favourite hero, Anodos in *Phantastes*.[21]

As the poet struggles to align her own image with that of MacDonald's Anodos, it is precisely the pre-Platonic sense of *anodos* that is blocked from view. But without a model of self and rebirth that thinks identity (and transcendence) in female terms, not only is the "I" lost – but also the sense of her female identity. Thus, in the diaries and letters that survive Mary Coleridge often seems to refer to herself as "he" and Anodos:

Anodos has over and over again been conscious, both for good and evil, that he was being rented by a spirit not his own, and when his body goes to sleep, he is in all probability animating another one at the Antipodes. Of course he cannot be found out in this Box and Cox arrangement; he cannot even find out himself.[22]

This use of the masculine pronoun – and this sense of being shuttled between two bodies – is particularly poignant given that in this same set of notebooks Coleridge also refuses to disown her sense of being distinctively *female*:

I don't think we are separate only in body and in mind, I think we are separate in soul too, and that a woman's prayer is as different from a man's as a woman's thought or a woman's hand. I cannot think of souls that are not masculine or feminine ... but just as the negation of sex is inconceivable to me, so is its unification; I cannot think we shall be men as well as women, and men women as well as men. If we do not retain sex I don't see how we can retain identity. Male and female we were created; it is the very essence of our nature.[23]

Mary Coleridge seems caught in a web of inconsistencies. She needs to think sexuality in order to think identity; but her sense of identity is intangible enough for her to describe herself (to herself) as "he" and suppose that she inhabits different bodies as she sleeps. Indeed, in this same set of notebooks personal identity itself becomes a fiction, secured by the transitory nature of the body, not the soul:

Personal Identity? People are fools that doubt it? Upon my word, I think we are much greater fools to believe in it. It is only the stupid transitory flesh in which we walk around about that makes us. We believe for others, not for ourselves.[24]

Unable to think of herself as *both* female and androgynous (in the manner of the male Romantics), Coleridge swings wildly between describing herself as having no identity and having an identity that is sexed to her very soul.

Mary Coleridge's writings are fissured and fractured by tensions that erupt as she struggles to align her own body and mind against the dominant models of the self – and the narratives of male desire and that which is beyond (male) desire – that exist in Western modernity. Her oeuvre is not an instance of "feminine" writing where "feminine" is understood as involving the breakdown or transcendence of ego. On the contrary, I would suggest that what makes Mary Coleridge an instance of a female (not feminine) writer is that she has no self as self is understood in the Kantian and Lacanian tradition. Far from having an (apparently) firm and auton-omous ego that reassures itself of its own identity by the rigorous exclusion of otherness (and then longs nostalgically for that other), Coleridge is wildly variable in her attitudes to the "I" because she has never made a sharp division between "I" and other. Thus in Kantian/Lacanian terms Mary Coleridge has no "I." She occupies a position not *beyond* ego, but *before* ego.

In this respect it is extraordinary to read the journals that Mary kept when she was eight to eleven years old. For although there are plenty of "I" pronouns in the tiny pages of these note books, there are no particular feelings that are special to the "I." The experience of others (her sister, her father, mother etcetera) are reported with as much vividness (and uncanny distance) as the "experiences" of her childhood self.[25] Gilbert and Gubar chose an unfortunate example when they picked Mary Coleridge as the embodiment of a female subject who had a sense of "the authority of her own experience" and "an invincible sense of her own autonomy, her own interiority."

There are, however, models for thinking ego other than those that describe the self as forming itself via the thrusting away of all that is "other." The twistings and turnings of the female subject who tries (and fails) to fit her mind and her body either side of the self/other divide does not mark the end of all subject-positions. Instead, it opens up the possibility of thinking subjectivity otherwise and thinking the self (in Irigarayan fashion) in terms that do not make woman either excessive or lacking with respect to the male. It is, therefore, intriguing to notice that it is in the Thesmophoria that John J. Winkler finds a model for a social order in which "men do not constitute the world and are not in fact its ruling norm but are rather a distinct sub-category of the world."[26] For him, a different understanding of female subjectivity can appear via adopting a different perspective on the rites of *anodos* and the "laughter of the oppressed".

In *Beyond Feminist Aesthetics* Felski rejects the notion that there is some trans-historical feminine consciousness. My willingness to register the existence of pre-Platonic (or anti-Platonic) forms of *anodos* does not mean that I would disagree. Nor do I think that Irigaray is right when she looks back only to pre-patriarchal Greece (and to non-Western cultures) for the expression of a subject-position that does not negate female bodies and birth.[27] By contrast, I see the problem of the female subject-position to be one that is linked to modernity and to the notions of individuality, autonomy and agency that became dominant during the late eighteenth-century period. Since the norms of personhood that defined the (white) male subject were only problematically able to embrace women, there were distinctively female responses as women authors and artists explored the spaces and trajectories of their own exclusions.

Of course, it is not just women writers who have a purchase on the fractured self, the double self and the multiple self. Nor do women across historical epochs and cultures always reverse (or use) mirrors or doubling in the same ways. However, there seems to me no need to conclude, as Felski does, that there can be no privileged relationship between being female and particular kinds of literary structure, style or form. For it is the varieties of response to this metaphysical and historical predicament that explains what is involved in writing as a woman.[28]

APPENDIX: The Other Side of a Mirror (1882)

> I sat before my glass one day,
>   And conjured up a vision bare,
> Unlike the aspects glad and gay,
>   That erst were found reflected there –
> The vision of a woman, wild
>   With more than womanly despair.
>
> Her hair stood back on either side
>   A face bereft of loveliness.
> It had no envy now to hide
>   What once no man on earth could guess.
> It formed the thorny aureole
>   Of hard unsanctified distress.
>
> Her lips were open – not a sound
>   Came through the parted lines of red.
> Whate'er it was, the hideous wound
>   In silence and in secret bled.
> No sigh relieved her speechless woe,
>   She had no voice to speak her dread.
>
> And in her lurid eyes there shone
>   The dying flame of life's desire,
> Made mad because its hope was gone,
>   And kindled at the leaping fire
> Of jealously, and fierce revenge,
>   And strength that could not change nor tire.
>
> Shade of a shadow in the glass,
>   O set the crystal surface free!

Pass – as the fairer visions pass –
Nor ever more return, to be
The ghost of a distracted hour,
That heard me whisper, "I am she!"

Mary Elizabeth Coleridge (1882)

Notes

1 Rita Felski, *Beyond Feminist Aesthetics* (London: Hutchison Radius, 1989), pp. 19, 3, 160.
2 Otto Weininger, *Sex and Character* [1903] (London: Heinemann; New York: Putnam, 1906) p. 189. And see Christine Battersby, *Gender and Genius: Towards a Feminist Aesthetics* (London: The Women's Press; Bloomington: Indiana University Press, 1989), pp. 113–119.
3 See *Gender and Genius*, pp. 3–4, 117–119.
4 See *ibid.*, p. 91.
5 See *The Collected Poems of Mary Coleridge*, ed. Theresa Whistler (London: Rupert Hart-Davis, 1954), pp. 88–89.
6 Luce Irigaray, *Speculum of the Other Woman* [1974], trans. Gillian C. Gill (Ithaca: Cornell University Press, 1985).
7 Sandra M. Gilbert and Susan Gubar, *The Madwoman in the Attic* (New Haven; London: Yale University Press, 1979), p. 15.
8 *Ibid.*, pp. 15–16.
9 Felski, *Beyond Feminist Aesthetics*, p 28.
10 Whistler, introd. to *Collected Poems*, pp. 62–63.
11 George MacDonald, *Phantastes: A Faerie Romance for Men and Women* (London; New York: Dent, Everyman, 1915), p. 2. Page number references cited in the text are to this edition.
12 Irigaray, *Speculum*, p. 337 (my revised translation).
13 The red blood/white blood imagery is introduced in the chapter on Hegel (*Speculum*, pp. 214–226) and then recurs to the end.
14 See Christine Battersby, "Stages on Kant's Way: Aesthetics, Morality and the Gendered Sublime," in *Feminism and Tradition in Aesthetics*, eds. P. Brand and C. Korsmeyer (Pennsylvania: Penn State University Press, 1995), pp. 88–111. A companion essay is my, "Unblocking the Oedipal: Karoline von Günderode and the Female Sublime," in *Political Gender*, eds. Sally Ledger, Josephine McDonagh, and Jane Spencer (London: Harvester Wheatsheaf, 1994), pp.129–143.
15 Jacques Lacan, *The Ethics of Psychoanalysis, 1959–60* (*Seminar VII*) trans. Dennis Porter (London: Routledge, 1992), pp. 286ff. (and 257ff. for the beautiful).
16 See Jacques Lacan, *Feminine Sexuality*, trans. and eds. Juliet Mitchell and Jacqueline Rose (London: Macmillan, 1982), especially p. 147 (from Seminar XX).
17 See, for example, John J. Winkler, *The Constraints of Desire: The*

271

Christine Battersby

Anthropology of Sex and Gender in Ancient Greece (New York; London: Routledge, 1990), pp. 193–209, and Anne Baring and Jules Cashford, *The Myth of the Goddess* (New York; London: Viking Arkana, 1991), pp. 374–377. See also "Avoδos" in *Pauly's Real-Encyclopädie der klassischen Altertumswissenschaft* (1894 edn.) and "Thesmophoria" by J. G. Fraser in the *Encyclopaedia Britannica* (9th, 1870 edn.).

18 See Winkler, p. 196 for contemporaneous descriptions of the rites as "shameless" and elaboration on the detail of their sexual nature.
19 Irigaray, *Speculum*, pp.147–149.
20 See Luce Irigaray, "Women, The Sacred and Money," trans. *Paragraph* viii (October 1986), pp. 6–18 and "Language, Persephone and Sacrifice," Interview trans. *Borderlines* iv (1985–6), 30–32. Also Luisa Muraro "Female Genealogies" in *Engaging with Irigaray* eds. Carolyn Burke *et al.* (New York: Columbia University Press, 1994), pp. 317–333.
21 Mary Coleridge, *Gathered Leaves from the Prose of Mary E. Coleridge*, ed. Edith Sichel (London: Constable, 1910), pp. 23–24.
22 *Ibid.*, p. 221. The entry of June 3rd 1888 (p. 222) makes it utterly clear that the "he" and "Anodos" signify Coleridge herself.
23 *Ibid.*, pp. 233–234.
24 *Ibid.*, p. 221.
25 MSS in Coleridge Collection, Diaries, 1870–9, in 6 notebooks, 670 pp., Humanities Research Centre, University of Texas at Austin.
26 Winkler, *Constraints*, p. 208.
27 I have argued this more fully in Christine Battersby, "Just Jamming: Irigaray, Painting and Psychoanalysis," in *New Feminist Art Criticism* ed. Katy Deepwell (Manchester University Press, 1995), pp. 128–137.
28 I would like to thank Carolyn Steedman for bringing Mary Coleridge's juvenile diaries to my attention; Angela Hobbs for help with opening lines of Plato's *Republic*; and also Richard Eldridge for his editorial comments.

12

Scene: An exchange of letters

PHILIPPE LACOUE-LABARTHE AND JEAN-LUC NANCY
translated by Maiko Behr

Dear Philippe,

Since we have been asked to contribute a work on "the scene" [*la scène*], I'd like to sieze the occasion to revive a debate which we have broached several times, long ago. I will, then, summarize the theme in the Greek word *opsis,* which designates, in Aristotle's terms, just about what we call "staging" [*mise en scène*]. ("Just about": here already is a problem of translation, and consequently of meaning and nuance. It can also be translated by "performance" [*spectacle*]. We will be able to return to this problem later.)

The *opsis* is one of the six "parts" of the tragedy, according to the *Poetics* (50a), which, "involves everything," listing the five other parts. A passage to be interpreted delicately, it could simply mean that when there is performance, there is everything else as well, plot, text, etc. (cf. the note of R. Dupont-Roc and J. Lallot; I will note their edition simply with a P). A little further along, when Aristotle details the nature of these parts, he declares that the *opsis* is on the one hand "seductive" ("psychagogical", 50b17), but, on the other hand, foreign to art (*atekhnotaton),* and not at all in its rightful place in the *Poetics.* If there is, in this case, *tekhnē,* it is that of the prop master (*skeuopoios*), not that of the *poiétés.* For "the tragedy achieves its finality even without enactment and without actors" (50b18). Consequently, its entire effect is found only in its reading. (I would remind you, in passing, that this signifies, for a Greek, reading aloud, which implies something quite different from our silent reading.)

In the continuation of the *Poetics,* the *opsis* appears at times valued, at times, as we see here, devalorised. Perhaps we can return to the detail of the texts. For the moment, I would like to ask you this:

(1) In our debate I always take the side of the *opsis* and you the

side of the "solitary reading," having neither of us ever really elucidated the reasons or the more or less clear motives of these preferences, nor fully analyzed their risks. As for the rest, paradox rules that it be you who has taken to practicing "staging" [*mise en scène*], while I for my part am in general rather unreceptive to the performance of theater. (As you know, I would have liked to play the role of comedian on the stage.) For the moment, before searching for these explanations, I would simply like to ask whether you still take the same "side," and why.

(2) The question of the *opsis*, or of the "staging" [*scène*], seems to me to relate in a precise and decisive manner to a more general question of the "figure" which preoccupies us both. For you, it evokes suspicion toward what you have termed "onto-typology," that is to say toward a figural and fictional assignation of the presentation of the being and/or of the truth. It is, after all, as an extension of this problem that I had spoken of the "interruption of the myth" as an element or decisive event for an actual idea of the being-in-common [*l'être-en-commun*]. But it seems to me that our divergence on the subject of the *opsis* comes into play again here: to state it quickly, you still tend toward an effacement of the "figure" (you speak voluntarily of "de-figuration," again in "Il faut" in fig. 6, 1991, where you invoke also an "extinction" of the figure, like some sort of extra-figure), while I find myself always brought back to the demand for a certain figuration, because the "interruption" of the myth does not seem to me a simple cessation, but rather a cutting movement which, in cutting, delineates another area of enunciation.

As for the rest, perhaps the beginning of the business is here: between a "figure" thought of initially as (re)presentation, and a "figure" thought of initially as a place of emission and as an enunciatory presence (inseparable, then, from a voice).

Pushing to the extreme, one could also consider it a question of the qualities of an identity *versus* the openness of individuality. Almost the same thing, and therefore, as is fitting, an irreconcilable difference.

What, then, is a "stage" [*scène*] if it is always a place for figures, and if there are no figures except on a stage? What happens to these two modes of the figure? (Whether figure is the right word or not is another affair entirely. We would have to speak also of images and the different relationships we have with them, you and I, and then also of sketches – but that will be for later.)

Or must we even think of two modes of the stage? And is it out of this duality that we must approach the question of the stage – of the theatrical stage, the political stage, the analytical stage?

My dear Jean-Luc,

Let us then return to our discussion; it's a good idea. But this will hardly rejuvenate us. It is a discussion we had twenty years ago, between '70 and '72, I believe. And in my memory at least, it did not concern theater specifically, but opera, of which we were great "consumers" at the time (we never stopped listening to it). Disappointed by all the "stagings" [*mises en scènes*] that I was able to see – including those of Wieland Wagner in Bayreuth in '69 (*Tristan,* the *Tetrology, Parsifal*), despite some unforgettable "moments" – I defended the "oratorio form" or the "concert version." I thought that all characteristically dramatic intensity was condensed in the *agony* of the voice and that, for what little the singers were visible, meaning that one attended the performance under technical (musical) constraints, the presentation – in the Aristotelian sense of the *mimēsis* – could still be perfect. Thus, nothing offended me more – indeed there is still nothing which offends me more – than the distortion, if not the contradiction, which appeared so violently at times between some wording or other, either harsh or sweet, and the disproportionate mimicry to which the singing was forced. I was driven to tears to know that such a soft word of love required such contortions of the face or mouth, or that on the other hand a declaration of hatred – a voice suddenly turned white – could, in the height of brutality, make do with an impassive face. The rest – props, costumes, even lighting, not to mention the acting, often pitiable or grotesque, of the actors – singers – seemed to me *accessory* . Moreover, I have rediscovered the same impression when mixing in theater, thus becoming more and more attentive to the *work* (of the body, in short) required in the utterance of feeling – a public, amplified, forced utterance. I am not far from thinking that it is there that the question of "staging" resolves itself, but we must come back to this term.

You warned, then, against this (vague) intuition, the *opsis,* which word, if not the concept, you took from the *Poetics* of Aristotle, as you recalled in your letter. You say that it "designates, in Aristotle's terms, just about what we call 'staging'" adding in parentheses "('Just about': here already is a problem of translation, and consequently of meaning and nuance. It can also be translated by 'performance'. We will be able to return to this problem later.)" Actually, I sat down to reread the *Poetics* and have remained, I must confess, quite perplexed.

Obviously we are neither going to embark upon a commentary of the *Poetics*, nor redouble the minute and enlightening notes of the Dupont-Roc and Lallot edition. I will settle then for a few isolated comments.

The first is to say that to me "staging" [*mise en scène*], at least in the sense that we understand it today, does not seem capable of translating *opsis*. In the passage from chapter 6 to which you refer (501b), *opsis* probably signifies nothing more than "performance" [*spectacle*], that is, simply the act of seeing or, for one thing, offering to view. (The nuance of this second is moreover largely attested to in the vocabulary of tragedy.) It is "presentation" in the most banal sense of the term: that which one attends at the theater. Since tragedy is of the genre of drama, presentation is inherent in its definition and it is normal that it include everything that is implied by this term, that is, the other five parts constituting tragedy as it is defined by Aristotle: story, characters, expression, thought, and song. But also since the true finality of the tragedy, its veritable *telos*, is the *catharsis* of terror and pity, and since the reading (aloud, of course; this is very important) suffices to cause this *catharsis*, the representation – from the exclusively Aristotelian point of view, that of a poetics – is not at all necessary. It is what Aristotle says most explicitly and most coherently, which is: "As for the performance, which exercises the greatest seduction, it is totally foreign to art and has nothing to do with poetics, for tragedy achieves its finality even without 'happening,' and without actors." And it is not less coherent when he adds later (I am modifying the translation slightly): "In addition, for the finishing (*apergasia*) of the performance, the art of the property maker is more decisive than that of the poets." The allusion to a rubric of "décor and costumes" is perfectly clear, and there are other occurrences of this elsewhere: for example in chapter 4 where you will recall that Sophocles introduced a third actor and painted sets (49a). All this raises again what Aristotle calls the organization or the arrangement of the performance (*ho tès opseôs kosmos*), which, it seems to me, confirms a passage from chapter 18 where Aristotle, who distinguishes between four types of tragedy (complex tragedy, "consisting entirely of the *coup de théâtre* and of recognition," tragedy of violent effects, tragedy of character), reserves the word *opsis* to designate the fourth type, "for example the *Phorcides, Prometheus* and all that which unfolds in Hades"

(56b, 32 sq.): otherwise known as tragedy "of great show" [*à grand spectacle*] or of "special effects" [*effets spéciaux*].

I think the distinction between "performance" [*spectacle*] and "staging" [*mise en scène*] must be held firmly. As we have learned from a recent history, theater is not in the performance, even less in the spectacular: one has been able to attend stunning performances (from the point of view of scenery, lighting, illusion or "realistic effect") above all in the last decade when the concurrence with cinema has been considerably aggravated without as much as the appearance of the least hint of staging. Moreover, you know how tedious this genre of "theater" is. Once the surprise of the spectacular has passed (one has a "full view" of it really), and in spite of several predestined "events" from time to time to renew interest, one remains there to listen to a text which one does not even hear because he is in the presence of actors who, *visibly*, do not know what to do with it; and it is fatal. (You, in general, always left before the end ...) Now, if I hold so strongly to this distinction, it is only because I am under the impression – perhaps false, we must discuss it – that it is precisely by this distinction that Aristotle governs himself, in particular in the famous passages where he seems to contradict himself, now, as you remarked, valorizing the *opsis*, now devalorizing it – a little bit depending, let us say, on its place in the thread of his argument. The text of the *Poetics* is not very reliable, no doubt, but on this point I have great difficulty finding either contradictions or incoherence, or even what one would ordinarily call "hesitation." I will attempt to explain myself as briefly as possible.

It is clear that Aristotle does not like what I call here – out of convenience but, I hope, without too much insistence – the spectacular. We have the best example of this in chapter 26 when Aristotle condemns very severely those actors (but moreover the singers, the musicians, and the rhapsodists as well) who "make too much of it": who "overact" as we say; and it is clear there that the spectacular equals redundance, which Aristotle calls "overloading of signs," or, in a probably archaizing sense of the term "pantomime." But this condemnation is neither one of "movement" in general (the fact of "acting" a text), nor of recourse to "corporeal figuration" (*ta skhemata*). It is not a condemnation of the *opsis* – the word appears once again – no more, in any case, than of music: tragedy, says Aristotle, "has all that the epic has ... with, in addition (and it is not a negligible factor), music and those elements which depend on

277

performance, from which are born the keenest pleasures" (62a, 14–16). And he adds: "And then it has all its vivacity (*to enarges*) at once both in the reading and on the stage." What Dupont-Roc and Lallot render "on the stage" is the Greek *epi tôn ergôn,* more faithfully restored in the notes as "set in action." And there, it is undoubtedly a question of the staging as we understand it, that is to say of the "presentations" (*mimēsis*) of an action and the actualisation of a dramatic form. Of the performance [*spectacle*], obviously, but where the essential is the play [*le jeu*]. But if the play consists of acting a text – and if the tragic text, for Aristotle, is first one of feeling – what is decisive in the presentation or the staging (*ta theatra*, we read in chapters 4, 49a, 8) is the enunciation or the utterance, to which all the rest is subordinated. All the rest: all that which *visibly* supports the setting in action: gestures, movement, mimicry, and corporeal figuration – and additionally the accessories (I am not forgetting music, but because it is more tied to the orchestral, it poses a slightly different problem). Aristotle does not condemn, or devalorize, staging: he expresses a principle of *restraint* in art. (I am purposely employing this term out of Hölderlin and passed on to us by Brecht).

This, to my mind, explains two things: on the one hand the emphasis placed by Aristotle on art, *tekhnē* or *poiesis.* The question which underlies the entire *Poetics* is: what is it in tragedy, in dramatic art, that is derived from or is not derived from art itself? And the answer, on this point, seems to be quite clear: restrained staging derives from art. This is so true that in chapter 17, when he discusses composition, Aristotle says that "it is necessary [for the tragic author] to place the scene before his own eyes as much as possible," or, more literally, to place (objects) before his eyes (*pro ommatôn*) – even adding a bit further on (55a, 32) that he must "polish it through gesture (*tois skhēmasin*) as much as possible". As Dupont-Roc and Lallot analyze so well in a long note (P, pp. 281–284), we see the linguistic (rhetorical) and the corporeal (oratory) sense of the *figure* combined in the term *skhēma*, associated throughout the passage with *lexis,* or expression. Gesture and speech. (This necessitates a very close reading of this entire first paragraph of chapter 17 which seems to contradict – but does not, at least in my opinion – the principle of restraint which I mentioned earlier. Perhaps we will come back to this.)

On the other hand, there is the celebrated concurrence of the simple reading and the presentation, or rather the performance (the *opsis*). What exactly does Aristotle say? This, which one finds at the beginning of chapter 14:

Fear and pity can surely be born of the performance (*opsis*), but they can also be born of the plan of story itself [the famous *sustatis tôn pragmatôn*:] There lies the process which holds the highest rank and reveals the best poet. Indeed it is necessary that the story be established independently of the performance such that as the facts present themselves, one shivers or is overcome with pity before what is taking place: it is what was felt upon *hearing* [emphasis mine] the story of Œdipus.

It is still the same principle: primacy of the text (of the word), meaning of what is heard. This is why reading – aloud, which never excluded the *gestus* for an ancient – which is an initial staging in the sense I am trying to make understood, suffices to carry out the tragedy to its proper effect. And to attempt to bring about the *catharsis* by other methods, that is by sole recourse to methods of performance, is not faithful to the essence of tragedy. I quote again, modifying the translation on one point:

Producing this effect through the means of the performance depends very little on art; it is an administrative [I hazard this word for *khorègia*] matter. Those who, by means of the performance, produce not the frightening but only the monstruous have nothing to do with tragedy.

It seems to me that there is here not only a very great coherence, but an extremely fitting apprehension for the theater, still true today. One could say: theater implies a "stage" [*scène*], but this stage – the setting in action [*la mise en acte*], the *enunciation* – is always anterior to the initiation of the performance. This defines a sort of *archi-theater*. And, after all, the one who understood this best is, as you well know, Mallarmé: the Book, provided that it be rendered orally, replaces all theater.

You will undoubtedly object that my interpretation, assuredly much too quick, comes back to a truism of the genre: good theater cannot be made of a bad text. And you will find in the *Poetics* a number of propositions of the same nature, starting with all those in which Aristotle distinguishes between "cultivated" (or "high") theater and "vulgar" theater. You will remember that Pautrat remarked, when we were working together on the *mimēsis*, that the audience which Aristotle considered was one of philosophers, of those who understand and take pleasure in understanding. And he contrasted this "elitism" with Brecht's position, which still does not seem to me to be too different except to suggest that the vocation of authentic theater is to make any audience a "philosophic" one. Or perhaps you will object that my "archi-theater" – which I pull from Aristotle not because I am an "Aristotelian," but because I see in him a profound intuition about the theater – is a sort of pious desire, an ideal condemned to hurl itself incessantly against the harsh reality of the stage [*scène*] (of the place, of the actors, and of the publication). Objection sustained. But I still argue that there is no dignified theater which does not strive toward this "archi-theater," and in any case, if I have dared try my hand at dramaturgy and staging – whatever the results – it was with this idea in mind. Or this question: how to break the performance?

At this point I must go on to your second question – which, I can imagine, is more important to you than the first. From my present viewpoint, I would be tempted to cut my response short and say: as we must break the performance, so we must also break – I was about to write the figure (what a plan!). Let us rather say: one must try to check the fictional process. There are days when I say to myself – in these great moments of simplification with which we are all familiar, whether through anger or through lassitude – that *figuration* is in fact the bad luck of the Occident, indeed of the "human world" in general (but the Occident alone has made of it a more or less complacent theory which one can call, in a certain light, a philosophy). You are correct to ascribe this hostility toward the figure not to my Calvinist past (even though ...), but to the suspicion I have held toward what I have called onto-typology, "that is to say toward a figural and fictional assignation of the presentation of the being and/or of the truth." This is one of the rare philosophic intuitions with which I have been gifted (you know that I do not claim to be a philosopher) and this is what has allowed me – in a complex manner because it was Heidegger who set me off in the right direction – to enter into a *dispute* with Heidegger himself and, with him, an entire philosophic tradition (which, I admit, is not necessarily the only philosophy, but which even so has, for the most part, dominated Europe these last three or four centuries). You say that it is with this bias that you spoke of the "interruption of myth." During the same period, I spoke of the interruption of art, or of poetry (and a bit before that I attempted to use the Hölderlinean word "cæsura" with similar intentions), when speaking of Celan. But we have not finished with this matter. In any case, I am trying to carry on with this Heideggerian interpretation of poetry, which seems to me to be a frenzied endeavor – and not at all innocent politically, ethically, etc.

– of (re)mythologization of (re)fictionalization. But you say: "I find myself always brought back to the demand for a certain figuration, because the 'interruption' of the myth does not seem to me a simple cessation, but rather a cutting movement which, in cutting, delineates another area of enunciation." I know that in saying this you have in mind all the implications – political, ethical, pedagogical, even religious – of this affirmation; and it seems to me that on the whole – I am not speaking then of divergences of detail, which are, at times, severe – we are in agreement on this point. I subscribe anyway to the *logic* of your proposition and actually, I realize now, it is even this logic which makes me defend, apropos Aristotle, an archi-theater. When you write that: "the beginning of the business is here: between a 'figure' thought of initially as (re)presentation, and a 'figure' thought of initially as a place of emission and as an enunciatory presence (inseparable, then, from a voice)," I can only say: "Oh, yes! However, however ..." – I have, or I think I have several reservations, perhaps because I did not understand you very well. At least two:

1. When I speak of "de-figuration" (the word is no doubt maladroit), I am making explicit reference to the ornate concepts of *Entymythologiesierung* and *Entkunstung*, but beneath them I also see the expression used by Benjamin in 1915, with respect to Hölderlin's late poetry: *Verlagerung des Mythologischen*, deposition of the mythological. Such a deposition, Benjamin stresses, is not a destruction of the myth itself, or of the mythological element that is the "mode of speech" where a truth of experience or existence can state itself, speech which controls – essentially as an enunciative posture – the great lyrical utterance. The deposition of the mythological is the deposition, even the wording, of the figural petrification of the enunciatory possibility: in the case examined by Benjamin, it is the deposition of the role of the poet as mediator between the gods and men (the people) – thus, precisely that which would exalt Heidegger twenty years later ... This provides the occasion once again for a figure: Benjamin calls *Gestalt* the "tenor" (*Gehalt*) of the poem, which he moreover very rigorously considers the transcendental schema, the figural possibility of the poem. But this needed figurality cannot – or rather must not – broaden itself into figuration. The freedom of a new enunciation implies the deconstruction of a previous figure which is, each time, a stiff inductor of conduct in the occurrence of poetic practice. But not alone, here's the evidence: the nuances of this business are none other than atheism, up to and

including the politics where figuration reimposes itself these days –
and it is a fatal figuration.

2. My hostility toward the figure is thus toward figuration – as, in
the order of strict language, it is toward terms. ("Sacred terms are
missing," etc.) Stated slightly differently: something about the figure
from the moment that it starts to become fixed too much in the
purely figural function (of schematization) necessary to all production, whatever it may be, lends itself inevitably to sacralization or
mythologization. You well know that I believe in a sort of figurative
spiritual exercise, even though I have on the other hand a passion for
"tailored images" in any genre (on the condition, of course, that they
no longer be "active" or no longer pretend to be so). And consequently I have more of a tendency than you to stress the break: the
cæsura – the "antirhythmic suspension" – *organizes* well a verse, a
sentence, even an entire work or story. It does not hinder until
afterward, which is no longer the same. Is this what you call an
"irreconcilable difference"? Is this where you let pass the difference,
which I do not yet grasp very well, between identity and individuality? (Ordinarily I would immediately think that they are very
much the same, for the effects of assignation and designation seem
very powerful to me in the latin *ipse*.) I don't know. All I can say, to
restate your last question and close this first exchange, is that yes,
there are certainly two stages, of which one is assuredly the stage of
the *exhibition* of figures, and the other, which I do not know how to
name, is in withdrawal of the exhibition. But this is not necessarily
an objection to what you propose.

Dear Philippe,

Indeed, your response does not constitute an objection to what I
was trying to indicate, even less as a thesis to be posed than as a
question to be examined. On the contrary – without wanting to
perform a simple unanimism which would not escape being judged
as questionable – you have enlightened me as to the true nuances of
this question. I can see more and more how much it is a question not
of contrasting the "figure" and the "non-figure," or the "stage" and
the "non-stage" (or the "ob-stage" [the French "ob-scène"]), but
rather of refining and complicating each of these concepts. Not for
the (doubtful) pleasure of the complication, but because, indeed,
there is in our actuality, in a way surely more insistent and more
urgent than it seems, a question of the "figure." This question is at
once philosophical, political, ethical, and psychoanalytical. This is a

lot and I am not seeking, at least for the moment, to go into the details. But our discourse on the "stage" seems particularly appropriate for trying to indicate the general or synthesized principle of the entire affair.

I will attempt, in rejoining this discourse by responding to you, to lay down things thus: an historic necessity (which I no longer seek to qualify or to explain here) entered us into a period of generalized non-presentation. Of the "being" or of the "real thing," of the "meaning," or even of the "truth" – in this respect distinguishing these terms means very little. There is no possible presentation, or no presentation supportable without considerable risks: telltale inveigling, spectacular allurement, representative illusion, imaginary tangles. Nothing, in fact, has become more foreign to us than Aristotle's tranquil affirmation, virtually the opening of the *Poetics*, according to which "men have, inscribed in their nature, at once a tendency to represent ... and a tendency to find pleasure in representation" (48h, 5–10). Or at least this affirmation would not work for us without an accompanying suspicion that the "tendencies" are dangerous, if not unhealthy. We will see, in short, something like the Kantian *Trieb* of reason, this incorrigible but eminently *criticizable* impulse to want to give oneself the unconditioned as an object (that is, to represent it).

(Moreover, behind this lies a long and complex tradition of interdiction of representation, of iconoclasty or of misicony with which we will one day have to explain ourselves.)

The strangeness of Aristotle's affirmation, for us, does not work without serious difficulties: all *mimēsis* is suspect, either by reason of indigence (if it is a matter of *mimeisthai*, shall we say of some transcendence) or by reason of superfluity. (We remain *properties*, as you say, of the "performance" – and also making use of a word from the old theatrical lexicon, the German *Requisit*, for which Benjamin reserves a discussion in the *Trauerspiel*. I recall this to you without malice since you make reference to Benjamin, and since I then wanted to know what the importance of the "Trauerspiel" was for you, the concept, not the book, seeing that it constitutes such an essential link with the "spectacular". But I am moving too quickly; everything is becoming jumbled. It is true that we are pressed for time to submit this text: too bad. Let us play the game, the play of improvisation.) In effect, everything occurs in this sluggish, Platonic – and precisely non-Aristotelian – tradition, as if we had remained before something pure and unpresentable, consequently deprived of "face," depriving ourselves of the "face-to-face," removing the spectator from the spectacle. Delivering oneself from the "subject of the representation," one would only have gained the pure and simple rejection of all representation: in an extreme sense, accomplished "nihilism" itself.

As you can imagine, I am not going to plead for one of these blockhead "return of or to the subject" which some strove to extol some time ago. I am, on the contrary, fully convinced that we are at the end of a subjectivity understood as a self-presence which supports presentations and brings them back as one's own – this subjectivity being, precisely, unpresentable. But I would say rather that the unpresentable is itself thus perhaps nothing but an effect programmed by the system of subjectivity. And I ask myself, consequently, if the *place* of this subject does not remain to be occupied at new costs, or even to state it perhaps less badly, if this place, as a location "face-to-face" with the world, "vis-à-vis" manifestation in general, does not remain openable for disposal in some other manner.

Vis-à-vis: one could pause on this point, know what it is that allows this difference of subject, *for* which there is the performance – the phenomenon – but which is not *seen, sighted by*, the phenomenon, which is itself neutralized by objectivity. The difference then of the subject: what I have for the occasion voluntarily called the *spectator* is only what he is because he is so seen/sighted by what he views or contemplates, and thus is taken – taken and shared – in a game, in an exchange, in a circulation, and in a community which depends on an economy completely different from that of subjective representation. In the "archi-theater" of which you speak, I believe that one would have to know to analyze how the archi-spectator is *seen* from the archi-stage, all the while viewing it himself. That is to say, after all, how do both myth (on the chance of returning to this term) and the group reciting it *come to him*, the archi-spectator.

I would be tempted thus to understand that the "pleasure" (*chairein*, to rejoice, from that which pleases, that which is beautiful, favorable, benevolent, that which renders thankful ...) of which Aristotle speaks indicates that "man" in the "nature" to which he belongs is not a "subject of representation" but rather a being defined by a certain being-outside-of-oneself, by a participation in, or by a sharing of manifestation as such, that is of that which puts something, in general, outside the self – identical and different, or even neither simply identical nor simply different (it is thus that at this very place Aristotle describes the *mimēsis* which causes us to "rejoice"). That which tears from the immanence of the being and exposes it in the appearance of being. The Aristotelian *spectator* is, in his turn, exposed there, or rather, the two expositions are taken one in the other, indissociable and irreducible to a subject to object relationship.

(I am adding here after having reread your letter: it is what I wanted to indicate, for better or for worse, by a distinction between identity and individuality, more or less taken from Bataille, which is in fact undoubtedly not very solid in its wording. Once more it is a matter of the question: what to call one who is not a subject and even less singularly *one*?)

It is here that I would see the first archaeological stratum of what you call "archi-theater." Something, in fact, which owes nothing to the "performance" understood as a representative exterior, as decoration and make-up. But as such, something which, in an essential manner, has something to do with an exteriority, with an appearance – with the appearance *of* the being, indeed *as* being. And this implies the figure. Or rather: the figure – and the stage – *are* inscribed in this archi-necessity of being, or, if you prefer, in this *ontological mimēsis* which should well be in one way or another in the background of the *Poetics*. A background in opposition to the Platonism which I brought up a moment ago (to which Plato would, no doubt, not lower himself, as would suggest his own complications with the *mimēsis*, concerning which you are an expert).

It is certainly not by accident that today the theater knows less of a "crisis" than a sort of generalized suspense. It has been struck full force by the fulfillment of this Platonism. This is why it is shared, or rather torn, between spectacularity and effacement. The "full view," as you call it, and the "nothing to see" (followed by, "Move on! there is no longer a place of assembly of the citizens!"). The pure appears in its most banal meaning, or the being is even driven back in pure immanence to himself.

Beyond the suspension between spectacularity and effacement (this was, no doubt, in his own manner, Beckett's question), re-opening a scene or even opening a new scene implies opening or reopening the space of an *ontological figurality* (of which I imagine Aristotle was aware, just like you imagine him to have had a "profound intuition about the theater" as you understand it. What we project upon him or not is of little importance ...). It seems that these are the essentials of this matter. This ontological figurality would not come under what you have christened "onto-typology." It would resemble it, if you will, but as its exact opposite and as evidence of what the model imposes.

But then again, *space* cannot be a frivolous word, or a stylistic clause. What is in question – the "stage" itself – requires the opening of the exterior as such, of "outside" as "outside": that is, for me, of that which makes a "meaning" a "meaning," its articulation, its utterance. Very simply, and still quite closely, I think, to what you write me, an enunciation rather than a statement. The *fact* that it is uttered (stated, phrased), and *how* it is uttered. Or, more precisely, *that* it is means *how* it is. The fact that the enunciation is indiscernible from its modality – from its pragmatism, we would say today. This modality forms not the accessory, but if I may say the transcendental condition of the emission of a meaning as a meaning. Both its "public," or "communicative," meaning and its recognizant condition (by which it touches on *mimēsis*). As in all circumstances, including the most humble, what counts is how it is said.

And as you yourself indicated, without my having solicited it for my part (if I remember my first letter correctly) it is a matter of "body." I will not insist too much on this word, concerning which I know your reservations and your defenses.

(There is, no doubt, between the Calvinism which you evoke and the Catholicism which I could evoke, as, no doubt, there is between a Hellenism and some other – let us use as a marking device "Plato"/ "Aristotle" – or between Judaism and some other – "Torah"/ "Kabbal" – an extremely complex line of division along which our entire tradition cracks and sutures itself: the line of the "body," the outline of the "figure," the delimitation, as well, of the "stage." One could well show how such a line organizes everywhere an intimate division and synthesis of all our identities or individualities: for example, looking at the most outstanding *figures*, those called "Dante," "Montaigne," "Rousseau," "Hegel," "Mozart," "Picasso." Returning to the theater, this entire history of the theater which since the '20s has been divided according to the double polarity of a return to the text, of the "oratory" type if I may say so, and a corporeal exhibition or exaltation to the point of gesticulation and vociferation. Artaud is, of course, at the crossroads, or on the cross, with Beckett once again. But one must also look back to Shakespeare.)

I can, then, grant you a lot on the breadth of the "signifying" *body* (and of all the "signifying bodies"), on the weight of the opposition to a "soul" no less sticky. Leaving the fact that, moreover for me, "body" is still the least fit to designate this *figural extension of the being without which, quite simply, the being* would not be (and, no doubt, it isn't, as Heidegger says; but I meant to say – and you understood – : *without which he couldn't make the being exist*).

"Body," meaning *already a stage.* The archi-theater which you refer to seems to me necessarily to have to do with this minimum of "*Inszenierung*" or of "*Darstellung*" which is the enunciation of a text – or perhaps even better, which is the text inasmuch as it pronounces itself or is pronounced. A minimum which furthermore is perhaps at the outset a maximum – which, in any case, constitutes perhaps the transcendental or the axiomatic of any "staging" and thus of any "performance." According to a motif which is a little bit haunting for me, this extension figures (...), in a privileged manner, into the opening of a mouth which speaks, sings, or shouts (or laughs). Of course, something grandiloquent could come out of that right away. In that case I wouldn't say anything. It seems to me an inevitable risk with which one can no doubt not cease to negotiate and against which one cannot cease to measure oneself. Also, one cannot dispense with the mouth which speaks – for it is already speaking *the very words of the text* (and here, perhaps, is where there is no contradiction between two aspects or tendencies of the declarations of Aristotle).

At this point I must add that the motif of the *opsis* falls back, in fact to a certain secondary role, or rather that it transforms itself into a *tactile* motif (which also haunts me a bit). Speech touches, if you will – there, for me, is the primitive stage (another name for archi-theater). Or: that which, in a text, can touch, is necessarily the mouth which speaks it, through which it is spoken. But one must even say, perhaps: the mouth which *is* the text.

(Here arises the whole question of dramatic text as such, of its eclipse today, in the sense of stagings of texts not written for the theater – in short, of what makes a text "dramatic" or not, that is unquestionably of what allows that it already be staged in its "textuality," and that it is only because of this that it can be *performed*, and even that it requires that it be performed.)

So, here is the point: it cannot touch without realistic extension. From which we get the mouth as the actual mouth of the actor, if need be *per-sonans* in a mask. In other words, that the text *touches* (moves) cannot remain metaphorical through and through. In the same way that pleasure is always physical, as Kant likes to repeat with Epicurus, so the *charismatic* pleasure which we take in the *mimēsis* cannot be without a certain *hedonistic* pleasure, even if Aristotle doesn't mix the two and reserves the second for the "performance" (Dupont-Roc and Lallot emphasize this, but to me it is precisely the impossibility of not linking the two which must be introduced in Aristotle).

It is not metaphorical to speak of touch and of the body here because, indeed, if it were a matter of transport – of meta-phore – it is really a matter of the realistic transport of the meaning. The meaning is not communicated without effectively touching, even if this touch remains at a distance and even if, I readily concede, "to touch" remains at the same time a metaphor. The important thing is that *at the same time* it ceases to be, precisely. (It is also through similar logic, but in the opposite sense, that it is not possible, as I have tried to say elsewhere, to speak of "body" without adopting a pose specifically of enunciation or of writing.)

The "stage" would be the location of this transport of meaning, inasmuch as it is at once a figural and non-figural location (and also taking the figure in the sense of extensive diagram and the figure in the sense of figurative meaning). I do not fail to recognize the risk: one could let slip here, insidiously, a new metaphysical (in the Nietzscho-Heideggerian sense) claim of propriety and appropriation. Similarly, I don't fail to recognize that touch can take on the most "metaphysical" properties of sight. "To touch" in Greek is *haplo*. The *haptic* can always be confused with the *optic* (Descartes provides a good example). But perhaps the nuance is precisely to draw the *optic* toward the *haptic*, if this latter is understood as the (possibly uncertain?) conjunction of the proper and the improper, of the immediate and the indirect, of presence and distance – and are these not the risks of the theater?

At this point I will add only one thing, to finish for today (but I don't know if we will have time for another exchange).

As I just mentioned, as much as the text of the theater must be, as text, already in play, already on a stage (one can see that it is the very principle of the written device of the dramatic play, with the names of the characters situated syntactically outside of the text. But beyond that it is a matter of many other aspects of writing, which I would be incapable of formulating) – so, it seems to me, at the opposite extreme, that of public dramatic execution, it is no doubt never completely simple to separate the "performance" [*le spectacle*] from the "play" [*le jeu*] in the sense in which you propose. I mean to say that there is also already necessarily performance in the play of enunciation, and that it can remain enunciation even in the most "accessoried" or the most "brilliant" performance. This could be called the "question of the false jewel"; the "fake," does not have its use merely at the cabaret (and indeed the cabaret itself …?). There is perhaps "fake" in all theater. The Greeks, if they must be referred to once again, needed more than we to make the most of all sorts of coarse contrivances (although "make the most of" is not the correct wording). First of all Aristotle – which did not prevent him from having the intuition of the theater which you say he has.

This is why I am not sure I can be satisfied with the demarcations which you place between a "figuration" remaining faithful to the enunciation and to the play, and a "petrification" or a "thickening" of the figure. This type of disagreement always leaves the line of demarcation in shadows: *where* does it become "petrified"? I think you would respond with precise examples. You would be correct: but that would also show that there is no a priori jurisdiction for that. Perhaps one must say it is a question of *taste* – but in the least subjective and relativistic sense possible. There could be material for another entire chapter.

This brings me to one last remark, concerning the principle of *restraint* which you invoke. I would like to try to give it more defined terms. For the moment, I propose this: first, restraint is not opposed, in a simply exterior and formal sense (for where, precisely, does form begin?), to overwork or to intoxication. It signifies first that it is not a matter of belief in an alcohol of words and forms, of which the vapors would give access to some revelation. Restrained art is opposed to mystical art – ultimately mystifying. Some examples of mystical art, perhaps (chosen without too much thought): the paint-ings of Gustave Moreau (which I like, nevertheless), the music of Wagner (in which there is also something I like – but you know that better than I), the poetry of Char, the theater of Claudel. But one realizes quickly that it is difficult to not discover something of it just as easily in Mallarmé, for example, as anywhere else. Again, how to define a demarcation?

In a general way, the opposition in question concerns two postures or two styles of "poetry". In the "poetic", it is most often the "mystical" which one wants to indicate: I know that this coincides with your present work on Heidegger, and on what he is seeking in the *Dichtung*, namely in terms of the "mytheme" not the "poem." I subscribe to your words, even more so because I tried once to dismantle the system of reading which functions in *Dichterisch wohnt des Mensch*. But that makes me add here, as for our present exchange: what Heidegger (and what, no doubt, philosophers as such) deducts from the poem, when he has it speak in the "mind," is precisely what presents itself, at least at first, as the ornamentation or as the poetic staging. (I know that I am simplifying Heidegger's gestures and intentions outrageously – but I am passing beyond that for the moment.) Thus, it is the philosopher who could, at the limit, pass for the one who puts art in restraint. Restraint which certainly would confuse itself with the Hegelian gray on gray, which Hegel names not only in the page of the *Philosophy of the Right* on Minerva's bird, but also in the *Aesthetics* under the heading of the contrast between the "past" era of art and the present era of the idea.

All this to say that we must still understand each other concerning "restraint": it cannot simply be "prosaïsm." Or moreover, I don't believe it is necessary to renounce intoxication, not simply or unconditionally in any case. But, we mustn't think that it leads to some mysterious vision. What I call "intoxication" is not necessarily orgiastic either, even less grandiloquent. But it is at least a certain transport, even deportment which is perhaps indissociable from the "play" and from the "stage" in which we are in agreement to situate them. It happens that one must cry out, as actor, and/or as spectator – even though I detest that particular vociferating practice which is encountered at times at the theater. At times the utterance *must* be "excessive." When you criticize, after the "petrification" and "thickening," that which "starts to become fixed too much in the purely figural function (of schematization)," I agree *and* I ask myself where and how to designate this "excess" (where and how, then, to mark the *purity* which remained unviolated).

In other words: schematization? Yes – but it is precisely because the "hidden art" of the schematism of pure reason remains "forever" out of reach that Kant would have taken the schema all the way to the avatars which he knew in the third *Critique*, and to a certain "sublimity" for which the "stage," if it could have one, would be for Kant "oratorio, tragedy in verse, didactic poetry." All right for oratorio, which you choose at the beginning of your letter as a "restrained" form, "purely" figural – but the two others, above all in the mind of Kant, are they truly restrained? It does not suffice to say that Kant has bad taste, even if, incidentally, it is true.

But, as Hyperion says, that's enough for today. We will talk more some other time.

Dear Jean-Luc,

Will we be capable of a dispute? I have just been imagining it. I admit it would at least be a healthy sign, a means of not obscuring our difference – an undeniable one – of activating things, of recommencing the discussion. And by the time which passes, it would not be a luxury. But here it is: I read your response and do not very well see immediately what I would restate in return. I am rather for the most part confused, as is often the case when one must intervene, reply, object (tortures of conversation, for which the sole, terrifying rule is to have "something to say"). At first reading, then, I object to nothing. Or rather (the nuance is not useless), I have no objections. At the second reading, however, in the after-shock, it is different. It takes some time, but there comes a moment when I say to myself: "Ah, no!", a means of signifying, without articulating it, a disagreement or a protestation. But, naturally, I don't trust myself. It could be a purely reactionary motion, comparable – I exaggerate – to a gesture of anger or annoyance. We would be in a suffocating economy of rivalry; it would be a matter of *a scene* [*scène*]. And the risk, in our excitement, would be the "whatever," like in the "infantile" disputes with no basis but to last a very long time – or very late. (I'm not forgetting that our first readers will be psychoanalysts. I offer them the said *scène*; they have seen many others and will know, in any case, why it returns between us.)

I still choose – once is not by habit – the "reaction." It is the final state of things. And consequently, I object.

To what do I object? To two theses, essentially, or to two propositions. (I place in parentheses, provisionally, everything which, from an idiosyncratic point of view – if you will – remains completely foreign to me – and therefore that, I know very well, you hold to very strongly: the thematic of the mouth, of the mouth which touches, of the mouth as text – or the reverse, etc. I think I can grasp what you try to think of in this manner: in short an absolutely native spatiality: Being [*l'être*] as separation and distinction of beings [*étants*]; or existence as a singularity. I am not able to, or more exactly do not have any interest in "emphasizing," if that can be said, this or that – "noble", *natürlich* – part of the body. The smile from the psychoanalysts acknowledged, more than acknowledged even. But it is true that this disgusts me a little, and I cannot think for an instant that the mouth or any other part of the body could be a concept, except to *impose upon* the catachresis (of the type of the "mouth of truth"). Subject or object of a painting, of the plan of a film, of a poem, yes. Of

291

an "interrogation" as well. And of a phantasm, of course. I am, like any individual the first to be warned, in all senses of the term. I am equally very sensitive to the motif of "touch" in its reputed "mystic" meaning: that happens. But don't make of it a philosophy, or then it becomes a watermark. One fear: that an effusion, a complacency toward some life, an expressionistic weakness (it is, perhaps, a question of style after all) would cast into pieces the work of thought. Let's not gush in sentimentality: and the mouth, I am given to believe, is a sentimental concept. By its difference from enunciation or utterance or any other *abstract* thing of the same order. Let us take this step gained: abstraction, that is concreteness itself, the real, if *res* is not a frivolous word. How to say it? An impeccable, irreproachable – thirty years ago they would have said rigorous – restraint is necessary in philosophy as it is elsewhere. This is not (above all) a lesson in morality – how can I present it? But there is vehemence, this I don't hide. You didn't raise this point again last time: but our task, I am convinced, is to be resolutely *atheist*, even – or first of all – in our writing, that is in our manner of speaking.

I return to my two objections since I have said that I have them.

The first touches on interpretation – and consequently on translation – (of the concept) of *mimēsis*. It is a question which has "worked" me for a very long time. Since, in fact, I discovered, thanks to a book by Kohler, that it was Schlegel who proposed to render *mimēsis* by *Darstellung* in order to tear the word from the context of its Latin interpretation (*imitatio, Nachahmung*). We can see the whole point of the operation, and one can guess, in any case, what Schlegel sought to solicit: the negative or perjorative value that is attached to *nach* – or to the French [and English] "re-" inasmuch as it indicates or signifies duplication and after-shock (as in "reproduction," for example). Which, I note in passing is not the case with our "representation" where the "re" usually retains, even if no one remembers or thinks about it, its ancient active worth: "re-present" is not "present a second time", it is "render present". This is moreover why it is not wrong to translate *Darstellung* by "presentation." I'll say for one thing: to mime – a very correct word coming from the alleged Greek onomatopoeia – is not *to copy* (redo). It is to do – if it is present. But do what? There is the entire problem and the origin of my reticence. To say it as well as I can: I don't see why we have entered "into a period of generalised non-presentation," nor at the same time why the distrust we hold toward a certain stage or a certain type of figuration only authorized itself by an obscure mystique of the unpresentable, itself referred to a late Platonism (or to an anti-Platonism) or thought of as a betrayal of Aristotle.

To simplify, and it is, no doubt, excessive: at least, it is said, when presentation is spoken of – it is what Heidegger tries to say in the '30s to return to the "remarkable fatality" which dominates "any theory of art and aesthetics" from the Greeks (Plato) up to our day (Hegel and his following): art presents nothing in the sense of a "presentation of something supersensible in a sensuous material subjected to a form." Or if it presents, it never presents except to say that *there is* a presence. Citing one of the versions of *The Origin of the Work of Art*: "The work of art never presents anything and this for the simple reason that it has nothing to present, being itself that which first creates what enters, for the first time thanks to art, into the open." In other words, art is the presentation of the single *Thisness* [*Dassheit*], an absolutely paradoxical presentation (the possibility of the impossible, thinks Schelling), since the *Thisness* which is not an unpresentable thing located no one knows where, only presents itself as the presence of what is present, which obviously doesn't make it anything. (On this point I imagine we agree.) There is the interpretation of the *mimēsis* which I will call "maximalist". It could no doubt be authorized by some very general statement or other from Aristotle, in Book B of the *Physics* on the relationship between *physis* and *tekhnē*, but certainly not in the *Poetics*. And besides, this interpretation doesn't allow much to be said about art – about the works of art, about what the artists do or attempt to do (Heidegger's Van Gogh is nonetheless dismaying and I will say nothing, keeping on the subject, of his contempt for theater). What it does allow to propose is that if we didn't have art (*tekhnē*), if this grace (*kharis*) had not been given to us, we would have nothing present around us and we would not even be present to – or rather for – ourselves, with all the immense distance (and the immense proximity) which that assumes. It is already a lot. But as much as that is, that does not mean that the "being" or the "thing itself" or the "meaning" or the "truth" are unpresentables. They cannot present themselves by definition. But that there be beings, things, language and thought is obvious – and constantly presented: Heidegger calls this a "world," and even if I contest the historico-political connotation that he attributes to this word (which he uses readily in the plural, as with languages, myths, gods, peoples, etc.), I cannot say that I disagree fundamentally: there is very well a world – I mean *one* world – and art, if I may

293

say, presentation, is certainly not there for nothing. In a word: man is a being which presents. And which, consequently, makes exist. Hail to the artist.

Or rather, to return to the thread of my argument, by *mimēsis* (presentation, always) is understood simple simulation: the record of the appearance, of the "as if" (you know all this by heart): the theater, in short, and frankly I think this is what Aristotle speaks of in the *Poetics*. To designate this concept, and thus to translate, Genette suggests "fiction." The word bothers me slightly for a reason I will try to explain. But it is accurate if we understand by it that which we know not to be – at present – real: the story of Œdipus or of Julien Sorel, the body of Olympia or the "archaic torso of Apollo." Even the crucified Christ. It is present; it doesn't refer to any unpresentable fact (except, perhaps, let's hold off on this case, for Christ, crucified or not). But we cannot forget – from which arises the pleasure we obtain from it – the stage or the book (the narration), the painted canvas or the carved stone de-realize what they present, that is, remove from presence that which they are presenting. We return to the same notion of (absolutely) paradoxical presentation, the more paradoxical because it assumes that nothing is unpresentable. (Except, in the Christian theology, where the "finitization" of God, thought of as the "in-finite," is like a frantic desire for presentation of the unpresentable.) Tradition thinks of *tekhnē* as a surplus: an "addition" to nature as Mallarmé says – and refuses to say. I suspect that it is the opposite and that it changes everything. It is, in particular, of incalculable consequence in terms of the distinction – which we all make spontaneously, but without really knowing what to make of it, precisely – between art and technique. Everything that I tried to say the last time under the title of archi-theater, about the non-spectacular, restraint, etc. stems from this theory of subtraction, or rather *reserve*. Art reserves nature, what is, the ensemble of the present being – and thus presents presentation.

Granted, when you say presentation, you say – or are immediately tempted to say – that the presentation in question is that of something which has not yet (or not already) been presented. Or which is present here or there but which you present a second time. From which stems the immense confusion about *mimēsis*. But it is not that at all: the whole adventure of modern art shows this constantly. Art presents nothing presented or presentable, actual or potential. It makes a *presentation* in indenting [*en échancrant*] everything which is of – or is presumed to be of – the present order. This is why, and this is my second objection, I don't agree with you about the necessity of the figure. But I must proceed in order.

First, I am not at all convinced that the scene inevitably produces the figure, nor that, in reverse, any figure be the consequence of an "effect of the scene." We must understand each other nonetheless concerning the extension of these concepts, and attempt, be it only out of discipline, to settle the question of their metaphoric use (and too often abuse). I would be happy if there were no scene except at the theater, and if any device where agents and audience, or more broadly receivers, were distinguished from each other could be called a scene. I would also be happy if we could call a scene any place where there occured an imaginary (or vain) action perceived as such: we said, for example, the "theater of the world." But things are moving very quickly. If we want to retain some sort of strictness in dealing with these grave questions (I am serious about this), I believe we must constrain ourselves to defining a scene as a place reserved for an imaginary production, which is quasi-redundant. There can be, in this sense, a "political scene" or a "scene of politics" (even though, for reasons I have already mentioned, I prefer to speak of the "performance" [*spectacle*]), but certainly not, for example, an "analytical scene," as was often spoken of years ago. Or, if you will, all "de-realized" space, in the words of Lyotard, does not necessarily constitute a scene. It must accommodate or be able to accommodate (imaginary) action. A museum is not a scene, unless performances are authorized to be held there.

The same for the figure, although the problem is the inverse so to speak. One can define figure, in this context, at least, as any fictional being. But obviously, the philosophical usage of the term is much more restricted, when the semantic harmonics of French (of Latin) or of German come into play (but *Gestalt* has always been thought of as an equivalent of *figura*). To be sure, a fictional being is called a figure, this time in a very broad or very abstract sense (I would like to say: it is not necessarily always a "character," but if it isn't or it doesn't seem to be, like in Hegel – let's say the unhappy consciousness – it is, in fact, a quasi-character), but such that: (1) there be condensed, even incarnated in it, in a symbolic sense, a meaning (the meaning of an era, for example); and that: (2) by virtue of this symbolic condensation of meaning, it be recognized as having a rectional or directional function concerning the conduct of men. In this sense, the mythical hero is a figure *par excellence*, inasmuch as he incarnates a quality (courage in battle for Achilles, fidelity for

Penelope) and serves as an example to this name. In this sense again, Christ is the ultimate figure, that is to say God as a figure. And you see where I am heading: how, under these conditions, to decide – my great concern – *on the inside* of the figure, as you propose? How to avoid, if one affirms as you do the necessity of the figure, withholding all mythological elements, that is to say – because for me it is the same thing – religion? None of the moderns who dared or who were constrained to discuss figural production – even under the claim of atheism, as is separately the case with Nietzsche (Zarathustra), Freud (Œdipus), Marx (the proletariat), or Jung (the working class), and even Bataille (Acephalus) – knew how to avoid this barrier, neither for himself, nor for his successors – which amounted to many people.

Once again, this is not a lesson in morality, and above all not in "atheist morality." But the question must be asked: what do we do with religion when we try to think a bit about ethics and politics? You know that my initial tendency is one of refusal. But for all that I am not forgetting that this attitude is probably "dictated" – there is nothing like literature for secreting religion – and I also am well aware that on the other hand you can't settle problems by denying them. The question I would like us to ask (but it would require an entire book, or in any case much more space) is a real question – even if I present it with an obsession proper to myself: are we capable of a practice which is not, or is no longer, religious?

If I have held myself to these two objections, and to this question, it is because otherwise I subscribe for the most part to what you propose or suggest in your response. Including, and perhaps this will surprise you, what concerns restraint. But it is also because I do not want to prolong this exchange uselessly or render it wearisome. I believe that we have progressed: a problem has in any case been set up, and that in itself is not so bad. I trust in you to find the most precisely condensed expression of it. *A piu tarde.*

Dear Philippe,

Of course there is a dispute here, and not a small one. But it is not new either: I believe, in fact, that it is the one which has always organized all the *scenes* between us, preferrably, as you know, on the grounds of literary and political judgments, and it is also one which long ago found a privileged point of fixation or of crystallization in the question of the Aristotelian *opsis*. However, it is remarkable that when we manage to develop it a bit more for itself, we bring to light a dissociation, to which your last letter bears witness, and which is not new either, between two levels: that of a rather broad philosophical agreement, and that of this dispute, which I will for the moment call aesthetic, before returning to it later, and which moreover for this reason I will rather call a dissent (understood in the strongest sense: an antinomy, if you will, of perceptions and affections).

Which gives me a remarkable preliminary note: if there can be agreement in the theoretical judgment and disagreement of judgments of taste, that implies, if we go all the way and aren't content to accept thoughtlessly a pure and simple heterogeneity in the two levels, *that something is still missing in terms of the theoretical agreement* . It is not invalidated, far from it. It has meaning and import – and I will return in a moment to the problem which comes out of it and which, in fact, flows from one to the other. But the statement of it is still no doubt missing a certain punch, or a touch to make it – to make it what? not "complete" (in a sense, at the conceptual level, it is, perhaps), but to make it a *statement.* In other words, it is missing its *staging* [*mise en scenè*], or its "dramatization" in a certain "style" and through a certain "pathos": which I am very careful not to confuse with a simple "idiosyncrasy," like the one which you invoke only in parentheses, unless questions of the "idio-" in general must be specifically integrated into the problem. For they are caught up in it, and in a very integral manner, as is proven by the fact that your twenty-five line parenthesis conceals the vein of your response.

If I were to look for the most abridged formula for nuance, I would say it concerns the *idiopsis*. A matter of "seeing in proper" or "properly seeing" (it being understood that "seeing" could be "touching" or "being touched" and that "proper" puts into play a fearsome, even exhausting complexity, which the Heidegger of the *Er-Enteignis* gave the launching push). Or even also "presenting," but how? that is to say first, how would the presenter not be in the presentation *himself*? and would he be, somewhere, "himself" if there were no presentation?

The mass of questions to list here is such that I must interrupt – to say this, more simple but no less decisive: our dissent, and the fact that it is expressed, as if by chance, today and not fifteen years ago (it was there, it is even legible, tangible in the common and uncommon workings of the period, but we would tend rather to de-emphasize it, to treat it as a "simple" dispute of tastes and colors – which it *also* is, I must add, because that is a part of the infinite complexity and delicacy of the problem), testify, among many other traits of the period, to today's sharp insistence on the question of style. I say *style* in order to proceed quickly, but under the imperative indication of Borgès' biting irony against "style in the acoustico-decorative meaning of the term," a formula so well ingrained in me that I have forgotten the reference. In a word, "style" would mean: the "how" of a presentation is "consubstantial" to it. We are, it seems, in agreement. But we are in dissent precisely concerning the "how," and consequently also certainly concerning the mode of "consubstantiality," and thus, finally, of the "substance" in question, or of the "thing itself" or of the "matter" in play. And *yet*, it is not doubtful, either, that we are in agreement about the *same* thing. And thus that we must examine closely the sameness of this thing, its mode of sameness. And that the dissent be a part of it – without my slipping in here some cunning dialectical resolution.

If there is something missing from the discussion today, it is the matter of style approached in this manner. Or even, it is limited to the contracted affronts which contemporary art, or what we have hastily baptized "culture," bears the cost of at the moment. But it is enough to examine literary and artistic criticism: little or no risk of style, or at least in a position of minor importance. But this is also an issue in philosophy, and there also the most visible actuality has forgotten the essence of it. I say "forgotten" because, in short it was style in particular which very clearly was at issue in the philosophical invention, say of the post-Sartrean (with no disparagement intended: it is about an historical movement; but it is not a coincidence that Sartre was fascinated by a literature which he obstinately subjected to something other than what we will call for the moment "presentation" or "stage." Sartre's theater, the simple fact that there *is* theater by Sartre, would itself be a plan of research for one part of the book which we would have to, as you say, consecrate to all this!). A simple listing of names: Blanchot, Barthes, Derrida, Deleuze, Lacan. It is more than ever a question of these. All the laborious philosophic restaurations (*in significatu politico*) can achieve nothing.

I interrupt once again. Before returning to the dissent, I want to reconsider for a moment the terms on which we agreed, for a few definitions.

Yes, it concerns presentation and the presentation of the being, or rather the being as presentation – that is to say existence inasmuch

as its *meaning* is in its representation. I made myself wrongly understood by you on the subject of the "period of generalized non-
presentation." I meant to say that a discussion of this "non-presentation" would have characterized a moment (calling itself "post-
modern") which, all in all, would have remained, even, in the
opposite position, in obedience to the "presentation *of* something"
(no less showing, thus, a movement, an historical displacement, one
which designates more or less the "end of philosophy" philosophy,
if we take the time to understand it that way). But there is no
"presentation *of*". There is – is exactly that, the *there is* – what I
prefer more and more to call the "coming into presence," reserving
thus a sort of permanent, repeated initiality, and a differ*a*nce from
the said "presence" (this "neither-word-nor-concept" of Derrida's
imposes itself here: not as a solution, but as a work plan more open
than ever). In essence, it concerns nothing other than what you
evoked when you spoke of *archi*-theater: that the "archi" in general,
the origin or the foundation, does not occur, does not happen, except
in its very repetition. Or in its *Ur-teil*, in its division and decision
which occur for nothing, which do not occur for the primordial One
(here could be our true deviation from idealism, or from philosophy
in this sense), the decision which comes upon and surprises itself.
(In fact, and to anticipate any particular motives, no religion is
possible here: what you call "atheism" is there *in nuce*, and in this
respect I don't see why you feel the need to preach[!] to the convert
[!!] which I am much more than you think[!!!].)

Otherwise, I would also say this: if there hasn't been, up to now,
any other available definition for art than that of the "sensuous
presentation of the Idea," it is only worthwhile if it is also added
that *in its presentation the idea disappears as an idea*. It is what
Hegel cannot recognize, although as the first he does everything for
that (whereas Kant, in spite of everything, remains far from it).
And this retreat of the idea is essential to it. There is thus an
"aesthetic" which is the internal delimitation of "idealism" itself,
of its original "spacing." Body, then, if you will (or will not). Or
"stage," "archi"-stage.

Here I raise another point of your letter: your distrust of the generalized use of "scene." You are right, but you musn't contradict
yourself. If it is appropriate to call *mimēsis* "presentation" (and you
do not say why, once you have finished with the question of
"imitation," you keep this word where I feel the original doubling
and spacing are retained), it is because there is some original

299

"stage," "scenography," or "scenery." *But* there is no less a uniform display of the staged [*du scenique*] on all determinations of existence. On the contrary, "the" scene must divide and distribute itself into scenes (the political, for example, which I don't see any reason to limit as "performance," or the analytical, for which I don't see why you refuse your own definition of the scene) – among which there is a place, at least, specifically of exhibition of the "scenic" as such. The theater, then.

Once rejoined to the proper necessity of the theater in this manner, I would ask even more of it than you do in your letter. I would like – but we cannot do it here – for us to analyze the final judgment of the dramatic text, starting with its most visible (a)syntax. I mean to say what allows the text to present itself as follows:

PHILIPPE
Let us stop a moment, in this presentation
I can see well, Jean-Luc, a lack of precision ...

I don't know whether much has been written about the position of the name of the character, which complicates, in my eyes, the Platonic schema, for the *mimēsis* in Plato's sense does not begin until *after* this name. But this "asyntactic" positioning of the names of the speakers is what disappears on the stage, where the speaker presents himself. Once again space and body, a body not mimicking of mime. From there I would like to go much further into dramatic writing, into what makes a piece of writing "dramatic" in the most precise sense of the word. Let's leave this for another time.

And let us return to our dissent. Its first provision is the figure. This word is bothersome because it retains, perhaps inevitably, that of which you spoke: God, the hero or the myth. I thought you had understood that I used this word, in spite of everything, because I had no other word for *that which stands out on a stage*, and *in a scene*. And because a refusal of the figure (you go back and forth continually between this refusal and a differentiation between figure and figure ...) returns, in my opinion, quite exactly to the acceptance of what you suspect passes unnoticed or betrays itself with me: to the religion of the unpresentable, then, and to a sort of ecstasy which resonates no less of those suave or exquisite harmonics, in any case traversed by a shiver of unpronounceable ascension in order to detail itself in the words of a moral (in spite of everything) of austerity and rigor. Perhaps it is very revealing (is this the place to say this?) that everyone finds too much religion in his neighbor ... For the moment, I will say this: religion is the (melancholic or triumphal) intropathy of the figure, its identifying consumption by which every figure can become the Figure, where the spacing of the origin disappears. What you call "atheism" (the word seems to me uselessly reactionary: we are no longer there, despite the political menaces of fundamentalism, which I do not take lightly: nothing remains of the gods but the places, really – and it is not the remains of *them*, it is they who have remained somewhere, nowhere: nothing to fear), is the free tracing of figures (phrases, schemes, designs, allures, styles). At this point, it is "free" and "delineation" which we must take back to the drawing board ...

Here, I must add something that is very dear to me: art has never been religious. In the religions which used it, it was always the part which was secretly taken away from the religious as such. But I cannot say more here.

Second item of dissent: the purely aesthetic point. It is your aversion (your dis-gust) for a certain taste. Here the whole question of the *idiopsis* must be readdressed. And, at the same time, the question of a necessary diversity, even more a necessary disparity and a necessary dissent of tastes and styles. Without thinking of teaching subjectivism, and without opening up to the sort of norma-tivity which you seem to touch on, but considering this rather: that figural and staged spacing bring with them the spacing of genres, and of styles (also of arts, according to a spacing of tangible *meanings*). This spacing itself has its moments, its variable configurations, its occasions, its leaps and its ruptures. At a period when a certain gloomy and serious discourse begins to hum again, I don't find it useless to falter (protest, grumble, "misstep"). Not without risks: I see very well those of the word "mouth," for example. But fear not, I don't make it a concept: I take it rather as an obstacle or as a difficulty which the language places ... in my mouth – in the phrase, like a resistance to what I call significant figuration, and like an appeal to non-meaning, to the open and outlined figure. I am moving far too quickly, but finally: the nuance of "body" is nothing more than that of *sense* as a limit of signification, like what passes beyond signification. No question, in this sense, of treating "mouth" as a concept, or of placing it in "expressionism" and "watermark." But it is then at once a matter of the style of writing and of the style or disposition of reading. Of taste, which must, one of these days, once again be "radically" taken into question.

It is much too late to do it today. The fax waits to devour these letters for the printer. A Dieu vat! (heavens! what did he say).

In finishing, and out of pure malice, I am opening a book which I know well is not to your taste, *Finnegan's Wake*, and "Virgilian fate" led me to this: "Face, speak now; eye, feign sadness. Mouth, sing in mimicry."

Yours . . .

Index

Addison, J., 205
Adorno, T. W., 13–14, 16, 70, 242
Alexander, J., 90
Althusser, L., 5
Altieri, C., 16–17, 18, 23, 28, 66–89
anamnesis, 16
Anaxagoras, 135
Anaximander, 135
Antigone, 40–46, 52–53, 55, 61–62,
    264
Arendt, H., 56–59, 62
Aristotle, 7, 28, 75, 122, 208–209,
    273–281, 283–285, 287–289,
    293–294
Arnold, M., 220
Artaud, A., 286
articulation, 16–17, 18, 22, 23, 25, 30,
    75–8, 82–4
Austin, J. L., 96
Averill, J., 237
Ayer, A. J., 92

Balzac, H., 76
Barrell, J., 195
Barthes, R., 146–147, 298
Bataille, G., 296
Bates, S., 21–22, 23, 27, 28, 151–174
Battersby, C., 25–27, 28, 249–272
Baym, N., 200–201, 214
Beckett, S., 285, 286
Beethoven, L., 152
Behr, M., 273
Belsey, C., 3
Benjamin, W., 65, 187, 281, 283
Bernstein, J. M., 14–16, 22, 24, 25, 28,
    34–66, 187
Bildung, 11–13
Blake, W., 209, 251
Blanchot, M., 77, 298

Bonaventura, 142
Borges, J.-L., 298
Bowen, D., 201, 204
Brecht, B., 279
Briggs, J., 145
Burke, E., 158, 219

Cascardi, A., 134, 148
Cavell, S., 18, 72, 92–99, 102, 166, 169,
    215, 233–234
Celan, P., 107, 118–119, 122, 129, 130,
    280
Cezanne, P., 68, 77
Chamfort, S. R. N., 141
Chandler, J., 235, 239, 241
chaos theory, 142–149
Chisholm, R., 91
Chomsky, N., 3
Cixous, H., 250
Coleridge, M., 25–27, 251–264,
    267–271
Coleridge, S. T., 24–25, 167, 210,
    216–217, 232–234, 254, 259
    "The Rime of the Ancient Mariner,"
    216, 220–221, 222–228, 233–238,
    293–294
    Osorio, 221, 222, 223
contracts, frustrated, 23, 108–114,
    126–127, 131
Crawford, D., 127

Danto, A. C., 17–18, 19, 28, 90–106
Davidson, D., 90, 91, 118–122, 126,
    129–130
Deane, S., 219
Debussy, C., 115, 132
Deleuze, G., 298
Dennett, D., 91
DeQuincey, T., 234–235, 240, 242

Index

Derrida, J., 16, 22, 66, 72, 73, 171, 172, 298, 299
Descartes, R., 3, 6, 11, 17, 21, 97, 166, 167, 288
Dewey, J., 91, 92
Dickens, C., 218, 239
dogmatism, 2, 6, 20, 163, 176
Dostoyevsky, F., 182

Eagleton, T., 66, 72
Einstein, A., 107
Eldridge, R., 22, 23, 28, 175–196
Emerson, R. W., 21, 96–97, 167–172
Erinnerung, 13
Ewell, B., 200, 201–202

Felski, R., 249, 253, 269, 270
Fichte, J. G., 38, 133, 178
Fischer, M., 22–23, 28, 197–215
Fleischacker, S., 19, 28, 107–132
Fodor, J., 91
Foucault, M., 5, 140
fractals, 143–146
fragment, 13, 20, 133–137, 139–145, 147, 240
French Revolution, 24, 135, 137, 211–213, 217–220, 244
Freud, S., 5, 171, 296
Frost, R., 93–94

Gadamer, H.-G., 91
genius, 68–69, 73, 250–251
Gilbert, S., 197, 252–253, 269
Gleick, J., 133, 146, 148
Godwin, W., 235, 239, 242
Goethe, J. W. von, 259
Goodman, N., 91
Grice, H. P., 96
Gubar, S., 197, 252–253, 269
Guyer, P., 127–128

Habermas, J., 36–37, 187
Hacking, I., 1
Hampshire, S., 105
Harding, D. W., 241
Hayles, K., 143
Hegel, G. W. F., 2, 8–10, 14–16, 17, 21, 34–66, 151, 156, 160–166, 168, 169, 290, 293, 295, 299
Heidegger, M., 2, 16, 17, 22, 29, 38, 72, 91, 92, 97, 122, 124, 171, 280, 281, 287–290, 293, 297
  on Hölderlin, 187–188, 189
Heine, H., 165, 259
historicism, 163–165
Hobbes, T., 184

Hölderlin, F., 22, 23, 122, 175–176, 185–193, 280, 281
Horkheimer, M., 16
Hume, D., 20, 177

idealism, linguistic, 4
indifferentism, 13
Irigaray, L., 25–26, 250, 251, 252, 262–267
irony, Romantic, 38–39, 72, 137–139, 146–147

Johnson, S., 95
Johnston, K. R., 24–25, 28, 216–248
Jordan, J., 84
Joyce, J.
  Finnegan's Wake, 302
Jung, C., 296

Kant, I., 2, 10–14, 19, 20–23, 27–29, 35, 49, 66, 69, 70, 72, 75, 84, 95, 104, 122, 125, 134, 145, 151–161, 163–166, 168–169, 175–184, 190, 205, 262, 264, 268–269, 283, 287, 290, 299
  Copernican revolution of, 152, 154, 158, 160
  on aesthetic judgement, 114–117, 134, 208
  on phenomena and noumena, 154–160
  on reflective judgment, 117–118, 126–128
  on the transcendental ego, 153–155, 161, 178
Kiefer, A., 115
Kierkegaard, S., 22, 164, 165, 167, 171, 172
Kripke, S., 91, 92–94, 102, 129
Kristeva, J., 250
Kuhn, T. S., 112

Lacan, J., 5, 73, 77, 78, 187, 262–265, 268–269, 298
Lacoue-Labarthe, P., 11, 21, 22, 27–30, 136–137, 139, 140–141, 145, 151, 273–302
Lang, B., 136, 147
Levinas, E., 73
Levinson, M., 195, 227–228, 235, 240–241
Lombroso, C., 251
Longinus, 16, 75–77
Lowes, J. L., 233
Lyotard, J.-F., 6, 134, 295

MacDonald, G., 253–262, 265

Mackie, J. L., 3
Mackintosh, J., 219, 242
Magnuson, P., 225
Mallarmé, S., 279, 289, 294
Malthus, T., 240, 242
Mandelbrot, B., 143
Mannheim, K., 164
materialism, cultural, 4–5
Marx, K., 5, 22, 171, 184, 188, 227, 296
McGann, J., 227, 235, 239–240, 241, 242
Meier, R., 101
Merleau-Ponty, M., 2, 17
Miall, D., 236
Mill, J. S., 38
Milton, J., 80, 167
mimesis, 7, 286, 294, 299–300
Modersöhn-Becker, P., 76

Nancy, J.-L., 11, 21, 22, 27–30, 72,
    136–137, 139, 140–141, 145, 151,
    273–302
Napoleon, 220, 224, 240
Naquet, P. V., 185
naturalism, 3–4, 57–59
Nietzsche, F., 22, 29, 30, 38–40, 144, 167,
    171–2, 184, 288, 296
Novalis [Friedrich von Hardenburg], 133,
    136, 139, 259
novel, Romantic, 141
Nussbaum, M., 72

Peat, F. D., 145
Peirce, C. S., 171
performativism, 12–13, 28, 29, 36, 277,
    279
Phillips, A., 197
Pippin, R., 12, 193
Plato, 7, 254–257, 259–263, 266–267,
    285, 293, 300
pleasure, aesthetic, 67–68, 70–71, 73,
    115–117
poiesis, 6–9, 11, 13–17, 27, 30, 145,
    175–176, 216–217, 232, 242–244,
    278, 289–290
Pollock, J., 19, 77, 115, 116, 132
Putnam, H., 91

Quine, W. V. O., 3, 91, 171

Rawls, J., 36–37, 96, 105
representationalism, 1–3, 6, 17, 133–139,
    145–146, 217, 274
Reynolds, J., 208–209
revenge, 55–59
Richter, J.-P., 259
Robespierre, M., 23, 212–214, 242

Roe, N., 240, 241
Romanticism, 11, 20, 22, 26–27, 36, 66,
    69–70, 133–148, 151–152, 157–158,
    164, 169, 175–176, 180, 216–220,
    223, 240–241, 244, 249–253, 259,
    264
Rorty, R., 1, 4, 19, 72, 73, 91, 198
Rousseau, J.-J., 46, 184, 235

Santner, E., 186–187
Sartre, J.-P., 298
Saussure, F. de, 4, 5
Schelling, F. W. J., 293
Schiller, J. F., 69, 70, 72, 147, 182–183,
    186, 189, 190, 194, 259
Schlegel, A. W., 140
Schlegel, F., 20, 27, 29, 133, 135–141, 292
Schliermacher, F., 259
Schopenhauer, A., 70, 166
Searle, J., 91
Seyhan, A., 20–21, 22, 27, 28, 133–150
Shakespeare, W., 286
    King Lear, 51
    Othello, 17, 73, 84–86, 238
    Richard II, 77
Shelley, P. B., 19
Shorey, P., 7
Showalter, E., 197, 198
Smith, B., 198
Stein, G., 77
Stevens, W., 22, 82
sublime, 22, 29, 75–76, 88, 147, 165–168
    Kantian, 158–160, 264

Tarski, A., 119
Taylor, C., 2, 17
Thesmorphoria festivities, 265–267, 269
Thales, 135
theoria, 7
Thompson, E. P., 219
Thoreau, H. D., 97
Tintoretto, 76

Valéry, P., 107, 125
Vernant, J.-P., 185

Walton, K., 75
Warnock, M., 127
Watson, R., 218, 242
Weber, M., 187
Weininger, O., 251
Whalley, G., 241
Williams, B., 3, 74–75
Williams, W. C., 22
Wilson, E. O., 3
Winkler, J., 269

Wittgenstein, L., 2, 17, 18, 91–96, 102, 117, 129, 171
Wood, A., 184, 194, 195
Wordsworth, W., 22–25, 177, 192, 196, 259
   The Borderers, 220–223, 241, 244
   "Ode: Intimations of Immortality . . . ," 238

"Preface to *Lyrical Ballads*," 198–210, 213–214
Prelude, 202, 210–213, 222, 243
"The Ruined Cottage," 216–217, 220–245
"Simon Lee," 206–207, 238

Yeats, W. B., 16–17, 79–84, 210